"Laughter, a famous Irishman once said, 'is wine for the soul.' Imbibe this book forthwith. You'll clap. You'll cheer. You'll smile. You'll stagger. You'll feel better about business life. You'll remember its lessons for ever. Probably."

—*Prof. Stephen Brown, Ulster University*

"Humor is pervasive in a multitude of situations, and business settings are no different. Buying, selling, and promoting are just a few of the commercial domains where the positivity of humor comes into its own. This original book explores the role of humor in a wide range of marketable dealings and from an extensive variety of perspectives. From psychology to media studies and from marketing to linguistics, contributors are leading international experts from diverse academic fields thus rendering the collection both interdisciplinary and well and truly global, too."

—*Prof. Delia Chiaro, University of Bologna and President of the*
International Society of Humor Studies 2015–17

"The editors have brought together leading scholars from a variety of disciplines who work in academic and applied settings to produce the most comprehensive volume of cutting-edge, up-to-date research on the social functions of humor in organizational settings. This book is an important resource that tops the list of 'must reads' for basic and applied researchers, and students of humor and organizational psychology. This well-written volume demonstrates that humor can be a double-edged sword within an organization, showing that an organization's humor climate can be either *positive* or *negative*, having beneficial or detrimental effects on organizational culture by affecting the psychological well-being and performance of individual employees and by affecting the quality of interactions among workers, as well as the function of the organization as a whole. In addition to looking within an organization, this volume addresses the ways that companies use humor in marketing and advertising to relate to and engage the general public."

—*Dr. Thomas E. Ford, Western Carolina University and Editor*
of Humor – International Journal of Humor Research

T0313254

Not All Claps and Cheers

Scholars from various disciplines have studied humor since antiquity. Yet, over the centuries, these researchers have also struggled to conceptualize a viable, well-accepted notion of humor. Beyond pleasure and amusement, people use humor for a variety of social functions. On the one hand, humor can cause others to like the humorous source more, attract regard, ease conversations, promote expression and the exchange of ideas, introduce new topics of discussion, or smooth interactions. On the other hand, in aggressive forms, humor can halt verbal interactions, modify the usual rules of conversation, communicate critiques, or contribute to the creation of subversive environments.

Not All Claps and Cheers: Humor in Business and Society Relationships is an original research anthology that considers different angles from which to address the use of humor by individuals, groups and business actors in their interactions within, around, and across organizations—that is, at the interfaces of business and society. Accordingly, the research anthology is organized in four sections—"Humor, Business and Society," "From Society to Business: Humor's Use and Roles in Activist Movements," "From Business to Society: Humor's Use and Roles in Marketing, Corporate Communications, and Public Relations," and "Society within Business: Humor's Use and Roles in the Workplace and in Organizations."

This ground-breaking research anthology draws on material from marketing, communications, human resources and stakeholder theory to throw light on this poorly understood facet of human business behavior.

Dr. François Maon received his PhD in 2010 from Catholic University of Louvain (Louvain School of Management). After a visiting scholarship at the University of California, Berkeley, he now works as an Associate Professor at IESEG School of Management where he teaches strategy, business ethics, and corporate social responsibility. He is widely published in academic journals and books including *Journal of Business Ethics* and *A Stakeholder Approach to Corporate Social Responsibility*.

Dr. Adam Lindgreen is Professor of Marketing at Copenhagen Business School where he heads the Department of Marketing. Dr. Lindgreen received his PhD from Cranfield University. He has published in *California Management Review*, *Journal of Business Ethics*, *Journal of Product and Innovation Management*, *Journal of the Academy of Marketing Science*, and *Journal of World Business*, among others.

Dr. Joëlle Vanhamme is Professor at the Edhec Business School. Dr. Vanhamme received her PhD from the Catholic University of Louvain. She has been Assistant Professor at

Rotterdam School of Management, Associate Professor at IESEG School of Management, and a Visiting Scholar with Delft University of Technology, Eindhoven University of Technology, Hull University's Business School, Lincoln University, and the University of Auckland's Business School. Her research has appeared in journals including *Business Horizons, California Marketing Review, Industrial Marketing Management,* and *International Journal of Research in Marketing.*

Dr. Robert J. Angell is a Lecturer and Associate Professor in Marketing Research at Cardiff University. After working as a research executive for the Ordnance Survey, he went on to participate in research projects in Beijing and New York. Dr. Angell previously worked as a lecturer at Plymouth University where he also earned his PhD in marketing and statistics. An accomplished consultant and educator, Dr. Angell is widely published in internationally recognized journals.

Dr. Juliet Memery is a Professor in Marketing at Bournemouth University and previously Associate Professor and Marketing & Entrepreneurship Group Leader at the University of Plymouth. Professor Memery received her PhD in consumer behavior and marketing from the University of Plymouth with a thesis that examined the role of ethical and social responsibility issues in food and grocery shopping decisions in the United Kingdom. Her research findings have been published in journals such as *European Journal of Marketing, Journal of Business Research,* and *Journal of Marketing Management.*

Not All Claps and Cheers

Humor in Business and Society Relationships

Edited by François Maon, Adam Lindgreen, Joëlle Vanhamme, Robert J. Angell, and Juliet Memery

LONDON AND NEW YORK

First published in paperback 2024

First published 2018
by Routledge
4 Park Square, Milton Park, Abingdon, Oxon OX14 4RN

and by Routledge
605 Third Avenue, New York, NY 10158

Routledge is an imprint of the Taylor & Francis Group, an informa business

© 2018, 2024 selection and editorial matter, François Maon, Adam
Lindgreen, Joëlle Vanhamme, Robert Angell, and Juliet Memery;
individual chapters, the contributors

The right of François Maon, Adam Lindgreen, Joëlle Vanhamme, Robert
Angell, and Juliet Memery to be identified as the authors of the editorial
material, and of the authors for their individual chapters, has been asserted
in accordance with sections 77 and 78 of the Copyright, Designs and
Patents Act 1988.

All rights reserved. No part of this book may be reprinted or reproduced or
utilised in any form or by any electronic, mechanical, or other means, now
known or hereafter invented, including photocopying and recording, or in
any information storage or retrieval system, without permission in writing
from the publishers.

Trademark notice: Product or corporate names may be trademarks or
registered trademarks, and are used only for identification and explanation
without intent to infringe.

Publisher's Note
The publisher has gone to great lengths to ensure the quality of this reprint
but points out that some imperfections in the original copies may be apparent.

British Library Cataloguing-in-Publication Data
A catalogue record for this book is available from the British Library

Library of Congress Cataloging-in-Publication Data
A catalog record for this book has been requested.

ISBN: 978-1-138-24343-9 (hbk)
ISBN: 978-1-03-283850-2 (pbk)
ISBN: 978-1-315-27728-8 (ebk)

DOI: 10.4324/9781315277288

Typeset in Bembo
by Swales & Willis Ltd, Exeter, Devon, UK

For Yvonne, a true connoisseur of all kinds of humor—Adam

For all these friends who often don't understand my jokes. They will recognize themselves (or maybe not)—François

For my lovely daughters, Victoria and Zazou—Joëlle

For Sebastian, for whom fun is part and parcel—Robert

For Reg, Jill, and Rachel, for providing the humor that underpins family life!—Juliet

Contents

Figures

Tables

About the editors

François Maon

François Maon received his PhD in 2010 from Catholic University of Louvain (Louvain School of Management). After a visiting scholarship at the University of California, Berkeley, he is now an associate professor at IESEG School of Management, where he teaches strategy, business ethics, and corporate social responsibility. In his research, Dr. Maon focuses mainly on topics linked to corporate social responsibility, learning, implementation, and change-related processes; cross-sector social partnerships; and stakeholder influence strategies. He has published articles in various international journals, such as *California Management Review, European Journal of Marketing, European Management Review, International Journal of Management Reviews, Journal of Business Ethics*, and *Supply Chain Management: An International Journal*. He has co-edited several special issues of academic journals and books, including *A Stakeholder Approach to Corporate Social Responsibility* (with Lindgreen, Kotler, and Vanhamme) and *Sustainable Value Chain Management* (with Lindgreen, Vanhamme, and Sen). He serves on the editorial board of *M@n@gement* and is the founder and coordinator of the IESEG Center for Organizational Responsibility (ICOR).

Adam Lindgreen

After his studies in chemistry (Copenhagen University), engineering (the Engineering Academy of Denmark), and physics (Copenhagen University), Adam Lindgreen completed an MSc in food science and technology at the Technical University of Denmark. He also finished an MBA at the University of Leicester. Professor Lindgreen received his PhD in marketing from Cranfield University. He has served as Professor of Marketing at Hull University's Business School (2007–2010); the University of Birmingham's Business School (2010), where he also was the research director in the Department of Marketing; and the University of Cardiff's Business School (2011–2016). Under his leadership, the Department of Marketing and Strategy at Cardiff Business School ranked first among all marketing departments in Australia, Canada, New Zealand, the United Kingdom, and the United States, based upon the hg indices of senior faculty. Since 2016, he has been Professor of Marketing at Copenhagen Business School, where he also heads the Department of Marketing. He is also a research associate with University of Pretoria's Gordon Institute of Business Science.

Professor Lindgreen has been a visiting professor with various institutions, including Georgia State University, Groupe HEC in France, and Melbourne University. His recent publications have appeared in *Business Horizons, California Management Review, Industrial Marketing Management, International Journal of Management Reviews, Journal of Advertising, Journal of Business Ethics, European Journal of Marketing, Journal of Business and Industrial Marketing, Journal of Marketing Management, Journal of the Academy of Marketing Science, Journal of Product Innovation Management, Journal of World Business, Psychology & Marketing,* and *Supply Chain Management: An International Journal.*

Professor Lindgreen's books include *A Stakeholder Approach to Corporate Social Responsibility* (with Kotler, Vanhamme, and Maon), *Managing Market Relationships, Memorable Customer Experiences* (with Vanhamme and Beverland), and *Sustainable Value Chain Management* (with Maon, Vanhamme, and Sen).

The recipient of the Outstanding Article 2005 award from *Industrial Marketing Management* and the runner-up for the same award in 2016, Professor Lindgreen serves on the board of several scientific journals; he is co-editor-in-chief of *Industrial Marketing Management* and previously was the joint editor of the *Journal of Business Ethics'* section on corporate responsibility. His research interests include business and industrial marketing management, experiential marketing, and corporate social responsibility. Professor Lindgreen has been awarded the Dean's Award for Excellence in Executive Teaching. Furthermore, he has served as an examiner (for dissertations, modules, and programs) at a wide variety of institutions, including the Australian National University, Unitec, University of Amsterdam, University of Bath's Management School, University of Lethbridge, and University of Mauritius.

Professor Lindgreen is a member of the International Scientific Advisory Panel of the New Zealand Food Safety Science and Research Centre, as well as of the Chartered Association of Business Schools' Academic Journal Guide (AJG) Scientific Committee in the field of marketing.

Beyond these academic contributions to marketing, Professor Lindgreen has discovered and excavated settlements from the Stone Age in Denmark, including the only major kitchen midden—Sparregård—in the south-east of Denmark; because of its importance, the kitchen midden was later excavated by the National Museum and then protected as a historical monument for future generations. He is also an avid genealogist, having traced his family back to 1390 and published widely in scientific journals (*Personalhistorisk Tidsskrift, The Genealogist,* and *Slægt & Data*) related to methodological issues in genealogy, accounts of population development, and particular family lineages.

Joëlle Vanhamme

Dr. Joëlle Vanhamme is a professor at the Edhec Business School. Dr. Vanhamme received her PhD from the Catholic University of Louvain (Louvain School of Management). She has been assistant professor at Rotterdam School of Management, associate professor at IESEG School of Management, and a visiting scholar with Delft University of Technology, Eindhoven University of Technology, Hull University's Business School, Lincoln University, and the University of Auckland's Business School. Dr. Vanhamme's research has appeared in journals including *Business Horizons, California Management Review, Industrial Marketing Management, International Journal of Research in Marketing, Journal of Advertising, Journal of Business Ethics, Journal of Consumer Satisfaction, Dissatisfaction and Complaining Behavior, Journal of Customer Behaviour, Journal of Economic Psychology, Journal of Marketing Management, Journal of Retailing, Marketing Letters, Psychology & Marketing, Recherche et Applications en Marketing,* and *Supply Chain Management: An International Journal.*

Robert J. Angell

Robert Angell is a Lecturer and Associate Professor in Marketing Research at Cardiff University. After working as a research executive for the Ordnance Survey, he went on to participate in research projects in Beijing and New York. Prior to joining Cardiff University, he worked as a lecturer at Plymouth University, where he also earned his PhD in marketing and statistics. An accomplished consultant and educator, Dr. Angell has worked with brands such as Sage and Brittany Ferries; he was also awarded the Dean's Award for Excellence in Teaching on more than one occasion. His work has been published in internationally recognized journals such as *Industrial Marketing Management, European Journal of Marketing, Journal of Advertising Research, Journal of Business Research, Journal of Marketing Management,* and *Journal of Retailing and Consumer Services.* When Dr. Angell is not involved in academic or consultancy activities, he is an avid golfer (with a single-figure handicap) and committed follower of domestic football (Southampton FC, season ticket holder).

Juliet Memery

Juliet Memery is Professor in Marketing at Bournemouth University. She was Associate Professor and Marketing & Entrepreneurship Group Leader at the University of Plymouth prior to joining Bournemouth. Professor Memery received her PhD in consumer behavior/marketing from the University of Plymouth, with a thesis that examined the role of ethical and social responsibility issues in food and grocery shopping decisions in the United Kingdom. Expanding on this early work, she continued to research consumer behavior and decision making in relation to consumer choice, focusing in particular on the ethical considerations associated with food shopping behavior in both Europe and Australia. Themes emerging from this research resulted in further explorations of local, regional, and seasonal food; her current work addresses food security, sustainable fish, food waste, and consumer decision-making models. Professor Memery has received external funding for several studies related to food and drink consumption and has disseminated her research findings through publication in journals such as *European Journal of Marketing, Journal of Business Research,* and *Journal of Marketing Management.* Prior to entering academia, she worked in design departments for companies based in both Europe and Africa. She has continued to maintain close links with industry through her consultancy, research collaboration, and knowledge transfer partnerships.

About the contributors

Helena Ahola

Helena Ahola, Lic (Econ), is Principal Lecturer of Marketing at Oulu University of Applied Sciences, where she currently teaches research methods and marketing. Her research interests include services marketing, service design, e-business, and Internet marketing. She has been involved in e-business and service design-related projects, and she has published and presented her research on marketing, value creation, and e-retailing in several international Internet and service-related conferences.

Sari Alatalo

Sari Alatalo is a Senior Lecturer of English Business Communication at the Oulu University of Applied Sciences. She is also a doctoral candidate in international business at the University of Oulu, Oulu Business School. She recently published in *Israeli Journal of Humor Research*. Her research interests include communication in various contexts, including business and education, the use of humor and playfulness in communication, and well-being at work. Alatalo is currently working as a project manager for the multidisciplinary research project HURMOS—Developing Humor as a Strategic Tool for Creating Innovative Business. HURMOS is a joint project of two universities, namely, Oulu University of Applied Sciences and University of Oulu. Alatalo is also involved in FINNIPS (Finnish Network for International University Programmes) examination processes.

James Barry

James Barry is Associate Professor of Marketing at Nova Southeastern University's Huizenga Business College. Dr. Barry received his DBA from Nova Southeastern, MBA from DePaul University, and BSEE from University of Notre Dame. He has published in *European Journal of Marketing*, *Journal of Personal Selling and Sales Management*, *Journal of Business & Industrial Marketing*, *Journal of Marketing Management*, *Journal of Services Marketing*, *Journal of Global Marketing*, *International Journal of Emerging Markets*, and *International Business Research*, among others. His book, *Social Content Marketing for Entrepreneurs* (Business Expert Press) was released in 2015. His research interests include social media marketing, online thought leadership, humor in advertising, and cross-cultural relationship marketing. Prior to his academic career, he served as an executive strategic marketer for GE, Rockwell Collins, AT&T, and BFGoodrich.

Yoann Bazin

Yoann Bazin is Associate Professor of Management and Business Ethics at the ISTEC Business School in Paris, where he is also Dean of Research. His areas of research interest include practice-based studies, critical thinking, philosophy, business ethics, management education, and a business–in–society perspective. He has published several articles in *European Management Review*, *Scandinavian Journal of Management*, and *M@n@gement*. He is co-editor-in-chief (with Yvon Pesqueux) of the *Society and Business Review*.

Michael Billig

Michael Billig was Professor of Social Sciences at Loughborough University, where he worked for more than 30 years. He is the author of *Laughter and Ridicule: Towards a Social Critique of Humour* (Sage, 2005). He has published books on a variety of subjects, including psycho-analytic theory, fascism, humor, rhetoric, the history of rock-'n-roll, and eighteenth-century theories of mind. His latest book is *The Politics and Rhetoric of Commemoration*, written with Cristina Marinho (Bloomsbury Press, 2017). His book *Learn to Write Badly: How to Succeed in the Social Sciences* (Cambridge University Press, 2013), criticizing the over-use of technical language in social sciences, has been well received in some quarters but sparked opposition in others. To date, it has not had any noticeable effect on the way social scientists write.

Marcel Bogers

Marcel Bogers is Professor of Innovation and Entrepreneurship at the University of Copenhagen. He works in the Unit for Innovation, Entrepreneurship and Management, within the Department of Food and Resource Economics (Faculty of Science). He has published in *Journal of Management*, *Research Policy*, *Journal of Product Innovation Management*, *Long Range Planning*, *California Management Review*, *MIT Sloan Management Review*, *Industry and Innovation*, and *Creativity and Innovation Management*, among others. His research interests include openness and participation in innovation and entrepreneurial processes within, outside, and between organizations; he has studied specific issues such as open innovation, business models, family businesses, and university–industry collaborations. He has been guest editor at several journals, such as *Journal of Engineering and Technology Management*, *California Management Review*, and *R&D Management*, and he serves on the editorial board of multiple journals, including *Journal of Product Innovation Management* and *Creativity and Innovation Management*.

Alexander Brem

Alexander Brem holds the Chair of Technology Management at the Friedrich-Alexander-Universität Erlangen-Nürnberg. Moreover, he is Honorary Professor at the University of Southern Denmark (Sønderborg, Denmark).

Carla Canestrari

Carla Canestrari is a researcher and assistant professor in general psychology at the University of Macerata (Italy). Dr. Canestrari received her PhD from the University of Macerata. She has published in *Frontiers in Psychology, Journal of Cognitive Psychology, Discourse Processes, Humor, Discourse Studies, Europe's Journal of Psychology, Language and Dialogue,* and *Review of Cognitive Linguistics,* among others. Her research interests include humor studies and, in particular, the perceptual and cognitive processes involved in understanding humorous and ironic texts, as well as the discursive strategies used to build humorous communication. She is a member of the *EPhPLab* (*Experimental Phenomenology of Perception*) group at the University of Verona, Italy.

Valerio Cori

Valerio Cori received his PhD from the University of Macerata (Italy). He has published in *Journal of Cognitive Psychology* and *Gestalt Theory*. His main research interests include humorous communication and irony. He is currently involved in a research project concerning sensory perception in agri-food and pharmaceutical fields.

Danielle J. Deveau

Danielle J. Deveau is a lecturer in Media and Communication at the University of Waterloo's Department of English Language and Literature. She has published articles related to humor, cultural scenes, cultural mapping, and creative industries in *International Journal of Cultural Studies, Culture and Local Governance, Media Culture & Society, Cultural Studies,* and *Humor: International Journal of Humor Research,* among others. She co-edited a special issue of the *Canadian Journal of Communication* related to cultural production in Canada (with Zoë Druick) and has published chapters in a variety of edited anthologies. Her research interests include creative industries, digital mapping, urban cultural scenes, humor, and communication.

Margherita Dore

Margherita Dore is a research fellow and adjunct lecturer in the Department of European, American and Intercultural Studies and the Department of Oriental Studies at the University of Rome La Sapienza, Italy. She received her doctoral degree in linguistics (audiovisual translation [AVT]) from Lancaster University (2008) and holds an MSc in translation and intercultural studies from UMIST (2002), as well as a BA in English and Latin-American studies from the University of Sassari, Italy. Dr. Dore is the editor of *Achieving Consilience: Translation Theories and Practice* (CPS, 2016); she has also published a series of papers relating to the use of AVT humor in television series such as *Friends, The Simpsons, Misfits,* and the Italian series *Montalbano.* Her research interests include AVT and literary translation, humor, and cognitive linguistics.

Hershey H. Friedman

Hershey H. Friedman is Professor of Business at Brooklyn College's Koppelman School of Business. Dr. Friedman received his PhD from the Graduate Center of the City University of New York. He has held both the Bernard H. Stern Chair of Humor and the Murray Koppelman Professorship. He has published in *Decision Sciences, Journal of Business Ethics, Journal of the Academy of Marketing Science, Journal of Advertising Research, Psychosociological*

Issues in Human Resource Management, Journal of the Market Research Society, Journal of Statistical Computation and Simulation, Journal of Leadership and Management, and *Journal of Leadership Studies,* among others. His latest book, *God Laughed: Sources of Jewish Humor,* co-authored with Linda Weiser Friedman, was published by Transaction Publishers (2014). His research interests include biblical leadership, business ethics, and humor.

Linda Weiser Friedman

Linda Weiser Friedman is Professor of Information Systems and Statistics at Baruch College's Zicklin School of Business and the Graduate Center, both of the City University of New York. Dr. Friedman received her PhD from the Polytechnic Institute of New York (now NYU Tandon School of Engineering). She has published in *Computers & Information Science, Communications of the Association for Information Systems, Journal of Business Ethics, Journal of the Operational Research Society,* and *Argumentation,* among others. Her books include *Comparative Programming Languages: Generalizing the Programming Function* (Prentice Hall, 1991); *The Simulation Metamodel* (Kluwer, 1996); and *God Laughed: Sources of Jewish Humor* (Transaction, 2014), with Hershey H. Friedman. Her research interests include humor studies, Jewish studies, simulation, online education, and social media.

Matthew Gorton

Dr. Matthew Gorton is Professor of Marketing at Newcastle University Business School. Dr. Gorton received his PhD from Plymouth University. He has published in the *Journal of Advertising, Environment and Planning A, Industrial Marketing Management, World Development,* and *Food Policy,* among others. His research interests include sponsorship, food policy and marketing, and small businesses and rural development. He is an associate editor of the *Journal of Agricultural Economics* and the coordinator of the EU H2020 project Strength2Food.

Sandra Graça

Sandra Graça is Assistant Professor of International Business in the Collegium of Comparative Cultures at Eckerd College. Dr. Graça received her DBA from Nova Southeastern, as well as her MBA and BA from Western Michigan University. She has published in *Journal of Personal Selling and Sales Management, Journal of Business & Industrial Marketing, International Journal of Emerging Markets,* and *International Business Research.* Dr. Graça's chapter in *Emerging Markets and the Future of the BRIC Nations* (Edward Elgar Publishing) was released in 2015. Her research interests include communication across cultures, B2B relationship capital, relationship marketing in emerging markets, and humor in advertising. Prior to academia, she founded and managed a cross-cultural exchange organization.

Rob Hecker

Rob Hecker is a senior lecturer in the Tasmanian School of Business and Economics at the University of Tasmania, following a long term as Academic Director, Postgraduate. He researches the behavior of people on both sides of a firm's boundary, reflecting his long career in customer services and marketing, as well as his own consulting business, after he had earned a PhD in psychology. He is an associate fellow of the Australian Marketing Institute and a recently retired board member of the Australian and New Zealand Academy of Management. He contributes to journals such as *International Journal of Human Resource Management, Personnel Review*, and *Journal of Business Ethics*, as well as to international conferences.

Trine Heinemann

Trine Heinemann is project coordinator for the E-ferry project, funded by the EU Horizon 2020 program (e-ferryproject.eu). With a background in linguistics and conversation analysis, she has worked for many international universities in the United Kingdom, Sweden, The Netherlands, Denmark, and Finland. She has published in a range of journals and edited volumes, including *Research on Language and Social Interaction, Design Studies, CoDesign, Artificial Intelligence for Engineering Design, Analysis and Manufacturing, Journal of Pragmatics, Language in Society, PNAS*, and *Learning, Culture and Social Interaction*. She has also edited several special issues and one book. Her research focus includes anything that involves interaction, whether between humans or among humans, technology, and objects, as well as whether those interactions take place in the context of design, innovation, everyday life, service encounters, or caregiving situations.

Marc Järvinen

Marc Järvinen graduated with a bachelor's degree in international business and administration from Oulu University of Applied Science in 2013. His research interests included innovative business processes in marketing and the use of humor as a communication strategy. Armed with his own healthy sense of humor, Järvinen conducted a case research into the use of humor in marketing communications with the Finnish company Varusteleka. This research was later refined and presented at the 23rd Nordic Academy of Management Conference in Copenhagen in 2015. He now studies a master's degree in marketing at Oulu Business School and will continue his research on humor and viral marketing.

Roger J. Kreuz

Roger J. Kreuz is a Professor of Psychology at the University of Memphis. He received his PhD from Princeton University. He has published in *Psychological Science, Journal of Experimental Psychology: General, Cognition, Discourse Processes*, and *Journal of Language and Social Psychology*, among others. His books include *Becoming Fluent: How Cognitive Science Can Help Adults Learn a Foreign Language* (MIT Press, 2015), and *Getting Through: The Pleasures and Perils of Cross-Cultural Communication* (MIT Press, 2017), both with Richard Roberts. His research interests include discourse processing and pragmatics, nonliteral language, cross-cultural communication, and computer-mediated communication. He currently serves as an Associate Dean in the College of Arts and Sciences at the University of Memphis.

Nicholas A. Kuiper

Nicholas A. Kuiper is Professor of Clinical Psychology at the University of Western Ontario in London, Ontario, Canada. Dr. Kuiper received his PhD in psychology from the University of Calgary in 1978. Over the past two decades, his main research interests have focused on explorations of the sense of humor and its relation to psychological well-being and psychopathology. Professor Kuiper has published several research articles in *Humor: The International Journal of Humor Research*, *Personality & Individual Differences*, and *Motivation & Emotion*, as well as book chapters on various aspects of humor, personality, and mental health. In addition to editing three special journal issues on humor research and theory, published by *Europe's Journal of Psychology*, he has authored several encyclopedia entries on humor and laughter topics. He is a member of the International Advisory Board for the series on *Topics in Humor Research*.

Nadia B. Maiolino

Nadia B. Maiolino is a doctoral candidate in the Clinical Psychology program at the University of Western Ontario. She received her Masters of Science there and completed her undergraduate training at Brescia University College. The majority of her published works examine positive personality characteristics and their relation to psychological well-being. Her major research interests also include psychological models of psychopathology and vulnerability to mania in the context of bipolar disorder. She has published research on humor in various scholarly journals, including *Translational Issues in Psychological Science*, *Israeli Journal of Humor Research: An International Journal*, and special journal issues on humor research and theory published by *Europe's Journal of Psychology*. She has also served as a reviewer for *Europe's Journal of Psychology* for contributions focused on humor and positive personality characteristics.

Angela Martin

Angela Martin is an adjunct professor at the Tasmanian School of Business and Economics and Principal Consultant at Pracademia, a research translation business. She earned her doctoral degree in organizational psychology, and has more than 70 peer-reviewed publications related to factors that promote well-being at work, in journals such as *Human Resource Management*, *Human Relations*, and *Academy of Management, Learning and Education*.

Eeva-Liisa Oikarinen

Eeva-Liisa Oikarinen is a doctoral candidate in Marketing at the University of Oulu, Oulu Business School. She has published in *Journal of Service Management*, *Corporate Reputation Review*, *Australasian Marketing Journal*, and *International Journal of Innovation Management*, among others. Her research interests include consumer advertising, corporate and employer brand communications, service encounters, social media marketing, humor, and well-being. Currently Oikarinen is working as a project manager of the multidisciplinary research project HURMOS—Developing Humor as a Strategic Tool for Creating Innovative Business.

Daryl Peebles

Daryl Peebles is an honorary associate with the University of Tasmania's Tasmanian School of Business and Economics. After a 40-year professional career in human resource management, corporate communications, and media, and a parallel career as a writer and performer of humorous material for theater and comedy venues, he blended these two aspects of his working life through a research-based PhD examining the use and value of humor in Australian workplaces. He is a past chair of the Tasmanian Division of the Australian Institute of Training and Development and a founding member of the Australian Human Resources Institute.

Barbara Plester

Barbara Plester is Senior Lecturer in Management at the University of Auckland's Business School. Dr. Plester received her PhD from Massey University in 2008. She has published in journals such as *Employee Relations* and *Humor, Culture and Organization*, among others. She recently published a book that encapsulates 12 years of her humor research (*The Complexity of Workplace Humour: Laughter, Jokers and the Dark Side*, Springer, 2016). She has also contributed book chapters to *Humor: Emotional Aspects, Role in Social Interactions and Health Effects* (Nova Science Publishers, 2016) and *Routledge Handbook of Language and Humor* (Routledge, 2017). Her research interests include humor and fun at work; the organization as a food environment; and how the relationship between technology and emotions interacts with workplace outcomes such as stress, burnout, and well-being.

Daniel Putz

Daniel Putz is Professor of Organizational Psychology at the Rhenish University of Applied Sciences, Cologne, Germany. He received his PhD from RWTH Aachen University. He has published in *Management Learning*, *German Journal of Counselling and Academic Studies*, and several peer-reviewed books. His research interests include humor in the workplace, learning from errors at work, and vocational interests and career goals. He serves as a reviewer for several peer-reviewed journals, including *Human Relations* and *German Journal of Work and Organizational Psychology*.

Tabea Scheel

Tabea Scheel is currently Interim Professor for Work and Organizational Psychology at Europa-Universitaet Flensburg, Germany. Dr. Scheel received her PhD from the University of Leipzig and conducted research as a postdoc at the University of Vienna, Austria. She has published in *European Journal of Work and Organizational Psychology*, *Human Resource Management*, *Frontiers in Psychology*, and *Humor: International Journal of Humor Research*, among others. Her research interests include humor in the work context, human resource management and psychological contracts, new ways of working (e.g., coworking, crowdsourcing), motivational processes at work (e.g., procrastination), and change readiness. She reviews for a range of peer-reviewed journals (e.g., *Applied Psychology: An International Review*, *European Journal of Work and Organizational Psychology*, *Nonprofit and Voluntary Sector Quarterly*).

Elena Tavella

Elena Tavella is Assistant Professor of Organization Studies at the University of Copenhagen. Dr. Tavella received her PhD from the University in Copenhagen. She has published in the *European Journal of Operational Research* and *Journal of the Operational Research Society*, among others. Her research interests include strategizing and decision-making processes, facilitation, and top-management teams.

John White

John White is Associate Professor in Marketing at Plymouth University. His work has been published in *Journal of Advertising*, *European Journal of Marketing*, and *Industrial Marketing Management*, among others.

Katharina Wolf

Katharina Wolf is an academic with Curtin University in Perth, Western Australia (WA), where she serves as the course coordinator for the public relations program. Dr. Wolf has 20 years of communication and media experience as an educator and practitioner. Her industry experience spans media, communication, and research roles in Germany, Spain, the United Kingdom, and Australia. She has published in *PR Review*, *Journal of Communication Management*, *Higher Education Research & Development*, and *Asia-Pacific Public Relations Journal*. Her research interests focus on activism and (community) advocacy, diversity, and employability.

Rebecca Scott Yoshizawa

Rebecca Scott Yoshizawa specializes in the sociology of science, transdisciplinary collaboration, bioethics, and reproduction, along with her other interests in cultural studies. She is an instructor in Sociology at Kwantlen Polytechnic University. She has published articles on the intersections of science and society in *Body & Society*, *Feminist Theory*, *Placenta*, and *Journal of Empirical Research on Human Research Ethics*.

Foreword and acknowledgment

Because humor is an ageless phenomenon, "philosophers, literary critics, literary biographers and historians, sociologists, folklorists, psychologists, physicians and scholars from various other disciplines have studied humor since antiquity" (Apte, 1988: 8). Yet over the centuries, these researchers have also struggled to conceptualize a viable, well-accepted notion of humor. The challenge continues to confound us and elude clear definition. Taking diverse forms at various times and in different situations, with an all-pervasive scope, humor does not always look the same—even if a reasonable consensus indicates that it involves some "intentional verbal or nonverbal message which elicits laughter, chuckling, and other forms of spontaneous behavior taken to mean pleasure, delight and/or surprise in the targeted receiver(s)" (Booth-Butterfield and Booth-Butterfield, 1991: 206).

Beyond pleasure and amusement, people use humor for a variety of social functions. For example, it might facilitate and enhance learning processes; help reorient perceptions, attitudes, and behaviors; and facilitate social relationships (Dziegielewski, Laudadio, and Legg-Rodriguez, 2004). Graham, Papa, and Brooks (1992) emphasize two central functions of humor: facilitating communication in specific contexts and spreading aggressive messages (Bonaiuto, Castellana, and Pierro, 2003; Hay, 2000). On the one hand, humor can cause others to like the humorous source more, attract regard, ease conversations, promote expression and the exchange of ideas, introduce new topics of discussion, or smooth interactions. In business-related communications, interactions, negotiations, and public relations, being funny can draw attention, especially as a means to stand out from the massive amount of information that characterizes hyper-connected societies. In turn, it can exert strong influences on a situation and other actors. On the other hand, in aggressive forms, humor can halt verbal interactions, modify the usual rules of conversation, communicate critiques, or contribute to create subversive environments.

In this context, the mobilization of humor by individuals, groups, and businesses constitutes a research field of increasing interest. Extant research seeks to highlight why and how actors use humor within organizations and its effects on organizational members and processes (e.g., Mesmer-Magnus, Glew, and Chockalingham, 2012; Romero and Cruthirds, 2006; Sobral and Islam, 2015), as well as the utility of humor as a persuasive tool in external corporate communication or marketing campaigns, with impacts on consumers (e.g., Eisend, 2009; McIlheran, 2006; Spielmann, 2014). However, the use of humor by business actors in interactions with external stakeholders other than consumers, and the ways external stakeholders similarly use humor to influence business actors, remain poorly addressed (cf. Kutz-Flamenbaum, 2014; Westwood and Johnston, 2013; Wolf, 2014).

In particular, research that focuses on developing a constructive understanding of business and society relationships and interactions lacks specific analyses of the use of humor, even though humor is growing in popularity and use among external stakeholder groups that address corporations. The role of humor and the comic frame in criticisms targeted at the business world and in the expression of associated aspirations for systemic adaptation and corporate social change is significant, in line with the proscription that "criticism had best be comic" (Burke, 1984: 107).

This research anthology considers different angles from which to address the use of humor by individuals, groups, and business actors in their interactions within, around, and across organizations—that is, at the interfaces of business and society. Accordingly, this research anthology is organized as follows:

- Part 1, entitled "Humor, Business and Society," comprises two introductory chapters that delineate and critically reflect on the notion of humor, on the one hand, and the business and/in society field on the other. The goal is to provide a constructive basis and interesting routes to approach the three other sections and 15 remaining chapters contained in this research anthology.
- Part 2, "From Society to Business: Humor's Use and Roles in Activist Movements," addresses how external stakeholders and civil society initiatives have mobilized humor in their efforts to highlight and denounce negative corporate impacts, change the status quo from the outside, or rebalance business and society relationships. This section also evokes potential utopian or disillusioning aspects that may characterize such crusades and how humor can play a role in this context.
- Part 3 is labeled "From Business to Society: Humor's Use and Roles in Marketing, Corporate Communications, and Public Relations." It features chapters that aim to highlight, analyze, and synthetize the ways that companies engage in developing humor-laden signals, messages, and practices when interacting with and trying to influence their external stakeholders—particularly, their customer bases.
- Part 4, entitled "Society within Business: Humor's Use and Roles in the Workplace and in Organizations," addresses the internal life of the business organization and the ways that humor, in its diverse forms, can influence activities, relationships, and the organization's functioning in society. The chapters in this last section scrutinize the potential positive effects and impacts of humor-related attitudes and initiatives on organizational life, as well as the darker, toxic sides of humorous activity that can develop within organizational settings—just like in broader society. The related mechanisms entail asserting the superiority and dominance of some organizational members and groups over others, as well as control- and power-related dynamics in organizations.

Humor, business, and society

As Michael Billig explains, positive psychology is one of the fastest growing perspectives in psychology, and it has influenced many industrial and economic advisors. "Positive Psychology: Humour and the Virtues of Negative Thinking" takes a critical look at the way that positive psychologists view humor. According to leading positive psychologists, such as Martin Seligman and Barbara Fredrickson, humor is an essential component of the sort of positivity that prompts personal happiness and economic productivity. Although the proponents of positive psychology claim that their views are purely scientific and based on empirical evidence, this article asserts that such views are actually narrow and deeply ideological. Moreover, positive psychologists' use of self-reported questionnaires is flawed, in that they do not reveal how people actually use humor. In contrast with the present fashion for positivity, this chapter argues for the value of negative thinking.

Yoann Bazin instead imagines that "Friedman and Tocqueville Walk into a Bar. . .: Deciphering the Business *and* Society Discourse." This chapter seeks to decipher the influence of libertarian thought, as manifested in the voice of Milton Friedman, on the "business and society" perspective, as well as to offer a response. Using Alexis de Tocqueville's writing to deconstruct Friedman's views, Bazin notes that they appear so focused on freedom that these views cannot account for the key questions of equality and justice. This chapter thereby contributes to a shift from a business *and* society approach to a more inclusive and democratic business *in* society perspective.

From society to business: humor's use and roles in activist movements

Moving on to a conceptual study, located at the crossroads of humor and social movement theories, François Maon and Adam Lindgreen offer a dual integrative framework of the use and role of humor in contemporary counter-corporate social movements (CCSMs) in "How to Take the Joke: Strategic Uses and Roles of Humor in Counter-Corporate Social Movements." To begin, the framework introduces a two-dimensional taxonomy emphasizing four distinct, movement-level strategic roles for humorous messages in CCSMs: (1) clarification and affirmation, (2) cohesion and mobilization, (3) condemnation and challenging, and (4) designation and differentiation. Then the second part of the framework pertains to the individual, psychological level, where participants in CCSMs can use humor to foster (1) mutual coping, (2) mutual stirring, (3) public mourning, and (4) public protesting. On the basis of this framework, the authors discuss the paradoxical status of humor as an expression of resistance and renunciation in CCSMs that has the potential to affect the status quo at the interface of business and society.

To provide a first-hand insight into the use of humor in activist–business engagement, "Clowning Around: A Critical Analysis of the Role of Humor in Activist–Business Engagement," by Katharina Wolf, offers an in-depth case study, extensive secondary data analysis, and participant observations. The author challenges the notion of humor as a tool for reaching consensus and collaboration, thereby recommending a reconsideration of community activism and its drivers and aims. Humorous activism is not (necessarily) about engagement with corporate representatives or reaching a compromise. Instead, activist–business engagement may be based on irreconcilable differences. The use of humor in grassroots activism primarily seeks to build the activist community and its support network, while challenging existing distributions of power, by drawing greater attention to an issue. When business actors dismiss community activists as unprofessional, immature, or ineffective, they are relying on the assumption that organizations are the targets of the activists' humorous actions. But humor may be a communication strategy in its own right, not as a power leveler or tool to negotiate a common ground but rather as a resistance tool that can confront power and challenge the status quo. In this view, corporate headquarters and organizational representatives represent the stage setting and props.

From business to society: humor's use and roles in marketing, corporate communications, and public relations

The empirical study "A Typological Examination of Effective Humor for Content Marketing" by James Barry and Sandra Graça explores the effectiveness of humorous television advertisements recast on YouTube. From a sample of 2,135 advertisements screened for humorous content and high performance metrics, a typology of ten humor types is derived and analyzed for its effectiveness in terms of grabbing audience attention and stimulating engagement. The inductively derived typology details the incongruity, mockery, and arousal mechanisms used to create humorous content. Overall, social unruliness, as espoused by superiority and relief theories, performs best for attracting attention. The use of absurdity and surprise, as suggested by incongruity theory, performs well for attracting attention and engagement. More disparaging humor, such as putdowns and malicious joy, has less impact on these two outcomes.

Sari Alatalo, Eeva-Liisa Oikarinen, Helena Ahola, and Marc Järvinen next offer a case study of a Finnish online army store to describe the use of humor and its role in ethical brand building for digital content marketing, in "SMEs' Ethical Branding with Humor on Facebook: A Case Study of a Finnish Online Army Store." The case company's online narratives reveal how humor, even in its disparagement form, can build and communicate corporate brand images, based on ethical values. The preliminary three-dimensional framework contributes to an understanding of how ethical values and meaningful topics in society can be communicated through different types of humor in social media. In particular, the ethical brand of the case company currently highlights ethical values such as responsibility and quality, which the company attempts to convey through its use of humor in its Facebook communication. Among the humor types, this company favors wit and satire. This research thus combines considerations of humor and ethical branding, which is a novel contribution to branding literature.

In "With a Genuine Smile? The Relevance of Time Pressure and Emotion Work Strategies for the Adoption of Humor in Customer Contact," Daniel Putz and Tabea Scheel argue that in modern service societies, employees must display organizationally desired emotions, which in turn can increase customer satisfaction and help local retail stores gain and secure customers and sales, especially relative to mobile and e-commerce. Employees might create pleasant customer interactions through the deliberate use of humor, which involves self-regulatory activities. However, the consumption of self-regulatory resources caused by stressful job demands can impair these efforts, as well as employee well-being and mood. This chapter therefore investigates the relationship between time pressure, as a typical demand factor, and the use of positive and negative humor, as mediated by employees' emotion work strategies (i.e., deep and surface acting). This cross-sectional, quantitative study across four German retail stores relies on a regression-based mediation-analysis with bootstrapping. Time pressure is not related to positive humor use or deep acting but relates directly to negative humor use, in an association partially mediated by surface acting. Deep acting also relates positively to positive humor use, and surface acting is positively associated with negative humor use. These results indicate the beneficial effects of deep acting and the undesirable effects of surface acting (and time pressure) for interpersonal customer service performance. Encouraging employees to engage in deep acting thus may prove beneficial, especially for stressful work situations.

Robert J. Angell, Matthew Gorton, and Juliet Memery address the notion of newsjacking—referencing of news stories in paid-for communication—in "Did You

Get It? Newsjacking: What It Is and How to Do It Well." Humor may play a key role in its successful application, but its effectiveness as a marketing tool also might rely on people recognizing the related news story to understand the advertising. This empirical study investigates whether newsjacking might only be as beneficial as the number of people who understand its underlying reference to a news story. With stimuli from a real-life newsjacking advertisement, a survey of 126 people reveals that people with greater news involvement are more likely to recognize the related news story, and then display better attitudes toward the advertisement, brand attitudes, and purchase intentions. Various factors have notable influences, but the findings of this study indicate that the ability to decode the newsjacking message is a critical antecedent of building brand affect. People do need to understand and decode the underlying message for newsjacking advertising to work.

Another use of humor in advertising entails "Promoting, Informing, and Identifying: The Case of Foody, the Humorous Mascot of Expo Milan 2015." Carla Canestrari and Valerio Cori focus on the humorous portrayal of Foody, the mascot of Expo Milan 2015, an impressive business event with a global impact. The Arcimboldesque mascot Foody aims to express the values of the global event it represents. This chapter analyzes these humorous communicative strategies and their functions, in terms of the communicative actions in a corpus of 11 animated cartoons produced by Disney Italia, each starring one of the fruits and vegetables that make up Foody's face (i.e., his friends). Cognitive linguistic and perceptual perspectives of humor have been used to single out the humorous occurrences, and a further analysis based in multimodal discourse highlights their discursive dynamics. Humor can be used in association with an anthropomorphic mascot to promote values and information related to the represented event, as well as to build the identity of the mascot and amuse for the sake of entertaining.

According to Margherita Dore, humor can be used to enhance or challenge interpersonal and social relations in naturally occurring conversations or scripted texts such as jokes or comedy. In advertising, humor promotes products or services (and thus the brand or company that provides them) while seeking audience involvement. However, humor is an idiosyncratic phenomenon, which also varies according to individual cultures and historical time. Using humor in advertising thus can be risky, especially due to its potential offensiveness, which may be inadvertent or intentional. In modern hyper-sensitive settings, such campaigns set out to address their target clientele, so any (unexpected) reaction is worth exploring. Therefore, "Controversial Humor in Advertising: Social and Cultural Implications" focuses on the use of controversial humor in advertising and, in particular, a series of advertisements considered offensive by their receivers at local, national, or global levels, in relation to their themes, language, and culture-specific references. This analysis shows that controversial humor involves a great deal of surprise, but it may not result in a positive customer response to the product or a trade-off effect for the brand itself.

Society within business: humor's use and roles in the workplace and in organizations

Moving to an organizational perspective, "Humor styles in the workplace," by Nicholas A. Kuiper and Nadia B. Maiolino, provides a theoretical–empirical examination of the application of a humor styles model in the workplace. This model reflects a multidimensional approach that specifies both adaptive and maladaptive humor styles, whether self- or other-focused. The use of these humor styles can lead to very different outcomes, ranging from beneficial to detrimental. This model has been used as a theoretical framework to guide empirical investigations of several workplace topics, including job-related stress reduction, organizational commitment, satisfaction with co-workers, work persistence, and effective leadership. Building on such research, this chapter seeks to expand the humor styles model to include consideration of the broader humor climate in the workplace. A further extension of this model details the use of derogatory humor in the workplace. This expanded model can be employed to further understanding of broader societal issues that are of particular relevance to the workplace, such as diversity, sexism, prejudice, racism, and discrimination.

Daryl Peebles, Angela Martin, and Rob Hecker focus on "The Value of Positive Humor in the Workplace: Enhancing Work Attitudes and Performance," noting that the use of humor in workplaces remains a contentious issue in management theory. Some academics and philosophers praise humor and encourage its use; others see it as a frivolous distraction from the job at hand. This chapter reviews literature pertaining to the intersection between humor as a positive human attribute and its possible impact on contemporary workplace management practices. Contributions to arguments that support the benefits of workplace humor come from a clarification about preferred humor styles and the potential of humor as psychological capital (PsyCap). The PsyCap construct emerges from the field of positive psychology and is based on capacities of self-efficacy, resilience, hope, and optimism associated with improved organizational productivity. Researchers can look specifically at workplace humor that is predominantly affiliative, inclusive, and uplifting, to determine if this specific style is valuable for improving workers' attitudes and performance, which would lead to improvements in productivity. The chapter explores the relationship between PsyCap and positive humor, as well as indicators of employee work attitudes and performance, and the potential organizational issues that arise from the use of inappropriate (negative) humor.

Innovation processes also increasingly rely on the collaboration between different stakeholders across various boundaries (e.g., functional, hierarchical, organizational). Such boundary-crossing interactions rely on different mechanisms, activities, and boundary objects. Therefore, in "Laughing Out Loud: How Humor Shapes Innovation Processes within and across Organizations," Marcel Bogers, Alexander Brem, Trine Heinemann, and Elena Tavella consider how humor might act as an appropriate managerial tool to shape these objects, because it affects the social positions of and relationships among individuals. This chapter presents a case study of the use of humor at the micro-level of collaborative innovation processes. With data from workshops, in which participants work together to construct new business models for a particular company, the authors apply conversation analysis to determine that humor (and laughter in particular) can be an important condition for the acceptance of proposals at the interactional micro-level of innovation processes. Company-internal representatives' use of humor differs from that of company-external participants, in terms of their orientation toward different rights and responsibilities in the innovation process.

In contrast, Danielle J. Deveau and Rebecca Scott Yoshizawa challenge the notion of humor as a positive tool for business management in "Laughing Apart: Humor and the Reproduction of Exclusionary Workplace Cultures," by considering the often problematic role of humor in workplace culture. Humor frequently acts as an index of other systemic issues; furthermore, it plays a gatekeeping function for reinforcing workplace cultures and compositions. Scholars tend to emphasize subjective joke perceptions when considering conflicts that arise over workplace humor, thereby overlooking the role of humor for creating inequality, producing in- and out-groups, and reinforcing systemic biases or exclusions (e.g., sexism, racism). To illustrate these points, this chapter considers three recent Canadian discussions of workplace humor as gender harassment: a controversial "humorous" video promoted by Simon Fraser University; the use of pornographic material as a "joke" during a firefighter training course; and the release of the Deschamps Report, which showed that sexual harassment is rampant in the Canadian Armed Forces. In turn, this chapter reveals that humor (1) reinforces social hierarchies, (2) is intimately related to gender harassment in the workplace, and (3) can contribute to a hostile environment in the workplace.

Asking, "Does Verbal Irony Have a Place in the Workplace?" Roger J. Kreuz notes that though people frequently employ verbal irony and sarcasm, there is little consensus about whether the use of such nonliteral language is beneficial or harmful for social relationships. Typically, irony and sarcasm involve saying the opposite of what is literally true, and such statements can be used to mock and disparage others. However, this form of language serves many other purposes too. Irony and sarcasm are also strongly associated with humor and expressions of negative emotion in socially acceptable ways. These forms of language tend to be used by intimates, as a means to foster or invite intimacy. Sarcasm can even facilitate abstract thinking, which may be a requirement for creativity. Face-to-face interactions tend to make ironic communication more successful, because ironists can employ a variety of vocal and visual cues to mark their nonliteral intent. However, these cues are not available in computer-mediated communication, where the successful interpretation of nonliteral language can be particularly challenging. Some aspects of irony and sarcasm are relatively formulaic, and machine classifiers can exploit them to identify such language online. Emoticons also have evolved as a way to signal nonliteral intent, but the effectiveness of such cues has been debated. Verbal irony defies easy categorization, in that it is a pragmatically complex form of language that can be used in the workplace for good or for ill—in some cases, at the same time.

Linda Weiser Friedman and Hershey H. Friedman acknowledge that humor can be a useful tool in the workplace. It helps create a sense of belonging and contributes to group solidarity. Humor can facilitate team building and strengthen relationships; it can help remove barriers that separate management from employees; it can enhance trust and improve morale; it can reduce job stress; and it can help increase creativity. But in "Just Kidding: When Workplace Humor Is Toxic," they also highlight the dark side of humor, such that it can cause great harm in the workplace and be used as a tool to hurt, bully, or exclude others. This chapter reviews the many ramifications of humor and how it can be used in both positive and negative manners.

In "Just a Joke! A Critical Analysis of Organizational Humor," Barbara Plester identifies humor as ubiquitous in modern Western organizations but also argues that because workplace humor occurs within contexts of power, control, resistance, and authority, some complex and ambiguous dynamics are involved. Drawing on a variety of empirical research, this critical analysis considers the ways that humor might be used at work and the implications of humor use by managers and workers in everyday interactions and activities. Specifically, this chapter reveals managerial attempts to control workplace humor, as well as outlining an idiosyncratic organizational context in which humor is the primary method for dominating and controlling subordinate workers. Furthermore, this chapter discusses the use of humor by workers who resist or challenge managerial power. Using humor in this latter way does not significantly change organizational power and control but can temporarily disrupt managerial discourse and domination. Humorous disruption can provide workers with some relief from tension and pressure that may even restore some goodwill in adversarial management–worker interactions. Workplace humor thus ranges from fun, pleasurable interactions to dark, biting, confrontational events disguised by being framed as "just a joke." Considering the critical effects of workplace humor may help organizational members negotiate the complexity of workplace relationships conducted within contexts of tension, status, patriarchy, and power.

Closing remarks

We extend a special thanks to Routledge and its staff, who have been most helpful throughout this entire process. Equally, we warmly thank all the authors who submitted their manuscripts for consideration. They have exhibited the desire to share their knowledge and experience with the book's readers—and a willingness to put forward their views for possible challenge by their peers. We also thank the reviewers, who provided excellent, independent, and incisive consideration of the anonymous submissions.

We hope that this compendium of chapters and themes stimulates and contributes to the ongoing debate surrounding humor's use and roles in business and society. The chapters in this book can help fill some knowledge gaps, while also stimulating further thought and action pertaining to the multiple aspects that surround humor's use and its roles: in activist movements, in marketing, in corporate communications, in public relations, in the workplace, and in organizations.

François Maon, PhD
Lille, France

Adam Lindgreen, PhD
Copenhagen, Denmark

Joëlle Vanhamme, PhD
Lille, France

Robert J. Angell, PhD
Cardiff, Wales

Juliet Memery, PhD
Bournemouth, England
January 31, 2018

References

Apte, M. (1988). Disciplinary boundaries in humorology: An anthropologist's ruminations. *Humor: International Journal of Humor Research*, 1(1), 5–25.

Bonaiuto, M., Castellana, E., and Pierro, A. (2003). Arguing and laughing: The use of humor to negotiate in group discussions. *Humor*, 16(2), 183–223.

Booth-Butterfield, M. and Booth-Butterfield, S. (1991). Individual differences in the communication of humorous messages. *Southern Communication Journal*, 56(3), 205–218.

Burke, K. (1984). *Attitudes toward History*. Berkeley, CA: University of California Press.

Dziegielewski, S.F. Jacinto, G.A., Laudadio, A., and Legg-Rodriguez, L. (2003). Humor: An essential communication tool in therapy. *International Journal of Mental Health*, 32(3), 74–90.

Eisend, M. (2009). A meta-analysis of humor in advertising. *Journal of the Academy of Marketing Science*, 37(2), 191–203.

Graham, E., Papa, M., and Brooks, G. (1992). Functions of humor in conversation: Conceptualization and measurement. *Western Journal of Communication*, 56(1), 161–183.

Hay, J. (2000). Functions of humor in the conversations of men and women. *Journal of Pragmatics*, 32(6), 709–742.

Kutz-Flamenbaum, R.V. (2014). Humor and social movements. *Sociology Compass*, 8(3), 294–304.

McIlheran, J. (2006). The use of humor in corporate communication. *Corporate Communications: An International Journal*, 11(3), 267–274.

Mesmer-Magnus, J., Glew, D., and Chockalingam, V. (2012). A meta-analysis of positive humor in the workplace. *Journal of Managerial Psychology*, 27(2),155–190.

Romero, E.J. and Cruthirds, K. (2006). The use of humor in the workplace. *Academy of Management Perspectives*, 20(2), 58–69.

Sobral, F. and Islam, G. (2015). He who laughs best, leaves last: The influence of humor on the attitudes and behavior of interns. *Academy of Management Learning and Education*, 14(4), 500–518.

Spielmann, N. (2014). How funny was that? Uncovering humor mechanisms. *European Journal of Marketing*, 48(9), 1892–1910.

Westwood, R. and Johnston, A. (2013). Humor in organization: From function to resistance. *Humor*, 26(2), 219–247.

Wolf, K. (2014). Beyond the corporate lens: The use of humor in activist communication. In L.A. Lievrouw (Ed.), *Communication Yearbook: Challenging Communication Research*, pp. 91–105. Bern: Peter Lang Publishing, Inc.

Part 1

Humor, business, and society

1.1 Positive psychology

Humour and the virtues of negative thinking

Michael Billig

In his essay on Karl Kraus, Walter Benjamin compared genuine satirists with the "scribblers who make a trade of mockery and in their invectives have little more in mind than giving the public something to laugh about". Satirists like Kraus, wrote Benjamin, have "firmer ground under their feet" than those who merely seek to elicit laughter. Never was this truer, continued Benjamin, than in a world in which humanity "has run out of tears but not of laughter".[1] The world today is very different from the Germany of 1931, when Benjamin's essay was first published. We live in a pragmatic age. There are experts to advise us on the positive psychological benefits of laughter and tears. We should be grateful to those experts who seem to care about our possibilities for happiness. Yet, there is just as much need to find the firmer ground from which a critique of laughter – even a satire of laughter – can be proposed.

As Benjamin's colleagues in the Frankfurt School argued, if we want to understand the ideological nature of common-sense, then we should try to try to stand outside the positive virtues of accepted sense by taking upon ourselves the requirement to think negatively. According to Herbert Marcuse, negative thinking should function "to break down the self-assurance and self-contentment of common-sense, to undermine the sinister power and language of facts".[2] This applies to laughter and humour. In the false society of the culture industry, wrote Adorno and Horkheimer with more than a touch of cultural elitism, laughter "is a disease" and the laughing audience, obediently responding to those humorous products that have been mass-produced for their benefit, is merely "a parody of humanity".[3]

The notion of thinking negatively is particularly pertinent in the present case, for the ideas to be examined go under the heading of 'positive psychology' and they express the virtues of positive thinking. Included under the rubric of positive thinking is the recommendation to laugh – or at least to laugh and to appreciate humour in a positive manner. In the abstract, how could anyone doubt the worth of laughter, rather than tears, or being positively happy, rather than negatively miserable? However, these views need to be understood in their wider context, rather than being treated as eternal verities.

The ideas of the positive psychologists, and particularly their ideas about humour are being promulgated at a particular time in a particular economic context. They belong to what William Davies has identified as the successful "happiness industry", which is a major profit-making business, as well as being an important feature of today's managerial practices. Previously, happiness was seen to be the consequence of money: if people had money, then they were more likely to be happy. Today, according to Davies, means and ends have been reversed. The happiness of employees is now a means to profitability and, in consequence, companies invest in management consultants and happiness experts to increase the happiness of their employees.[4] More generally happiness is on the agenda of governments around the world.[5] For the past twenty years, positive psychology has been a successful and important part of this trend. Given the extent to which universities act like businesses in the contemporary world, the success of positive psychology can be described in economic terms.[6] It is said to have attracted hundreds of millions of dollars in research grants and has been described as the largest growth industry in psychology.[7]

Positive psychology should not be treated straightforwardly as a scientific theory, as many of its advocates might wish. It can be considered as an ideology, which fits the neoliberal thinking of advanced capitalism. This is "ideological positivism" – not to be confused with "logical positivism", a philosophy which dismissed all non-empirical statements as nonsense and to which no-one subscribes today. Ideological positivism, it will be argued, represents a conformist view. It suggests that there are no basic contradictions within the values and structures of contemporary society. Therefore, if individuals want to achieve their maximum potential for happiness, they need to learn how to change themselves, rather than to change the world. They must learn how to be positive whatever their circumstances; and having a suitable sense of humour is a crucial part of the recommended positivity.[8]

In calling this outlook an 'ideology' we are not suggesting that this is a political ideology that advocates support for a particular party. It is an ideology in the sense of being a form of common-sense that appears to be entirely 'natural' but that in crucial respects reflects the world as it is today. However, this reflection does not represent an undistorted reflection of the world, for, as will be argued, positive psychology involves a science that is limited in its powers of observation. Positive psychologists claim that their views on humour are firmly based upon empirical science and that they are merely being factual when they advocate their positivism. But in practice we will see that there is a gap between the claims of being scientific and the practice of positive science.

Regarding humour, the science that the positive psychologists are creating is a science that avoids looking too closely at what people might be doing when they are being humorous. This avoidance is not chance – it characterises an ideological outlook. Herbert Marcuse wrote that positive thinking can only be explored from a firm ground of negative thinking. This means interpreting what is present in terms of what is absent, and to confront "the given facts with that which they exclude".[9] What positive psychologists say about humour and the examples that they offer to bolster their theories must be understood in terms of what they do not say and the sorts of examples that are significantly absent in their writings.[10]

The science of positive psychology

Positive psychologists like to emphasise how different they are from previous academic psychologists. Martin Seligman, widely recognised to be the pioneer of positive psychology, claims that psychologists used to concentrate on "deficits and disorders", devoting themselves to finding solutions for problems such as depression, alcoholism and other psychological afflictions.[11] By focussing on negative issues, previous psychologists – and Seligman includes his youthful self in this category – ignored the positive psychology of well-being. Now, positive psychologists explore how people can be optimistic, happy and at ease with the world. As a movement, positive psychology has not brought a new psychological method or paradigm in the way that Gestalt psychology in its battle with behaviourism offered very different theoretical assumptions, methodological techniques and conceptual language. Positive psychologists are innovators to the extent that they have applied the orthodox methods and constructs of psychology to a new set of problems.

When Seligman and others commend the power of being optimistically positive, they write in ways that recall the sort of self-help books inspired by Norman Victor Peale's *The Power of Positive Thinking* – a work that has influenced Donald Trump, whose parents attended the church in which Peale preached. Peale advocated that everyone should apply the principles of positive thinking to their lives and that if they do, they will succeed personally and economically. The general message might resemble that of today's positive psychologists, but there is one big difference: the positive psychologists claim that their message is scientifically based. For example, Seligman writes: "The appeal of what I write comes from the fact that it is grounded in careful science: statistical tests, validated questionnaires, through researched exercises, and large, representative samples."[12] The word 'science' is seldom far from the writings of positive psychologists. When in an academic lecture Seligman cites the work that he and his colleagues have been doing, he refers to it as "the kind of science that is done in positive psychology".[13] He produces a scientific formula to describe his theory of happiness: $H=S+C+V$.[14] Critics have mocked the scientific pretensions of the formula, declaring it to be meaningless.[15]

Many of the scientific findings that Seligman and other positive psychologists cite in support of their ideas have come from scales which have been devised to assess phenomena such as optimism, happiness, positive thinking, resilience, psychological health, and so on. Positive psychologists seek to discover positive correlations between these measures of positive variables. Those who score highly on one measure are likely to score highly on others. It is as if it is possible to win the jackpot with a row of winning scores. This is not some sort of imagined pure science that is derived entirely from mathematical formula and statistical analyses. Rhetoric has its part to play. If not all measures of happiness are correlated with the other positive measures, then the researchers will sometimes divide up the troublesome variable into several variables. They will label those variables that win the correlational jackpot with rhetorically positive terminology. Thus, Seligman claims that "authentic happiness", as contrasted with inauthentic happiness, is correlated with other positive variables. The terminology is not haphazardly selected but it functions rhetorically to strengthen the impression that the positive goodies complement each other.[16]

The scientific display can be maintained by using metaphors as if they were literal descriptions. Barbara Fredrickson describes one of her studies in which volunteers improved their ability to concentrate if they "were injected with positivity".[17] Of course, they were not literally injected with positivity, or indeed with anything. They were given a small bag of chocolates. Talking of injecting with positivity closes the gap between what actually occurred and the language of medical and scientific theory.[18] It treats the so-called injection as if it were an objective fact and shuts down other explanations why those who have just been given a present might be more attentive to their surroundings. Fredrickson's choice of language suggests that it was the injectable "positivity" that made the scientific difference.

Distinguishing between authentic and inauthentic experiences, such as between authentic happiness and the non-authentic varieties, is not peculiar to positive psychology. The negative thinkers of the Frankfurt School did much the same when they claimed that the laughter elicited by the culture industry was inauthentic.[19] Positive psychology makes a very different link between authentic emotion and economics. They suggest that a positive outlook can bring economic success to individuals. Seligman writes that the "most important resource building human trait" is probably "productivity at work".[20]

He argues that those who are generally happy are likely to be happier at work and are, in consequence, likely to be more productive; and this in turn increases their earning power, leading to further authentic happiness. It is a benevolent circle resulting in financial and psychological jackpots, as well as consulting contracts for the experts in positive psychology. It is as if all the positive cherries can come up in a line on the fruit-machine of life.

In this way, positive psychology exemplifies an ideology as well as being a psychological theory. It advises individuals how to maximise their economic productivity. This is not by individuals seeking to change the world in which they have to work but by positively and happily fitting themselves to that world. The web-sites that promote positive psychology reinforce this impression. The University of Pennsylvania Positive Psychology Centre, whose director is Seligman, advertises that "Positive psychology is the scientific study of the strengths that enable individuals and communities to thrive".[21] The Penn Resilience Program, which is part of the Centre, claims to have worked with individuals, teams, and leadership groups from a variety of organisations; these include "Military, Corporations, First responders including police officers, Government. . ."[22] The list is revealing for its absences, as much as its presences. The Centre does not mention work with teams from trade unions, radical parties or other organisations that want to change the world. The groups that the Centre is proud to mention are those that superintend, or profit from, the world as it is.

Humour and ideological positivism

It still remains to be seen how the specific topic of humour fits in with the general approach of positive psychology. Theoretically it is one of the core elements. According to Seligman, there are twenty-four "signature strengths" that positive psychology aims to improve in people. In *Authentic Happiness*, he describes these strengths as "measurable and acquirable".[23] He includes a shortened version of his VIA Scale (or values-in-action scale) so that readers can identify their own signature strengths. The abbreviated questionnaire includes for each strength the two "most discriminating questions" from the complete scale. One of the key strengths measured by the scale is "playfulness and humour". People with this strength are described as liking to laugh and to bring smiles to other people.

The two questions measuring this trait are: "I always mix work and play as much as possible" and "I rarely say funny things". For each question there are five possible answers. Seligman tells his readers how to score their selected two answers: "this is your humour score". One might note that the first of the two questions not only assumes that responders will have work but that it is possible for them to find playfulness in their work. It does not presume work to be unremitting toil that is closely supervised. It assumes, in the manner of contemporary employment and productivity strategies, that fun is permissible at work.

There are several problems with determining "humour scores" in this way. Most crucially the measure relies on two self-report questions, neither of which asks about what sorts of things the respondents might find funny. Certainly the assessment does not include a behavioural element with respondents being observed either telling jokes or listening to them. In short, the questionnaire does not say anything about the nature of the respondents' sense of humour or 'humour style'.

Self-report questions can be problematic, especially when there are issues of social desirability, because respondents have to be trusted to answer honestly. Given the general social value placed on having a good sense of humour, the question "I rarely say funny things" is asking respondents to admit to a trait that is hardly socially desirable. Regarding humour, there is a specific problem of trust, which Freud in his great work *Jokes and Their Relation to the Unconscious* posed clearly. He distinguished between tendentious jokes, which break social taboos, and innocent jokes, which only use word-play or what Freud called joke-work. Freud argued that we tend to laugh more at tendentious jokes than at innocent jokes such as puns. Because tendentious jokes share the same sort of word-play as innocent jokes, the greater laughter that they evoke must be related to the themes of the joke and the release of wishes that cannot normally be expressed in conversation. However, if you ask someone why they are laughing at a tendentious joke, they will always cite the joke-work, not the topic. No-one is likely to justify their laughter at a lavatory joke by saying, "I always find jokes about poo uproariously funny". This means, according to Freud, that we deceive ourselves by believing that we are only laughing at the cleverness of a joke, not at its capacity to allow the unsayable to be momentarily said.

Seligman dismisses Freud. He claims that Freud's notion that childhood events determine adult lives is "worthless". He even writes inaccurately that, according to Freud, even our jokes are "strictly determined by forces from our past".[24] That characterisation fails to acknowledge Freud's distinction between tendentious and innocent jokes, as well as his careful analyses of joke-work. It also ignores the fact that Freud's ideas have been supported by the sort of experimental study that Seligman usually likes to describe as "scientific".[25]

Freud, as is well known, loved jokes, especially Jewish jokes.[26] Yet, it is possible to detect signs of self-deceit in his own understanding and appreciation of humour – a self-deceit that paradoxically confirms his theory. Freud saw the Jewish joke as an act of rebellion against the logic of the gentile world. More generally, he claimed that humour "is not resigned; it is rebellious".[27] In writing like this, Freud was ignoring the conservative, disciplinary force of humour. Many sociologists have claimed that people observe the minor but restricting codes of everyday behaviour, because they fear the social embarrassment that would ensue from a breach. Behind the fear of being embarrassed lies the fear of being laughed at, for, in many social situations, people will laugh at those who fail to observe everyday codes.[28] An instance can be found in Freud's own writing. He recounts when Little Hans, the young child of a close friend and psychoanalytic follower, was staying at a hotel on a family holiday.[29] The other guests were outwardly amused when at mealtimes the boy tried to catch the attention of a little girl, the only other child of the same age in the hotel. The adults laughed and the boy became embarrassed. To the guests, and later to Freud, it seemed as if the boy was behaving just like an adult in love, and he was becoming embarrassed because his desires were being observed. Freud did not notice a lonely little boy, wanting to make a friend, but embarrassed by the adult mockery as he flouted the grown-up codes of polite behaviour in a hotel dining-room. The more embarrassed the child became, the greater the adult fun. In not noticing this, Freud was failing to note the disciplinary, and certainly non-rebellious, functions of laughter. He did not notice that the adult laughter, carrying across the separate tables, was itself flouting the dining-room codes. The adults were enjoying themselves too much to notice.[30]

The episode in a middle-class, middle-European hotel in the early years of the twentieth century shows the difficulty of analysing humour. Things are frequently not quite as they appear, especially as they appear to those enjoying the laughter. At first sight what seems to be a moment of innocent amusement can, if one looks more closely, turn out to have disturbing undercurrents. As Freud suggested, we need to suspect what people say about their own laughter, not because they wish to deceive others but because they are deceiving themselves. There is social pressure to have a good sense of humour, although what constitutes a good sense of humour is socially unclear. To this end all of us want to believe that our laughter is a sign of playfulness, good spirit and harmless fun, not cruelty or what Henri Bergson called "a momentary anaesthesia of the heart".[31]

Attempting to distinguish between positive and negative humour

Despite positive psychologists claiming that humour is a signature strength of positivity, early results did not show strong correlations between humorousness and other positive variables. Rod Martin showed that the widely publicised links between humour and health were at best weak and mainly non-existent. He was also perplexed by other failures to show links between humour and other strengths of positivity.[32] However, Martin did not give up on the idea that humour is an important aspect of positivity. He believed that the failure of previous measures was that they treated humour as a unitary phenomenon and, in so doing, they failed to distinguish between positive and negative types of humour. In his view, only the positive types of humour would be correlated with the other measures of positivity. Therefore, he set out to develop a questionnaire to distinguish between positive and negative types of humour. The result was the Humour Styles Questionnaire (HSQ), another self-report measure.[33] The questionnaire, its wording and its construction bear close examination in order to see how ideological assumptions run through both the aims and the methodology of the scale.

In order to distinguish between different forms of humour, Martin concentrated on humour's functions rather than on its contents. He distinguished between the positive and negative functions of humour, as well as the intrapsychic and interpersonal functions of humour. Intrapsychic functions referred to the effects of humour on the self, and interpersonal functions referred to the effect on people's relations with others. This gave rise to four distinguishable types of humour based on these two sets of functions.

Affiliative humour positively bolsters one's interpersonal relations by bringing people closer together in a benevolent way. According to Martin, "individuals who are high on this dimension tend to say funny things, to tell jokes, and to engage in spontaneous witty banter to amuse others, to facilitate relationships, and to reduce interpersonal tensions". In the HSQ, affiliative humour was to be gauged by questions such as "I laugh and joke a lot with my closest friends". *Aggressive* humour, by contrast, is used to demean others and as such it can be presumed to have a deleterious effect on relations with others. Aggressive humour was assessed by questions like "If someone makes a mistake, I will often tease them about it".[34]

As for the two intrapsychic forms of humour, the beneficial form was *Self-enhancing* humour. This refers to humour that enhances one's sense of well-being without harming others and helps the person to overcome obstacles in life. According to Martin, it represents "a tendency to be frequently amused by the incongruities of life, and to maintain a humorous perspective even in the face of stress or adversity". In the HSQ this dimension was assessed by questions such as "If I am feeling depressed, I can usually cheer myself up with humour". *Self-defeating* humour occurs when people use humour to mock or demean themselves in harmful ways, for example if they do so in order to try to gain favour with others. It was assessed by questions such as "I will often get carried away in putting myself down if it makes my family or friends laugh".[35]

Martin does not use neutral scientific categories to describe these four types of humour. By and large, he employs everyday categories which are value-laden: categories such as "deleterious", "benevolent", "amuse", "harm", "witty banter", etc. Even the names selected for the four types of humour capture everyday values. It is better to affiliate with others than to be aggressive towards them; to be enhanced is preferable to being defeated. In the same way the contrasting terms "adaptive" and "maladaptive", which Martin and his colleague use to describe respectively the positive and negative functions of humour, assume the desirability of being adaptive and the undesirability of being maladaptive.

Martin argues that previous humour questionnaires failed to recognise the maladaptive forms of humour. He ends his article about the construction of the HSQ with the hope that research with the new questionnaire "may provide better understanding of the ways in which humour may function as an adaptive resource for psychological health, as well as the ways in which it may interfere with healthy adjustment and impair relationships with others".[36] As is customary in this type of writing, the author does not explain what is meant by "adjustment" and "maladjustment", nor specify what exactly a person might be adjusting to or failing to adjust to. The category "healthy adjustment" is taken to be self-evidently desirable. Moreover, other positive psychologists have taken up this difference between adaptive and maladaptive humour. For example, one positive psychologist who links humour with resilience writes: "In contrast to these two adaptive humour styles, the maladaptive humour styles tend to be detrimental to either the self (self-defeating humour) or others (aggressive humour)."[37] There is a further semantic move when researchers equate the positive forms of humour with a "good sense of humour", although nothing about the content of the humour has been mentioned.[38]

These general distinctions, which can also be found in pop psychology and everyday thinking, provide the basis for this development in the positive psychology of humour. Of course, the development itself is highly technical. Martin's questionnaire emerges from some of the features that Seligman equates with science: statistical tests and large representative samples (although the representativeness of Martin's sample can be questioned, because a large proportion of his respondents were students). The technical development provides the evidence for the distinctions that originally motivated the search for the evidence. It is an example of what Herbert Marcuse, that champion of negative thinking, had in mind when he wrote that "empiricism proves itself as positive thinking".[39]

Ignoring contradictions

Those believing in ideological positivism aim to show that everybody can make their personal world of positivity, in which the various virtues of positivity are attainable. All it requires is personal rather than social change. "Adaptive" is assumed to be a benefit. There is no hint that adapting to a world that is itself maladaptive might be maladaptive. This type of positivism represents more than a theory, for it expresses an outlook that involves overlooking a series of existing contradictions. This is where the methodology of self-report questionnaires can be ideologically revealing.

The HSQ assumes that friendly teasing can be separated from aggressive teasing. Martin writes that "although friendly teasing and playfully poking fun at others may be a way of enhancing cohesiveness in more benign forms of affiliative humour", this did not count as aggressive humour which intends "to belittle others, albeit often under the guise of playful fun".[40] Thus, the playful and the aggressive types of humour can be distinguished. However, things are not so simple in real life. There is evidence that in close relationships those who tease their partner wrongly believe that their partner enjoys the good fun of being teased.[41] Such teasing can be an exercise of power and the victims risk being branded as lacking a sense of humour if they protest. There is nothing new in this. Over three hundred years ago, Jonathan Swift wrote that the victim of mockery in conversation "is obliged not to be angry, to avoid the imputation of not being able to take a jest".[42]

Of course, the methodology of self-report questionnaires cannot uncover the complex operation of power in such situations. The researcher has to take the respondents at their word, including the victims who hide their hurt, and the perpetrators who deceive themselves that their bullying is enjoyed by the victims. Although researchers such as Martin might acknowledge the difficulty of identifying the precise spot where friendly teasing shades into aggressive teasing, their methodology is designed to treat the two forms as if they were entirely distinct, rather than being inherently contestable. Yet the methodology does not fully succeed in satisfying the aims. The dimensions of affiliative and aggressive humour are not entirely separate. Martin's own study reveals that for male participants there was a .28 correlation between the two dimensions, while with female participants there was a .22 correlation (with both correlations being statistically significant). Subsequent researchers have tended to dismiss such correlations, even without describing what they might be. For example, Kuiper claims that "evidence is. . .strong that the four scales of the HSQ are distinct from one another, with intercorrelations being in the low to modest range".[43] It is as if researchers wish to avoid recognising that affiliative humour might be aggressive, as groups draw together by laughing at outsiders, foreigners or even scapegoats within their midst.

There is one omission that particularly underlines the inherent conservatism of ideological positivism. The functions of mockery that Martin seeks to identify are those that might harm the self's own psychological health or harm the person's interpersonal relations. The social world shrinks to the individual and the individual's personal relations. Humour relating to the wider social world does not feature in the HSQ. The socially rebellious function of humour that Freud stressed is theoretically and methodologically absent. There is no attempt to identify the firmer grounding that Walter Benjamin attributed to Kraus and to Swift and that gives their satire deeper meaning. Neither in the VIA nor in the HSQ are there questions about using humour for social critique: nothing in the style of "I find it funny when the powerful and the corrupt are satirised" – nothing about the way that mockery might help to establish justice in an unjust world. Instead, the positivity of the wider world is taken as an unspoken assumption. It is individual adjustment that matters.

Humourless writing

There is a further absence in the writings of positive psychologists on humour. They stress the positive value of humour – at least, the right type of humour – but when they write on humour, they tend to be humourless, despite the value that they place on humour. Martin's article about the development of the HSQ contains no illustrative jokes nor humorous passing remarks. All is seriously earnest. This is quite different from Freud's *Jokes and Their Relation to the Unconscious*. The author's love of jokes is clearly apparent. Freud knew that there was no inherent opposition between wit and serious investigation. Being funny can be a way of being serious.[44] It is possible for analysts of humour to be seriously funny, especially when mocking the work of others from a firm alternative grounding.

There is much to find funny in positive psychology, as Barbara Ehrenreich demonstrates in the witty sarcasm she uses in *Smile or Die*, especially when she discusses her meetings with Martin Seligman.[45] I must admit that some of Seligman's self-aggrandising comments have made me smile, even laugh. Towards the end of one chapter in *Authentic*

Happiness he asserts that the chapter ideally represents a win–win situation: "If I have done my job well, I grew intellectually by writing it, and so did you by reading it."[46] In each of Seligman's three works that are cited in the present piece, he mentions that he was once elected president of the American Psychological Association. His pride is clear, especially when in *Authentic Happiness* he describes at length how he nervously waited for the results to be declared. And there is no false modesty as he claims in *Flourish*: "I was elected by the largest majority in history."[47] To adapt Oscar Wilde's comment on the death of Little Nell: one must have a heart of stone – or a mind of mush – not to laugh at this self-enhancing tale of triumph.

Occasionally a joke slips through. Then we can see why so few do. Barbara Fredrickson provides an instance in *Positivity*, when she is discussing amusement as one of ten forms of positivity. She provides some hypothetical examples of amusement. One occurs when a neighbour "shares her latest favourite joke ('What do you call an agnostic, dyslexic insomniac?')". Amusements are not serious, Fredrickson writes, and "heartfelt amuse-ment" brings the "irrepressible urge" to share your joviality with others. When you laugh at your neighbour's joke, you signal that "you find the current situation to be safe and light-hearted and that you'd like to build connections with others".[48] Another win–win situation in which genuinely positive emotions broaden and build.[49]

Fredrickson gives the answer to her joke/riddle in a footnote, which is physically separated from the question by almost two hundred pages: "Answer: Someone who lies awake at night wondering if dog exists."[50] What Freud would have called the 'joke-work' depends on swapping the word 'dog' for 'god'. The joke assumes that teller and hearer are able to distinguish between the two words but they imagine that dyslexics cannot or might not; in reality, rather than in the stereotype that the joke plays upon, this is not an error that dyslexics are likely to make. The joke is an instance of what some analysts call 'superiority humour': the joke-teller and their audience assume the inferiority of dyslex-ics, who make mistakes that teller and hearers do not. And that makes the joke funny.[51] Accordingly, the joviality, the heartfelt amusement, the safety and the building of social connections depend on mocking imagined inferiors. All the positive win–wins in the hypothetical situation demand an anaesthetic of the heart.

No wonder positive analysts of humour do not encourage researchers to conduct in-depth studies of actual examples. They would then find that the categories, which are separated in the self-report questionnaires, are intermixed in real life. Positive psycholo-gists might champion the values of amusement and a good sense of humour but we have to take the nature of these phenomena on trust from the scientists, just as they take on trust what their respondents tell them. In this way, the research is conducted at a distance from everyday practice. A more sceptical position, which no doubt the positively-minded would disparage as hopelessly negative, allows us to see the ideological character of this outlook. There is no doubting that positive psychology today is successful both academi-cally and economically. It presents itself as a serious science with seriously profitable appli-cations, but, all the same, it's a funny business.

References

1 Walter Benjamin, "Karl Kraus", in *Reflections* (New York: Harcourt Brace Jovanovich, 1978), pp. 239–272.
2 Herbert Marcuse, "A note on dialectic", in *The Essential Frankfurt School Reader*, ed. A. Arato and E. Gebhardt (Oxford: Basil Blackwell, 1978).
3 Theodor Adorno and Max Horkheimer, *Dialectic of Enlightenment* (London: Verso, 1979).

4 William Davies, *The Happiness Industry* (London: Verso, 2015).

5 Laura Hyman, *Happiness: Understandings, Narratives and Discourses* (London: Palgrave/Macmillan, 2014).

6 Brendan Cantwell and Ilkka Kauppinen (eds), *Academic Capitalism in the Age of Globalization* (Baltimore, MD: Johns Hopkins University Press, 2014); Sheila Slaughter and Gary Rhoades, *Academic Capitalism and the New Economy* (Baltimore, MD: Johns Hopkins University Press, 2004).

7 Kristján Kristjánsson, *Virtues and Vices of Positive Psychology* (Cambridge: Cambridge University Press, 2013).

8 Michael Billig, *Laughter and Ridicule* (London: Sage, 2005).

9 Marcuse, op. cit., p. 447.

10 See Michael Billig and Cristina Marinho, *The Politics and Rhetoric of Commemoration* (London: Bloomsbury Books, 2017) for a discussion of the value of examining discursive and social phenomena in terms of significant absences.

11 Martin E. P. Seligman, *Authentic Happiness* (London: Nicholas Brealey, 2003), p. 21.

12 Martin E. P. Seligman, *Flourish: A New Understanding of Happiness and Well-being* (London: Nicholas Brealey, 2011), p. 1.

13 Martin E. P. Seligman, *Flourish: Positive Psychology and Positive Interventions*. The Tanner Lectures on Human Values (Chicago, IL: University of Michigan, 2011), p. 234.

14 Seligman, *Authentic Happiness*, p. 45.

15 Barbara Ehrenreich, *Smile or Die* (London: Granta, 2009); Andrew Anthony, "The British amateur who debunked the mathematics of happiness". *Observer*, January 19 (2014), https://www.theguardian.com/science/2014/jan/19/mathematics-of-happiness-debunked-nick-brown.

16 Kristjánsson, op. cit., chapter two.

17 Barbara Fredrickson, *Positivity* (London: Oneworld, 2009), p. 48.

18 See Michael Billig, *Learn to Write Badly: How to Succeed in the Social Sciences* (Cambridge: Cambridge University Press, 2013) for a more general critique of this type of rhetoric in psychological and social scientific writing.

19 See Adorno and Horkheimer, op. cit.; Herbert Marcuse, *One Dimensional Man* (London: Sphere, 1968). Positive psychologists who value the positive benefits of optimism would be unsurprised that the negatively thinking Frankfurt School members were generally pessimistic about the possibilities for transforming the society that they criticised: John Abromeit, *Max Horkheimer and the Foundations of the Frankfurt School* (New York: Cambridge University Press, 2011); Stuart Jeffries, *Grand Hotel Abyss* (London: Verso, 2016).

20 Seligman, *Authentic Happiness*, p. 40.

21 Accessed at http://ppc.sas.upenn.edu/.

22 Seligman also advises educational establishments. In January 2017 the University of Buckingham, one of the few private universities in Britain, welcomed Seligman as its new official advisor. Henceforward, all tutors would be trained in positive psychology and all students at the university would be required to take a module in positive psychology. https://www.timeshighereducation.com/news/happiness-expert-advises-uks-first-positive-university?utm_source=the_editorial_newsletter&utm_medium=email&utm_content=other_stories&utm_campaign=the_editorial_newsletter.

23 Seligman, *Authentic Happiness*, chapter nine.

24 Seligman, Ibid., pp. 66–67.

25 See, for example, Dolf Zillmann, "Disparagement humour", in *Handbook of Humour Research*, vol. 1, ed. P. E. McGee and J. H. Goldstein (New York: Springer, 1983).

26 Theodor Reik, *Jewish Wit* (New York: Gamut, 1962); Ruth R. Wisse, *No Joke: Making Jewish Humour* (Princeton, NJ: Princeton University Press, 2013).

27 Sigmund Freud, "Humour", in *Art and Literature*, Penguin Freud Library, vol. 14, ed. S. Freud (Harmondsworth: Penguin, 1985).

28 Billig, *Laughter and Ridicule*.

29 Sigmund Freud, "Analysis of a phobia in a five year old boy ('Little Hans')", in *Case Histories, I*, Penguin Freud Library, vol. 8 (Harmondsworth: Penguin, 1909/1990).

30 Billig, *Laughter and Ridicule*, chapter seven.

31 Henri Bergson, *Laughter* (London: Macmillan, 1911).

32 Rod A. Martin, "Humour, laughter and physical health: Methodological issues and research findings", *Psychological Bulletin*, 127(4) (2001): 504–519.

33 Rod A. Martin, P. Puhlik-Doris, G. Larsen, J. Gray and K. Weir, "Individual differences in uses of humour and their relation to psychological well-being: Development of the Humor Styles Questionnaire", *Journal of Research in Personality*, 37(1) (2003): 48–75.

34 Ibid., p. 53.

35 Ibid.

36 Ibid., p. 73.

37 Nicholas A. Kuiper, "Humour and resiliency: Towards a process model of coping and growth", *Europe's Journal of Psychology*, 8(3) (2012): 475–491.

38 For example Kuiper, op. cit.; Arnie Cann and Chantal Collette, "Sense of humour, stable affect, and psychological well-being", *Europe's Journal of Psychology*, 10(3) (2014): 464–479.

39 Marcuse, *One Dimensional Man*, p. 139.

40 Martin et al., op. cit., p. 52.

41 Dacher Keltner, R. C. Young, E. A. Heerey, C. Oemig and N. D. Monarch, "Teasing in hierarchical and intimate relations", *Journal of Personality and Social Psychology*, 75(5) (1998): 1231–1247. See also Billig, *Laughter and Ridicule*, pp. 160ff.

42 Jonathan Swift, "Hints towards an essay on conversation", in *Tale of the Tub and Other Satires* (London: J. M. Dent, 1909).

43 Kuiper, op. cit., p. 482.

44 Patricia Cormack, James F. Cosgrave and David Feltmate, "A funny thing happened on the way to sociology: Goffman, Mills, and Berger", *Sociological Review*, 65(2) (2017): 386–400; Aída D. Bild, "The Finkler question: Very funny is very serious," *Atlantis*, 35(1) (2013): 85–101.

45 Ehrenreich, op. cit.

46 Seligman, *Authentic Happiness*, p. 44.

47 Seligman, *Flourish: A New Understanding*, p. 61.

48 Fredrickson, *Positivity*, p. 45.

49 For Fredrickson's broaden and build theory of positive emotions, see *inter alia* Barbara Fredrickson, "What good are positive emotions?" *Review of General Psychology*, 2(3) (1998): 300–319; Barbara Fredrickson and Thomas Joiner, "Positive emotions trigger upward spirals toward emotional well-being", *Psychological Science*, 13(2) (2002): 172–175.

50 Fredrickson, *Positivity*, p. 238.

51 John Morreall, *Taking Laughter Seriously* (Albany, NY: State University of New York Press, 1983). For an analysis of jokes about dyslexics, see Andrew Goatly, *Meaning and Humour* (New York: Cambridge University Press, 2012), pp. 29ff.

1.2 Friedman and Tocqueville walk into a bar. . .

Deciphering the business *and* society discourse

Yoann Bazin

This is an honest introduction. Thanks to the editors of the present book, I went and properly read Milton Friedman. I was hoping to make a joke out of him—after all, this is a book about humor—by taking a few inflammatory extracts and shredding them to pieces, in the way that some overly casual referencing in our scholarship (and in some student essays) has done over the years. Was I wrong. . . Instead, I discovered a precise and honest thinker—more so than many authors that I admire and agree with. As a result, I had to question myself and dig deeper to find something to make my way back to my comfort zone. For that intellectual journey, I start this chapter with something unusual: absolutely no thanks to the editors for the emotional and intellectual distress this caused me.

Milton Friedman walks into a bar and presents his thesis. . . and then, many opportunistic academic followers, corporate executives and hasty journalists go on to caricature his words, pick and choose some extracts, and serve their own purpose. I have to admit that I was one of them until recently[1] and for that I express some regrets. Not complete ones, because in my caricature I hope I have contributed to limiting the work of these opportunists who use Friedman to advance their private interests against the ones of less powerful citizens. But there are some regrets nonetheless. What I would like to present here therefore is a synthesized, but closer reading of *Capitalism and Freedom* (Friedman's famous 1962 book), and explain how I crawled my way out of that particular libertarian 'black hole.'

Because after Milton Friedman walked into the bar, he saw Alexis de Tocqueville sitting in a dark corner. Indeed, I will aim to show how, helped by a conversation with de Tocqueville, but also Michael Sandel, it is possible to contradict the libertarian argument Friedman advanced. This is not in relation to its internal logic, for *Capitalism and Freedom* is astonishingly sound on that score. Neither is it in relation to its consequences, since its defenders have become good at finding creative alternative causes to many of them, for instance that the sole origin of the Global Financial Crisis is the Federal Reserve and its non-libertarian approach to markets. The same goes for the rise of social and economic inequalities in Western countries since the 1980s or the invasion of corporate and managerial rationales in our lives. I will do so by taking a wider point of view of democratic societies offered by Tocqueville's *Of Democracy in America*, which perhaps surprisingly, even Milton Friedman partly agrees with.

In doing so, I will work to decipher the 'business & society' academic discourse in management and organization studies, and show that it encompasses two streams, one of which I will defend as being in fact about business *in* society.

Milton Friedman walks into a bar. . .

Free capitalism or tyranny! A gentle libertarian warning

In Friedman's perspective, capitalism is fundamentally *the* economic system that puts freedom at its very core. In his words, "exchange can therefore bring about co-ordination without coercion. A working model of a society organized through voluntary exchange is a free private enterprise exchange economy what we have been calling competitive capitalism."[2] Any kind of regulation, for instance, will be considered under this measuring gaze: the extent to which it limits freedom. Given that freedom is *the* fundamental value—the one and only, as we will see later—any such limitation is problematic, no matter how popular it can be. As he notes,

> the citizen of the United States who is compelled by law to devote something like 10 per cent of his income to the purchase of a particular kind of retirement contract, administered by the government, is being deprived of a corresponding part of his personal freedom. (. . .) True, the number of citizens who regard compulsory old age insurance as a deprivation of freedom may be few, but the believer in freedom has never counted noses (. . .) A citizen of the United States who under the laws of various states is not free to follow the occupation of his own choosing unless he can get a license for it, is likewise being deprived of an essential part of his freedom.[3]

Pushed to the radical status of an ideology, liberty and freedom thus become libertarianism.

Importantly, as a true, that is holistic, libertarian, Milton Friedman does not only preach freedom for corporations—as many opportunist readers have tried, and still try to pretend. Instead, this is extended to all forms of markets, and even the rest of society. In this way, he is much more intellectually coherent than many of his self-appointed heirs. In Friedman's framework, liberty and freedom are untouchable values that infuse all structures, from economics to politics, and even education. This is where his economic doctrine becomes highly political.

For Friedman, this is a consequentialist concern. In particular, as soon as we contemplate limiting freedom in any manner, we are on a slippery slope leading quickly to tyranny:

> Because we live in a largely free society, we tend to forget how limited is the span of time and the part of the globe for which there has ever been anything like political freedom: the typical state of mankind is tyranny, servitude, and misery.[4]

Resultantly, his perspective tends to make him paint the world in black and white, with absolute freedom on one side and liberticidal rigid constraints on the other. As he argued,

> fundamentally, there are only two ways of co-ordinating the economic activities of millions. One is central direction involving the use of coercion—the technique of the army and of the modern totalitarian state. The other is voluntary co-operation of individuals—the technique of the market place.[5]

Absolute freedom or dreadful tyranny. Not quite a subtle depiction of the world, is it?

In this somehow ontological take on freedom, the onus is instead on individuals, who must be left alone "to wrestle with" the ethical dilemmas they face. A libertarian like Friedman therefore cannot be simply either a conservative or a social liberal, as any pre-determination or limitation of individuals' agency by any kind of system would be a contradiction. Indeed,

> in a society freedom has nothing to say about what an individual does with his free-dom; it is not an all-embracing ethic (. . .) The 'really' important ethical problems are those that face an individual in a free society—what he should do with his freedom.[6]

This take on ethical dilemmas is quite appealing and seems self-evident. Importantly however, it also leads to a view of markets and society as deprived of any politics, or even anthropology.

An a-political view of the social

To Friedman, free markets are the ideal place for the freedom of individuals to be expressed, through the exchange of goods and services. In these markets, no pressure or distortion should occur. But how idealized and utopic does the following description sound?

> Indeed, a major source of objection to a free economy is precisely that it does this task so well. It gives people what they want instead of what a particular group thinks they ought to want. Underlying most arguments against the free market is a lack of belief in freedom itself.[7]

In this ideal, there are apparently no influential power plays by international corporations and no manipulative marketing campaigns, for instance.

When looked at closely, the world viewed by Milton thus entirely lacks any kind of anthropology. Although it is never phrased this way, it is far from being hidden. As he wrote in the first paragraph of the introduction, "to the free man, the country is the col-lection of individuals who compose it, not something over and above them."[8] He adds a little later that "in its simplest form, such a society consists of a number of independent households, a collection of Robinson Crusoes, as it were."[9] In Friedman's mind, we are all castaways—who happen to be living on the same island.

Consequently, society appears as no more than a play or a set of rules followed by individuals. There is no community beyond—in a sense of something that would be part of these individuals. In his telling,

> the day-to-day activities are like the actions of the participants in a game when they are playing it; the framework, like the rules of the game they play. And just as a good game requires acceptance by the players both of the rules and of the umpire to interpret and enforce them, so a good society requires that its members agree on the general conditions that will govern relations among them, on some means of arbitrat-ing different interpretations of these conditions, and on some device for enforcing compliance with the generally accepted rules.[10]

In his libertarian view, therefore, individuals in society have no anthropological aspects, no cultural or common parts of themselves they would share with other members of the tribe. Their realities merely contain external constraints, which they freely choose to respect, or not.

This last aspect leads Friedman to what I found to be the weak point of his argument: justice. In particular,

> the liberal conceives of men as imperfect beings. He regards the problem of social organization to be as much a negative problem of preventing "bad" people from doing harm as of enabling "good" people to do good; and, of course, "bad" and "good" people may be the same people, depending on who is judging them.[11]

Indeed, how can you conceive a non-relativist system of justice without any core value other than freedom? This is especially since any judgment or limitation of what individuals do with their freedom is considered close to tyrannical. In addition, following this, how can you imagine a system of social responsibility and accountability for corporations in which such freedom is protected, without the prevention he himself refers to?

The libertarian influence on the relation between business and society

It is only after considering in some detail the thesis offered by Friedman that we can, in all intellectual honesty, assess his frequently quoted maxim:

> Few trends could so thoroughly undermine the very foundations of our free society as the acceptance by corporate officials of a social responsibility other than to make as much money for their stockholders as possible. This is a fundamentally subversive doctrine.[12]

The infamous position, based on which we can paint Milton as an awful defender of corporations.

The very idea of a corporate social responsibility as a principle or a value predates Friedman's 1962 classic. Indeed, critical examinations of the links between businesses and society can be traced back to the early 1920s. It can be argued that it led to an academic field in itself with the birth of the academic journal *Business & Society* in 1960. In his study of this field, Frederick[13] found that scholarly works on the link between businesses and societies shifted slowly, moving away from the idea of responsibility toward the notion of responsiveness. He thus offers the underpinnings to understand CSR as an ability to account for, to respond and to react to the organizations' environment and stakeholders. His non-normative take shows that a 'business & society' view is not necessarily anti-libertarian. Far from it, since many stakeholder analyses are strategic—if not opportunistic—rather than being about ethics or politics. Indeed, the famous "stakeholder theory" was initially offered in a strategic management perspective,[14] therefore casting an ambiguous shadow over what the relation between business and society should be when it comes to corporations' accountability and responsibility. As Wicks and colleagues noted,

> one of the assumptions embedded in this world view is that the "self" is fundamentally isolatable from other selves and from its larger context (. . .) The parallel in business is that the corporation is best seen as an autonomous agent, separate from its suppliers, consumers, external environment, etc. (. . .) These definitions all share the implicit premise that the basic identity of the firms is defined independent of, and separate from, its stakeholders.[15]

In his seminal article, Carroll in turn offered a clear statement defining what he thinks CSR is: "the social responsibility of business encompasses the economic, legal, ethical, and discretionary expectations that society has of organizations at a given point in time."[16] It is worth noting that the categories mentioned (economic, legal, ethical and discretionary) are neither mutually exclusive, nor additive, but rather an evolving continuum of responsibilities organizations have to face. Here again, the approach seems to be strategic, in the sense of facing and managing expectations, and does not necessarily consider any built-in normative duties for corporations and corporate officers.

Such fluidity has consequences. For Wood, for instance, the expression "business and society" carries an ambiguity about the hierarchy between the two words.[17] As a result, it tends to place first and foremost the corporation, its own constraints and its cherished objectives. Here he identifies a critical point: as a result, there could very well be some kind of "libertarian CSR." This echoes Buchholz and Rosenthal (1997) according to whom such an assumption has actually "infused" and "plagued" the academic field of business & society. As they outlined,

> this position is called atomic individualism which is based on the view that the individual is the basic building block of a society or a community, and that the society is no more than the sum of the individuals of which it is comprised.[18]

As such, it could be argued that Friedman's Robinson Crusoes view of society is somehow constitutive of the "business & society" perspective, since the latter's very title implies these are separate entities, which can be dissociated and eventually put on the same level.

In the same vein, Matten and Moon[19] explain the different conceptions of CSR in the US, where they describe it as "explicit," and in Europe, where it would be "implicit."

If Friedman were to tolerate one column, given his principles as recounted, it would clearly be the explicit one, as it leaves the most space for freedom of executives and stockholders to run their companies in the way they intend. If they were to incorporate some elements of responsibility in their decisions, it would only be "voluntary" and strategic, and result from their own "motivated" reasons. Put differently, the idea of implicit CSR would rely far too much on constraints imposed by society at large, or the community, not to impinge on freedom as a central value.

Table 1.2.1 Conceptions of CSR

Explicit CSR	*Implicit CSR*
Describes all corporate activities to assume responsibility in society	Describes all formal and informal institutions of a society which assigns and defines the extent of corporate responsibility for the interests of an entire society
Consists of voluntary corporate policies, programmes and strategies	Consists of values, norms and rules which result in (chiefly codified and mandatory) requirements for corporations
Motivated by the perceived expectations of all stakeholders of the corporation	Motivated by the societal consensus on the legitimate expectations towards the role and contribution of all major groups in society, including corporations

Adapted from Matten and Moon (2008)

However, Friedman did not stop at the infamous quote I mentioned earlier. He went on to finish the paragraph. I shall quote it at length, as it is far too rarely presented as such:

> If businessmen do have a social responsibility other than making maximum profits for stockholders, how are they to know what it is? Can self-selected private individuals decide what the social interest is? Can they decide how great a burden they are justified in placing on themselves or their stockholders to serve that social interest? Is it tolerable that these public functions of taxation, expenditure, and control be exercised by the people who happen at the moment to be in charge of particular enterprises, chosen for those posts by strictly private groups? If businessmen are civil servants rather than the employees of their stockholders then in a democracy they will, sooner or later, be chosen by the public techniques of election and appointment.[20]

Here Friedman says something that is too rarely mentioned, namely, if we ask corporations to be responsible, aren't we putting too much non-democratic power in their hands? Aren't we putting them in charge of deciding what justice should be?

This issue led me to pin-point what I think is one of the biggest blind spots of Friedman's framework: justice *vis-à-vis* freedom. Taken as it is, it has an intellectual flawlessness: it is all-encompassing. If you accept the premise however that freedom is *the* one and only important value and that any other should be secondary, if not rejected, then Friedman has trapped you in the corner of our metaphorical bar, making it almost impossible to escape. However, if you notice that he struggles with the notion of justice in his view of the world, then you might have a Tocquevillian way out.

And sees Tocqueville in a dark corner. . .

Equality in Friedman's blind spot

Going through *Capitalism and Freedom*, a quantophrenic reader would count the word 'freedom' 205 times. In comparison, outside of the tenth chapter on the distribution of income, 'equality' only appears 18 times, and 'liberty'—freedom's political synonym—even less (8 times). Moreover, in the aforementioned chapter, 'equality' is half the time written under its form '*in*equality.' Finally, all such references are about economic income, not justice in society. In summary, in Friedman's view, equality in the political sense does not exist, or has very little space.

This is why, in a libertarian perspective, government has no role to play in insuring equality amongst citizens, as it would impair their fundamental freedom. That being said, Friedman recognizes that it can and should serve one practical purpose: ensuring the respect of the rules of the game. In his telling,

> we cannot rely on custom or on this consensus alone to interpret and to enforce the rules; we need an umpire. These then are the basic roles of government in a free society: to provide a means whereby we can modify the rules, to mediate differences among us on the meaning of the rules, and to enforce compliance with the rules on the part of those few who would otherwise not play the game.[21]

In such a view, government is only secondary to markets and to corporations, but also to individuals freely exchanging; a mere practical necessity. As he puts it, "the role of government just considered is to do something that the market cannot do for itself, namely, to determine, arbitrate, and enforce the rules of the game."[22] Importantly, these rules should be limited to the absolute minimum, i.e. to ensuring the sustainability of the game itself, as capitalism requires the protection of capital, a legal framework for contracts and some kind of labor law. A "business & society" perspective in this telling could thereby perfectly prioritize markets and corporations over the social contexts they are embedded in, hence the ambiguity noticed by Wood (1991).

It is unsurprising then to find the equality ensured by government being mostly depicted in a pejorative light. As Friedman puts it, "but in the process (of regulating through standards), government would replace progress by stagnation, it would substitute uniform mediocrity for the variety essential for that experimentation which can bring tomorrow's laggards above today's mean."[23] Friedman thus sees equality as evidence of government intervention, which is almost always a bad thing since it is synonymous with some limitation of freedom. Here, freedom and equality are thought to be in strict, mutually exclusive opposition, almost never capable of coexisting:

> the catchwords became welfare and equality rather than freedom. The nineteenth-century liberal regarded an extension of freedom as the most effective way to promote welfare and equality; the twentieth-century liberal regards welfare and equality as either prerequisites of or alternatives to freedom.[24]

Consequently, and this is key to understanding how one can escape Milton's libertarian vortex, democratic societies should be based on freedom, and freedom alone.

Published in 1962, *Capitalism and Freedom* carries the stigma of an opposition between capitalist societies—considered as free and democratic—and socialist ones—that can only be anything but. As Friedman puts it, "a society which is socialist cannot also be democratic, in the sense of guaranteeing individual freedom."[25] However, and this is the beauty of Friedman's intellectual honesty, he recognizes that there can be economies "that are fundamentally capitalist and political arrangements that are not free."[26] Following the same line of honesty, he goes as far as respecting the right for someone to be a communist (something that was not exactly in fashion in the 1960s): "His freedom includes his freedom to promote communism."[27] You can disagree with the man, but you have to acknowledge his coherence.

Analyzing the democratic rationale, Friedman asserts that markets in capitalist democratic societies could be seen as a legitimate system for the representation of citizens. He argues that "from this standpoint, the role of the market, as already noted, is that it permits unanimity without conformity; that it is a system of effectively proportional representation."[28] To him, it is even less flawed than the idea of voting: "fundamental differences in basic values can seldom if ever be resolved at the ballot box; ultimately they can only be decided, though not resolved, by conflict."[29] This makes for brutal coherence, doesn't it?

Having equality in his blind spot however, Friedman sees citizens in a democracy only as being free, and nothing else. He therefore struggles in his second chapter with the notion of justice and the majority principle—as do many promoters of corporations' rights and values in democratic societies. Although his argument is more than sound from a logical and purely economic point of view, it remains unbalanced and awkward as a political system. To me, it therefore presents no issue to see it as an intellectual contribution relying on a libertarian ontology, but I shudder when some use it as an unproblematic ideology, in order to promote politics in its mould.

Of democracy in markets?

According to Michael Sandel, "the case for free markets typically rests on two claims": "letting people engage in voluntary exchanges respects their freedom" and "free markets promote welfare."[30] But in arguing against this simplistic view, he reminds us that choices and decisions made by actors involved in markets are far from being always 'free.' Through a few concrete examples, especially the case of volunteering in the army, he shows how class discrimination and economic disadvantages can constrain people to some decisions despite the appearance of a free exchange. Through this argument, Sandel brings back the question of equality as an absolute requirement in building a system that is not only 'free,' but also 'fair.' As he phrases it, it is all about "how much equality is needed to ensure that market choices are free rather than coerced?"[31]

This simple idea is key to countering the libertarian, freedom–obsessed perspective, by stressing that for people to be free, a certain level of equality needs to be achieved. Here, Sandel is not the first, a fact he fully recognizes, as he knows very well the work of Jean-Jacques Rousseau. The latter argued in 1762 in the second book of his *Social Contract* that

> if we enquire wherein lies precisely the greatest good of all, which ought to be the goal of every system of law, we shall find that it comes down to two main objects, *freedom* and *equality*: freedom because any individual dependence means that much strength withdrawn from the body of the state, and equality because freedom cannot survive without it.[32]

Crucially, this conceptual articulation between freedom and equality underlies the Tocquevillian perspective on democracy.

In his analysis of the American society of the early nineteenth century, Alexis de Tocqueville grounds democracy in two core values: freedom and equality. In doing so, he does not oppose them, but shows their necessary interactions and interdependence in democratic society. As he noted,

> it is possible to imagine an extreme point at which freedom and equality would meet and blend. Let us suppose that all the people take a part in the government, and that each one of them has an equal right to take part in it. As no one is different from his fellows, none can exercise a tyrannical power, men will be perfectly free because they are all entirely equal; and they will be perfectly equal because they are entirely free.[33]

But before this extreme point, an articulation has to be achieved in order to build a fair and democratic society.

Tocqueville considers equality as the very fundamental norm of all relationships in a democracy. If hierarchies and differences can obviously exist—between employers and employees for example—they shall not be constitutive of the individuals' identities as citizens. Consequently, social positions should never interfere in individuals' exercise of political sovereignty. According to Tocqueville, this aim for equality in rights will be anchored in an "imaginary" equality in the minds. This is an equality that cannot ever be perfectly reached, but that instigates a core process: the equalization of conditions. In his words,

> in democracies servants are not only equal amongst themselves, but it may be said that they are in some sort the equals of their masters (. . .) Why then has the former a right to command, and what compels the latter to obey?—the free and temporary

consent of both their wills. Neither of them is by nature inferior to the other; they only become so for a time by covenant. Within the terms of this covenant, the one is a servant, the other a master; beyond it they are two citizens of the commonwealth—two men.[34]

Put differently, although differences will arise from the other core value of democracy—freedom—fairness will be insured by a duty of individuals to respect this idea that they are all equals, and therefore should be treated equally.

This echoes Sandel's take on justice, which he strongly connects to duty, and the risk of its commodification leading to its demise. Referring back to Jean-Jacques Rousseau's *Social Contract*, he shows how a society of citizens solely involved in free exchanges and without any sense of a higher purpose than their individual interest leads to the disappearance of democratic justice. As Rousseau suggested, "as soon as public service ceases to be the chief concern of the citizens and they come to prefer to serve the state with their purse rather than their person, the state is already close to ruin."[35] Importantly, Sandel sees in the libertarian obsession with free exchange between individuals an inversion of, if not a risk for, justice. He argues that "we are inclined to view the state, with its binding laws and regulations, as the realm of force; and to see the market, with its voluntary exchanges, as the realm of freedom."[36] Notably, his phrasing could not be closer to Friedman's, which we saw in the first section.

In the Tocquevillian perspective, freedom is the other core value in democratic societies, but only as another pillar, not in itself. Even further, Tocqueville sees equality and freedom as the remedies for one another: "but I contend that in order to combat the evils which equality may produce, there is only one effectual remedy—namely, political freedom."[37] Freedom in itself can therefore not be the sole source for justice in a democracy. An environment that would over-emphasize its importance would quickly disrupt the status of equality amongst citizens, and lead to a slow demise of democracy itself as a political system.

The idea therefore is not to reject freedom, but to refuse Friedman's assertion that anything short of absolute freedom is a move toward tyranny. Jean-Jacques Rousseau cherishes it as one of the highest values mankind should aim for:

> to renounce freedom is to renounce one's humanity, one's right as a man and equally one's duty. There is no possible quid pro quo for one who renounces everything; indeed such renunciation is contrary to man's very nature; for if you take away all freedom of the will, you strip a man's actions of all moral significance.[38]

However, being less radical than libertarians—and probably less terrified by communism—he sees in the State (the institution encompassing and insuring the existence of a social contract) a way to achieve a balance. In his phrasing,

> power shall stop short of violence and never be exercised except by virtue of authority and law, and, where wealth is concerned, that no citizen shall be rich enough to buy another (. . .) Such equality, we shall be told, is a chimera of theory and could not exist in reality. But if abuse is inevitable, ought we not then at least to control it? Precisely because the force of circumstance tends always to destroy equality, the force of legislation ought always to tend to preserve it.[39]

But what place remains for the State in a "business & society" debate mostly concerned with entities such as 'the social,' 'the community,' or even 'the stakeholders'? What kind of "business & society" does this recognition demand? And what lessons does this hold for our scholarship?

Concluding on a drift: from business *and* society to business *in* society

According to Siltaoja and Onkila, the ideas of business *and* society and business *in* society refer to different understandings of what corporations consider to be their social responsibility.[40] For the defenders of the "in" articulation, corporations ground their legitimacy and their *raison d'être* in the mandate delegated by society to operate on segments of economic activities that give them the right to operate and to create value.[41] In this perspective,

> businesses and other organizations have been understood to interact with society because they are part of it and are in partnership with other focal actors—emphasizing the view we call *business in society* (. . .) The distinctive elements of this kind of 'European CSR' are the inclusion of regulated industrial relations, labour law and corporate governance.[42]

Although respecting the rights of individuals *vis-à-vis* free enterprise, this perspective clearly bounds their freedom within a democratic framework that ensures equality is respected—or at least that inequalities are limited. Following this reasoning, for instance, since taxes and other fiscal apparatus are one of the ways nation states ensure and finance social justice, tax evasions practices would be considered anti-democratic, and tax opposition highly questionable.

Instead of understanding corporations as being ontologically and morally free to act however they want—or not—, and thus to be accountable—or not—for what they do, the "business *in* society" perspective thus puts society first, as source and frame of economic activity that also needs to respect and contribute to equality. In a somehow Tocquevillian perspective, Breton and Pesqueux, for example, strongly state that they "start by refusing to consider shareholders as the alpha and omega of the corporation while placing society, which is supposed to have the first and the last role in our western democracies, at the origins of every entrepreneurial activity."[43] The wider point is that understood as social institutions, corporations cannot only claim their freedom; they have to also acknowledge the environments in which they are embedded and the State that structures them.

A "business *in* society" perspective is therefore a counter-point to the current managerialist trend, and its major development that is New Public Management, according to which every institution in society could, and should, apply managerial models and tools.[44] This trend is a direct heir to Friedman's radical libertarianism, only it replaced his intellectual honesty and coherence with an opportunistic strategy to serve the interest of a few. Scholars working on the "in" perspective tend to question the legitimacy of corporations, to interrogate their responsibility and accountability, and call for a fine-grained understanding and integration of their multiple impacts. In such a vein, Buchholz and Rosenthal, for instance, offer to leave what they call "atomic individualism" in the past and instead turn to American pragmatism, since in this perspective, "the relationship between business and society is inherently relational, for no business organization can

Table 1.2.2 Business in society, or corporations living in societies

Living in	*Living* with
Philosophy of the age of Enlightenment	Liberal philosophy
Rousseau and Kant	Hobbes and Locke
Representative democracy and liberty	Communitarian utopia
Law, its genesis, validation and application	Standards and interests
Universality	Self-regulation, self-judgment and self-sanctioning
Justice as an institution	Justice as a production
The wise man, the judge	The expert
Politics and morality	Politics and ethics

Adapted from Breton and Pesqueux (2006)

exist in isolation from society or from its environment, and society is what it is in relation to its constituting institutions."[45]

One could thus place the business in society perspective within the opposition, offered by Breton and Pesqueux,[46] between the "live in" inspired by the Enlightenment (of which Alexis de Tocqueville is an heir), and the libertarian "live with" (which Milton Friedman would consider closer to his program):

The "business *in* society" approach is fully grounded in the perspective opened by Shocker and Setii, according to whom

> any social institution—and Business is no exception—operates in society via a social contract, expressed or implied, whereby its survival and growth are based on: (1) the delivery of some socially desirable ends to society in general, and (2) the distribution of economic, social or political benefits to groups from which it derives its power.[47]

This forces us to critically engage with the very notion of responsibility. In particular, it often leads to what Solomon considers to be a trap,

> beginning with the assumption of the corporation as an autonomous, independent entity, which then needs to consider its obligations to the surrounding community. But corporations, like individuals, are part and parcel to the communities that created them, and the responsibilities that they bear are not products of argument or implicit contracts but intrinsic to their existence as social entities.[48]

Surprisingly enough, this position is not far from Friedman's, when one extends his quote to the full paragraph as we did earlier:

> Is it tolerable that these public functions of taxation, expenditure, and control be exercised by the people who happen at the moment to be in charge of particular enterprises, chosen for those posts by strictly private groups? If businessmen are civil servants rather than the employees of their stockholders then in a democracy they will, sooner or later, be chosen by the public techniques of election and appointment.[49]

However, as an heir of Tocqueville and Rousseau rather than Friedman, I advocate for a shift from "business & society" to "business *in* society" thus conceiving corporations as social institutions fully embedded in societies. Although refusing the libertarian assumption that these corporations would be above or outside societies—even if they are *multi national*—it acknowledges their necessary autonomy and their multiple contributions. Its aim is therefore to analyze their place and role as organizations within society today in a relational manner, not as autonomous entities. Consequently, the expansion of the managerial rationality—the infamous managerialism and its New Public Management—ought to be one of its main points of focus. In short, business *in* society offers a perspective understood in the wider sense (both conceptually and internationally) of critical analysis (understood as a position of distance and discernment) of the links and interactions between societies (their history, their culture, their laws and their State) and the businesses (in their diversity of form and aim) that operate within them. Moreover, the role of the State needs to be conceptualized, not as something that should only be reformed through economics and management, but as a key social institution—rather than an annoying limiter of freedom. For a more refined approach, one that takes both Friedman and Tocqueville seriously, such investigations are both analytically and politically necessary.

References

1 Bazin, Y. (2016). Editorial. *Society and Business Review*, *11*(2), pp. 106–109.
2 Friedman, M. (1962/2002). *Capitalism and Freedom*. University of Chicago Press, p. 13.
3 Ibid., pp. 8–9.
4 Ibid., p. 9.
5 Ibid., p. 10.
6 Ibid., p. 12.
7 Ibid., p. 15.
8 Ibid., pp. 1–2.
9 Ibid., p. 13.
10 Ibid., p. 25.
11 Ibid., p. 12.
12 Ibid., p. 133.
13 Frederick, W. C. (1994). From CSR1 to CSR2: The maturing of business-and-society thought. *Business & Society*, *33*(2), 150–164.
14 Freeman, R. E. (1984). *Strategic Management: A Stakeholder Approach*, Pitman; Carroll, A. B. (1979). A three-dimensional conceptual model of corporate performance. *Academy of Management Review*, *4*(4), 497–505.
15 Wicks, A. C., Gilbert, D. R., & Freeman, R. E. (1994). A feminist reinterpretation of the stakeholder concept. *Business Ethics Quarterly*, *4*(04), 479.
16 Carroll, A. B. (1979). A three-dimensional conceptual model of corporate performance. *Academy of Management Review*, *4*(4), 500.
17 Wood, D. J. (1991). Corporate social performance revisited. *Academy of Management Review*, *16*(4), 691–718.
18 Buchholz, R. A., & Rosenthal, S. B. (1997). Business and society: What's in a name? *The International Journal of Organizational Analysis*, *5*(2), 181.
19 Matten, D., & Moon, J. (2008). "Implicit" and "explicit" CSR: A conceptual framework for a comparative understanding of corporate social responsibility. *Academy of Management Review*, *33*(2), 404–424.
20 Friedman (1962/2002), p. 133.
21 Ibid., p. 25.
22 Ibid., p. 27.

23 Ibid., p. 4.
24 Ibid., p. 5.
25 Ibid., p. 8.
26 Ibid., p. 10.
27 Ibid., p. 20.
28 Ibid., p. 23.
29 Ibid., p. 24.
30 Sandel, M. J. (2009). *Justice: What's the Right Thing to Do?* Penguin, p. 75.
31 Ibid., p. 84.
32 Rousseau, J.-J. (1762/2004). *The Social Contract.* Penguin revised edition, p. 58.
33 Tocqueville, A. (1835/1998). *Democracy in America.* Wordsworth, p. 201.
34 Ibid., p. 266.
35 Rousseau (1762/2004), p. 111.
36 Sandel (2009), p. 87.
37 Tocqueville (1835/1998), p. 186.
38 Rousseau (1762/2004), p. 8.
39 Rousseau (1762/2004), pp. 58–59.
40 Siltaoja, M. E., & Onkila, T. J. (2013). Business in society or business and society: The construction of business–society relations in responsibility reports from a critical discursive perspective. *Business Ethics: A European Review, 22*(4), 357–373.
41 Wood, D. J. (1991). Corporate social performance revisited. *Academy of Management Review, 16*(4), 691–718.
42 Siltaoja & Onkila (2013), pp. 359–360.
43 Breton, G., & Pesqueux, Y. (2006). Business in society or an integrated vision of governance. *Society and Business Review, 1*(1), 7–27, 8.
44 Kilkauer, T. (2013). *Managerialism: A Critique of an Ideology.* Palgrave Macmillan.
45 Buchholz and Rosenthal (1997), pp. 193–194.
46 Breton and Pesqueux (2006), p. 16.
47 Shocker, A. D., & Setii, S. O. (1974). An approach to incorporating social preferences in developing corporate action strategies, in Sethi, S. P. (Ed.), *The Unstable Ground: Corporate Social Policy in a Dynamic Society.* Melville, pp. 67–80, p. 67.
48 Solomon, R. (2008). Business ethics, corporate virtues and corporate citizenship in Scherer, A. G., & Palazzo, G. (Eds.), *Handbook of Research on Global Corporate Citizenship.* Edward Elgar Publishing, p. 126.
49 Friedman (1962/2002), p. 133.

Part 2

From society to business

Humor's use and roles in activist movements

2.1 How to take the joke

Strategic uses and roles of humor in counter-corporate social movements

François Maon and Adam Lindgreen

"As John Cleese said, there is a tendency to confuse seriousness with solemnity. Serious causes can and must be approached with good humour, otherwise they're boring and can't compete with the Premier League and Grand Theft Auto. *Social movements needn't lack razzmatazz."*

—Russel Brand [comedian, radio host, author, and activist]

"Humor is the shortest path between one man and another."

—Georges Wolinski [cartoonist and comic author, co-founder of *Charlie Hebdo*]

Introduction

Among calls for more stakeholder-based, externally oriented investigations of stakeholder influences, the need for theories that can explain changes at the interface of business and society is highly pertinent (Lee, 2008). Scholars demand models that can describe how (and why) stakeholder groups influence the nature and level of a firm's corporate social change activities (e.g., den Hond and de Bakker, 2007). Some research efforts offer partial answers and explicate specific stakeholder influence processes, such as those that reflect a utilitarian-based, resource dependence perspective (e.g., Frooman, 1999; Mitchell et al., 2007) or those that build on identity or institutional theories (e.g., King, 2008; Rowley and Moldoveanu, 2003). Yet such approaches cannot provide sufficient analytical insights into actual choices by stakeholder groups that proactively seek to influence corporate actors. In particular, it has become highly relevant to analyze and understand "the strategies and tactics that secondary stakeholders can deploy to engage in stakeholder politics" (de Bakker and den Hond, 2008: 11), as well as the outcomes of these strategies and tactics aimed at contesting the corporate status quo (de Bakker et al., 2013).

In this line of research, among the societal dynamics and diverse actors that interact with corporate actors, we focus on new anti-corporate or counter-corporate social movements (CCSMs) that began to take shape in the closing years of the 20th century and the early years of the 21st (Crossley, 2002; Kraemer et al., 2013; Schneiberg, 2013). In line with McCarthy and Zald (1977: 1217–1218), we assume that social movements manifest "a set of opinions and beliefs in a population which represents preferences for changing some elements of the social structure and/or reward distribution in society." Although they may contain some formally organized groups, which often serve as movement-dedicated mobilizing structures, social movements by definition are not organized groups. The approaches and methods associated with any particular movement thus might be widely divergent and varied.

In particular, participants in social movements might rely on humorous messages to formulate, build, and spread the arguments that constitute the heart of those movements' mobilization and development. Despite significant growth in studies of social movements, we find that humor, as a "lighter" side of CCSMs, has been widely neglected, even as its presence, in the form of humorous messages and behaviors in CCSMs, is evident. For example, in a study of Occupy Wall Street protestors' signs, Morris (2012) identifies 27% of them that featured jokes or humorous content. For a CCSM such as the Occupy Movement (OM), humor helped increase the visibility and energy of the movement; countless informational and humor websites reposted the funny slogans of the protestors or even ranked the funniest, most creative posters and costumes exhibited by protest participants (e.g., Cosme, 2011; Edwards, 2011).

We critically review emerging literature on humor and social movements to develop a two-dimensional framework that describes the use and role of humor in modern CCSMs, which we illustrate through the example of humorous messages during OM protests. The first part of our framework highlights the strategic role that humor has at the movement level. Our two-dimensional taxonomy in turn emphasizes four distinct, movement-level strategic roles of humorous messages in CCSMs: (1) clarification and affirmation, (2) cohesion and mobilization, (3) condemnation and challenging, and (4) designation and differentiation. Then in the second part of our framework, we introduce a second two-dimensional taxonomy at a more individual, psychological level, to detail how humor can be used by CCSM participants to foster (1) mutual coping, (2) mutual stirring, (3) public mourning, and (4) public protesting. Finally, we specify humor as an expression of both resistance and renunciation in CCSM.

By drawing on humor-focused behavioral research together with social movement theory, we thus contribute to burgeoning literature at the crossroads where social movements, business and society relationships, and stakeholders' influence strategies meet, with consequential influences on corporate social change (de Bakker et al., 2013; Frooman, 1999; King, 2008). We examine humor as a neglected yet critical resource that is increasingly being mobilized by modern social movements (Varol, 2014).

Theories of humor

Reasonable agreement exists that humor involves an "intentional verbal or nonverbal message which elicits laughter, chuckling, and other forms of spontaneous behavior taken to mean pleasure, delight and/or surprise in the targeted receiver(s)" (Booth-Butterfield and Booth-Butterfield, 1991: 206). Yet scholars also have long had difficulty conceptualizing this ageless phenomenon, which eludes clear-cut definitions (Dziegielewski et al., 2003). Philosophers, literary theorists, psychologists, and other "humorologists" thus have framed humor variously "as a psychological effect . . ., as a mental state or as a stimulus. . . . Others yet define it as a response . . . or as a disposition" (Cardena and Littlewood, 2006: 286). This ambiguity also is evident in the variety of terms used to describe humor (e.g., comic, incongruity, absurdity, ridicule, playfulness, funny) and the multiple categories of humor that have been identified, including wit, satire, sarcasm, parody, mimicry, formal jokes, and practical jokes (Norrick, 1993; Roeckelein, 2002). Humor takes diverse forms in different situations, so no general theory of humor really exists (Chapman and Foot, 1976). Rather, existing theories can be helpful for framing the understanding of humor's use and effect on and within societal and personal dialog, by explaining "what causes individuals to experience or express humor (i.e., what motivates humor) as well as the processes by which people evaluate humor (i.e., how they judge whether or not a humor instance is enjoyable)" (Cooper, 2008: 1094).

The plentiful theories of humor elicitation tend to be categorized into three theoretical perspectives: incongruity theory and its cognitive foundations, superiority theory and its sociological basis, and relief or arousal theories and their psychophysiological nature. An incongruity theory perspective seeks to describe the humor object (i.e., stimulus that is humorous, such as a joke), so the basic phenomenon for explaining humor is humorous amusement, or the enjoyment of incongruity (Morreall, 1983). A simple premise underlying this theory is that people enter communication situations with a set of particular expectations, and when something happens in an unanticipated or surprising manner, or is odd in a nonthreatening way, it is perceived as funny (Berlyne, 1960). The situation features two customarily incompatible contexts or some duality of meaning within a common setting (Bergson, 1956), which thereby singles out the violations of a rationally learned pattern. As Morreall (1983: 15) explains, "we live in an orderly world, where we have come to expect certain patterns among things, their properties, events, etc. We laugh when we experience something that does not fit these patterns."

The two other theories address conditions that might motivate humor within people. Superiority theory, traced back to Plato and Aristotle, identifies laughter as a form of scorn directed at someone else as a form of derision or expression of superiority. People laugh at others' shortcomings, inadequacies, and misfortune because they feel some kind of triumph over those others (Meyer, 2000). A person seems funny when she or he is regarded as "inadequate according to a set of agreed-upon group or societal criteria" (Lynch, 2002: 426). Such laughter also might arise from a feeling of superiority over one's own position or circumstances, such as laughing after making a mistake, such that "we can laugh at ourselves and at groups with which we identify" (McCauley et al., 1983: 818). Self-directed humor may even be particularly appealing. As Hobbes (1840: 46) realized as early as the 17th century, "the passion of laughter is nothing else but sudden glory arising from a sudden conception of some eminency in ourselves by comparison with the infirmity of others, or with our own." Superiority theory thus remains extremely useful because of its congruence with research findings related to communication, media, and power (Mills, 2011; Peifer, 2012).

Finally, the relief theory of humor encompasses a variety of insights from psychological and physiological domains, based on the conviction that people experience humor in response to tense or difficult events (Morreall, 1983). From this perspective, a release of stress and repressed emotion and a venting of superfluous nervous energy occurs through reactions such as laughter (Shurcliff, 1968; Spencer, 1860). People use humor and tell jokes in a delicate conversation to defuse a potentially tense situation or increase trust and facilitate further interactions (O'Donnell-Trujillo and Adams, 1983). The physiological manifestations of humor are "most important to this view, which holds that humor stems from the relief experienced when tensions are engendered and removed from an individual" (Meyer, 2000: 312).

According to Buijzen and Valkenburg (2004), there is no consensus about which of these three sets of theories is the most viable or can best explain instances of humor. Modern thinking about humor indicates that their respective, specific foci make these theories more complementary than rivalrous; many instances of humor can be explained by more than one set of theories (Berger, 1993; Meyer, 2000).

Humor and social movements

A humorous experience essentially should cause amusement, pleasure, or relief, at least to some parties to an interaction (Dunbar et al., 2012). At first glance, humor and politics may appear oppositional, if not antithetical, such that "politics is often understood as serious, important, and grave, while humor is perceived as lighthearted and frivolous" (Kutz-Flamenbaum, 2014: 294). Yet, beyond pleasure and amusement, humor can serve various social functions, such as facilitating and enhancing learning; reorienting perceptions, attitudes, and behaviors; and enabling social relationships (Dziegielewski et al., 2003). Graham et al. (1992) highlight two central functions of humor: facilitating communication in specific contexts and mediating aggressive interactions to make them smoother (see Bonaiuto et al., 2003; Hay, 2000). From this view, humor and politics might be "not only compatible but perhaps inseparable" (Wildavsky, 2003: xix). The association of serious politics with laughter as a reality accordingly goes back to Aristotle, Socrates, and Aristophanes (Dmitriev, 2008), and the resulting "tension between humor and seriousness, importance and frivolity, and legitimate and dismissible" (Kutz-Flamenbaum, 2014: 294) is at the heart of many modern social movements. In social movement literature, specific analyses of humor use have been relatively scarce, though with some important contributions (Fominaya, 2007; Hart, 2007; Hiller, 1993; Kutz-Flamenbaum, 2014; Mersal, 2011; Olesen, 2007; Sorensen, 2008; Varol, 2014; Young, 2013).

In particular, some authors address the purpose and potential functions of humor in social movements, such as when Varol (2014) highlights its significance for advancing the purposes of a social movement. When deployed properly by social movements protesting against oppressive regimes, humor can pierce a culture of fear and "provoke the regime into reactionary conduct that ironically legitimizes the protestors' objectives" (Varol, 2014: 573). In addition, Varol proposes that within a movement, humor can support political mobilization, provide an effective coping mechanism, and increase the self-esteem of the oppressed population. These considerations reflect Sorensen's (2008) more general arguments—developed in the context of the Serbian Otpor movement, which used humorous actions as a part of its strategy to remove Slobodan Milosevic from power—that humor as a serious strategy of non-violent resistance to oppression can serve three central objectives. First, humor can first facilitate outreach and mobilization, enabling the movement to "attract more members; it becomes more fun to be involved, and it brings energy" (Sorensen, 2008: 175). Second, it can facilitate a culture of resistance at both organizational and individual levels, where members support one another and overcome political and individual apathy. Third, Sorensen contends that when humor deals directly with the relationship between oppression and resistance, it contributes to turn the oppression upside down, by presenting the situation in a new frame.

Building on such purpose-focused preliminary analyses of the use of humor in social movements, Kutz-Flamenbaum (2014) presents two broad categories of social movement humor, according to their audiences. Humor directed outside the group, to multiple audiences such as potential bystanders, the public, and the media, represents external humor, and it can communicate critiques in highly personalized, often embodied ways. Humor directed inside the group, or internal humor, instead functions to influence movement leadership, collective identity, sense of commitment, and emotional labor. Within these two broad categories, humor might be mobilized as an expressive strategy or as a more instrumental or relational one, as suggested by Hiller (1993). That is, humor can be "a vehicle to express a range of emotions as well as intellectual critiques" but also "an explicit strategy to attract media attention or an unplanned quip that dispels tension in a high risk situation" (Kutz-Flamenbaum, 2014: 302).

Uses and roles of humor in CCSMs: a dual framework

Building on and expanding this literature on humor and social movements, we propose a dual taxonomy to integrate, in an articulated fashion, the function-, audience-, and message-related dimensions of humor in social movements. We seek to provide a more comprehensive tool for understanding and analyzing the use and role of humor in social movements, with a particular focus for this conceptual study on humor in CCSMs. For this purpose, we use the OM to illustrate our conceptual development. The first part of our proposed dual taxonomy refers to what we designate as the central, strategic movement-level roles of humor in CCSM. The second part deals with its secondary (less explicit, more psychological) roles, at the level of individual participants in the movement.

Movement-level strategic roles of humor in CCSMs

At the movement level, the consideration of two central dimensions helps explain the expressive and instrumental roles of humorous messages in the development of CCSM. Building on Kutz-Flamenbaum's (2014) distinction between internal and external humor, we assert that the first dimension relates to the *orientation of the humorous messages*, which may be either intra-oriented, directed at movement participants and potential supporters, or extra-oriented, focused at corporate actors as opponents and targets, as well as other individual and organizational members of society who are deemed non-supporters of the movement. Because messages convey two levels of information (Burgoon and Hale, 1984; Watzlawick et al., 1967), we also propose that a second central dimension to consider relates to the *level of action of the humorous messages*, which pertains to either the expressive dimension of the message (i.e., content, denotative meaning of an utterance) or its relational dimension (i.e., information an utterance provides about the nature of the relationship and interaction between actors). The analytic combination of these two central dimensions produces four movement-level strategic roles of humorous messages in CCSM, as summarized in Table 2.1.1: (1) a clarification and affirmation role, (2) a cohesion and mobilization role, (3) a condemnation and challenging role, and (4) a designation and differentiation role.

Clarification and affirmation role

Humor can be a vehicle to stimulate meaningful insights, such as words of wisdom, through recollections of past events or similar situations. Humor represents a gentle way to state or reaffirm what might represent a difficult truth or potentially complex information; it can also elicit shared laughter, to signal that the information "is more than just

Table 2.1.1 Movement-level strategic roles of the use of humor in CCSMs

		Level of action of the humorous message	
		Expressive (content)	*Relational (interaction)*
Orientation of the humorous message	*Intra-oriented*	Clarification and affirmation	Cohesion and mobilization
	Extra-oriented	Condemnation and challenging	Designation and differentiation

a personal gripe—and therefore warrants serious attention" (Barsoux, 1996: 502). For example, protestors and activists, to make their point heard, comically play with signs and symbols in an effort to share ideas with fellow protestors and activists, as well as to spread them to passive supporters or bystanders. Humorous lines "gets more play on radio and television newscasts than does a thorough presentation of positions" and "serve to express one's views creatively and memorably because they are presented incongruously or unexpectedly" (Meyer, 2000: 319). Through humor-laden framing, members of the movement can fashion their intended view of the world and themselves.

In the case of the OM, handmade signs offered "accessible and low-risk ways for individuals to express their personal critique of an issue" (Kutz–Flamenbaum, 2014: 297), as well as a key source of movement humor. At OM events across the United States, protestors rejected the Supreme Court's well-known *Citizen's United* decision in similar ways, asserting for example, "I'll believe corporations are people . . . When Texas executes one." This "classic" OM sign and its humorous message helped highlight, concisely and clearly, the limitations of the legal conception of corporate personhood, enabling them to (over)simplify the complex question and stimulate critical thinking. The humor in this case stems from the incongruity between a concept involved in a certain situation and the real objects thought to be in some relation to the concept. A protestor in Zucotti Park in New York City (photographed by the author) displayed a small, somewhat dirty paper plate, reading "My other sign was outsourced," playfully and symbolically noting how the outsourcing strategies of U.S. corporate actors could be deemed excessive and detrimental to average workers and citizens.

Cohesion and mobilization role

This social dimension of the movement arises because digressive talk can contribute to build *esprit de corps*. The use of humor in the form of private or inside jokes can increase cohesion and defend against the infiltration of strangers (Morgan et al., 1986), giving participants a sense of belonging and acting as a social identification mechanism (see Ashforth and Mael, 1984). Accordingly, the use of humor can contribute to establish a collective identity (Fominaya, 2007), a process by which social actors give meaning to their own experiences and develop emotional attachments to their fellows (Polletta and Jasper, 2001). In this view, humor functions as the cement to connect people from diverse backgrounds and allow individual members to establish what otherwise might be difficult-to-form relationships. For example, using cross-generational, cross-society, fictitious characters to spread messages can bring people from different origins and backgrounds together. The "Occupy Sesame Street" Internet meme leveraged the central characters of a long-running, popular children's show, such as when one Twitter user tweeted, "Truly outrageous that 99% of the cookies are consumed by 1% of the monsters on PBS." This use of humor exemplifies Varol's (2014: 568) contention that humor can "create a collective identity for a popular movement by integrating individuals into the humorist's broader intellectual in-crowd."

Along similar lines, humor can mobilize new supporters, because it makes involvement seem more fun (Fominaya, 2007). Humor attenuates people's resistance and renders them more amenable to being influenced (Meyer, 2000). A handwritten sign displayed by a woman taking part in an OM rally read, "You know things are messed up when librarians start marching," such that it activated both amusement and self-reflection among readers who likely started to think about their own mobilization. For the OM, both conventional and social media attention appeared particularly attracted by this humorous dimension, such that these channels rapidly and widely spread humorous messages and actions of OM participants. They could reach thousands of potential supporters in a matter of seconds through a single tweet or Facebook post. New recruits could also join the movement more readily, having been prompted and motivated by humorous messages relayed by real-life and virtual connections and friends. As suggested by Varol (2014), the contagious quality of humor in such a context can provide a mobilizing structure, through which individuals engage in collective action (McAdam, 1996), reflecting "the mechanisms that pool individual inputs of the movement" (King, 2008: 27).

Condemnation and challenging role

The need for a humorous check on (economic) power has long been recognized. With an extra-oriented, content-focused perspective, humor provides a means to communicate frustrations or fears to a target group, by denouncing the current or proposing an alternative reality in a "safer" (i.e., not completely true or serious) way (see Mulkay, 1988). That is, humor offers a low-cost entry point to protest for potentially risk-averse people, who can entertainingly blame and condemn the perceived motivations and actions of powerful members of society, as well as the consequences of those actions. This tangible, non-violent avenue for conveying discontent and undermining traditional methods of repression allows "subordinates," such as the OM's 99%, to challenge hierarchical power relationships within the system. A rather classically dressed, seemingly well-mannered, polite woman holding a cardboard sign in New York illustrated this point with her sign, inspired by Jay Z's song: "Dear 1%, you got ninety-nine problems and this bitch is one."

Here, humor's main source of power is "its ability to turn things upside down and present them in a new frame" (Sorensen, 2008: 185), as exemplified by several collective initiatives by the OM. For example, for the corporate zombies walk, protestors dressed as zombies in suits, with white faces and hollowed eyes, stumbled through Manhattan's Financial District holding fistfuls of fake money, to the amusement of onlookers. The protestors thus humorously framed and denounced what they considered a grim reality. Conversely, humor can depict and envision an alternative, more cheerful reality, because "by distorting proportion and scale of difficulties, humor allows the unimagined to become imaginable" (Varol, 2014: 573), which can trigger radical challenges to existing situations. What starts as a pun or satire over time may signal an achievable potential future (Hart, 2007). A widely shared photograph taken in Times Square in New York illustrates this contention: An OM protestor deferentially holds a large cardboard sign, referring to the relatively disorderly state of the square: "Sorry for the inconvenience: We're trying to change the world." This actual episode shows that, as suggested by Bonaiuto and colleagues (2003: 214), humor "serves the two rhetorical actions par excellence: criticism and justification."

Designation and differentiation role

Beyond strengthening the sense of "we" within the movement, the use of humor may serve to define its conscious (and unconscious) opponents by ridiculing them. In this argument, "enhancing group identity often comes at the expense of an outgroup, and humor can be used in an aggressive manner, in essence, to laugh 'at' others" (Dunbar et al., 2012: 472). In the OM, humor often functioned to defame, say, bankers, as illustrated by an alluring protestor holding a whip and a sign that read "Naughty bankers need a spanking. . ." in September 2012 in Manhattan. This tone served not only to stigmatize bankers' or corporate leaders' behaviors but also to call out and mock indifferent or enthusiastic supporters of the status quo. The ironic sign, "Everything is OK: Please continue shopping," was reproduced in several demonstrations, disparaging unengaged citizens who were going about their daily lives.

Humor used to elevate one group and deride another also contributes to build boundaries that "can be erected and patrolled by humorously degrading those who are outside" (Quinn, 2000: 1165). By stressing the contradictions of designated "others" and highlighting their differences with members of a movement (see Schutz, 1977), such humor can establish a powerful form of differentiation. The pseudo-launch of the satirical "Occupy Occupy Wall Street" counter-protest group, with its own website and YouTube channel, used slogans like "Investment bankers, unite!" or "Status quo! Status quo!" Caricaturing Wall Street investment bankers, in favor of keeping the current economic situation and urging OM protestors to stop the "woe is me mentality" and "instead of holding a sign, go to business school," the two comedians who originated the prank satirically impersonated and laughed at those they identified as the clichéd representatives of the "others," the OM 1%. In doing so, they confronted audiences with an incongruous situation and message and drew the attention of bystanders, protestors, and the media.

Individual-level, psychological roles of humor in CCSMs

The first part of our taxonomy suggests that, at the movement level, the use of humor represents a potentially powerful strategic tool, in line with the argument that humor can contribute to affirm the inversion of the central premises, such as rationality and hierarchy, of a dominant culture (Cardena and Littlewood, 2006). Beyond such movement-level strategic considerations, we introduce two new dimensions, at a secondary, more individual, psychological level. The first dimension again relates to the *orientation of the humorous messages* (i.e., intra- or extra-oriented nature). Building on Hiller's (1993) conceptualization of conflict humor, we posit that a second central dimension at the individual level is the *tacit level of resistance of the individual sender of the humorous message*. This dichotomous dimension features contrasting positions regarding the sender's conception and attitude toward the status quo, at the interface of business and society: active resistance (i.e., defying the existing state of affairs, with the belief that it can be changed) or passive resistance (i.e., accepting the existing state of affairs, with the belief that it cannot be changed significantly). An analytic combination of these two central dimensions produces the four individual-level psychological roles of humorous messages in CCSM that we summarize in Table 2.1.2: (1) a mutual coping role, (2) a mutual stirring role, (3) a public mourning role, and (4) a public protesting role.

Mutual coping role

Humor often is just a way to adjust to confusion, disorder, fear, or uncertainty. It helps participants in a social movement see the amusing side of things. In line with relief or arousal theories, humor can be used as a coping mechanism "to avoid conflict, allowing people to remain safe until they are ready to deal with the painful events in life"

Table 2.1.2 Individual-level psychological roles of the use of humor in CCSMs

		Level of resistance of the sender to the humorous message	
		Passive resistance (acceptance)	Active resistance (defiance)
Orientation of the humorous message	*Intra-oriented*	Mutual coping	Mutual stirring
	Extra-oriented	Public mourning	Public protesting

(Dziegielewski et al., 2003: 79), as well as letting them become "accustomed to their fears and even conquer them" (Varol, 2014: 573).

In this sense, humor functions as a sort of social balm, through which people find ways to support one another, as well as finding outlets for their pent-up emotions (Hiller, 1993). This mutual coping mechanism was exhibited clearly by a woman in an OM protest whose sign read "$96,000 for a BA degree in Hispanic transgender gay and lesbian studies and I can't find work. . ."—using a self-deprecating, ironic message to depict the complex situation of young college graduates in the employment market. Humorous messages along these lines, which are not directed at outsiders, contribute to help fellow members acknowledge and release tension, providing a "welcome relief" (Fominaya, 2007: 247) or "a momentary respite from a collective task" (Hiller, 1993: 259) that is often characterized by serious, grave ambitions and that demand lengthy concentration. However, these uses typically have very limited potential to break taboos or actually alter the status quo.

Mutual stirring role

A positive use of humor can enable members of the movement to stimulate themselves and bring more energy to the movement (Fominaya, 2007). Humor can be a source of excitement, emotion, optimism, and self-esteem (Thorson et al., 1997). In the OM, the broad use of creative chants, costumes, masks, and comic artifacts stimulated participants to inspire and amuse one another in multiple ways that can "help to alleviate burnout and discouragement" (Kutz-Flamenbaum, 2007: 301). Carnivalesque events and behaviors, though often short-lived and temporary, enabled participants to take a break from their ceaseless efforts, perceive the world from a different standpoint, and find spaces beyond conventional perceptions of the status quo.

These humorous efforts also contribute to strengthen individual members' active support of the movement and its goals, because they are intentionally, explicitly fun, triggering sincere enjoyment that can contribute to the motivation to take part in the protests. Protestors with silly signs in OM demonstrations teased, "I am so angry I made a sign!" or "So, do you come here often?" Such humor likely intended to "promote good feelings" (see Meyer, 2000), and this enjoyment helps them maintain enthusiasm while also defusing potentially difficult situations in ways that can support continued, active commitment (Fominaya, 2007; Olesen, 2008).

Public mourning role

There is also a less positive, more pessimistic use of humor in social movements. Extra-oriented messages depict how protestors and activists publicly leverage cynicism and humor, in a way that represents a form of public renunciation or half-hearted acceptance of the status quo, which can seem less threatening than direct criticism. It is comparable to interpersonal relationships, in which romantic partners may use humor to criticize their partners, then claim later, "I was only kidding."

Humor that pokes fun at some aspects of society or the movement might lack some cutting or critical edge though. Hiller (1993: 258) suggests that "making fun of one's plight or lot in life may be a symptom of resignation to that social position." In a CCSM context, protestors might endeavor to generate laughter to keep from crying (see Stevenson, 1993). Identical posters in protests across the United States thus evoked people's lack of faith in a better future, explaining that "Due to recent budget cuts, the light at the end of the tunnel has been turned off." Another OM protestor used wordplay to express his perception of modern hopelessness: "20 years ago we had Steve Jobs, Bob Hope and Johnny Cash.

Now we have no jobs, no hope, and no cash." In power-conditioned relationships, such humor can function to help people save face while still releasing tension (Smeltzer and Leap, 1988). However, it can also convey to message recipients, whether opponents or bystanders, a lack of potency or confidence by the sender (Buhler, 1991; Crawford, 1994), which may reinforce their own dominant position.

Public protesting role

Finally, humor can reside within social interactions as "an abiding critique of the status quo, a reminder to people of alternatives and as capable of energizing resistance" (Westwood and Johnston, 2013: 228). By publicly using humor to confront dominant actors, the sender seeks to use humor as an efficient objection and form of demonstration, that is, a true "weapon of the weak." One OM protestor defiantly embraced this role, dressing up as Jesus Christ in a demonstration while holding a sign that read "I threw out moneylenders for a reason" (referring to an episode in the Christian New Testament when Jesus enters a temple, throws out anyone who was selling or buying therein, and upturned the moneychangers' tables).

Humor in this function can signal the individual's willingness to be defiant and protests of apparent social meanings and established structures of power. In this context, the aim of the mobilization of humor might be not solely to suggest ways to improve society but also to publicly protest and defy those who exert power and the institutions that support them.

Discussion: humor as a double-edged sword for CCSMs

We draw on humor-focused behavioral research and social movement literature to advance understanding of contemporary stakeholders' influence strategies and the tactics aimed at shaping corporate social change. By emphasizing the ways that wit and laughter can be used strategically by contemporary social movements and their supporters, as well as their motivation for doing so, this study brings to light the significance of a widely overlooked, critical resource that is increasingly being mobilized to address and criticize corporate actors and their representatives.

In particular, our dual taxonomy of the use and role of humor in CCSM emphasizes that humorous messages directed at participants and potential supporters of the movement and those directed at outsiders and opponents can have both strategic significance at the level of the movement and psychological importance at the level of the individual. We emphasize how humor can represent a strong force for change. However, it can also represent a divergent path, causing activists or protestors to get lost and potentially contributing to hindering existing efforts and attempts at seriously changing the status quo at the interface of business and society.

In a movement like the OM, humor has diverse, beneficial functions, though our conceptual analysis of its use suggests its primary role, at least at the individual level, as a means to release tension. In many cases, similar to that in the OM, humor might never constitute a serious challenge to the domination or status quo. Paradoxically, it even might deter serious considerations, by the public or external actors, of the power and legitimacy of the claims and demands of the movement. By not taking themselves seriously, participants who rely on humor might have some negative impacts. Our study thus elucidates that humor is not always productive; in some cases, it can even divert attention away from the central and critical demands of a movement or protest.

By simplifying complex situations and demands and sometimes unsubtly degrading outsiders through mockery (in line with the superiority theory of humor), protestors also might foment or amplify societal rifts and undermine the effectiveness of their movement, especially if it intended to bring about reforms on a broad scale (Varol, 2014). As Collinson (2002) indicates, humor contains subversive potential, but that power often remains potential, without ever truly changing the status quo. The OM relied heavily on creative and humorous utterances, and ultimately, it was dismissed by many outsiders as a joke (King, 2012). Humor's actual transformative capacity thus remains somewhat indeterminate in a social movement context. We suggest that humor can even reaffirm the status quo (see Westwood and Johnston, 2013), by overcoming "the contradictions and ambiguities inherent in complex social structures, and thereby contributes to their maintenance" (Coser, 1960: 90). At the end of the day, the joke might be on the joker.

Further research on the way humor can be used effectively in a movement like the OM to encourage the development of the movement and actual consideration of its claims and demands is thus urgently needed. In particular, the conditions and objectives of the use of humorous messages in a social movement should be discussed more thoroughly, to define the circumstances and conditions in which the use of humor promises to be more productive for activists and protestors who aim at altering the corporate domination and significantly affecting the status quo, as it exists at the interface of business and society.

References

Ashforth, B. and Mael, F. (1989). Social identity theory and the organization. *Academy of Management Review*, 14(1), 20–39.

Barsoux, J. (1996). Why organizations need humor. *European Management Journal*, 14(5), 500–508.

Berger, A. (1993). *An anatomy of humor*. New Brunswick, NJ: Transaction.

Bergson, H. (1956). Laughter. In W. Sypher (Ed.), *Comedy* (pp. 61–190). Baltimore, MD: Johns Hopkins Press.

Berlyne, D.E. (1960). *Conflict, arousal, and curiosity*. New York: McGraw-Hill.

Booth-Butterfield, M. and Booth-Butterfield, S. (1991). Individual differences in the communication of humorous messages. *Southern Communication Journal*, 56, 32–40.

Bonaiuto, M., Castellana, E., and Pierro, A. (2003). Arguing and laughing: The use of humor to negotiate in group discussions. *Humor*, 16(2), 183–223.

Buhler, P. (1991). Wanted: Humor in the workplace. *Supervision*, 52(7), 21–23.

Buijzen, M. and Valkenburg, P.M. (2004). Developing a typology of humor in audiovisual media. *Media Psychology*, 6(2), 147–167.

Burgoon, J.K. and Hale, J.L. (1984). The fundamental topoi of relational communication. *Communication Monographs*, 51, 193–214.

Cardena, I. and Littlewood, R. (2006). Humour as resistance: Deviance and pathology from a ludic perspective. *Anthropology and Medicine*, 13(3), 285–296.

Chapman, J.A. and Foot, H.C. (1976). *Humour and laughter*. New York: Wiley.

Collinson, D. (2002). Managing humour. *Journal of Management Studies*, 39(2), 269–288.

Cooper, C.D. (2008). Elucidating the bonds of workplace humor: A relational process model. *Human Relations*, 61(8), 1087–1115.

Coser, R. (1960). Laughter among colleagues: A study of the social functions of humor among the staff of a mental hospital. *Psychiatry*, 23, 81–95.

Cosme, S. (2011). The 40 funniest signs from Occupy Wall Street. *Complex*, October 24 [Available at http://www.complex.com/pop-culture/2011/10/the-40-funniest-signs-from-occupy-wall-street; last accessed April 6, 2017].

Crawford, C.B. (1994). Theory and implications regarding the utilization of strategic humor by leaders. *Journal of Leadership Studies*, 1(4), 53–68.

Crossley, N. (2002). *Making sense of social movements*. London: Open University Press.

de Bakker, F. and den Hond, F. (2008). Introducing the politics of stakeholder influence: A review essay. *Business and Society*, 47(1), 8–20.

de Bakker, F., den Hond, F., King, B., and Weber, K. (2013). Social movements, civil society and corporations: Taking stock and looking ahead. *Organization Studies*, 34(5), 573–593.

den Hond, F. and de Bakker, F. (2007). Ideologically motivated activism: How activist groups influence corporate social change activities. *Academy of Management Review*, 32(3), 901–924.

Dmitriev, A.V. (2008). Humor and politics. *Russian Social Science Review*, 49(1), 53–89.

Dunbar, N., Banas, J., Rodriguez, D., Liu, S.-J., and Abra, G. (2012). Humor use in power-differentiated interactions. *Humor*, 25(4), 469–489.

Dziegielewski, S., Jacinto, G., Laudadio, A., and Legg-Rodriguez, L. (2003). Humor: An essential communication tool in therapy. *International Journal of Mental Health*, 32(3), 74–90.

Edwards, J. (2011). The 13 best protest signs seen at Occupy Wall Street. *CBS News*, October 5 [Available at http://www.cbsnews.com/news/the-13-best-protest-signs-seen-at-occupy-wall-street; last accessed April 6, 2017].

Fominaya, C.F. (2007). The role of humour in the process of collective identity formation in autonomous social movement groups in contemporary Madrid. *International Review of Social History*, 52, 243–258.

Frooman, J. (1999). Stakeholder influence strategies. *Academy of Management Review*, 24(2), 191–205.

Graham, E., Papa, M., and Brooks, G. (1992). Functions of humor in conversation: Conceptualization and measurement. *Western Journal of Communication*, 56(1), 161–183.

Hart, M. (2007). Humour and social protest: An introduction. *International Review of Social History*, 52, 1–20.

Hay, J. (2000). Functions of humor in the conversations of men and women. *Journal of Pragmatics*, 32(6), 709–742.

Hiller, H. (1983). Humor and hostility: A neglected aspect of social movement analysis. *Qualitative Sociology*, 6(3), 255–265.

Hobbes, T. (1840). *Thomas Hobbes, human nature* (The English works of Thomas Hobbes, vol. 4). London: John Bohn.

King, B. (2008). A social movement perspective of stakeholder collective action and influence. *Business and Society*, 47(1), 21–49.

King, J. (2012). Has Occupy Wall Street finally achieved "joke" status? *The Village Voice* [Available at http://www.villagevoice.com/news/has-occupy-wall-street-finally-achieved-joke-status-668 1914; last accessed April 6, 2017].

Kraemer, R., Whiteman, G., and Banerjee, S.B. (2013). Conflict and astroturfing in Niyamgiri: The importance of national advocacy networks in anti-corporate social movements. *Organization Studies*, 34, 823–852.

Kutz-Flamenbaum, R.V. (2014). Humor and social movements. *Sociology Compass*, 8(3), 294–304.

Lee, M-P. (2008). A review of the theories of corporate social responsibility: Its evolutionary path and the road ahead. *International Journal of Management Reviews*, 10(1), 53–73.

Lynch, O. (2002). Humorous communication: Finding a place for humor in communication research. *Communication Theory*, 12(2), 423–445.

McAdam, D. (1996). Conceptual origins, current problems, future directions. In D. McAdam, J.D. McCarthy, and M.N. Zald (Eds.), *Comparative perspectives on social movements* (pp. 23–40). New York: Cambridge University Press.

McCarthy, J. and Zald, M. (1977). Resource mobilization and social movements: A partial theory. *American Journal of Sociology*, 82, 1212–1241.

McCauley, C., Woods, K., Coolidge, C., and Kulick, W. (1983). More aggressive cartoons are funnier. *Journal of Personality and Social Psychology*, 44, 817–823.

Mersal, I. (2011). Revolutionary humour. *Globalizations*, 8(5), 669–674.

Meyer, J.C. (2000). Humour as a double-edged sword: Four functions of humour in communication. *Communication Theory*, 10, 310–331.

Mills, B. (2011). "A pleasure working with you": Humour theory and Joan Rivers. *Comedy Studies*, 2(2), 151–160.

Mitchell, R.K., Agle, B.R., and Wood, D.J. (1997). Toward a theory of stakeholder identification and salience: Defining the principle of who and what really counts. *Academy of Management Review*, 22(4), 853–886.

Morgan, B., Glickman, A., Woodward, E., Blaiwes, A., and Salas, E. (1986). *Measurement of team behaviors in a Navy environment* (NTSC Tech. Rep. No. TR–86-014). Orlando, FL: Naval Training Systems Center.

Morreall, J. (1983). *Taking laughter seriously.* Albany, NY: State University of New York Press.

Morris, P.K. (2012). Occupy Wall Street signs: Visual reflections of hidden social issues. *International Communication Association.* Phoenix, AZ, May 2012 [Available at: http://works.bepress.com/pamela_morris/9; last accessed January 10, 2014].

Mulkay, M. (1988). *On humor: Its nature and its place in modern society.* New York: Basil Blackwell.

Norrick, N.R. (1993). *Conversational joking: Humour in everyday talk.* Bloomington, IN: Indiana University Press.

O'Donnell-Trujillo, N. and Adams, K. (1983). Heheh in conversation: Some coordinating accomplishments of laughter. *Western Journal of Speech,* 47, 175–191.

Olesen, T. (2007). The funny side of globalization: Humor and humanity in Zapatista framing. *International Review of Social History,* 52, 21–34.

Peifer, J.T. (2011). Can we be funny? The social responsibility of political humor. *Journal of Mass Media Ethics,* 27, 263–276.

Polletta, F. and Jasper, J.M. (2001). Collective identity and social movements. *Annual Review of Sociology,* 27, 283–305.

Quinn, B.A. (2000). The paradox of complaining: Law, humor, and harassment in the everyday work world. *Law and Social Inquiry,* 25, 1151–1185.

Roeckelein, J.E. (2002). *The psychology of humor: A reference guide and annotated bibliography.* Westport, CT: Greenwood Press.

Rowley, T. and Moldoveanu, M. (2003). When will stakeholder groups act? An interest- and identity-based model of stakeholder group mobilization. *Academy of Management Review,* 28(2), 204–219.

Schneiberg, M. (2013). Movements as political conditions for diffusion: Anti-corporate movements and the spread of cooperative forms in American capitalism. *Organization Studies,* 34, 653–682.

Schutz, C.E. (1977). *Political humor.* London: Associated University Press.

Shurcliff, A. (1968). Judged humor, arousal, and the relief theory. *Journal of Personality and Social Psychology,* 8, 360–363.

Smeltzer, L.R. and Leap, T.L. (1988). An analysis of individual reactions to potentially offensive jokes in work settings. *Human Relations,* 41, 295–304.

Sorensen, M.J. (2008). Humor as a serious strategy of nonviolent resistance to oppression. *Peace and Change,* 33(2), 167–190.

Spencer, H. (1860). On the physiology of laughter. *Macmillian's Magazine,* 1, 286–311.

Stevenson, R. (1993). We laugh to keep from crying: Coping through humor. *Loss, Grief, and Care,* 7(1–2), 173–179.

Thorson, J., Powell, F., Sarmany-Schuller, I., and Hampes, W. (1997). Psychological health and sense of humor. *Journal of Clinical Psychology,* 53(6), 605–619.

Varol, O. (2014). Revolutionary humor. *Southern California Interdisciplinary Law Journal,* 23, 555–594.

Watzlawick, P., Beavin, J.H., and Jackson, D.D. (1967). *Pragmatics of human communication.* New York: Norton.

Westwood, R. and Johnston, A. (2013). Humor in organization: From function to resistance. *Humor,* 26(2), 219–247.

Wildavsky, A. (2003). *The revolt against the masses: And other essays on politics and public policy.* Piscataway, NJ: Transaction Publishers.

Young, D.G. (2013). Political satire and Occupy Wall Street: How comics co-opted strategies of the protest paradigm to legitimize a movement. *International Journal of Communication,* 7, 371–393.

2.2 Clowning around

A critical analysis of the role of humor in activist–business engagement

Katharina Wolf

Introduction

This chapter provides a first-hand, in-depth insight into humor-based activist–organization interaction based on a single case study. Although extensively examined in social science literature,[1] humor is arguably not a characteristic that is frequently associated with activism in mainstream Western culture and psyche. Historically, business and communication scholars have examined the activist–business relationship primarily through an organizational lens. In providing an alternative—activist-focused—perspective, this chapter addresses an existing gap in the literature. It challenges current understanding and assumptions, and hence the way businesses seek out to engage with activists and 'manage' opposition. Based on in-depth observations I argue that comedy, wit and hilarity have traditionally performed a crucial role in activist communication and continue to do so today. However, the communication styles and tools utilized by activists tend to differ from those used by professional organizations, which employ humor for very specific and distinct purposes. The unfamiliarity and adverse connotations associated with street theater, clowning and playful communication in a business context may lead to activists being injudiciously misunderstood or dismissed as unprofessional and amateurish. However, much of this conclusion may be based on misconceptions and the assumption that humorous protests are targeted at and performed for the benefit of organizational representatives, which is being contested in this chapter.

Street theater inspired actions and small protest are not unique to Australia and are certainly not uncommon, ranging from localized protests to international, humor-based campaigns by established networks and non-government organizations (NGOs). Nevertheless, these types of 'actions'—in particular at a community level—tend to take the business community by surprise, as they represent a dramatic contrast to the way corporations communicate, negotiate and function on a day-to-day basis. Within a business context, humor is largely used as a means to an end, for example as ice breaker at the start of meetings or discussions, or as part of team building exercises and staff development. Although the benefits of comedy and in particular clowning are recognized within professional contexts, such as health[2] and even corporate staff training (see e.g. www.nosetonose.com and www.circusunique.com.au), the concept of humor remains undertheorized and frequently misunderstood within the context of professional and/or business communication.

By providing an alternative perspective on activist–organization engagement and its drivers, this chapter challenges the use of humor as *leveler* and bridging tool. Instead, the author argues that within this context humor arises naturally out of irreconcilable differences and the lack of a common ground. I thereby question the business community's assumptions and 'best practice' approaches related to activists' interest in being consulted and co-opted into projects and developments, encouraging a review of approaches and the allocation of resources.

Activist–business engagement

This chapter investigates professional communication and activist–business engagement from a public relations perspective. As a multidisciplinary field, the public relations perspective enables scholars to draw on relevant literature and scholarly insight from a range of related subject areas, including management, organizational behavior, business studies, linguistics, psychology and marketing. Furthermore, a key focus of public relations is organizational engagement with a wide range of key stakeholders, in this case between business representatives and community activists. Moreover, activist–business engagement and activist communication represent one of the largest bodies of knowledge in the public relations literature, therefore providing useful and relevant insights for the purpose of this chapter.

Best practice communication theory has traditionally been built on the concept of (symmetrical) two-way communication[3] and the assumption that a compromise is the desirable best practice outcome for any form of stakeholder engagement.[4] Within this context it is important to note that the public relations activism research agenda has historically been largely limited to the corporate perspective, motivated by a focus on issues management and damage limitation.[5] Activists have been predominantly framed as entities that disrupt meaningful engagement. Hence, they need to be managed, quieted, and moved on, so that organizations, corporations and governments can engage with those communities that may be less confrontational and more inclined to seek out a compromise. More recently, critical scholars have strongly questioned the notion of negotiating a 'middle ground' or 'win–win zone' as a desirable goal of 'excellent' public relations, as a 'compromise' may not appeal to those activist groups who are entirely opposed to a business proposition or policy decision.[6] The author argues that there are some activists, particularly those interested in broader (global) issues, who are not interested in engagement at a meso level. There is no such thing as a middle ground for networks like the no coal alliance or—as in this case study—the anti-uranium movement, i.e. groups that are entirely opposed to the future of mining of certain raw materials. Instead, the aim of their communication efforts is to raise awareness and challenge the status quo. Hence, what may be perceived as a humorous action performed for the benefit of organizational representatives is a crucial means for activists to strengthen their internal bonds, re-energize themselves and raise awareness of an issue amongst the broader community. Furthermore, the concept of balanced, two-way communication as championed in the extant literature essentially ignores the unequal distribution of power between activists and organizations,[7] which is usually in favor of the commercial entity.

The role of humor in business communication

Although multidisciplinary by nature, 'humorology' has evolved into a field of research in its own right, with dedicated scholarly journals, such as *Humor: The International Journal of Humor Research*, *The European Journal of Humor Research* and *The Israeli Journal of Humor Research*. Scholars refer to humor as a "powerful communication tool."[8] Its use—and positive effects—have been particularly highlighted within the context of business negotiations[9] and any other form of communication where persuasive techniques may be required,[10] such as meetings with key external stakeholders, or internal (e.g. pay) negotiations. Within this context humor acts as a power leveler[11] and can be used to "diffuse tension, mitigate a possible offense, introduce a difficult issue, and thus to pursue one's own goals."[12] Its use can aid in lowering defenses and hence invite others to open up to new perspectives.[13] Research has furthermore suggested that humor can compensate (to some extent) for weak arguments.[14] However, scholars warn that some types of humor are more effective than others. For example, studies identified persuasive benefits specific to the use of irony,[15] which may explain why some studies have identified the use of ironic exaggerations as the most common type of humor used in (business) meetings.[16]

Additionally, humor contributes to social cohesion in the workplace, by increasing feelings of solidarity[17] or collegiality between co-workers,[18] i.e. humor aids in breaking down existing hierarchies and potential barriers by creating communities of shared understanding and a sense of belonging. However, there is consensus amongst scholars that styles and dominant types of humor depend on the context, initiators and the overall aim of humor use. Hence, existing studies suggest that different communities of practice have dissimilar ways of *doing* humor.[19] This observation is arguably particularly relevant within the context of this study, where two distinct ways of communication and styles of humor collide as community activists confront business representatives in the reception area of their head offices, as will be described later in this chapter.

Beyond its much celebrated benefits, multiple studies have highlighted the drawbacks and challenges of humor use in (business) communication. For example, communication scholars have traditionally warned against the pitfalls of using humor in cross-cultural communication, due to translation difficulties and differing preferences in terms of humor styles,[20] which may essentially result in a reduction of communication effectiveness. Furthermore, multiple studies refer to the double-edged nature of humor use. As much as it is recognized for its ability to unite communicators and facilitate collaboration, humor simultaneously has the ability to alienate and divide, through the (re)enforcement of norms and delineation of social boundaries.[21] For example, in meetings, humor does not tend to challenge existing power relationships, which are usually predetermined and relatively static.[22] The acceptable and chosen style of humor therefore tends to be determined by an already powerful group,[23] which may result in the emergence of sub-groups and collusion against each other.[24] Hence, humor can have a dual purpose; both as a unifier and divider: as much as it can be used positively to promote inclusion, it may equally have negative effects, through the facilitation of collusion, exclusion and the emphasizing of differences between participants.

The use of humor in activism

Humor has a long history as a tool to "confront privilege, weaken the power of oppressors and empower resistance."[25] A classic example of this is the royal court jester, who could express critical thoughts about policies without fearing punishment.[26] Lievrouw[27] similarly argues that activists' political and artistic heritage is in Dada and situationism, which leads to the use of irony and humor as a means to confront power, challenge the status quo, and emphasize alternative points of view via, for example, culture jamming, flash mobs, or provocative media artifacts. Hence, humor is frequently employed by social movements and community activists as a communication strategy in its own right.

Scholars have argued that humor naturally complements other forms of activism, in particular political activism and protest.[28]

Within this context it is important to note that scholarly literature, industry publications and the media commonly refer to activism as a monolithic concept and practice, encapsulating well-established and funded international non-government organizations and mass demonstrations, as well as community groups, individual 'active' citizens and signatories of petitions. This conceptualization of activists as a homogenous entity implies that international NGOs, like Greenpeace and Amnesty International, can not only be studied in the same way, but are by implication comparable to other forms of activism, such as localized community groups or context-driven, heterogeneous social movements, such as the Arab Spring or Occupy Wall Street. It is not disputed that some international NGOs, such as the World Wildlife Fund, have deliberately positioned themselves to work with corporate entities to negotiate a compromise and hence sustainable solutions to business challenges. Within this particular context, the community building features of humor, as noted above, provide obvious benefits, by lowering defenses and encouraging both business representatives and activists to open their mind to the other party's suggestions and perspectives. However, the focus for this chapter is the use of humor in community or grassroots activism and what Smith and Ferguson[29] define as issue activists, i.e. individuals focused on border-spanning causes (e.g. global warming, landmines, or pollution). The author argues that within this context there is often no middle ground to negotiate, as activists are entirely opposed to a particular business proposition. Hence, I contend that contrary to best practice communication theory and industry assumptions, the anti-nuclear activists observed as part of this study do not use humor to engage and collaborate with business representatives. Instead, they use humor for their own purposes to illustrate differences in aims and priorities between commercial entities and the broader community, and to challenge the status quo.

Method

Activists' engagement in business contexts has traditionally been examined through a corporate lens, characterized by a heavy reliance on conceptual papers and minimal insights into the activist perspective. This study aims to address current gaps in the literature by gaining real-time, first-hand insights into activist communication. In this chapter the author sets out to challenge the common underlying assumptions of activists seeking some form of a compromise—or indeed any form of engagement—with business representatives within the context of humorous actions, by investigating activist–business engagement through the eyes of community activists.

This case study is part of a larger, longitudinal study into activist communication, which follows an ethnographic approach to explore the activities, interests and motivations of activists affiliated with the West Australian anti-nuclear movement (WA ANM). A range of methods have been employed, including participant observation for multiple, extensive periods at the movement's planning meetings and public actions; interviews with activists; and qualitative document analysis of activist texts (such as flyers and brochures), as well as media coverage such as newspaper articles, online reports, and broadcast programs, including audience comments and subsequent discussions. For the purpose of this particular case study, close attention was paid to activists' artifacts and the wider support community's online communication in response to first-hand insights into this particular humorous action, which targeted a local mining operation, as well as the (re)distribution of the resulting video and photos via social media. Despite the existence of a video channel and Twitter account, interaction and 'sense making' of public actions has traditionally been largely limited to Facebook, i.e. the group's profile, related accounts and comments from individuals in response to posts, photos, videos and others' statements. Face-to-face interactions and reflections at planning meetings, as well as at consequent actions further contributed to this case by providing insight into activists' interpretations of individual actions and engagement with business representatives that would not have been captured as part of a structured interview process.

A grounded theory approach was chosen for this study, as this is considered particularly suitable for the exploration of social organizations from the participants' point of view[30]—in this case, through the eyes of West Australian (WA) anti-nuclear activists, as opposed to the organization in the premises of which the action took place. To overcome the scarcity of existing knowledge and insights into humorous activist–organization engagement from the activist perspective, a single case study approach was selected, enabling the author "to collect 'rich,' detailed information across a wide range of dimensions."[31] This includes records of media reports and online engagement; images, photos and screenshots; personal notes on observations at public actions and group meetings; audio files of interviews and subsequent transcripts; as well as a reflective diary that was kept throughout the longitudinal study. Data have been stored and coded with the aid of the software package NVivo. The central storage location enabled the continuous analysis and coding of data throughout this study. It allowed the data to gain meaning in the form of key themes and helped to identify further areas for data collection.

The West Australian Anti-Nuclear Movement (WA ANM)

The WA ANM is a collective of not for profit organizations, community groups and individuals that are opposed to the use of nuclear technologies during any stage of the nuclear fuel cycle.[32] This covers the exploration, mining and export of uranium ore, as well as the use of uranium for the purpose of energy generation and warfare. The global anti-nuclear movement was arguably most active and visible during the 1960s and 1970s. Interest in and support for the anti-nuclear movement in Australia may have diminished since hundreds of thousands of supporters took to the streets in the 1980s to participate in mass rallies.[33] However, the anti-nuclear movement remains relevant due to the unique circumstances Australia finds itself in. On one hand, Australia is recognized as one of the world's major uranium exporters[34] and home to the world's largest uranium reserves.[35] However, on the other hand, despite much debate and speculation over the past decades, Australia does not have any nuclear power stations, with the exception of a research facility, which is largely used for medical purposes. A number of factors have ensured the anti-nuclear movement's continued activity and relevance: the framing of nuclear energy as an affordable, safe and—arguably most importantly—low carbon response to the threat of global warming by the nuclear lobby;[36] major international incidents such as the nuclear meltdown and release of radioactive material at the Fukushima Daiichi Plant in Japan following an earthquake and tsunami on March 11, 2011; increased calls for nuclear waste to be stored in the Australian outback; and reversals of state-based uranium mining bans, such as in Western Australia in 2008.[37] Hence, the WA ANM has been a prominent voice in Australian politics and social commentary for over four decades, although activists' focus may have shifted over the years from opposition to nuclear weapons testing to the prevention of the mining of uranium.

The movement has traditionally been characterized by its dedication to non-violent direct action (NVDA) and civil disobedience, which highlight the appropriateness of humor, street theater and satire as crucial campaign tools and recognizable characteristics of the WA ANM. However, the author argues that the concept of humor is largely misunderstood and underutilized within an organizational—and in particular a corporate—context, which can lead to activists' capabilities being underestimated or even dismissed as ineffective, childish and amateurish. Organizations fail to recognize the multiple, crucial roles that comedy, wit and hilarity perform in sustaining movements and community groups,[38] by wrongly assuming they themselves are a key target audience of—or even a vital participant in—humorous actions. In this chapter I argue that humor arises naturally out of the contrasting communication styles preferred by activists and the organizations whose practices they challenge. Business representatives and their offices provide merely the props and stage setting, whilst the true target audiences are fellow activists and the broader community.

This chapter challenges the role of humor as power leveler and community builder in activist-organizational engagement, arguing that its actual intention is the complete opposite. This theory will be further investigated and substantiated on the basis of a case study outlining observations of activist–organization engagement throughout the next part of this chapter.

Findings

Case study: Toxic Office Clean Up

Flanked by his office manager and front desk staff, the chief executive officer of a middle-sized mining company watches with astonishment as, without prior warning, five flamboyant characters empty multiple bags of bright yellow sand onto the polished floor tiles in front of him. Donning colorful wigs and scarves, feather dusters, buckets, mops and brooms, the representatives of what appears to be a '70s-style cleaning crew waste no time in spreading the fine sand throughout the otherwise pristine and arguably sterile reception area. The contrast between the clean cut, professional business environment and the five representatives of a local grassroots group gives the entire event a somewhat surreal effect. One activist attentively films every detail, as his peers embrace their characters and the chaotic atmosphere, without taking much notice of the small group of business representatives that has gathered—and continues to grow—behind the glass doors leading to the main offices. There is head scratching and bewilderment amongst the workforce. Some point their phones in the direction of the activists to record the strange events with the intention of sharing this experience with colleagues and peers. Others are on the phone to security services. However, all appear to be somewhat mystified about the scene in front of them, struggling to make any sense of it. The activists make no demands, nor any efforts to communicate or to raise any concerns. Less than four minutes after the group has confidently entered the reception area, they are escorted off the premises by two suited security guards. They do not protest, simply shout over their shoulders "clean up your mess," and spill giggling back onto the pavement, as their every move is recorded on a small handheld camera.

The events described above took place in late 2012 in the Central Business District (CBD) in Perth, Australia, and are just one example of a string of protest performances by local, national and international representatives of the anti-nuclear movement, opposing the exploration of uranium in (Western) Australia (and beyond). Through a professional communication lens, these activities appear to be pointless and fail to make any sense, especially as no attempt is being made to communicate or engage with representatives from the mining company. The spreading of the sand is later framed as vandalism in the local business news and activists are publicly condemned for their "irresponsible behavior" and "time wasted."[39]

However, these (public) interpretations of this short public action are entirely based on an organizational perspective. Through the eyes of participating activists and their wider support community the above scenario signified time and resources well invested, as illustrated in the resulting video and related online discussions, supporter comments on Facebook and references to the Toxic Office Clean Up in consequent email exchanges, planning meeting and their official records.

Cultural differences in humor use and appreciation

As discussed earlier, communication literature commonly cautions against the pitfalls associated with using humor in cross-cultural communication. This case study arguably emphasizes this point, as organizational representatives struggle to make sense of activists' actions, failing to understand what the activist community perceives as so hilarious about their Toxic Office Clean Up initiative. From an organizational perspective there is nothing humorous about the event. Instead, the incident appears childish and pointless, representing an unwelcome disruption to the workday with no clear objectives, demands or attempts to engage.

This brief scenario emphasizes that humor is ultimately culture-bound, i.e. dependent on what is considered to be amusing, or indeed appropriate behavior amongst a group of actors with shared values.[40] Although jokes may take place in virtually all organizations and groups, the appreciation of a joke usually requires a shared cultural background, assumptions and beliefs. Within this context culture should not be understood in the narrow sense of ethnic or national identity, but refers to a discourse community that individuals belong to and to which underlying stylistic conventions they prescribe. Conversely, humor can provide insights into the distinctive culture which develops in different workplaces or communities of practice.[41] In this case, both groups may be concerned with the mining of uranium and have similar subject knowledge; however, their interpretation of the world around them, associated values and priorities differ starkly. This context and shared understanding ultimately influence communication and humor styles.

For example, within the grassroots activism context there is a strong emphasis on clowning, carnivalesque actions and street theater,[42] which are forms of expression that are uncommon in day-to-day business contexts. Slapstick humor, dress ups, drama and colorful costumes are all integral parts of the WA ANM resources kit. Their contrast to the sterile business environment, decision makers in suits and perceived humorless attitude increase their attractiveness for activists and leads to humor arising naturally. However, I argue that in dismissing activists as ineffective, business representatives commonly misunderstand—or even overestimate—their own role in humorous activist actions. In interviews and informal discussions WA ANM activists emphasized a lack of interest in engagement with corporate representatives, largely driven by a fear of being co-opted into a project or business decision. (Corporate) Consultation processes were being interpreted as meaningless and tokenistic. Hence, humorous protest is not being enacted for the benefit of the business community. Business representatives' confusion and their apparent inability to see the funny side of the action, ultimately lead to hilarity among performing activists and the subsequent audiences' first-hand accounts of the 'action' in word, print, images and video. Although humor has the ability to become a unifier, breaking down existing boundaries and hierarchies, in this case humor is used as a divider, creating an 'us vs. them' scenario, which further strengthens the identity of and solidarity amongst activists and their broader support community. This is illustrated in on- and offline discussions following the Toxic Office Clean Up, where supporters shared in the hilarity surrounding corporate representatives' puzzlement.

The role of humor in activist–business engagement

Business scholars have highlighted the effectiveness of humor use in persuasive communication,[43] which may lead to the assumption that activists seek to engage with organizations—via humor and other means—in order to have their voice heard and to potentially contribute to some form of negotiation or compromise. However, a critical analysis of communication (email, social media, discussions at meetings, informal engagement and interviews) surrounding the Toxic Office Clean Up action indicates that community activists such as the WA ANM do not set out to persuade business representatives of their point of view. From an anti-nuclear perspective there is no room for negotiation or a compromise with mining operations. Company employees are merely discussed as bystanders and part of the stage setting. However, at no stage was any direct engagement or interaction with representatives of the targeted organization planned or even considered.

As discussed earlier, irony has been identified as the most common and effective form of humor in a business context.[44] However, within the context of the Clean Up action, irony does not arise from a common denominator, shared understanding, or similar values, but from the fact that business representatives do not understand WA ANM activists' actions. Hence, their confusion and bewilderment as captured in the video actively contribute to activists' amusement; both during the actual action, but even more so when recordings and photographs are shared and discussed with the wider support community in person and via social media. The stark contrast between the office environment and the clean-up crew, corporate dress and colorful costumes, the uneasiness of corporate representatives and confident determination of the 'clean-up crew' all add to the embedded irony and overall effectiveness of the stunt from the activist perspective.

Underlying power relationships do not tend to be dynamic, but dependent on available resources—both symbolic and financial. Humor can be utilized to overcome hierarchies and power differences; however, scholars emphasize that essentially the more powerful entity determines what is funny, what type of humor is acceptable, who can start a joke and—most importantly—if the style of humor is inclusive or exclusive of the less powerful group.[45] In choosing a style of humor that is unfamiliar to the corporate context, WA ANM activists effectively undermine existing power relationships and distribution, challenging norms and preconceptions. Essentially, their aim is not to convince business representatives of their point of view. At no point of this study have any objectives been set that relate to consultation, direct engagement with corporate representatives or the direct influence of business goals by the WA ANM. Humorous actions may contribute to individual activists' enjoyment of their involvement, but they ultimately exist to engage the broader community, which is illustrated by the fact that the action itself is recorded in video and stills and widely shared via social media and personal networks.

Different types of humor construct different types of relationships. According to Holmes and Marra,[46] humor is a means to maintain "sustained mutual relationships," which by nature can be harmonious, but may also be conflictual. Rogerson-Revell[47] similarly refers to humor's ability to reinforce solidarity, or to contribute to what she labeled *distancing*. Hence, whilst humorous actions like the Toxic Office Clean Up may contribute to harmony and feelings of solidarity amongst activists and their wider support community, they simultaneously serve as an acceptable vehicle to express subversive attitudes and negative feelings towards mining representatives. Therefore, preferred humor styles may act as boundary markers, which reinforce differences between activists and commercial entities.

Humor and laughter have traditionally served as powerful tools in social protest, contributing to social cohesion, a strong sense of unity and belonging.[48] However, within this context 'unity' does not refer to engagement and collaboration with the targeted mining company and its representatives, but to the strong internal community building features provided by comedy, hilarity and absurdity, which allow activists to strengthen the bond among participants, as well as to reach out to their supporters, networks and likeminded groups. On- and offline discussions prior to and after the Clean Up action indicate that there was no desire to utilize humor to engage with organizational representatives. Humor is invoked to make both alliances and distinctions.[49] It is used to highlight differences and strengthen connections within individual groups, especially as part of cross-cultural communication.[50]

Within the context of the Toxic Office Clean Up action, humor is utilized to distinguish activists from the mining business. This 'us vs. them' ideology contributes to the level of hilarity and increases the *stickiness* and appeal of resulting artifacts, such as photos, videos and first-hand accounts amongst activists and their wider support network. Recent studies have found that sarcasm and silliness are the most common and effective forms of humor used on social media networks, such as Facebook.[51] Furthermore, emotions evoked have been determined to be more important than the actual content in political satirical videos.[52] Hence, costumes, the clumsiness of the characters and the disruptive nature of the Toxic Office Clean Up action itself, as captured in humorous videos[53] and photos and subsequently shared online with the wider community, are therefore arguably more valuable and effective than any factual discussion about uranium mines or angry protests could ever be. Humorous actions empower audiences by making them laugh at the inability of corporate representatives to make sense of the clean-up action. Despite the limited subject-specific, educational content, records of the Toxic Office Clean Up action draw attention to the cause and encourage viewers to challenge the status quo, based on which corporate entities are assumed to hold the balance of power.

Discussion

Business and communication scholars have traditionally emphasized the notion of a compromise, or the negotiation of a win–win zone, as best practice in organization–activist engagement.[54] Hence, through a corporate lens, initiatives like the Toxic Office Clean Up appear to be unprofessional and immature, by failing to clearly outline objectives, demands and alternative viewpoints. This interpretation is clearly captured via the visual recording of corporate representatives' facial expressions and body language, as well as indirectly in the consequent criticism of the WA ANM's action in the business press. However, these interpretations are based on the assumption that the organization is the actual target of the brief performance, implying that activists actively seek to engage with corporate representatives in an effort to influence decision making (in this case their determination to pursue uranium exploration rights).

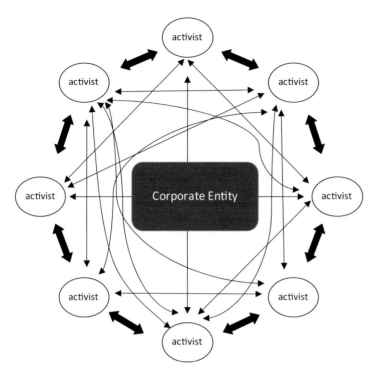

Figure 2.2.1 A visual representation of humor arising from activist–organization engagement

In lieu of the goal of persuasion, community activists such as the WA ANM use humor as a tool to confront, divide and ultimately to highlight irreconcilable differences between the business and activist perspectives. As illustrated in Figure 2.2.1, activists in this case study do not seek to engage with business representatives. Instead, humorous actions emphasize irreconcilable differences between participants and the business community and are targeted at likeminded people, i.e. fellow activists and the broader community of supporters. As traditionally powerless—or power lacking—entities in the organization–activist-relationship, community activists utilize the capabilities of humor to confront privilege and challenge preconceived assumptions. In doing so, they frequently employ different styles of humor to those employed in a business context, which may lead to organizational representatives dismissing activists as ineffective. However, this contrast in communication styles—hence styles of humor—and the resulting bewilderment by business representatives are key to the success of humorous activist actions, as they challenge preconceived power relationships and communication preferences. Rather than setting out to build solidarity and understanding, or to initiate further engagement, activists use organizational representatives as *props* and a crucial element of their *stage set*; both in real time and as part of resulting artifacts, such as videos, photos and first-hand accounts.

Conclusions

Business leaders feel somewhat helpless when confronted by a gaggle of clowns, a singing group of pensioners or other colorful characters, all of which are crucial elements of activist groups such as the WA ANM and similar collectives. Faced with a communication style which is entirely removed from their day-to-day expectations and assumptions, the business community is inclined to dismiss grassroots activists as unprofessional, ineffective communicators and time wasters, as detailed in related news articles and resulting commentary. 'Hippies,' 'tree huggers' and 'clowns' are some of the derogatory terms frequently used to describe participants in these types of actions in the (local) media, alongside the assumption that activists are unemployed and hence have nothing better to do with their time. This chapter challenges these preconceived assumptions by providing first-hand insights from the activist perspective, disputing the notion that businesses are the principal target of humorous actions. It furthermore challenges preconceived assumptions by the business community relating to 'best practice' approaches and activists' interest in being consulted and co-opted into projects and developments. If resources are to be used in a cost effective and productive manner, any relationship—including activist–organization engagement—needs to be examined from both sides and communication approaches tailored accordingly.

Based on observations, interviews and the analysis of related artifacts, I argue that in this context humor is an asymmetrical communication strategy intended to create conflict with, and encourage resistance to, dominant social discourses. Humorous actions by community activists, such as the Toxic Office Clean Up, challenge best practice communication theory and the notion that collaboration should be a core aim of activist–organization engagement. Instead, activists advocate conflict, resistance and irreconcilable differences as important contributors to democratic processes, by ensuring exposure of alternative perspectives and the drawing of attention to issues close to their heart (in this case uranium mining).

Drawing on more than two years of participant observation at planning meetings, actions, Annual General Meetings and industry conferences, the author argues that the business community has failed to understand the true drivers and motivators behind humorous activist activities. I challenge the notion that activists exist in opposition to organizations and instead argue that grassroots activists frequently do not seek to engage with business representatives and may instead even actively avoid being consulted or entering any form of relationship based on the notion of a compromise. Grassroots activists such as the WA ANM identify themselves as facilitators of democratic decision making. Their perceived role is not to convince business leaders of their point of view or to enter negotiations. Instead, they draw on humorous actions to raise awareness of issues that are close to their hearts in an effort to engage and possibly mobilize the wider community. Through the grassroots activist lens, the business community represents merely part of the stage setting. Corporate decision makers are not a target audience but purely 'props' that are being utilized to emphasize the humor inherent in a given action or situation.

Limitations

As an exploratory, single case study, this study has a number of limitations. Its insight is limited to one activist group, during a given period of time, within one cultural and economic context. Due to the focus on a specific research setting, the generalizability of this case study is limited. However, humorous, street theater inspired actions are not unique to (Western) Australia. Readers may be able to relate some elements of this case study to their own observations in different cultural contexts. Furthermore, due to space limitations this chapter does not provide detailed examples of the data itself, but rather presents conclusions drawn from the data available. Observations at actions and planning meetings, as well as the use of a reflective research diary provided the broader context that informed many of the interpretations and assumptions on which this chapter is based. This study provides a snapshot of what I as a researcher observed and experienced during the time of data collection. I acknowledge that many conversations and examples of communication would have taken place without my presence. Furthermore, the findings and in particular my conclusions rely on my personal ability as a researcher, as well as my own identity and cultural background (intersubjectivity). However, it is my actual presence and participation as a researcher that characterize this study and have enabled me to gain first-hand insights into grassroots activism from the activist point of view in the first place, thereby enabling me to provide an alternative viewpoint that challenges the extant body of knowledge. Strategies have been put in place to ensure the quality of the research findings. Further research based on different contexts, issues and groups is needed to confirm findings and conclusions drawn regarding the role of humor—and consequently the nature of the activist–organization relationship.

References

1 E.g. Bogad, L. M. (2010). Carnivals against capital: Radical clowning and the global justice movement. *Social Identities, 16*(4), 537–557; Bruner, M. L. (2005). Carnivalesque protest and the humorless state. *Text and Performance Quarterly, 25*(2), 136–155; Chvasta, M. (2006). Anger, irony, and protest: Confronting the issue of efficacy, again. *Text and Performance Quarterly, 26*(1), 5–16; Shepard, B. H. (2011). *Play, Creativity, and Social Movements: If I Can't Dance, It's Not My Revolution* (Vol. 57). New York: Routledge; Weissberg, R. (2005). *The Limits of Civic Activism: Cautionary Tales on the Use of Politics*. New Brunswick, NJ: Transaction Publishers.

2 Killeen, M. E. (1991). Clinical clowning: Humor in hospice care. *American Journal of Hospice and Palliative Medicine, 8*(3), 23–27; Mancke, R. B., Maloney, S., & West, M. (1984). Clowning: A healing process. *Health Education, 15*(6), 16–18; Schamberger, M. (2014). Compassionate clowning: Improving the quality of life of people with dementia. In S. Shea, R. Wynyard, & C. Lionis (Eds.), *Providing Compassionate Healthcare: Challenges in Policy and Practice* (pp. 139–154). Oxon: Routledge.

3 Grunig, op. cit.

4 See e.g. Smith, M. F., & Ferguson, D. P. (2001). Activism. In L. H. Robert (Ed.), *Handbook of Public Relations* (pp. 291–300). Thousand Oaks, CA: Sage.

5 E.g. Bunting, M., & Lipski, R. (2001). Drowned out? Rethinking corporate reputation management for the Internet. *Journal of Communication Management, 5*(2), 170–178; Deegan, D. (2001). *Managing Activism: A Guide to Dealing with Activists and Pressure Groups*. London: Kogan Page; Grunig, L. A. (1992). Activism: How it limits the effectiveness of organizations and how excellent public relations departments respond. *Excellence in Public Relations and Communication Management* (pp. 503–530). Hillsdale, NJ: Lawrence Erlbaum Associates; John, S., & Thomson, S. (2003). *New Activism and the Corporate Response*. London: Palgrave Macmillan; Turner, M. M. (2007). Using emotion in risk communication: The anger activism model. *Public Relations Review, 33*(2), 114–119; Werder, K. P. (2006). Responding to activism: An experimental analysis of public relations strategy influence on attributes of publics. *Journal of Public Relations Research, 18*(4), 335–356.

6 See e.g. Stokes, A. Q., & Rubin, D. (2010). Activism and the limits of asymmetry: The public relations battle between Colorado GASP and Philip Morris. *Journal of Public Relations Research, 22*(1), 26–48; Weaver, C. K. (2010). Carnivalesque activism as a public relations genre: A case study of the New Zealand group Mothers Against Genetic Engineering. *Public Relations Review, 36*(1), 35–41.

7 Coombs, W. T., & Holladay, S. J. (2007). *It's Not Just PR: Public Relations in Society*. Oxford: Wiley-Blackwell; Dozier, D. M., & Lauzen, M. M. (2000). Liberating the intellectual domain from the practice: Public relations, activism, and the role of the scholar. *Journal of Public Relations*

Research, *12*(1), 3–22; Jones, R. (2002). Challenges to the notion of publics in public relations: Implications of the risk society for the discipline. *Public Relations Review*, *28*(1), 49–62.

8 Meyer, J. C. (2000). Humor as a double-edged sword: Four functions of humor in communication. *Communication Theory*, *10*(3), 310–331, p. 328.

9 Vuorela, T. (2005). Laughing matters: A case study of humor in multicultural business negotiations. *Negotiation Journal*, *21*(1), 105–130.

10 Lyttle, J. (2001). The effectiveness of humor in persuasion: The case of business ethics training. *The Journal of General Psychology*, *128*(2), 206–216.

11 Duncan, W. J., & Feisal, J. P. (1989). No laughing matter: Patterns of humor in the workplace. *Organizational Dynamics*, *17*(4), 18–30.

12 Vuorela, op. cit.

13 Meyer, op. cit.

14 Cline, T. W., & Kellaris, J. J. (1999). The joint impact of humor and argument strength in a print advertising context: A case for weaker arguments. *Psychology & Marketing*, *16*(1), 69–86.

15 Lyttle, op. cit.

16 Vuorela, op. cit.

17 Rogerson-Revell, P. (2007). Humour in business: A double-edged sword: A study of humour and style shifting in intercultural business meetings. *Journal of Pragmatics*, *39*(1), 4–28.

18 Holmes, J., & Marra, M. (2002). Having a laugh at work: How humour contributes to workplace culture. *Journal of Pragmatics*, *34*(12), 1683–1710.

19 See e.g. Rogerson-Revell, op. cit.

20 Chiaro, D. (1992). *The Language of Jokes: Analyzing Verbal Play*. London: Routledge; Curtin, P. A., & Gaither, T. K. (2007). *International Public Relations: Negotiating Culture, Identity and Power*. Thousand Oaks, CA: Sage Publishing; Holmes, J., & Hay, J. (1997). Humour as an ethnic boundary marker in New Zealand interaction. *Journal of Intercultural Studies*, *18*(2), 127–151.

21 Meyer, op. cit.

22 Rogerson-Revell, op. cit.

23 Rogerson-Revell, op. cit.

24 Meyer, op. cit.

25 Branagan, M. (2007). The last laugh: Humour in community activism. *Community Development Journal*, *42*(4), 470–481, p. 470.

26 Hart, M., & Bos, D. (Eds.). (2007). *Humour and Social Protest* (Vol. 15). Cambridge: Cambridge University Press.

27 Lievrouw, L. A. (2011). *Alternative and Activist New Media*. Cambridge: Polity Press.

28 Bruner, op. cit.; Hart, & Bos, op. cit.

29 Smith & Ferguson, op. cit.

30 Glaser, B. G. (1998). *Doing Grounded Theory: Issues and Discussions*. Mill Valley, CA: Sociology Press.

31 Daymon, C., & Holloway, I. (2011). *Qualitative Research Methods in Public Relations and Marketing Communications* (2nd ed.). Oxon: Routledge, p. 115.

32 Kearns, B. (2004). *Stepping Out for Peace – A History of CANE and PND (WA)*. Perth, Australia: People for Nuclear Disarmament.

33 Murray, S. (2006). 'Make pies not war': Protests by the women's peace movement of the mid 1980s. *Australian Historical Studies*, *37*(127), 81–94; Wittner, L. S. (2009). Nuclear disarmament activism in Asia and the Pacific, 1971–1996. *The Asia-Pacific Journal*, *25*.

34 World Nuclear Association. (2016, May 22, 2015). World Uranium Mining Production. Retrieved March 11, 2016, from http://www.world-nuclear.org/information-library/nuclear-fuel-cycle/mining-of-uranium/world-uranium-mining-production.aspx.

35 World Nuclear Association. (2016, February 2016). Australia's uranium. Retrieved March 19, 2016, from http://www.world-nuclear.org/info/inf48.html.

36 Towie, N. (2010, February 1). Great science debates of the next decade: Spotlight on uranium. *Perth Now*; Switkowski, Z. (2009, December 3). Australia must add a dash of nuclear ambition to its energy agenda. *Sydney Morning Herald*.

37 O'Brien, A. (2011, August 6). Boom economy starts to feel spreading gloom. *The Australian*. Retrieved from http://www.theaustralian.com.au/national-affairs/boom-economy-starts-to-feel-spreading-gloom/story-fn59niix-1226108821447.

38 Wolf, K. (2014). Beyond the corporate lens: The use of humour in activist communication. In L. Lievrouw (Ed.), *Communication Yearbook: Challenging Communication Research* (Vol. 38, pp. 91–105). New York: Peter Lang Publishing, Inc.

38 Online news articles have since been removed by the relevant news organization, as news items are archived on a regular basis. The author has set up her own news and social media archive for research purposes.

40 Chiaro, op. cit.; Rogerson-Revell, op. cit.

41 Burns, L., Marra, M., & Holmes, J. (2001). Women's humour in the workplace: A quantitative analysis. *Australian Journal of Communication*, *28*(1), 83; Rogerson-Revell, op. cit.

42 See e.g. Bruner, op. cit.; Hart, & Bos, op. cit.; Weaver, op. cit.

43 Lyttle, op. cit.; Vuorela, op. cit

44 Lyttle, op. cit.; Vuorela, op. cit.

45 Rogerson-Revell, op. cit.; Vromen, A., & Collin, P. (2010). Everyday youth participation? Contrasting views from Australian policymakers and young people. *Young*, *18*(1), 97–112.

46 Holmes, & Marra, op. cit.; Holmes, J. (2000). Politeness, power and provocation: How humour functions in the workplace. *Discourse Studies*, *2*(2), 159–185.

47 Rogerson-Revell, op. cit.

48 Hart, & Bos, op. cit.

49 Meyer, op. cit.

50 Holmes, J., & Hay, J. (1997). Humour as an ethnic boundary marker in New Zealand interaction. *Journal of Intercultural Studies*, *18*(2), 127–151.

51 Taecharungroj, V., & Nueangjamnong, P. (2015). Humour 2.0: Styles and types of humour and virality of memes on Facebook. *Journal of Creative Communications*, *10*(3), 288–302.

52 Botha, E. (2014). A means to an end: Using political satire to go viral. *Public Relations Review*, *40*(2), 363–374.

53 Footprints4Peace. (2012, November 28). Toro Energy Clean Up AGM. Retrieved from https://www.youtube.com/watch?v=AAL-BJCOUQU.

54 E.g. Smith, & Ferguson, op. cit.; Grunig, J. E., & Grunig, L. A. (1997). Review of a program of research on activism: Incidence in four countries, activist publics, strategies of activist groups and organisational responses to activism. Paper presented at the Fourth Public Relations Research Symposium, Managing Environmental Issues, Lake Bled, Slovenia July 11–13.

Part 3

From business to society

Humor's use and roles in marketing, corporate communications, and public relations

3.1 A typological examination of effective humor for content marketing[1]

James Barry and Sandra Graça

Introduction

This chapter examines the effectiveness of applying various types of humor to advertising and social content from a derived typology of ten humor types. Interest in this subject stems from the fact that marketers are recognizing the power of connecting with their social audiences through storytelling, heartfelt inspiration, provocation and humor. In particular, humor in advertising dominates entertainment in spot television advertisements and social videos as social media metrics attest to its high performance in attention and engagement.[2]

Yet despite centuries of studying what makes a narrative funny, the complex nature of humor leaves questions as to its formula for success. Of the attempts to create useful typologies of humor for more concentrated research, most studies to date lack a foundation in which to appropriately categorize humor in line with well accepted theories. Attempts to categorize humor often result in an unmanageable number of humor techniques suggested for skit storyline manipulations and character portrayals.[3] Finally, a number of studies suffer from subjective measurement results and other sampling challenges related to pre-Internet experiments that depended on unwieldy methods for capturing advertisement content. Today, however, the statistics compiled on YouTube-posted advertisements provide a mechanism with which to measure audience engagement more efficiently.

Method

From a search of YouTube recasts of humorous TV advertisements, 2,135 videos were identified as having content intended to be humorous. Only advertisements featured over the past decade and with more than 50,000 views on YouTube were included in the sample. The advertisements were then defined and sorted into categories of comic devices that dominated the advertisement. Up to three comic devices were recorded for each advertisement. These devices (e.g., exaggerated stories, miscast personality, exaggerated performance, elderly acting out, etc.) were then consolidated in accordance with the cognitive, emotional and physiological aspects of humor, culminating in a typology that is aligned with three theories of advertising humor widely discussed in the literature: incongruity theory, superiority theory (disparagement) and relief theory (arousal–safety).[4]

Grouping humor types from comic devices and theory

First level consolidation of the comic devices was based on the face value discovery of in-group conceptual similarity and distinctiveness across groups. Further refinements to these

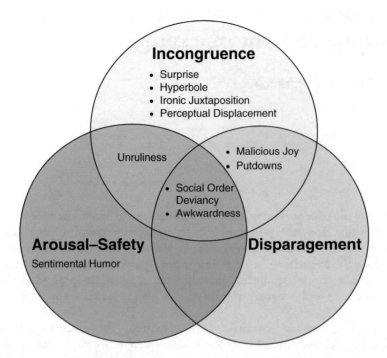

Figure 3.1.1 Humor typology

humor category assignments were then made to reflect comic device categories discussed in the literature.[5] Finally, examination of Speck's[6] humorous taxonomy identified additional humor categories derived from the combination of theory-derived concepts (e.g., full comedy comic devices resulting from the combined effects of incongruity, superiority and relief). As explained further, this led to a final list of ten humor types illustrated in Figure 3.1.1.

Theories of humor

1: Incongruity theory

The theory of incongruity attributes humor to the appearance of something seen as "out of sorts." Often referred to as comic wit, this humorous response to a cognitive shift takes on many forms. Our own examination of high performing humorous advertisements (videos with >50,000 views) shows that comic wit is most often manifested in the way we see or reflect upon anomalies in our surroundings. In this case, laughter is expressed in the form of an *"Ah-Hah."* Specifically, this research discovered that anomalies trigger comic wit primarily through audience detection of logical discords, odd behaviors and visual aberrations.

Researchers of comedy and humor have also discovered a number of incongruity mechanisms that consistently produced these anomalies. In particular, hyperbole, ironic juxtaposition, puns, surprise and perceptual displacement have been used to arouse

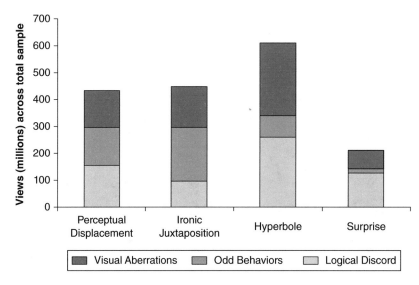

Figure 3.1.2 Summary performance of comic wit usage

laughter for centuries.[7] With the exception of puns, this research validates the popularity of these incongruity mechanisms for comic wit skit manipulations.

Figure 3.1.2 shows a distribution of comic wit videos by popularity (views) when examined across incongruity mechanisms and anomaly manifestations. These groupings were inductively derived from 64 comic devices recorded in Table 3.1.1 as attributes of humor associated with each video. Results show an even distribution of anomaly manifestations across visual aberrations, odd behaviors and logical discords. Among the incongruity mechanisms proposed in the literature, hyperbole stands out as the most effective, while puns were rarely used in any of the high performing videos.

Staying consistent with four of the five devices discussed in the literature (i.e., minus puns), these research findings propose a comic wit typology of the following types:

- Humor Type 1: *Perceptual Displacement* detected from visual, behavioral and logical discords.
- Humor Type 2: *Ironic Juxtaposition* detected from visual, behavioral and logical discords.
- Humor Type 3: *Hyperbole* detected from visual, behavioral and logical discords.
- Humor Type 4: *Surprise* detected from visual, behavioral and logical discords.

2: Superiority theory

The superiority theory suggests that we laugh in response to disparaging others usually after witnessing a well-deserved putdown; the enjoyment of others' misfortune; or awkwardness that relieves us from experiencing the same discomfort. This process starts with a mockery mechanism like sarcasm, outwitting, parodies and paybacks. When seen as well-deserved or innocent, the mockery mechanism often results in sensations of sudden

Table 3.1.1 Detailed performance of comic wit across comic devices

Incongruity Mechanisms	Comic Wit Manifestation					
	LOGICAL DISCORD		ODD BEHAVIORS		VISUAL ABERRATIONS	
	CDEs¹/Views²		CDEs¹/Views²		CDEs¹/Views²	
Humor Type 1: Perceptual Displacement	1. Misrepresented Context		3. Unusual Personification★, #		4. Bizarre Substitutions	
	2/1.0M	1a. Misplaced Metaphors & Idioms	42/89M	3a. Performing/Talking Babies	38/18M	4a. Object Replacement
	38/13M	1b. Humanized Depiction	36/27M	3b. Unlikely Animal Behavior	22/4.5M	4b. Sound Imitations
	81/40M	1c. Unusual Setting	9/13M	3c. Multiple Personalities	20/13M	4c. Animal Substitution
	15/11M	1d. Unconventional Routine	9/14M	3d. Foolishness★, #	184/99M	4d. Anthropomorphism
	2. Nonsense★, #					
	43/42M	2a. Ignorance★, #				
	53/20M	2b. Baffling Dialog				
	25/9.2M	2c. Irrelevance				
	12/18M	2d. Confusing Response				
Humor Type 2: Ironic Juxtaposition	5. Situational Irony★, #		6. Ironic Temperament★, #		8. Visual Irony	
	22/12M	5a. Anachronisms	2/0.9M	6a. Callous Turned Kind	28/24M	33. Cyborgs Acting as Humans
	46/42M	5b. Unexpected Outcome	49/64M	6b. Miscast Temperament	15/5.6M	34. Humans Acting as Animals
	26/6.6M	5c. Miscommunications	17/8.9M	6c. Soft Tough Guy	5/58M	35. Hypocritical Behaviors
	29/17M	5d. Misplaced Routine	21/36M	6d. Unlikely Friendliness	3/0.5M	36. Oxymorons
	32/17M	5e. Misunderstood Intentions★, #	10/17M	6e. Unusually Considerate	65/60M	37. Unusual Pairing
			7. Ironic Persona			
			29/17M	7a. Adult Acting Child		
			12/16M	7b. Childish Adult		
			62/39M	7c. Miscast Role		
			18/3.7M	7d. Mistaken Identity		
			3/0.3M	7e. Unlikely Hero		

Humor Type 3: Hyperpole	9. Exaggerated Outcomes★, #		11. Overreactions		12. Exaggerated Qualities★, #	
	72/100M	9a. Exaggerated Results	45/33M	11a. Extreme Measures	56/58M	12a. Exaggerated Body Reactions
	67/24M	9b. Exaggerated Response	3/1.3M	11b. Awestruck	110/124M	12b. Supernatural Performance
	9/6.1M	9c. Exaggerated Nightmares	40/29M	11c. Over Intense	20/38M	12c. Incredible Allure
	107/83M	9d. Exaggerated Stories	13/17M	11d. Over Heroic	103/48M	12d. Speed & Scale Distortion★, #
	10. Understatements					
	22/13M	10a. Unrattled				
	28/18M	10b. Exaggerated Simplicity				
	17/13M	10c. Exaggerated Concealment				
	4/1.1M	10d. Profound Grasp of Obvious				
Humor Type 4: Surprise	13. Conceptual Surprises★		15. Transformations★, #		16. Visual Surprise★, #	
	2/0.4M	13a. Wrong Answer	7/4.7M	15a. Age Transformation	45/52M	16a. Surprise Revelation
	15/7.2M	13b. Uneventful Conclusion	9/3.4M	15b. Magic	17/11M	16b. Creature Appearance
	59/26M	13c. Absurd Chain Reaction	17/11M	15c. Body Switch	15/3.7M	16c. Wishful Thinking
	14. Plot Trickery					
	77/87M	14a. Storyline Twist				
	33/33M	14b. Fantasy Turned Reality				
	11/4.8M	14c. Twist of Fate				
Puns	Puns★, # (low volume)					

1) Comedic Device Episodes (CDEs) refers to the number of times the comedic device (skit manipulation) was identified by two authors across the video sample

2) The total number of views garnered on YouTube across all videos in the category

★ Humor technique adopted from Buijzen and Valkenburg (2004)

Humor technique adopted from Berger (1993)

glory that make us laugh. In this case, laughter is expressed in the form of a "*Hah-Hah.*" Consistent with Speck's definition of satire, this sudden glory combines elements of incongruity and mockery. For example, we may delight in witnessing a celebrity featured in an unusual setting (incongruity) through a stereotyping parody that humbles the celebrity (mockery).

Although a number of mockery mechanisms have been used as a disparaging or aggressive form of humor, most can be categorized as putdowns or malicious joy. The latter is often referred to as schadenfreude or the "feeling of enjoyment that comes from seeing or hearing about the troubles of other people."[8] Malicious joy is normally situationally driven where the mockery is not necessarily directed at a certain stereotype. Putdowns, on the other hand, are directed toward certain personalities that audiences love to disparage.

Figure 3.1.3 shows a popularity distribution of high performing videos when examined across incongruity and mockery mechanisms. These groupings were inductively derived from 36 comic devices recorded in Table 3.1.2 as attributes of humor associated with each video.

Results show that putdowns and malicious joy represent about two-thirds and one-third, respectively, of the views associated with disparagement. This leads us to the following additions to our humor typology:

- Humor Type 5: *Putdowns* exemplified through satires, stereotype mockery and lofty conquests.
- Humor Type 6: *Malicious Joy* exemplified through deserved repercussions, spoiled hopes and ineptitude.

Of the supporting incongruity mechanisms, hyperbole performs the best in accentuating mockery. Irony performs especially well for malicious joy by setting the stage for the opposite expected (irony) consequences, but well-deserved mishaps suffered by those we loath.

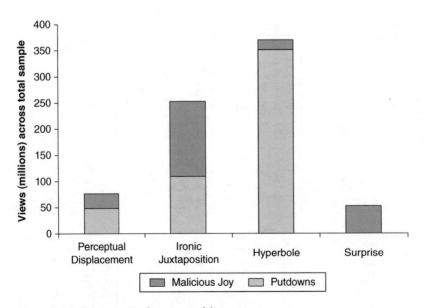

Figure 3.1.3 Summary performance of disparagement usage

Table 3.1.2 Detailed performance of disparagement across comic devices

Mockery Mechanisms	Incongruity Mechanisms							
	PERCEPTUAL DISPLACEMENT		IRONIC JUXTAPOSITION		HYPERBOLE		SURPRISE	
	CDEs[1]/Views[2]		CDEs[1]/Views[2]		CDEs[1]/Views[2]		CDEs[1]/Views[2]	
Humor Type 5: Putdowns	1. Stereotyping		2. Lofty Conquest		3. Mocked Peculiarities			
	1a. Dimwits	11/10M	2a. Outwitting★	58/28M	3a. Background Mockery/ Dramatic Irony	45/69M		
	1b. Sterotyped Professions	17/8.5M	2b. Macho Gone Sour	8/3.5M	3b. Illusory Superiority	24/62M		
	1c. Celebrity Impersonation	13/11M	2c. Arrogant Knockdowns	46/20M	3c. Maladroitness ★, #	52/57M		
	1d. Beauty Conquered Male	31/16M	2d. Unfair Advantage	72/56M	3d. Quirkiness	48/27M		
					4. Social Satire			
					4a. Cultural Nuance	68/42M		
					4b. Parodies★	93/71M		
					4c. Language Peculiarities	42/12M		
					4d. Cheeky Barbs	11/11M		

(continued)

Table 3.1.2 (continued)

Mockery Mechanisms	Incongruity Mechanisms			
	PERCEPTUAL DISPLACEMENT	IRONIC JUXTAPOSITION	HYPERBOLE	SURPRISE
	CDEs[1]/Views[2]	CDEs[1]/Views[2]	CDEs[1]/Views[2]	CDEs[1]/Views[2]
Humor Type 6: Malicious Joy★	5. Bungling Behaviors	6. Unlucky Happenstance	8. Cretins	9. Unanticipated Spoiler
	17/2.4M 5a. Accident Prone	5/3.4M 6a. Unfortunate Timing	4/3.5M 8a. Cavemen	12/15M 9a. Unexpected Danger
	23/11M 5b. Futile Attempts	29/22M 6b. Bad Idea	27/12M 8b. Grotesque & Deformed	12/16M 9b. Unexpected Injury
	23/8.0M 5c. Innocently Offensive	26/7.9M 6c. Lost Opportunity	3/1.1M 8c. Derelicts	20/12M 9c. Unexpected Damage
	3/7.7M 5d. Toxic Stupor	109/65M 6d. Unforeseen Consequences	14/2.5M 8d. Gross	11/8.4M 9d. Spoiled Romance
		7. Deserved / Repercussions		
		47/10M 7a. Paybacks		
		40/33M 7b. Backfires		
		2/1.0M 7c. Hangovers		
		10/2.6M 7d. Overextended		

1) Comedic Device Episodes (CDEs) refers to the number of times the comedic device (e.g., skit manipulation) was identified by two authors across the total video sample

2) The total number of views garnered on YouTube across all videos in the category

★ Humor technique adopted from Buijzen and Valkenburg (2004)

Humor technique adopted from Berger (1993)

3: Relief theory

Finally, the relief theory attributes humor to the tension released in the form of aggressive liberation, sexual allusion or fear/anxiety relief. According to this theory, humor is used mainly to overcome sociocultural inhibitions or other suppressed desires often vicariously imagined through fantasized rule breaking, dream exploits or unruly outbursts. Unlike the cognitive and emotional forms of humor represented by the incongruity and superiority theories respectively, the relief theory assumes humor is derived from a physiological state.[9] It follows an arousal–safety narrative, where laughter in the form of an "*Ahhh*" results after a fearful situation is resolved.

This research found that certain arousal mechanisms can lead to laughter as we imagine our own naughtiness or otherwise inappropriate behaviors. In particular, this research found that the injection of anxiety, taboos or acts of infantilism into a skit creates the best opportunity for this tension release. However, the form of humor varies in aggression. At one extreme are wild outbursts or unruliness that tend to shock viewers. The other extreme relates to a milder form of humor where audiences vicariously live out innocent fantasies. This is often referred to in the literature (e.g., Speck's typology) as sentimental humor leading us to the following typology additions:

- Humor Type 7: *Unruliness* exemplified through hysteria, belligerence and other forms of unleashed repression.
- Humor Type 8: *Sentimental Humor* exemplified through childlike fantasies, naughtiness and inner secrets.

Table 3.1.3 shows a classification of 28 comic devices across both arousal–safety extremes and narratives employing anxiety, taboos and infantilism. Figure 3.1.4 shows that skits manipulated for anxiety perform the best. Taboos, on the other hand, work especially well for sentimental humor.

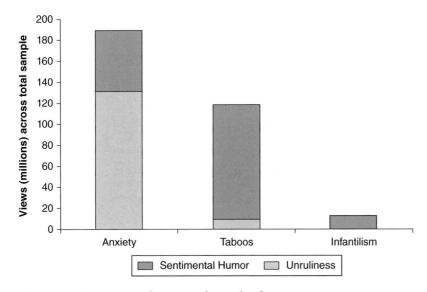

Figure 3.1.4 Summary performance of arousal–safety usage

Table 3.1.3 Detailed performance of arousal–safety across comic devices

Arousal Mechanisms			
ANXIETY	TABOOS	INFANTILISM*, #	
CDEs¹/Views²	CDEs¹/Views²	CDEs¹/Views²	

Humor Type 7: Unruliness	ANXIETY		TABOOS		INFANTILISM*, #
	1. Hysteria		4. Exercising Improprieties		
	14/9.7M	1a. Angry Yelling	4/1.0M	4a. Invasive Peeking	
	2/0.4M	1b. Nervous Breakdown	3/1.4M	4b. Unruly Pop Culture Lexicons	
	8/9.2M	1c. Sports Fanatical	3/4.1M	4c. Recalcitrance	
	25/16M	1d. Extreme Screaming	5/3.2M	4d. Unsightly Exposure	
	2. Impulsive Outbursts				
	14/13M	2a. Belligerance			
	13/3.0M	2b. Forceful Demonstration			
	19/9.0M	2c. Spontaneous Performance			
	57/54M	2d. Unleashing Repressed Impulses			
	3. Displaced Irritation				
	24/7.0M	3a. Annoying Natures			
	2/0.2M	3b. Incessant Talker			
	7/1.0M	3c. Ending the Annoyance			
	10/8.1M	3d. Annoying Repetitions			

Humor Type 8: Sentimental Humor	5. Fear & Anxiety Relief	6. Melodrama	7. Inner Secrets	8. Child Innocence
	5a. Narrow Escape — 28/22M	6a. Histrionic Behaviors — 8/3.6M	7a. Dream Exploits — 29/18M	8a. Youthful Discoveries — 30/9.5M
	5b. Trepidation — 24/14M	6b. Melancholic Behaviors — 24/9.5M	7b. Suggestive Sexual Allusion*, # — 59/90M	8b. Inner Child — 2/0.3M
	5c. Barely Escaped Detection — 15/8.1M	6c. Fervent Behaviors — 9/7.3M	7c. Contradicting Inner Voice — 2/0.8M	8c. Child Mimicry of Adulthood — 11/2.8M

1) Comedic Device Episodes (CDEs) refers to the number of times the comedic device (e.g., skit manipulation) was identified by two authors across the total video sample

2) The total number of views garnered on YouTube across all videos in the category

* Humor technique adopted from Buijzen and Valkenburg (2004)

Humor technique adopted from Berger (1993)

When combined with disparagement, these acts of tension relief create an additional form of humor that is emotional and physiological in nature. The combination of disparagement and tension relief leads to what Speck calls a full comedy. For example, we may laugh from outwitted censorship, slapstick or social order deviancy as we witness someone mocking society (disparagement) while releasing tension by breaking the rules (tension relief).

Two combinations of disparagement and arousal especially work well in creating laughter. Table 3.1.4 shows how the combination of taboos as an arousal mechanism and society satire (putdown) as a mockery mechanism creates laughter. Another combination involves the use of embarrassment as an arousal mechanism and unlucky happenstances (malicious joy) as a mockery mechanism. This adds the following to our typology:

- Humor Type 9: *Social Order Deviancy* exemplified through social irreverence, violating sacred barriers and unrefined behaviors.
- Humor Type 10: *Awkwardness* exemplified through remorseful quandaries, uncomfortable intimacy and the exercise of humility.

Resulting typology

Consistent with the literature previously mentioned and video examinations, the study results show that humor is derived from three distinct theories. Using inductive reasoning, this was demonstrated by assigning attributes to video narratives that epitomized the tenets of each theory. A total of 160 comic device attributes were compiled from the evaluations after screening each attribute for high usage (combined video views) and grouping them into sets of common characteristics. High order classifications were then made to reflect aspects of theory leading to a distinct, complete and parsimonious set of ten humor techniques.

The resulting typology suggests that humor theories are not mutually exclusive. Videos exhibiting aspects of comic wit and mockery, for example, give credence to both theories of superiority and incongruity. Similarly, videos displaying social order deviancy exemplify elements of all three theories. In effect, an incongruity is expressed in the form of irony or hyperbole to portray a social situation that seems out of order. The intended mockery of social rules is supported by the theory of superiority. Finally, the outburst is seen as an innate desire to unleash social restraints as suggested by the relief theory.

Perceptual displacement

Perceptual displacement represents a form of comic wit that was detected in 11% of the examined video episodes which, collectively, accounted for 20% of the total sample video views. But instead of showing extremes like that of hyperbole, perceptual displacement shows us something out of touch. Stemming from the theory of incongruity, this concept entertains us by contrasting what we see with what is routinely expected.[10] Mentally, we are asking ourselves: 'Did I see that correctly?'

This perceptual displacement can be realized in the form of visual anomalies like bizarre substitutions as well as unusual personifications, nonsense and misrepresented content. In each case, the audience detects a mismatch with common perceptions. In the case of unusual personifications, the audience laughs at the innocence of children or

Table 3.1.4 Detailed performance of arousal–safety and disparagement across comic devices

	Arousal + Mockery Mechanisms	
	AROUSAL (Taboos) + PUTDOWNS (Social Satire)	AROUSAL (Embarrassment) + MALICIOUS JOY (Unlucky Happenstance)
Humor Type 9: Social Order Deviancy	CDEs¹/Views²	Humor Type 10: Awkwardness★, # CDEs¹/Views²
	1. Social Irreverence	5. Remorseful Regrets
	3/30M 1a. High Society Satires★, #	4/0.6M 5a. Tough Predicaments
	3/0.6M 1b. Degrading the Honorable★, #	19/3.9M 5b. Regretful Actions
	15/7.2M 1c. Rule Breaking	12/2.5M 5c. Regretful Statements
	16/4.9M 1d. Undermining Authority	16/14M 5d. Caught Off Guard
	2. Forbidden Behaviors	6. Uncomfortable Settings
	17/45M 2a. Taboos & Sacred Barriers	3/0.3M 6a. Awkward Male Bonding
	11/2.1M 2b. Taking Professional Liberties	13/30M 6b. Uncomfortable Intimacy
	3/1.2M 2c. Exhibitionism	14/11M 6c. Awkward Conversation
	20/4.3M 2d. Face Slapping★, #	4/2.1M 6d. Creepiness
	3. Offensive Conduct	7. Exercising Humility
	4/52M 3 a. Odor Offensive	7/1.9M 7a. Wrong Impression
	3/1.1M 3b. Repulsive Behaviors	2/18M 7b. Exposed Privacy
	3/0.5M 3c. Unrefined Behaviors	9/1.6M 7c. Public Embarrassment
	6/6.3M 3d. Bleeped Language	3/0.5M 7d. Unveiled Feminine Side
	4. Unleashed Mania	8. Revealed Secrets
	6/2.5M 4a. Mad Science	3/5.7M 8a. Captured Glances
	3/17M 4b. Sadomasochism	2/31M 8b. Revealed Deceptions
	2/32M 4c. Public Disturbance	2/0.4M 8c. Exposed True Colors
	6/34M 4d. Swooning Women	40/38M 8d. Revealed Fantasies

1) Comedic Device Episodes (CDEs) refers to the number of times the comedic device (e.g., skit manipulation) was identified by two authors across the total video sample

2) The total number of views garnered on YouTube across all videos in the category

★ Humor technique adopted from Buijzen and Valkenburg (2004)

Humor technique adopted from Berger (1993)

animals acting as adult humans. Witnessing the character contrast, the laughter is created by a harmless cognitive shift where the audience often imagines an underdog putting others in their place.

Throughout the last decade, this concept has been played out with over-performances. Consider the babies in E-Trade and Evian that pose as adults. Several viral videos also feature animals going the extra mile to motivate themselves or their masters. A great example is the highly popular Nolan Cheddar video where a mouse driven by "Eye of the Tiger" musters up the energy to escape its trap (http://bit.ly/1s2NsFl).

Another technique used in perceptual displacement relates to our visualizing objects or scenes taken out of context. Some of the top viral videos show unconventional routines or unusual settings surrounding the highlighted activity. In other cases, the viral videos make the audience laugh when they imagine a human depiction of abstract concepts or literal interpretation of idioms. EDS's portrayal of cowboys herding cats (http://bit.ly/1m2HW0y) exemplifies such a technique well. In this case, the attempt at humor is based on audience detection of a mismatch with what their minds see as a common practice.

A concept similar to misrepresentation involves the substitution of animals or objects with a bizarre alternative. One popular technique includes anthropomorphism, where human attributes are ascribed to abstractions. Allstate used this form of humor to depict the concept of "mayhem" through the careless habits of an unruly actor who exemplified the dire consequences of poor insurance coverage.

Finally, one comic device used in perceptual displacement relates to nonsense. As a cognitive exercise, this form of humor starts with the audience's observance of something confusing and proceeds to a recognition of actor ineptitude or imbecility.

Ironic juxtaposition

Ironic juxtaposition represents a form of comic wit that was detected in 13% of the examined video episodes, which collectively accounted for 14% of the total sample video views. Much like any perceptual discord, irony is characterized by an outright contrast between expectations and reality.[11] It makes the audience laugh by showing the opposite or undesired intentions of someone's actions. Mentally, the audience is saying to themselves: 'I did not see that coming.' Irony can be realized in the form of visual anomalies (e.g., unusual pairing, wrong personas and temperaments, hypocritical behaviors) or conceptual incongruities (e.g., wild coincidences, misunderstandings or something scripted out of place). In each case, the audience detects a mismatch with what they expect to see.

Visual irony, or the use of two or more images that do not belong together, works well especially in content marketing. An unusual pairing of well-known characters or scenes, for example, make the audience laugh at the imagined conflict. These inevitable battles were played out well in the 1970s show *The Odd Couple*. The series featured a neurotic neat freak pitted against an untidy, cigar-chomping gambler. Audiences laughed at how the two mismatched friends could possibly share an apartment following their divorces.

Other examples of visual irony include the casting of humans as animals or cyborgs as humans. In both cases, the irony is enjoyed as the audience witnesses the acting out of a certain mismatch. Similarly, an oxymoron like the living dead, friendly adversaries or a screaming mime create laughter as the audience envisions the inherent conflict.

Another successful way to get laughter from irony is through the display of tempera-
ment anomalies such as the mellowing of cantankerous personalities (e.g., John McEnroe
and Bobby Knight). This can also be accomplished through the juxtaposing of characters
in contradicting or aberrant ways, such as a mother and daughter fiercely arguing over
each other's kind attributes as well as a beautiful woman admiring a man's unattractive
habits. A third technique used in irony involves the miscasting of character roles or intentions. This is often accomplished through the display of mistaken identities, adult-acting
children or childish-acting adults or when the audience witnesses the least likely character
as a hero figure. Finally, audiences often laugh over situational irony in which actions
have an effect that is contrary to what was expected. They laugh at the unexpected scene
or unorthodox routine such as when employees let loose in an office setting.

Hyperbole

What Speck and others refer to as exaggeration,[12] hyperbole is another approach to comic
wit that was detected in 18% of the examined video episodes, which collectively accounted
for 19% of the total sample video views. Dating back centuries as a comic device, it suggests that laughter results from seeing things blown out of proportion. Most people laugh
when they witness over-the-top demos or exaggerated stories. Perhaps the most famous
of viral videos in this area is the case of Blendtec. The founder, Tom Dickson, produced
a series of videos that grossly exaggerated how iPads, golf balls and even a garden rake
could be blended in his blenders (http://bit.ly/1k62WbE). After 186 videos, Blendtec's
retail sales increased 600%[13] while its YouTube site enlisted 200,000+ subscribers and
surpassed 200 million views. The preposterous demos were featured on *The Today Show*,
The History Channel, *The Tonight Show*, and *The Wall Street Journal*.

An effective technique used in exaggeration taps into the audience's emotional response
to over-reactive behaviors. In this case, individuals laugh at how others take such extremes
to make their point. Forceful demonstrations, for example, are often loaded with intensity
so that the audience can appreciate the peculiar nature of others. In a similar vein, some
of the top viral videos show scenes of extreme naiveté or over-protectionism where we
shamefully find ourselves or close ones exhibiting these same fanatic behaviors.

Finally, many brands and small companies have capitalized on the visual side of exaggeration. Seeing the visual anomaly, our brains often ask: 'can that really be true?' Some of
the most popular comic devices used in this form of wit include the display of supernatu-
ral performances, motion distortion, exaggerated body reactions and incredible allure.
The key to using this humor technique, however, is making it evident that the object of
exaggeration is beyond the realms of possibility.

The popularity of exaggeration as an entertainment device can be attributed to the
following:

* It rarely offends any particular audience.
* It can be easily grasped visually, emotionally or cognitively.
* It can be easily produced in low budget settings (e.g., Blendtec's budget <$10K).

Surprise

A surprise twist can cause the audience to laugh as they witness or experience a change in
course. This approach to comic wit was detected in 8% of the examined video episodes

which collectively accounted for 8% of the total sample video views. Stemming from the theory of incongruity, this concept entertains us through a distracting segue. Mentally, the audience is asking: 'Where did this come from?' This surprise twist can be realized in the form of visual anomalies (e.g., sudden appearances, changes or revelations) or conceptual incongruities (e.g., storyline twists or unexpected responses). In each case, the audience detects a mismatch with what they expect to occur next. This often occurs when the audience is stopped in their tracks after a scene or statement suggests that something is off track.[14]

This concept is not new. Years ago, Wendy's conducted a comical test taste of their hamburgers. In their famous 1989 advertisement featuring a trucker, the participant was asked to choose from a delicious looking hamburger A or a nasty looking hamburger B. The trucker unexpectedly picked hamburger B. This unexpected twist would be followed with comments like: "I'm a trucker, I could be eating this baby in Shaky Town and still tasting it in Salt Lake. . ."

Plot trickery is another successful method of stealing the audience attention by taking the viewer down a subliminal storyline that ends in an unexpected twist. Snickers capitalized on these techniques in their transforming of cranky actors (e.g., Betty White, Roseanne Barr, Aretha Franklyn, Don Rickles and Joe Pesci) into younger folks ready to return to action after eating a Snickers bar. Visual surprises can also include the sudden arrival of a new character (e.g., alien creature) or an unexpected object. Nationwide, for example, shocked their audiences with a surprise ugly substitute as when the fantasized Fabio turns into a wrinkled old man (http://bit.ly/1ZGNLpF).

Putdowns

Mockery through putdowns was detected in 15% of the examined video episodes, which collectively accounted for 15% of the total sample video views. This technique capitalizes on the audience's emotional reaction to watching others experience a well-deserved jibe. Stemming from the theory of superiority, individuals often experience sudden glory when dethroning others or elevating themselves at the expense of others' peculiarities. Of the viral videos featuring putdowns, most include satires, stereotype mockery and lofty conquests.

The use of mockery dates back centuries as audiences watched imbeciles and maladroits parade on stage or be the target of putdowns felt through background mockery. Geico capitalized on this with their mockery of a poor farmer who misspelled cow as c-o-w-e-i-e-i-o (http://bit.ly/1ZGNPpi).

A second technique used in putdowns taps into individuals' desire to dethrone the self-righteous, the popular, the pretentious and the hyper-masculine. Some of the top viral videos show scenes of some form of outwitting that shames the victim or proves our superiority over them (e.g., Miller Lite's macho moments gone bad: http://bit.ly/1rMDBm8).

A number of top viral videos feature the sudden glory the audience feels when our society is mocked. Individuals often relish the opportunity, for example, to poke fun at other cultures by exaggerating the cultural nuances or language peculiarities of audiences targeted by our sarcasm. Similarly, people poke fun at celebrated lifestyles with parodies of popular shows and sports events. Like satires, the use of mimicry and impersonations work well as putdowns. One of the most popular ways of doing this is through the stereotyping of blondes or provincial men. The latter are often portrayed as idiots or as hypnotized under the spell of seduction.

Malicious joy

Malicious joy, or schadenfreude, refers to the pleasure individuals derive from seeing others fail or suffer misfortune. This form of mockery was detected in 11% of the examined video episodes, which collectively accounted for 8% of the total sample video views. Also rooted in the theory of superiority, this feeling of sudden glory is often exemplified through deserved repercussions, spoiled hopes and ineptitude.

A common approach for entertaining audiences with malicious joy is to poke fun at someone notorious for their clumsy or incompetent behaviors. The 1950s sitcom *I Love Lucy* reached the highest popularity of any show at its time based on the bungling behaviors of Lucy. The naïve and accident-prone housewife had a knack for getting herself and her husband into trouble whenever she tried to make a name for herself.

Several viral YouTube videos are based on characters who are accident prone, drunk or oblivious and tend to say the wrong thing. Men, in particular, are often portrayed for their bungled behaviors resulting from their one-track minds. Another successful way to get laughter from malicious joy, based on the emotional theory of superiority, is through the portrayal of spoilers (e.g., spoiling of romance) and storylines that end with unexpected damage, injuries or danger. In addition, laughter is also evoked upon watching others experience the catastrophic consequences from bad luck, bad timing or foolish mistakes.

Similarly, many viral videos elicited laughter by featuring instances of well-deserved retaliation and paybacks against someone who is despised or who is unveiled of their devious intentions (e.g., Doritos' advertisement featuring a baby snatching the bag of chips from an annoying older sibling who incessantly teases the toddler (http://bit.ly/WPH61O)). On the lighter side, some sponsors use innocent repercussions to highlight the misfortunes of someone overzealous or careless. Lending Tree took this route in their depiction of Stanley Johnson, who shamefully reveals that his lavish lifestyle has put him in debt to his eyeballs (http://bit.ly/1n7zgWw).

Another, not so light, but effective use of malicious joy relates to the casting of cretins whose low-class demeanor elevates one's own status. For centuries, comedies of derelicts, the grotesque and the deformed have aroused fits of laughter from audiences. A number of sponsors have obtained high scores in views and engagement from the portrayal of people seen as physically deformed or mentally subnormal (e.g., Geico and FedEx Caveman: http://bit.ly/1u49isx and http://bit.ly/1oRuth3).

Unruliness

Unruliness refers to outrageous behavior and was detected in 5% of the examined video episodes, which collectively accounted for 4% of the total sample video views. The relief theory contends that laughter is created when individuals release tension or nervous energy, such as when they unleash suppressed desires. Consequently, the audience enjoys watching others act out uncontrollably or violate some social order, such as unleashing their anxiety through uncontrollable screaming and yelling. According to the relief theory, the audience is likely enjoying the observation of others acting out their own inhibitions through hysteria, impulsive outbursts, displaced irritation or exercising improprieties.[15]

Many viral YouTube videos include scenes of angry bosses losing their control or folks experiencing nervous breakdowns. Similarly, many of the popular sports-related advertisements show scenes of fanatics going over the edge to support their teams. Unruliness is often demonstrated through scenes of impulsive outbursts, forceful demonstrations, body explosions or outright belligerence. The tension relief can be explained as an innate desire individuals may have to act out their aggression.

In addition, some advertisements feature one's deep irritation and desire to fiercely lash out at others' annoying habits (e.g., incessant talkers) or scenes of one's wishful naughtiness, improprieties and forbidden behaviors such as invasive peeking.

Sentimental humor

Often exemplified through childlike fantasies, naughtiness and inner secrets, sentimental humor was detected in 6% of the examined video episodes, which collectively accounted for 6% of the total sample video views. This type of humor taps into the audience's emotions through an arousal–safety mechanism. For example, in the first stage of arousal–safety, emotions are aroused with sentimentality, empathy or some form of negative anxiety. As the storyline develops, the audience then sees this heightened arousal state as safe, cute or inconsequential. This shift from high arousal to relief is what creates laughter.[16]

Among the types of humor that capitalize on this arousal–safety mechanism are those involving false alarms, melodrama or childhood innocence. Children, for example, can easily arouse emotions with their youthful discoveries and mimicry of adulthood. The laughter tends to result when the audience watches them successfully overcome their struggles to get through complicated situations. These storylines usually start with a sentimental attachment or an empathetic feeling towards the child. The audience then laughs when they see how their first battles with courage, romance or independence conclude with a happy ending.

In some situations, the audience may be laughing at how the children's trials prove more fruitful than their own. This may be the reason why individuals love scenes of children reflecting their own inner self. Several viral YouTube videos are based on child innocence where the laughter results from children topping their adult counterparts as well as from one's vicariously living through their incorruptibility (e.g., Doritos' 5-year-old warning his mother's suitor to mind his manners: http://bit.ly/1s8p0mX).

Another successful way to get laughter from sentimental humor is through the relief of fear and anxiety. For example, just when an audience expects some disturbing outcome, a storyline then shows the fears to be baseless. The arousal–safety mechanism produces a swing in emotions which starts with a build-up of suspense causing fear (emotional response) and ends with something inconsequential (physiological release of anxiety). The technique is demonstrated in the Dirt Devil viral video of *The Exorcist*: http://bit.ly/1k9RATV.

Sentimental humor can also be created through melodrama. For example, a storyline may start with someone's passionate reaction to a mundane situation. In addition, the exposure of inner secrets and fantasies are also examples of how the arousal–safety mechanism elicits emotional swings in the audience that cause tension relief and consequently laughter.

Finally, inner secrets can produce laughter when the audience observes and hears a contradicting inner voice. In this case, individuals are likely experiencing an emotional shift when the imagined inner voice allows them to safely escape from a hostile or awkward situation.

Social order deviancy

One form of humor that combines aspects of all three humor theories involves behaviors that challenge social rules and expectations. In this case, the audience enjoys watching others unleash their innate desire to break the law, enter forbidden territory or simply act out their inhibitions. This social order deviancy is exemplified through narratives about social irreverence, the violation of sacred barriers and unrefined behaviors. As the highest in attention getting, this type of humor was detected in 3% of the examined video episodes, which collectively accounted for 8% of the total sample video views.

A popular technique for entertaining audiences with social order deviancy is to poke fun at the pompousness of those who take themselves to have a degree of social pre-eminence. Several viral YouTube videos are based on high society satires, rule breaking and undermining authority. Common to all is the release of tension experienced when we outwit the censorship imposed by honorable judges, pious clergymen or smug professors.

Another successful way to get laughter from social order deviancy is through the depiction of forbidden social behaviors such as witnessing the spoiling of sacred rituals and others break taboos, strip off clothing, break office rules, or slap a smug antagonist. Social order deviancy, in some instances, involves offensive behaviors such as bad manners or disgusting personal habits (e.g., foot odor, perspiration or flatulence). As the perfect target of one's tactless behavior, this works especially well when exposing the offense to those sensitive to protocol or classy surroundings.

Other categories of social order deviancy involve letting loose with craziness. Some of the oldest forms of humor involve the depiction of mad scientists' disruptive behavior in public places. Finally, the witnessing of women swooning over men in insane frenzies has been a highly successful humor technique over the years. In 1995, Diet Coke featured an office of ladies running to windows to get a glimpse of a sexy construction worker: http://bit.ly/1rNpyN4. Axe took this concept a step further in a video that garnered over 50M views by featuring hordes of bikini-clad jungle women closing in on their prey. In this case, the hunted was a man freshly deodorized with Axe: http://bit.ly/1pu7J5M.

Awkwardness

Rooted in superiority and relief theories, awkward moments are a disparaging form of humor that lead to a feeling of sudden glory when we displace our own histories of embarrassing moments onto others. Among the types of humor that capitalize on awkwardness are remorseful quandaries, uncomfortable intimacy and the exercise of humility. Scenes of awkwardness were detected in 4% of the examined video episodes, which collectively accounted for 5% of the total sample video views.

This technique evokes laughter through the depiction of embarrassing situations where victims are left speechless, such as Geico's advertisement featuring Abe Lincoln faced with a tough predicament of being honest or offending his wife (http://bit.ly/1xG20LJ).

Another successful way to get laughter from awkwardness is through scenes of discomfort that arise when someone gets too intimate or reveals too much information. A number of advertisements feature the discomfort that men in particular feel when other men get too close or expose their creepy behaviors. Doritos utilized this technique with their advertisement featuring a man licking another man's fingers (e.g., http://bit.ly/1PBh7yj). A similar sense of misfortune is realized when a young boy faces the dreaded kiss of an assertive girl or when a father is pressed to answer the question 'Where do babies come from?'

This same displaced embarrassment can also arise when the audience witnesses characters having to explain themselves after exposing their vulnerabilities. In this case, laughter results from a feeling of relief at not being the one who has to exercise humility. Southwest uses this technique in their "Wanna Get Away" campaigns. The storyline features characters often put on the spot publicly to explain their mistakes (e.g., http://bit. ly/25sNxGR). This technique works especially well when featuring men inadvertently exposing their feminine or child sides. The feeling of shame can also result when quiet words are broadcast publicly or when surrounding audiences get the wrong impression from seemingly perverted behaviors.

Another method used to create awkward moments involves the exposure of someone's embarrassing intentions. This often includes the unraveling of a character's foiled deceptions when caught red handed. This exposure may reveal a man's true colors or his inappropriate glances at another woman. In this case, the audience is likely laughing at men's behavioral hypocrisy as well as their misfortune at having a poor disguise.

Humor performance results

From the ten resulting humor archetypes, a perceptual map was compiled for each type with one axis measuring advertising attention (views) and the other measuring engagement (a normalized compilation of likes, dislikes and comments). The results displayed

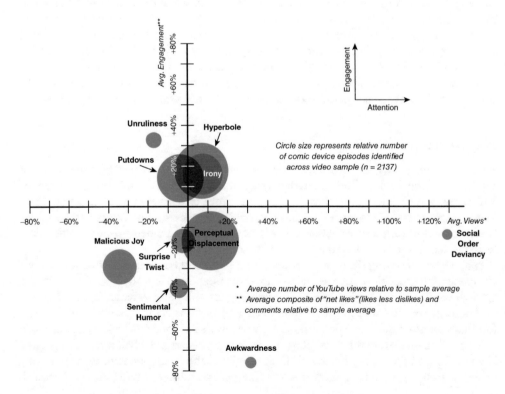

Figure 3.1.5 Perceptual mapping of humor archetype performance

in Figure 3.1.5 show that comic wit represents the largest dimension of humor and is the most effective in garnering attention. Narratives involving ironic juxtaposition and hyperbole, in particular, perform above average in attention and engagement.

Aggressive forms of humor like unruliness and putdowns score above average on engagement. This suggests that provocative forms of humor create more opportunities for audience response in the form of comments and gestures of approval than the more reserved forms of comic wit. Malicious joy, on the other hand, scores below average in engagement (as noted by below average likes), perhaps suggesting that poking fun at the innocent's misfortunes runs the risk of offending audiences.

Conclusions

Few would debate the growing influence of entertainment in creating audience interest in television advertisements. And with the vast majority of this study's advertising sample featuring some form of humor, it is no wonder that nearly $50 billion is spent annually on humorous advertisements worldwide.[17] What may be surprising, however, is the limited knowledge we have on what types of humor perform the best.

This research found ten humor types to represent the vast majority of high performing advertisements when measured by total views and social media engagement. Among the humor types that consistently score above average in attention and engagement are those based on incongruity theory. Consistent with the literature, people laugh at unexpected surprises that break the logical pattern or sequence of events. The cognitive process experienced by audience interpretation of the 'joke' contributes to increased advertisement effectiveness as measured by attention and engagement. Companies can utilize this humor technique to increase the life-span of the advertisement and to break through the noise in advertisement today. Humor techniques such as hyperbole and irony can be safely used to elicit 'clean and fun' laughter from the audience.

On the other hand, negative or aggressive humor are found to be less effective in grabbing the audience's attention and increasing the audience's engagement in the advertisement. Humor techniques such as malicious joy and putdowns should be used with caution as audiences may find them harmfully disparaging or socially inappropriate.

Finally, it is important to note that the humor type 'social order deviancy' scored the highest in increasing the audience's awareness. When applied appropriately (e.g., in good taste), this humor technique shows great promise as an attention getter. Its ability to garner likes and commentary from this initial attraction, however, remains questionable as the technique ranks below average in engagement.

Although this research does not consider differences in audience groups (e.g., gender, culture, age, etc.), when analyzing audience responses to the advertisements, the study provides a comprehensive typology that reveals the most prevalent forms of effective humor used in advertisement. From this typology, an examination was made of the performance to expect from each humor type as measured by audience attention and engagement.

References

1 Parts of this chapter have appeared in Barry, J., 2015, *Social Content Marketing for Entrepreneurs*, Business Expert Press; Barry, J. M. and Graça, S. S., 2013, 'A cross-cultural typology of advertising humor,' paper presented at the 15th Cross-cultural Research Conference, Antigua, Guatemala, December, 2013.

2 Barry, J. M. and Graça, S. S. (2013), A cross-cultural typology of advertising humor, *Proceedings of the 15th Cross-cultural Research Conference*, Antigua, Guatemala, December 8–10.

3 Berger, A. A. (1993), *An Anatomy of Humor*, New Brunswick, NJ: Transaction Books; Buijzen, M. and Valkenburg, P. M. (2004), Developing a typology of humor in audiovisual media, *Media Psychology*, 6 (2), 147–167.

4 Speck, P. S. (1991), The humorous message taxonomy: A framework for the study of humorous ads, *Current Issues & Research in Advertising*, 13 (1–2), 1–44.

5 Berger, op. cit.; Buijzen and Valkenburg, op. cit.

6 Speck, op. cit.

7 Weinberger, M. G. and Spotts, H. E. (1989), Humor in US versus UK TV advertisements: A comparison, *Journal of Advertising*, 18 (2), 39–44; Berger, op. cit.; Speck, op. cit.

8 Merriam-Webster Dictionary (2016), Simple Definition of Schadenfreude, available http://www.merriam-webster.com/dictionary/schadenfreude [accessed March 24, 2016].

9 Speck, op. cit.

10 Buijzen and Valkenburg, op. cit.; Speck, op. cit.

11 Buijzen and Valkenburg, op. cit.; Speck, op. cit.

12 Berger, op. cit.; Buijzen and Valkenburg, op. cit.; Speck, op. cit.

13 Walker, R. (2008), Mix It Up, available http://nyti.ms/1Rwv7eT [accessed March 24, 2016].

14 Buijzen and Valkenburg, op. cit.; Speck, op. cit.

15 Buijzen and Valkenburg, op. cit.

16 Buijzen and Valkenburg, op. cit.; Speck, op. cit.

17 Barry, J. and Hale, D. (2014), Humor determinants and relevance in high engagement social TV advertisements, in: Kubacki, K. (Ed.), *Ideas in Marketing: Finding the New and Polishing the Old: Proceedings of the 2013 Academy of Marketing Science (AMS) Annual Conference*, New York: Springer.

3.2 SMEs' ethical branding with humor on Facebook

A case study of a Finnish online army store[1]

Sari Alatalo, Eeva-Liisa Oikarinen, Helena Ahola, and Marc Järvinen

Introduction

This chapter discusses ethical branding through the use of humor. More specifically, we aim to describe the use of humor and its role as part of ethical brand-building in digital content marketing of one particular small and medium-sized enterprise (SME),[2] a Finnish online army store. The case company, Varusteleka, represents one of the many SMEs which account for 99% of all companies in the EU.[3] The company is known for its use of humor in its B2C (business-to-consumer) communication.

The present research is based on an empirical study of how the store deals with the complexities of humor in its communication on social media. Our case study of the company, a pioneer in e-business and content marketing in Finland, describes and provides further understanding of humor at a practical level through analyzing online narratives, i.e. the most recent Facebook posts. The goal here is to illustrate how humor, even disparagement humor, can be employed in building and communicating corporate brand identity with ethical values as part of it.

An unconventional way of promoting ethical values with humor has the potential to improve the visibility of a small company and help the company participate in a dialog about ethical issues between business and society while simultaneously contributing to the building of the corporate brand. The contribution of our study will be to bring the role of humor into the contemporary discussion of ethical branding; this, we believe, provides a unique perspective into the phenomenon, which remains fairly uninvestigated. In addition, our case study indicates that humor has become a more relevant topic in the emerging digital content marketing context which, in this study, refers to marketing as a management process responsible for identifying, anticipating and satisfying customer requirements through electronic channels.[4]

In order to build a framework for identifying and analyzing humor, we begin by discussing the types of humor, and the various mechanisms to generate humor generally and these specific types in particular. Humor has been widely studied in consumer advertising, and in this study, we have adopted a typology of humorous ad types by Beard[5] and employed it in a novel context. After this, we continue with introducing a corporate brand identity concept adopted in this study, and present the key ethical values chosen here as the building blocks of ethical branding. Finally, our case study provides a further understanding of how humor is used in building the ethical brand of the case company, previously known for its claims to play for the "good team!"

Origins of different humor types

When using intended humor in strategic marketing, humor is acknowledged to work as one of the widely studied advertising appeals, and to have positive effects on attention and attitudes towards ads.[6] However, the strategic role of humor has gained limited attention in research outside literature on advertising. In particular, when operating in the online environment, the scarce literature on the use of humor has focused on humor as a viral element.[7] Moreover, today companies are striving not to seem "faceless" in social media, and they are adding personality to their brand communication in order to create and develop a strong online corporate brand image.

Contemporary humor in advertising has become more non-playful, nonsense, satirical and aggressive,[8] i.e. more negative. We are interested in this new trend and the starting point of this study is to explore how unconventional and controversial, even disparagement, humor could be tailored to work in digital content marketing. Generally, it has become a key issue for the marketers to determine how to target the right people with properly tailored messages in social media.[9] To accomplish this, the kind of humor which is appropriate for the situation is of great importance. As for our empirical study, we give illustrative examples on how different humor types can communicate ethical brand values,[10] which, in turn, are part of corporate brand identity as identified by Urde.[11]

Different humor types can be described as combinations relying on different mechanisms of processing what is seen as humorous. Based on Speck's[12] depiction, Beard[13] has summarized the ideas of various researches into a concise model of humor mechanisms, humorous ad types and relatedness. To begin with, there are three well acknowledged theories on the mechanisms that generate humor, and the humor types can be perceived as the results of one or more of these mechanisms.[14] As shown in Figure 3.2.1, the model establishes five possible types of humorous ads as a result of the humor mechanisms working either alone or together.

When it comes to the mechanisms, the *incongruity-resolution theory* stipulates that humor is a result of a person confronting an incongruity between ideas or feelings and resolving that incongruity.[15] Research results suggest that the feature of inconsistency or surprise is frequently present in advertisements in various countries.[16] Another classical humor theory, the *arousal–safety model*, proposes that a situation may lead a person to perceive something to be humorous when that person experiences heightened arousal but evaluates this stimulus as safe or inconsequential.[17] The subsequent laughter is seen as a way to release physiological or emotional tension and consequently, this can be regarded as a release or relief theory.[18] Thirdly, the phenomenon of humor can be approached through *disparagement theories*, which have been called by other names such as superiority, hostility, aggression and derision theories.[19] These theories rely on the idea that humor is a tool for criticism, censure and control,[20] and as such there is a winner and a loser in every humorous situation.[21] All in all, these three mechanisms form the basis for the different humor types.

Figure 3.2.1 provides an overview of the humorous advertisement types generated by the classical humor processing theories. Moreover, the figure involves examples of the humorous advertisement types taken from the present research material. When it comes to the practical implications, it appears that the *comic wit* type of humor—e.g. jokes, parody, double entendres, puns, humorous stereotypes and absurdity as well as comic exaggeration and understatement—is frequently used in advertisements.[22] By contrast, the *resonant humor* advertisement type was found to be the least common type in US television advertisements.[23] This kind of humor can be embodied in a threatening situation of a minor kind

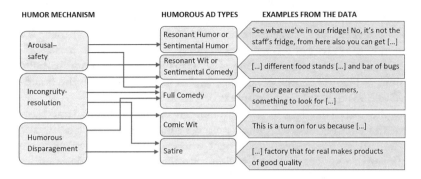

Figure 3.2.1 Humorous ad types generated by humor mechanisms (based on Beard; Speck[24])

resulting in a happy ending. In resonant humor there is no incongruity involved, whereas *resonant wit* results from a combination of incongruity—e.g. pun or exaggeration—and arousal–safety mechanisms. Together with disparagement, incongruity is also a humor mechanism contributing to the generation of *satirical* advertisement which often involves criticism or put down of someone. The use of satire in advertising is challenging since the disparagement may seem too harsh and therefore not funny to the consumer. As for the last type, *full comedy*, all three mechanisms play their part in generating such an advertisement. Just like satire, the full comedy type of advertisement encourages the consumer to adopt a critical view on someone or something, but unlike satire, the disparagement is in some way toned down.[25]

In the study, we approach the narratives of the case company from the viewpoint of these five humor types, which have previously been employed mainly in advertising studies and traditional ads. We found the presented typology of humor types applicable to our study since narratives generated by the company and published in the social media represent new forms of digital advertising in the emerging digital content marketing context.

Ethical branding in SMEs' digital content marketing

As names with power to influence,[26] brands are central to the creation of sustainable wealth.[27] Consequently, the building of such powerful brands is of great significance for companies. They are especially important for SMEs, even though, as suggested for example by Merrilees,[28] branding may be considered typical of big businesses while small business branding might be seen as unfeasible. The increasing amount of research focused on brand–building in SMEs[29] seems to indicate a change in this earlier approach of ignoring SMEs' branding. Traditional marketing frameworks that apply to large enterprises may not be that useful for SMEs[30] which is primarily due to the inherent characteristics of SMEs, e.g. limited resources in terms of finance, time and marketing knowledge,[31] elements which make them different from large businesses. Thus, further research into new angles related to SMEs' branding is needed.

It is widely recognized that there are distinctive characteristics to SMEs and these features set them apart from large organizations.[32] Firstly, *the owner-manager* is often deeply involved in the business,[33] which is reflected in the business by way of the owner-manager influencing branding and instilling their personality traits into the brand.[34] Owner-managers also tend to develop and utilize their networks in business, although there is a considerable variation in the extent of this network building.[35] When it comes to marketing, owner-managers of SMEs regard marketing as a means to create sales and to build customer relationships.[36] These are some of the aspects that have an effect on the brand-building of an SME and make it different from that of a large business.

In consequence, the brand-building in SMEs differs greatly from that of large businesses; it seems that the building of SME brands involves minimum brand planning and limited resources. Instead, an innovative, experiment-oriented and resourceful approach is applied.[37] An innovative approach to brand-building among SMEs can be detected for example in the contexts of using humor for ethical branding and operating in a digital content marketing context. The digital content marketing as the relevant context of this study is presented next.

Facebook: an effective channel for digital content marketing

According to Holliman and Rowley,[38] digital content in marketing requires brands to take a "publishing" approach, and thus to adopt a cultural change from "selling" to "helping" customers. The emergence of various social media channels has enabled companies to take a more active role as publishers of their own messages. Communication in a B2C context has also become more interactive over the past decades.[39] These changes, in turn, require different marketing skills compared to traditional marketing. Rather, organizations and companies need to adopt an "inbound" approach[40] which involves the idea that customers actively seek out a brand because this particular brand provides them with relevant, engaging content. It is suggested that another aspect of being a content marketer is the need to take on and learn the role of a publisher. Peppers and Rogers[41] identify four key elements of a content marketing strategy that could enhance trust: shared values (with the customer); interdependence (mutual value in the relationship); quality communication; and non-opportunistic behavior.

Social media has become an important part of an organization's marketing communications and branding. One type of marketing traditionally used by SMEs is 'Word of Mouth' marketing, but it is now being replaced by 'Word of Mouse' and social media.[42] There are plenty of social media channels available for the companies, such as Twitter, Facebook, LinkedIn, Instagram, Blogs, Webpage, YouTube and Snapchat. Some companies, such as the case company, seem to be particularly active on Facebook, and for this reason the present study focuses on Facebook and the posts generated by the company on their own Facebook profile.

Values and relationships as key ethical elements of corporate brand identity

In effect, there are two approaches to the defining of a brand: outside-in and inside-out, respectively represented by the market- and brand-oriented paradigms proposed by Urde et al.[43] and Urde.[44] In our case study, the focus is on one particular brand and we take an essentially inside-out perspective as we are concentrating primarily on narratives constructed by the case company. The outside-in (i.e. market-oriented) approach would address a brand from, for example, a consumer's perspective with a brand image as the key concept. Because here the viewpoint of the organization is of

primary importance, brand identity is the key concept, and, in essence, we are referring to a corporate brand which contributes to corporate brand identity. Still, we are
approaching the company from outside and, thus, inherently have an outsider's view on
what the company communicates.

As for the definition of a corporate brand, various understandings can be found in
the literature. For instance, it can be defined primarily by organizational associations,[45]
or by additional values associated with a corporation.[46] According to Balmer,[47] a corporate brand has its basis in the corporate identity; yet, it lives in the minds of people.
This view appears to incorporate the inside-out (i.e. corporate identity) and outside-in
(i.e. market-orientation) perspectives of a brand depicted by Urde et al.[48] and Urde.[49]
Furthermore, Gyrd-Jones et al.[50] have distilled the main dimensions of corporate brands
into the concepts of image, identity and culture. Of these components, brand identity
and the building of it through humorous narratives are the primary focus of this study.
In particular, we explore the way that the corporate brand, with the focus on key ethical values, is presently manifested through humorous narratives of the case company
on Facebook.

Corporate brand identity is constructed by many elements such as personality, vision,
culture and mission. However, based on Urde,[51] promise and core values are some of the
central components of corporate brand identity. As shown in Figure 3.2.2, there are various other interrelated elements to the building of corporate brand identity.

In this study, we consider the aspects of core values and relationships to constitute
some of the most relevant features behind corporate brand identity when operating in
a digital content marketing context. The rationale behind this is that the key elements
of content marketing strategy enhancing trust are based on shared values and interaction
with customers.[52] Moreover, with core values as the focal point, we suggest that ethical
values form part of the potential core values of a corporate brand identity. In consequence, we make the connection of ethical branding to corporate brand identity.

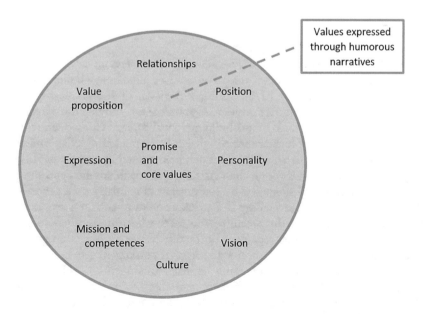

Figure 3.2.2 Elements of corporate brand identity (based on Urde[53]) and the present study

Ethical values

The underlying idea here is to study what kind of humor can be detected in the narratives and how the values of the case company are reflected in their use of humor. Hence, we are studying the way humor is used to promote brand-building in accordance with the expressed values of the company. The company owner has repeatedly expressed his aim to do the right thing,[54] which seems to relate to ethical behavior. Ethics, as described by Fan,[55] refers to moral principles according to which a person decides what is right or wrong; moreover, it needs to be recognized that ethical values vary between individuals and organizations. These are some implications of the wide range of ethical theories.

There are many theories about ethics ranging from normative to descriptive ethical theories. Within the framework of normative theories, one of the main types of non-consequentialist theories commonly applied to business ethics is the ethics of duty which is concerned with universally applicable rules or obligations.[56] In the field of non-consequentialist theories, Immanuel Kant is the most prominent figure, according to whom an individual should act in a way that would be possible for all people to act[57] without disrupting a stable civilization.[58] Kant also developed a theoretical framework from which the principles for ethical behavior can be derived.

Ethical branding is related to moral principles which make it possible to differentiate between right and wrong. In addition to economic or financial ones, a brand should also be evaluated based on moral criteria, and an ethical brand should contribute to the promotion of the public good. In the context of a corporate brand, ethical principles could include such attributes as *honesty, integrity, diversity, quality, respect, responsibility*, and *accountability*.[59] It appears these represent ethical aspects at a practical level, such as being honest, and therefore, they are some of the principles that the values expressed in the social media by the present case company will be reflected on. However, the analyzed narratives were approached with an open mind in case any other principles related to ethics could be detected.

Methodology

The methodology of the study is based on a *qualitative case study approach* which in this case, primarily for instrumental motivations,[60] is focused on the online brand-building of a case company. This study will contribute to the existing knowledge of the various ways of brand-building. An approach of this kind is considered applicable for studying the dynamics present in single settings,[61] for example brand-building in webpages.[62] Consequently, it is appropriate for studying the use of humor in the digital content marketing of an online shop, a phenomenon the dynamics of which is not much investigated in a single setting.

The case company is approached through their narratives about themselves and their operations. The word 'narrative,' as suggested by Riessman,[63] is regularly used synonymously with 'story,' which in oral storytelling is a structure with events in a sequence consequential for later action and for the meanings the teller wants the receiver to get from the story. She further explains that regardless of the differences, the one thing various definitions of a narrative have in common is the idea of contingent sequences, i.e. there needs to be a consequential linking of events or ideas. Brand stories, in line with Twitchell,[64] are commercial variants of storytelling, and they reduce complex ideas to the core of them. According to Shankar,[65] research indicates that the success of an

organization is at least partly dependent on how well they narrate their story. In consequence, narratives can contribute either to the success or the failure of an entrepreneurial
venture. Furthermore, these stories, for their part, are frequently used with the intention
of conveying brand values.[66] In this study, we are interested in the successful use of humor
in narratives in order to put forward the values of one business venture.

In this study, we are analyzing narratives, and how humor and ethical values can be
combined in brand narratives, i.e. how brand stories can be constructed and how they
contribute to the formation of an ethical corporate brand. The empirical material for
analyzing the ethical values and the humor types was gathered from the case company's
Facebook profile between September 15, 2015, and March 15, 2016. This is a snapshot
of the posts but it is relevant for describing a period of time when the company has been
active in digital content marketing. This case study also works as an illustrative example of
the company and presents the current state of its brand in relation to values and humor.

Case: Varusteleka

Our case company, Varusteleka, is a Finnish army and outdoor store, an e-retailer which
has become a phenomenon in Finland known for its rather unconventional, tailored
and powerful use of humor in social media. The company appears to be one of the
early adopters and developers of digital content marketing practices among online stores.
Currently the company has been successful in forming an active brand community with
about 85,000 likes by their followers on the Facebook page.[67] This social media marketing channel in particular seems to be effectively used for digital content marketing with
plenty of information shared and exchanged between the company and its customers. The
information range is wide, including product-related information, daily business activities
and segments intended purely for the sake of entertainment.

The entrepreneur and the owner, Valtteri Lindholm, is also very active as content
producer on Facebook. He was also awarded the Young Entrepreneur of the Year award
in 2015 by the Federation of Finnish Enterprises.[68] In the company, the founder and the
staff are actually all active online, and they have created communities where they express
their own ethical values. Humor can be seen in their products, product descriptions,
website, social media and customer service. This type of communication differentiates
the company from its competitors, and it also enables them to get their message through,
including their ethical values.

The following examples provide an idea of how the company has established itself in
the minds of Finnish consumers; simultaneously they demonstrate some of the values of
the company. There was a product called 'Wifebeater shirt.'[69] The idea however, was to
promote and support The Association against Domestic Violence in a manner which can be
described as unorthodox. Causing public turmoil with the use of unconventional humor is
a way to generate discussion and increase the visibility of the company. Another example is
the 'Genocide beret' which received a lot of publicity and provoked discussion, even negative, in social media.[70] Here the company aimed to criticize people who wore this beret
and who were involved in the violence that erupted in Eastern Europe in the 1990s. The
company has often humorously supported various significant themes in society such as the
rights of sexual minorities. These previous examples could be seen as communication of
ethical values which has been visible in the company's previous efforts of brand-building.

Research protocol

We have adopted a firm-centric approach, and the main focus is on firm-originated narratives[71] rather than consumer stories, although we recognize the fact that when operating in a social media context, there is no longer any clear distinction between those who are creating and those who are consuming a brand. The stories comprising the research data were selected on the basis of certain criteria. Firstly, the narratives were constructed by the case company and they were concerned with the company. Secondly, elements related to humor and values could be detected in these narratives.

The progression of the analysis encompassed multiple phases. In the selection of the research material, we employed the relatively lose definition of a narrative by Riessman[72] according to which a narrative contains contingent sequences. Based on the typology of humorous ads,[73] we then excluded narratives that did not contain any features of humor. Furthermore, we left out narratives with no signs of the Facebook post writer of the company expressing his or her views on what is right or wrong; these were specifically reflected on the ethical attributes suggested by Fan.[74] Still, we were open to other possible values being expressed but it appeared these ethical attributes quite comprehensively covered the values in the present data. We then adopted a thematic approach to determine the themes discussed in the narratives. In the end we looked for any specific features that would emerge from the analyses.

The Facebook posts were originally written in Finnish as the company is of Finnish origin. They were analyzed in their original language, but during the research process the relevant posts to illustrate the different humorous ad types were first chosen and then their contents were translated into English. The original posts employed features of spoken language, and in the translation process the aim was to preserve this characteristic.

Findings

We have analyzed narrative posts initiated by the case company on their Facebook profile. One of the posts included a link to the owner's own blog and this was also analyzed since it represented a continuation of a topic discussed earlier on in the posts. Additionally, the aim of the company was to put an end to a heated discussion, and it seemed to work as intended as there were no further posts on the subject. In general, the posts were predominantly concerned with the operations and products of the company. The posts about products could be taken for marketing but in them, the company manifested their values in quite an original manner; thus, they were also included.

The number of relevant posts involving humor amounted to 46, which accounts for 30% of all the posts during the time period of the study. Some of the posts contained more than one type of humor; at most three different humor types could be discerned in one post. Moreover, some posts included more than one occurrence of similar humor type concerned with a somewhat different topic. As Table 3.2.1 demonstrates, all humor types could be found in the posts but they were in no way evenly represented in the material.

From the table it can be concluded that several posts were characterized by comic wit and satire types of humor. Other humor types figured less frequently. Resonant humor, in turn, was practically non-existent as there was only one occurrence of such. The table also contains further information on the content of the posts, which will be discussed next.

Table 3.2.1 Findings of humor types and ethical values in Facebook posts of case company

Humor types	Number of posts with humor	Topic in the post	Ethical values expressed through the humor type
Comic wit	23	• Product-related	quality, responsibility, accountability, honesty, respect
		• Boobsgate★	honesty, responsibility, integrity
		• Operations-related	responsibility, honesty, respect
		• Extra activities	responsibility
Resonant humor	1	• Product-related	quality
Resonant wit	10	• Operations-related	honesty, responsibility
		• Product-related	responsibility, accountability, quality
		• Extra activities	responsibility
Satire	13	• Operations-related	responsibility, quality, respect
		• Boobsgate★	integrity, responsibility, honesty
		• Product-related	quality, honesty, responsibility
		• Others	honesty, integrity
Full comedy	7	• Product-related	respect, quality, diversity
		• Operations-related	honesty
		• Boobsgate★	integrity

★*explained in the subsequent text*

Comic wit

There was far more comic wit type humor than any other types. The topics of the posts involving this type of humor were mostly concerned with products. There were a couple of other incidents that could be categorized as not directly being about the products; namely "Boobsgate" (explained later), company operations and some extra activities the company is involved in.

The posts about products included such themes as testing products, information about incoming products, customization of products, unavailability of products, Flea Market and Restaurant Day as well as a beer bar which they were going to open in their premises. Quite a few of the posts emphasized the *quality* of their products or services. They did this in various ways, such as by letting the reader know they test their products themselves and by telling that they are now offering products that people have asked for. They also strived to add credibility to their claims by providing information about favorable opinions of people outside the company. These included implying they had high-profile customers and providing a link to an article in a magazine which had tested some of their products. Apart from quality, other values conveyed through the humorous tone of product-related posts encompassed responsibility, accountability, honesty, respect and integrity. In the example below, a couple of the values are expressed simultaneously.

Example 1:
  Jämä—Varusteleka's own product family made in Finland out of recycled material! Army surplus is usually very good as such but there is also a lot of stuff that, for one reason (small sizes) or another (Soviet design), don't sell although the materials

are really good. We also have quite a pile of this unsold junk, and because we have educated people who can sew working for us, we made a couple of simple designs which we sew whenever we have time left over from other tasks.

Our aim is to make this Jämä stuff extremely practical, durable and simple. Because real Finnish workforce is employed to sew these, every working minute is included in and can be traced to the price. [. . .] So, these are good, occasionally deformed stuff of which—classically—every item is an individual.

The passage above loses quite a bit in translation but the point here is that the Finnish word 'jämä,' which refers to leftovers, and the word 'junk' present a clear contrast to what the writer is actually saying. The company is basically explaining that these products are of high quality even though they are produced from leftovers provided by the armed forces. And even though the company does not emphasize it here, they are also acting in an eco-friendly way. They express this aim in other contexts.

'Boobsgate' was another topic which was quite thoroughly covered in February. The word 'Boobsgate' is a translation of the word they use in Finnish. This was an uproar created by one of their ads published on Facebook. In it they had a young woman having her naked breasts covered by hand warmers that the company sells. In their posts, the company and its owner in his own blog tried to convey their rationale behind the ad and their subsequent response on Facebook. They said their aim with the response was to have a reasonable conversation with the people who were offended by the ad. However, the whole thing spiraled out of control and quite a few comments by men ended up being hostile towards the women who had been offended by the ad. The company tried to calm down the heated conversation by, for example, acknowledging that the conversation had gone too far. In this context, they also tried to demonstrate consistency in their behavior and published a similar ad with a man posing in it.

The remaining two topics, company operations and extra activities, had various themes under them such as explaining their system of customer returns and giving information about the flea market they were about to organize. Of all the values, acting responsibly seemed to be related to these activities while quality as a value did not come up at all.

Resonant wit and resonant humor

Resonant wit and especially resonant humor were significantly less frequent than comic wit; ten posts contained features of the resonant wit type of humor while only one ad could be interpreted as having resonant humor with no characteristics of incongruity inherent in resonant wit. The topics of these posts were related to either company operations or products. Only one instance of a different type of topic could be detected, namely an announcement of the owner giving lectures on how they run their business.

The topics of company operations and company products were quite evenly represented among the type of humor discussed here. The one theme that dominated the Facebook posts about the company operations was that new computer software was to be implemented at the turn of January/February and the potential inconvenience caused by this to the customers. The company was quite open and honest about the consequences of this change, and they had even taken some measures to prepare for these problems as they had created a feedback form in advance for these instances. The company was also going to review its system of customer returns as well as its system of granting discounts to its customers. The idea seemed to be to make the system of customer returns more transparent, basically a positive change for the customers, but they planned to abolish the current way of allowing discounts which, they feared, would not please their regular customers. In these posts, they appeared to aim to act honestly and responsibly as they were frank about their intentions and explained their actions.

In posts about the products, the company discussed the availability of products and Restaurant Day. The values conveyed through humor were especially concerned with responsibility and quality. During the Restaurant Day they demonstrated their green attitudes by offering food made of insects; they called the place "Bar of Bugs." All in all, the values seemed to center around honesty and responsibility while quality of either products or service was, although occasionally present, not in focus here.

Satire

Posts with satirical humor were considerably fewer than posts with humor of the comic wit type, amounting to a total of thirteen posts. Still, it turned out that several posts involved more than one occurrence of satirical humor concerned with a different theme. The major topics of these posts encompassed company operations, "Boobsgate," products and a few others.

Satirical comments were provoked by, for example, laws and customs regulations concerning their plans to provide Finnish customers with locally brewed beer. These comments were directed at what the company sees as unreasonably strict laws and regulations applied to the sale of beer in Finland. Still, at the same time they proclaimed their willingness to pay all the "taxes, duties and whatever" required by the Finnish law which they seem to consider to be a responsible way of acting. In addition, as they were attempting to find a partner for another company, they stressed the quality of this company's products by stating the following:

> Example 2:
>   So, tricot made IN FINLAND, sewn into a garment IN FINLAND. A tiny bit more than many other things accredited with the Key Flag Symbol. And funnily enough, we in Varusteleka really like this! [. . .] it's really great that now we have found a factory that for real makes products of good quality from start to finish.

The Key Flag Symbol is a symbol indicating that the product is designed in Finland, and it is accredited by the Association for Finnish Work's Design. Consequently, the company was suggesting that some other companies did not meet their high criteria of products being Finnish. Here we see disparagement of these other companies. Furthermore, simultaneously with highlighting the quality of the products, they were also saying it is a responsible act to buy domestic products in order to "leave the money from these products in Finland."

Apart from company operations, products and a few unclassified topics, the satirical posts were about "Boobsgate," an incident already mentioned in connection with comic wit type humor. This topic was approached with some type of humor in four of their Facebook posts. Satire was quite extensively employed in these posts, mainly directing disparagement at people who had reacted negatively towards either the original ad or women's indignant comments on the ad. Facebook received its share of the satirical comments, as the original ad with the young woman was banned whereas a subsequent ad with a young man in similar circumstances was not. In several posts, the comments indicated that the company saw itself as acting coherently and being strong about what they believe to be the right behavior. This would suggest that the value they were trying to convey was integrity. Besides integrity, responsibility and honesty were also values detectable in their use of humor in this context.

Full comedy

Full comedy involving all the three mechanisms generating humor were chiefly concerned with three topics: products, company operations and, once again, "Boobsgate." In particular, new products were presented using full comedy to convey values such as respect for the customers' wishes, quality of the company's products and diversity. The last one was discernible in one post where customers were urged to participate in a competition the company was organizing. The competition involved customers taking pictures of themselves wearing the jeans produced by the company. In this context, women were especially encouraged to take part in the event as, compared with male customers, the company has considerably fewer female customers.

Full comedy was also used to convey respect for customers as the company wished to be honest about the problems they were having with their new online shop. Here they also used self-disparagement as they confessed to having made a mistake, in other words being "stupid." They also assured that they have made sure that this will "never ever happen again." Additionally, they employed full comedy to show integrity in "Boobsgate"; namely, someone had suggested that the problem is that the company did not have a similar ad aimed at women. They actually had this but recognized the fact that the same kind of ad does not work with women. In consequence, they challenged women to suggest what kind of steamy ad would work with women. The disparagement in all of these posts were softened in some way.

Discussion

The purpose of our study has been to explore ethical branding with humor in SMEs' digital content marketing. We approached the phenomenon through a case study of a Finnish online army store. This study creates some preliminary understanding about how ethical values can be communicated with humor on Facebook, which represents an ideal channel for digital content marketing. More fundamentally, we were able to determine how and what kind of humor the company employed in their social media (i.e. Facebook) communication.

As for the type of humor we found present in the Facebook posts, there are several interesting points. Firstly, incongruity is present in the vast majority of the posts, with only one exception in our research material. This is in line with the research results obtained by Alden et al.,[75] according to which most television ads contained incongruent contrast. Secondly, the most common (comic wit) and the least common (resonant humor) types of humor seem to comply with Speck's[76] results. Otherwise the results seem to differ, as the second most common humor type in our material is satire whereas it was only number four in Speck's material. It appears that the satirical kind of humor, generally more favored by men than women,[77] was quite prominently present in the case company's communication. Harsh disparagement is said to be rare in advertising but a satirical tone and more aggressive style are becoming increasingly common.[78] In terms of the topics, it seems that with the exception of resonant humor, all the humor types were used to discuss the topics of products and company operations. In addition, "Boobsgate" was discussed using three humor types, namely comic wit, satire and full comedy.

We were also able to identify some core ethical values and conclude them to be part of the case company's corporate brand identity (see Figure 3.2.2). Moreover, there are differences in the use of humor types in relation to these core values as well as to the topics. These results are quite clearly seen in Table 3.2.2.

If we take a closer look at this three-dimensional table, we are able to discern that the primary values the company is conveying at the moment are *quality* and *responsibility*. Quality is most often conveyed through the comic wit type of humor and is related to the products while responsibility is far more diverse in both aspects, i.e. responsibility is expressed through quite a few types of humor and in contexts of several topics. A clear number three, *honesty*, appears to be equally varied in terms of humor types and topics. However, the number of posts is limited, and this also applies to the other values—i.e. integrity, respect, accountability and diversity—detectable in the material. The ethical brand of this company seems to integrate all seven of the ethical attributes that Fan[79] refers to regarding ethical branding. However, some of these seem to have a more prominent role in the brand identity than others. Figure 3.2.3 shows the values and humor types found in our material.

The Facebook posts referred to all the ethical attributes presented by Fan[80] and all the humor types introduced by Speck as well as Beard.[81] The values as well as the humor types are included in Figure 3.2.3, and the more important or prominent ones are emphasized. As can be seen, responsibility and quality were the core values conveyed through humor. It is noteworthy that comic wit and satire were somewhat more common than other types of humor. Satire playing a significant role in the types of humor employed by the company is of special interest, and it might explain the perceived image of the case company. In consequence, the ethical brand of the case company is currently characterized by the company striving for responsibility and quality through the use of humor in its Facebook communication.

Table 3.2.2 Communication of case company: humor types, ethical values, and topics

Value/Topic of humor	Product-related	Operations-related	Boobsgate	Extra activities	Others	Total
Quality	11 (CW)+ 1 (RH) + 1 (RW) + 2 (S) + 1 (FC)	1 (S)				17
Responsibility	5 (CW) + 2 (RW) + 1 (S)	1 (CW) + 3 (RW) + 4 (S)	1 (CW) + 1 (S)	1 (CW)		19
Honesty	2 (CW) + 1 (S)	1 (CW) + 4 (RW) + 1 (FC)	1 (CW) + 1 (S)	1 (RW)	1 (S)	13
Integrity	1 (CW)		1 (CW) + 3 (S) + 1 (FC)		2 (S)	8
Respect	1 (CW) + 3 (FC)	1 (CW) + 1 (S)				6
Accountability	1 (CW)+ 1 (RW)					2
Diversity	1 (FC)					1

CW = Comic Wit; RH = Resonant Humor; RW = Resonant Wit; S = Satire; FC = Full Comedy

Figure 3.2.3 Values and humor types found in Facebook posts by Varusteleka

Conclusions and managerial implications

The intended contribution of our chapter is based on our aim to examine, at a practical level, how organizations may deal with the complexities of humor; in particular, we concentrated on the potential of ethical branding through the use of humor in an SME's digital content marketing. We approached the phenomenon through a case study of a Finnish online army store and applied the content analysis of narrative posts in a social media environment. As a conclusion, our contribution is to enrich the understanding about the role of humor in the contemporary discussion of ethical branding in the online environment. By providing an illustrative example of this, our contribution, we believe, is significant for both an academic audience and practitioners. We can learn a great deal from this unique emerging business practice and apply the knowledge in broader theoretical and practical contexts which are described in more detail next.

Apart from promoting the public good, ethical branding can give a competitive advantage for firms since consumers today are more conscious of ethical values.[82] Our empirical case illustrates that, in their ethical branding, some companies have indeed adopted humor-related practices which have previously been discussed mainly by social movement activists.[83] However, an approach combining humor and ethical branding in a company's brand-building has not been very prominently present in earlier literature and, hence, the objective of our study is to offer more insight into this research gap. All in all, our chapter aims to bring a new angle to the emerging discussion on *ethical branding*.

As a result of the present study, we introduce *one framework to approach the way ethical values can be communicated with the help of humor* by providing an illustrative example of an SME's digital content marketing. This case seems to integrate all the ethical values

Fan[84] refers to regarding an ethical brand. However, some of the values seem to have a more prominent role in the brand identity than others. Whether or not these are context-dependent findings should be confirmed in further research. However, this seems to be the present state of the case company's ethical brand conveyed through the use of humor. This kind of unconventional branding is in line with the ideas presented by Centeno et al.[85] about SMEs' branding being innovative, experiment-oriented and resourceful.

As for managerial implications, the presented framework involving the three aspects of humor types, ethical values and topic content may help managers in their digital content marketing efforts. For them, the framework offers a tool for evaluating and planning their ethical-based corporate communication. All in all, this study presents one potential way for owners/managers of SMEs with limited resources to develop and communicate their ethical values by unconventionally combining ethical values and humor in brand communication. Through our case study, we emphasize the fact that the significance of the use of humor in ethical digital marketing should not be ignored, and the present study makes a contribution to the discussion of SMEs' branding by offering a new perspective to our understanding of this area.

Limitations and recommendations for further research

Our study has limitations some of which open up new, intriguing avenues for research. To start with, our focus has been on Facebook communication of a single case company. The case itself was unique and it offers a fruitful starting point for further research on SMEs' use of humor to promote their ethical values in their digital content marketing. The empirical data of this unique company represent a snapshot of the phenomenon as it was limited in time (i.e. six months) and scope (i.e. Facebook). Consequently, a study on the development of the ethical brand over time in various social media contexts could be the next step.

Due to the case study nature, we would like to encourage researchers to conduct more case studies related to the topic of ethical branding with the help of humor. In addition to case studies, researchers could utilize and further develop our framework. In this way, we might deepen our understanding about the relationship between humor types and ethical values in digital content. The effectiveness of different humor types in communicating specific ethical values could also be tested experimentally in order to gain more insight into the effectiveness of the emerging communication practices of ethical branding.

As for the theories in this study, we selected ones that appeared to be most applicable in our context. For example, we used Balmer's definition of a corporate brand as it relates well to the Urde's model of the elements of a brand. As the primary goal in the study was to approach the brand from the viewpoint of brand identity (i.e. inside-out) the adopted model was appropriate in this context. Still, in further studies it would be possible to use Aaker's[86] brand personality which takes more of a consumer perspective to a brand. Furthermore, we based our ethical theory on Kant as he is a prominent figure in the field of non-consequentialist theories frequently applied to business ethics. However, business ethics could be an area worthy of further research in general.

On the whole, our approach to the phenomenon of building an ethical brand through humor was company-centered. This view excluded the perspective of a customer as a relevant actor in a brand-building process. Co-creation involving customers is becoming a recognized way to build brands.[87] Nowadays, social media enable customers to participate in brand-building. Furthermore, the way shared values of a company and its customers might contribute to the effectiveness of humorous communication is an interesting topic. These aspects, certainly, would be beneficial ways to proceed with the research in future.

References

1 Parts of this chapter were presented at the 23rd Nordic Academy of Management Conference, NFF 2015—Business in Society.
2 European Commission. *Growth. Entrepreneurship and Small and Medium-sized Enterprises (SMEs)*. Retrieved October 21, 2016. http://ec.europa.eu/growth/smes/business-friendly-environ ment/sme-definition_en.
3 Ibid.
4 Rowley, J. (2008), Understanding digital content marketing. *Journal of Marketing Management*, 24(5–6), 517–540.
5 Beard, F. K. (2008), *Humor in the Advertising Business: Theory, Practice, and Wit*. Plymouth: Rowman & Littlefield Publishers, Inc.
6 Weinberger, M. G. and Gulas, C. S. (1992), The impact of humor in advertising: A review. *Journal of Advertising*, 21(9), 35–59; Eisend, M. (2009), A meta-analysis of humor in advertising. *Academy of Marketing Science Journal*, 37(2), 191–203.
7 Veil, S. R., Petrun, E. L., and Roberts, H. A. (2012), Issue management gone awry: When not to respond to an online reputation threat. *Corporate Reputation Review*, 15(4), 319–332.
8 Weinberger, M. G., Gulas, C. S., and Weinberger, M. F. (2015), Looking in through outdoor: A sociocultural and historical perspective on the evolution of advertising humour. *International Journal of Advertising: The Review of Marketing Communications*, 34(3), 447–472.
9 Wright, E., Khanfar, N. M., Harrington, C., and Kizeret, L. E. (2010), The lasting effects of social media trends on advertising. *Journal of Business & Economics Research*, 8(11), 73–80.
10 Fan, Y. (2005), Ethical branding and corporate reputation. *Corporate Communications: An International Journal*, 10(4), 341–350.
11 Urde, M. (2013), The corporate brand identity matrix. *Journal of Brand Management*, 20(9), 742–761.
12 Speck, P. S. (1990), The humorous message taxonomy: A framework for the study of humorous ads. *Current Issues and Research in Advertising*, 13(1), 1–44.
13 Beard, op. cit.
14 Speck, op. cit.; Gulas, C. S. and Weinberger, M. G. (2006), *Humor in Advertising: A Comprehensive Analysis*. Armonk, New York: Sharpe; Beard, op. cit.
15 Suls, J. (1983), Cognitive processes in humor appreciation. In Goldstein, J. (ed.), *Handbooks of Humor Research*. New York: Springer-Verlag Inc., 39–57.
16 Alden, D. L., Hoyer, W. D., and Lee, C. (1993), Identifying global and culture-specific dimensions of humor in advertising: A multinational analysis. *Journal of Marketing*, 57(2), 64–75.
17 Rothbart, M. K. (1973), Laughter in young children. *Psychological Bulletin*, 80(3), 247–256.
18 Beard, op. cit.
19 Ibid.
20 Speck, op. cit.
21 Gruner, C. R. (1997), *The Game of Humor*. New Brunswick, NJ: Transaction Publishers.
22 Beard, op. cit.
23 Speck, op. cit.
24 Speck, op. cit.; Beard, op. cit.
25 Beard, op. cit.
26 Kapferer, J.-N. (2012), *The New Strategic Brand Management: Advanced Insights and Strategic Thinking*. London; Philadelphia: Kogan Page.
27 Clifton, R. et al. (2009), *Brands and Branding*. New York: Bloomberg Press; Lindemann, J. (2009), The financial value of brands. In Clifton, R. et al. (eds.), *Brands and Branding*. New York: Bloomberg Press, 26–44.

28 Merrilees, B. (2007), A theory of brand-led SME new venture development. *Qualitative Market Research: An International Journal*, *10*(4), 403–415.

29 Abimbola, T. and Vallaster, C. (2007), Brand, organisational identity and reputation in SMEs: An overview. *Qualitative Market Research: An International Journal*, *10*(4), 341–348.

30 Carson, D. and Gilmore, A. (2000), Marketing at the interface: Not 'what' but 'how.' *Journal of Marketing Theory and Practice*, *8*(2) (Spring), 1–7.

31 Gilmore, A., Carson, D., and Grant, K. (2001), SME marketing in practice. *Marketing Intelligence & Planning*, *19*(1), 6–11.

32 Culkin, N. and Smith, D. (2000), An emotional business: A guide to understanding the motivations of small business decision takers. *Qualitative Market Research*, *3*(3), 145–157; Gilmore et al., op. cit.; Resnick, S. M., Cheng, R., Simpson, M., and Lourenço, F. (2016), Marketing in SMEs: A "4Ps" self-branding model. *International Journal of Entrepreneurial Behavior & Research*, *22*(1), 155–174.

33 Dobbs, M. and Hamilton, R. T. (2007), Small business growth: Recent evidence and new directions. *International Journal of Entrepreneurial Behavior & Research*, *13*(5), 296–322.

34 Centeno, E., Hart, S., and Dinnie, K. (2013), The five phases of SME brand-building. *Journal of Brand Management, 20*(6), 445–457.

35 Gilmore, A., Carson, D., and Rocks, S. (2006), Networking in SMEs: Evaluating its contribution to marketing activity. *International Business Review*, *15*(3), 278–293.

36 Reijonen, H. (2010), Do all SMEs practise same kind of marketing? *Journal of Small Business and Enterprise Development*, *17*(2), 279–293.

37 Centeno et al., op. cit.

38 Holliman, G. and Rowley, J. (2014), Business to business digital content marketing: Marketers' perceptions of best practice. *Journal of Research in Interactive Marketing*, *8*(4), 269–293.

39 Leckenby, J. D. and Hairong, L. (2000), From the editors: Why we need the *Journal of Interactive Advertising*. *Journal of Interactive Advertising*, *1*(1), 1–3. Available http://jiad-org.adprofession.com/article1.html.

40 Halligan, B. and Shah, D. (2010), *Inbound Marketing: Get Found Using Google, Social Media, and Blogs*. Hoboken, NJ: John Wiley & Sons Inc.; Odden, L. (2012), *Optimize: How to Attract and Engage More Customers by Integrating SEO, Social Media, and Content Marketing*. Hoboken, NJ: John Wiley & Sons.

41 Peppers, D. and Rogers, M. (2011), *Managing Customer Relationships: A Strategic Framework*. Chichester, UK: John Wiley & Sons.

42 Resnick et al., op. cit.

43 Urde, M., Baumgarth, C., and Merrilees, B. (2013), Brand orientation and market orientation: From alternatives to synergy. *Journal of Business Research*, *66*(1), 13–20.

44 Urde, op. cit.

45 Aaker, D. A. (2004), Leveraging the corporate brand. *California Management Review*, *46*(3), 6–18.

46 Balmer, J. M. T. and Gray, E. R. (2003), Corporate brands: What are they? What of them? *European Journal of Marketing*, *37*(7/8), 972–997.

47 Balmer, J. M. (2010), Explicating corporate brands and their management: Reflections and directions from 1995. *Journal of Brand Management*, *18*(3), 180–196.

48 Urde et al., op. cit.

49 Urde, op. cit.

50 Gyrd-Jones, R., Merrilees, B., and Miller, D. (2013), Revisiting the complexities of corporate branding: Issues, paradoxes, solutions. *Journal of Brand Management*, *20*(7), 571–589.

51 Urde, op. cit.

52 Peppers and Rogers, op. cit.

53 Urde, op. cit.

54 Hämäläinen, K. and Ratilainen, J. (2015), *Yrittäjän taivas+helvetti: Vol. 3, Riko rajasi* (1. p.). Helsinki: One on One.

55 Fan, Y., op. cit.

56 Crane, A. and Matten, D. (2010), *Business Ethics: Managing Corporate Citizenship and Sustainability in the Age of Globalization*. Oxford: Oxford University Press.

57 Hoover, K. F. and Pepper, M. B. (2015), How did they say that? Ethics statements and normative frameworks at best companies to work for. *Journal of Business Ethics, 131*, 603–617.

58 Crane, V. and Mattern, D., op. cit.

59 Fan, Y., op. cit.

60 Stake, R. E. (2005), Qualitative case studies. In Denzin, N. K. and Lincoln, Y. S. (eds.), *The Sage Handbook of Qualitative Research*. Thousand Oaks, CA: Sage Publications, 443–466.

61 Eisenhardt, K. M. (1989), Building theories from case study research. *Academy of Management Review, 14*(4), 532–550.

62 Spence, M. and Essoussi, L. H. (2010), SME brand building and management: An exploratory study. *European Journal of Marketing, 44*(7/8), 1037–1054.

63 Riessman, C. K. (2008), *Narrative Methods for the Human Sciences*. Thousand Oaks, CA: Sage.

64 Twitchell, J. B. (2004), An English teacher looks at branding. *Journal of Consumer Research, 32*(2), 484–489.

65 Shankar, A., Elliot, R., and Goulding, C. (2001), Understanding consumption: Contributions from a narrative perspective. *Journal of Marketing Management, 17*(3/4), 429–453.

66 Lundqvist, A., Liljander, V., Gummerus, J., and van Riel, A. (2013), The impact of storytelling on the consumer brand experience: The case of a firm-originated story. *Journal of Brand Management, 20*(4), 283–297.

67 Varusteleka. Facebook page. Retrieved October 21, 2016. https://www.facebook.com/Varusteleka/.

68 Yrittäjä. (2015), Varusteleka Oy:n Valtteri Lindholm on vuoden nuori yrittäjä. Retrieved October 21, 2016. https://www.yrittajat.fi/tiedotteet/495691-varusteleka-oyn-valtteri-lindholm-vuoden-nuori-yrittaja.

69 Vihavainen, S. (2012), "Vaimonhakkaajapaitojen" myynti suomalaisessa verkkokaupassa aiheuttaa hämmennystä. *Helsingin Sanomat*. Retrieved October 21, 2016. http://www.hs.fi/kotimaa/a1305573029214.

70 Jauhiainen, I. (2013), Mainonnan eettinen neuvosto: vaimonhakkaajapaita on ok mutta kansanmurhabaretti ei. *Mainonta & Markkinointi*. Retrieved October 21, 2016. http://www.marmai.fi/uutiset/mainonnan-eettinen-neuvosto-vaimonhakkaajapaita-on-ok-mutta-kansanmurhabaretti-ei-6289384.

71 Ibid.

72 Riessman, C. K., op. cit.

73 Beard, op. cit.; Speck, op. cit.

74 Fan, op. cit.

75 Alden et al., op. cit.

76 Speck, op. cit.

77 Beard, op. cit.

78 Ibid.; Weinberger et al., op. cit.

79 Fan, op. cit.

80 Ibid.

81 Speck, op. cit.; Beard, op. cit.

82 Fan, op. cit.

83 Kutz-Flamenbaum, R. V. (2014), Humor and social movements. *Sociology Compass, 8*(3), 294–304.

84 Fan, op. cit.

85 Centeno et al., op. cit.

86 Aaker, J. L. (1997), Dimensions of brand personality. *Journal of Marketing Research, 34*(3), 347–356.

87 Mäläskä, M., Saraniemi, S., and Tähtinen, J. (2011), Network actors' participation in B2B SME branding. *Industrial Marketing Management, 40*, 1144–1152.

3.3 With a genuine smile?

The relevance of time pressure and emotion work strategies for the adoption of humor in customer contact

Daniel Putz and Tabea Scheel

Theory

Major parts of today's economy are based on service jobs that include the deliberate regulation of emotions during customer contact. Organizations aim at creating pleasant customer interactions in order to provoke desirable reactions (e.g., higher turnover, less cancellations and complaints) that may ensure and increase commercial success. At the same time, employees are often challenged with stressful job demands that may impair their subjective well-being and their actual capability to shape customer relations in a positive way. Therefore, the aim of the present study is to investigate the relationship between job demands and the quality of customer contact. Specifically, we investigate how time pressure is related to the adoption of positive and negative humor in interactions with retail customers, and whether the emotion work strategies of deep and surface acting mediate these relationships.

Given the focus on humor in the communication between employee and customer, our research is in line with humor definitions as a communicative activity. For instance, Romero and Cruthirds (2006) defined humor as amusing communications that create a positive cognitive and emotional reaction in a person or a group.[1] In addition, we differentiate between the potentially positive and negative sides of humor, thus following the humor styles introduced by Martin et al.[2] They conceptualized two positive (i.e., affiliative, self-enhancing) and two negative styles (i.e., aggressive, self-defeating) of using humor in everyday life. Given our focus on interpersonal communication, our positive and negative humor use in customer contact mirror other-directed humor, i.e., the affiliative and the aggressive styles.

The role of humor in customer contact

The creation of positive mood during customer contact may be regarded as a pivotal task of employees in customer service. Pleasant interactions with employees are likely to increase customer satisfaction, loyalty and recommendations.[3] The global PwC Total Retail Survey 2016 with nearly 23,000 participants from 25 countries highlights the relevance of satisfying customer contacts: with 40% approval, sales associates were qualified as the most relevant factor to increase in-store experience.[4] The creation of positive customer contacts may be among the most promising factors to face one of the main challenges for retailers today: operators of department stores and local shops are struggling to gain and secure customers and sales, while mobile and e-commerce offer permanent access to cheaper and more convenient purchasing opportunities.[5] Thus, service providers are faced with the question of how their employees can evoke and maintain comfortable feelings during customer contact. One effective way to do so may be the purposeful use of humor, which can be regarded as "amusing communications that produce positive emotions and cognitions in the person, group or organization."[6] Accordingly, service employees may smile to customers and banter with them during sales talks in order to create an enhancing and affiliative atmosphere. However, humor may also be used in a more negative way, such as mocking and making fun of customers, and can therefore also impair the quality of customer relations through aggressive or deprecating behaviors.[7] Thus, Martineau[8] stated that depending on the kind of humor used, it can both function as a social "lubricant," fostering closeness to other people and increasing social support, or as an "abrasive," creating a hostile atmosphere and disintegrating relationships. This differentiation between desired and undesired kinds of humor raises the question of what increases the likelihood of employees applying positive humor and avoiding negative humor in customer contact.

Time pressure threatens the purposeful adoption of humor in customer contact

The purposeful use of humor in customer contact involves a number of self-regulatory activities, such as:

- monitoring and interpreting the characteristics, behavior and emotional state of customers for potential links for jokes and their receptivity to humorous interactions in a given situation;
- keeping up professional communication while preparing for an amusing statement or action;
- adopting them at the right time and in an appropriate application rate to develop its humorous potential for the self and the other; and
- regulating one's own feelings in order to prevent the adoption of negative humor (e.g., by reducing annoying or aggressive impulses) and to facilitate positive humor (e.g., lightening up one's mood).

According to the Ego Depletion Theory,[9] stressful job demands reduce employees' self-regulatory resources and may therefore influence the adoption of humor. For instance, customer contact is often characterized by subjective time pressure. Customer requests can occur suddenly at any time during operating hours and are usually expected to be tended to immediately regardless of whether the responsible employee has other work obligations or not. Thus, "the sense that one's duties and responsibilities exceed one's ability to complete them in the time available"[10] is likely to occur and will permanently redirect a certain amount of employees' regulatory resources from current customer interactions to the monitoring of concurrent requirements and the preparation for future tasks. Due to the reduced amount of resources available, employees pressed for time may lack the essential attention and readiness to express a witticism with a right timing to make the customer laugh and to brighten up the atmosphere, or may fail to suppress an ironic reply or cynical remark that may harm or annoy a customer. Furthermore, the ongoing consumption of self-regulatory resources caused by stressful job demands such as time pressure is regularly accompanied by impairments in subjective well-being and increases in affective irritation.[11] This results in a prevailing mood readily accessible for aggressive and deprecating impulses. Employees need to actively suppress these emotions in order to enable affiliative and pleasant interactions. We therefore assume that time pressure impairs employees' ability to adopt humor in a functional way through the delimitation of self-regulatory resources and the impairment of subjective well-being resulting in less positive and more negative humor.

Hypothesis 1: Time pressure will be (a) negatively related to the adoption of positive humor and (b) positively related to the adoption of negative humor in customer contact.

Emotion work strategies mediate the effects of time pressure on humor

In modern service societies, emotion work, that is, the "emotional regulation [. . .] in the display of organizationally desired emotions"[12] has become a central job requirement for many employees. Customer contact is to be regarded as a prototypical type of emotion labor, requiring employees to actively regulate their emotions in order to display emotions that are desired by the organization and the customers. This involves ongoing self-regulatory activities, such as:

- understanding a client's emotional situation;
- activating the relevant social rules that determine which emotions should be suppressed or evoked in the given situation;
- perceiving one's own actual emotional state; and
- coping with the demand to suppress or amplify one's actual feelings or to express diverging emotions.[13]

Employees may apply different strategies in order to regulate their emotions, and these emotion work strategies may be one of the mechanisms linking time pressure to employees' adoption of humor in customer contact.

There are at least two distinct strategies to shape apparent emotions in a desired way: employees may either modify their facial expressions without regard to their actual emotional experience ("surface acting," e.g., smiling while feeling sad) or they may try to influence their inner feelings in a way that their emotional experience fits the requested emotional expression ("deep acting," e.g., cheering oneself up when being sad).[14] While surface acting refers to a behavioral strategy of changing emotional expression, deep acting attempts to adjust the emotional experience itself. As such, surface and deep acting do not only describe certain ways of adjusting emotional expressions, they also refer to different stages in the development of emotional experience.[15]

Deep acting aims at aligning a person's true feelings to the situational requirements before emotional cues can elicit behavioral, experiential, or physiological response tendencies.[16] Thus, deep acting can be regarded as an antecedent-focused emotion regulation strategy, i.e., a strategy that is applied very early in the timeline of the emotion process before an emotion entirely develops its experiential and behavioral potential. When a person becomes aware of an inconsistency between the emotional reactions directly provoked by situational cues and the emotional reactions required in the very same situation, he or she may engage in deep acting. This may be addressed in three ways:

- by changing the situation (e.g., addressing an annoyed customer in a different way in order to reduce his or her anger and to induce more positive reactions);
- by changing the perception of the situation by refocusing attention on situational aspects or thoughts more consistent with the required emotional reaction (e.g., focusing on the spending capacity of a rude and demanding customer or remembering the last pleasant interaction with a client); or
- by reappraising the situation (e.g., reframing the customer interaction as an opportunity to learn how to deal with challenging interaction situations which may increase sales counts in the long run rather than viewing it as a critical situation to immediately increase poor sales counts).[17]

As a consequence of these deep acting strategies, emotional experience is redirected in the desired way, thus immediately resolving the emotional conflict and triggering the required emotional expressions. People who tend to engage in deep acting report less negative feelings and show fewer expressions of negative affect while positive emotional experience and expressions are increased,[18] most likely resulting in a corresponding pattern of less adoption of negative humor and more use of positive humor in customer contact. Empirical studies show that deep acting is associated with closer and more positive interpersonal relations[19] as well as higher job satisfaction, emotional performance and customer satisfaction.[20] Accordingly, we assume deep acting to be positively related to the adoption of positive humor in customer contact.

While deep acting appears to be beneficial for the person and the organization, its effective adoption requires the person to immediately sense and rapidly react to the very onset of emotional conflicts in order to selectively redirect attention, reinterpret information, and inhibit emotional stimuli before emotional experience unfolds. Accordingly, Gross and John suggested that "occasionally, there may not be time to cognitively reevaluate a rapidly developing situation, making reappraisal an unworkable choice."[21] Especially under time pressure, when employees are occupied with several tasks simultaneously, the opportunity to perceive and respond to the development of undesired emotions is limited, thereby increasing the risk of missing the very limited time frame when deep acting can be effectively applied. We therefore assume that higher time pressure will be associated with less engagement in deep acting.

In contrast, surface acting describes a response-focused strategy of emotion regulation that can be applied rather late in the timeline of the emotion process. When an emotion has already developed and the person experiences an inconsistency between the expressive reactions associated with the actual emotional experience and the situational requirements, surface acting aims at suppressing undesired automatic reactions while amplifying or faking desired emotional expressions. Thus, surface acting enables people to manage emotional expression without adjusting their actual feelings[22] and may also be applied when the opportunity to deep act was missed. Time pressure should therefore increase the likelihood of surface acting.

Employees engaging in surface acting may be effective in masking negative feelings, but the negative experience itself remains unchanged and the emotional conflict between actual feelings and requested emotions persists, thus continuing to provoke undesired emotional reactions that need to be countered by further emotional regulation. Surface acting therefore permanently consumes cognitive resources to effortfully manage emotion response tendencies. Furthermore, while employees engage in surface acting the ongoing discrepancy between inner feelings and observable behavior is likely to trigger feelings of inauthenticity that also need to be countered by active emotional regulation, further

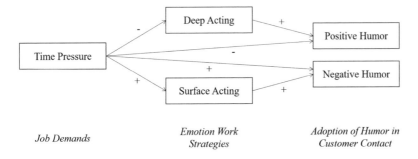

Figure 3.3.1 Research model

reducing the capability to effectively manage the emotional expression, interpersonal behavior and performance. In fact, people who tend to engage in surface acting not only report less positive affect and show less positive expressions but also experience higher levels of negative emotions resulting in less close and less positive interpersonal relations.[23] Furthermore, a meta-analysis by Huelsheger and Schewe[24] showed surface acting to be positively associated with burnout and strain and negatively related to job satisfaction and emotional performance. Accordingly, we assume that surface acting will increase the likelihood of negative humor use.

Altogether, we assume a mediating role of employees' emotion work strategies for the link between time pressure and humor use with customers. Our hypotheses are summarized in Figure 3.3.1.

Hypothesis 2: The relationship between time pressure and humor use in customer contact will be mediated by (a) deep acting for the adoption of positive humor and (b) surface acting for the adoption of negative humor in customer contact.

Method

Participants and procedure

We conducted a cross-sectional, quantitative study at four German retail stores in order to test our hypotheses.[25] Complete surveys of 170 employees were obtained (70.8% response rate). Surveys were administered personally to employees, completed during work time, and immediately collected. Anonymity and confidentiality were guaranteed.

Fifty-six participants were women (32.9%), and 106 were men (62.4%). Most of the participants were between 21 and 30 ($n = 68$, 40%) or 31 and 40 years of age ($n = 56$, 32.9%), nine were between 16 and 20 (5.3%), 26 were between 41 and 51 (15.3%), seven were between 51 and 60 (4.1%), and four were older than 60 (2.4%). Participants had worked in retail for an average of 11.4 years ($SD = 8.1$).

Measures

Time pressure

Time pressure was measured with the four-item subscale from the Instrument for Stress-Oriented Analysis of Work (ISTA)[26] on a 5-point Likert scale. Two questions (e.g., "How often are you pressed for time?") were rated as 1 (*very rarely/never*), 2 (*rarely/ approximately once a week*), 3 (*occasionally/approximately once a day*), 4 (*frequently/several times a day*), or 5 (*very often/almost continuously*). The answer choices differed for two questions: The question "How often do you have to delay or cancel your break due to too much work?" were rated as 2 (*rarely/approximately once a month*), 3 (*occasionally/approximately once a week*), 4 (*frequently/several times a week*), or 5 (*very often/daily*). The question "How often do you have to leave work later than planned due to too much work?" differed from the previous question in the anchors for the ratings of 3 (*occasionally/several times a month*) and 5 (*very often/almost daily*). Cronbach's alpha was .71.

Emotion work

Deep acting and surface acting were assessed with three items each.[27] A sample item for deep acting is "I try to actually experience the emotions that I must show" and for surface acting "I try to hide my true feelings." The items were rated on a 5-point Likert scale as 1 (*seldom/never*), 2 (*seldom/several times month*), 3 (*occasionally/several times a week*), 4 (*often/daily*), and 5 (*very often/several times a day*). Cronbach's alpha was .75 for deep acting and .82 for surface acting.

Adoption of humor in customer contact

Four questions had to be answered for positive humor in customer contact, and two questions for negative humor with customers. The questions were rated on the same 5-point Likert scale as applied for emotion work. For instance, participants were asked to answer "How often do you joke with the customers in a sales conversation?" (adoption of positive humor) or "How often do you poke fun at customers, directly in sales conversation?" (adoption of negative humor). Cronbach's alpha was .70 for positive humor with customers and the correlation of the two items of negative humor with customers was $r = .52$ ($p < .01$).

Control variable

As the adoption of emotion work strategies is likely to change with ongoing work experience, we controlled deep acting and surface acting for participant's tenure in retail.

Analyses

In order to test our assumptions that time pressure is related to the adoption of certain kinds of humor in customer service and that this relationship is mediated by emotion work strategies, we used Ordinary Least Squares (OLS) regression-based mediation-analysis with bootstrapping provided by the PROCESS software for SPSS.[28] PROCESS estimates the indirect effect of the predictor on the dependent variable through the mediator. If emotion work strategies mediate the effects of time pressure (predictor) on the kind of humor used in customer contact (criterion), this indirect effect becomes significant. PROCESS only provides unstandardized estimates. Therefore, we z-standardized all variables before entering them into the mediation analyses in order to facilitate interpretation of effects. In case of significant mediation, the amount of variance explained through the mediation process can be quantified by comparing the indirect effect to the direct effect of time pressure on the kind of humor used without taking emotion work strategies into account.

Results

Descriptive statistics and zero-order correlations for all variables are displayed in Table 3.3.1. Emotion work strategies show the assumed relations with the adoption of humor in customer contact with positive associations between deep acting and the adoption of

Table 3.3.1 Descriptive statistics and correlations between the variables

		M	SD	1	2	3	4	5	6
1	Tenure retail	11.40	8.11						
2	Time pressure	3.23	.75	.07	(.71)				
3	Deep acting	3.24	.89	.08	−.00	(.75)			
4	Surface acting	2.85	1.01	−.18*	.14	.16*	(.82)		
5	Positive humor adoption	3.40	.62	−.11	.08	.35**	.09	(.70)	
6	Negative humor adoption	2.34	.97	.02	.24**	.05	.23**	.24**	$r = .52$**

Note: $N = 169$–170. Pearson correlations, two-sided. Reliabilities (Cronbach's α) are on the diagonal in parentheses. *$p < .05$. **$p < .01$.

positive humor ($r = .35$; $p < .01$) and surface acting and the adoption of negative humor ($r = .23$; $p < .01$). The associations of time pressure with emotion work strategies were less distinct: time pressure was positively associated with the adoption of negative humor in customer contact ($r = .24$; $p < .01$). Although the correlation coefficient for time pressure and surface acting was also numerically positive it did not become significant ($r = .14$; *ns*). There was no direct association between time pressure and either the adoption of positive humor ($r = .08$; *ns*) or deep acting ($r = .00$; *ns*).

To test our hypotheses on the mediating effects of emotion work strategies, we estimated a mediation model[29] using 1,000 bootstrap samples and 95% bias-corrected bootstrap Confidence Intervals (CIs) for all indirect effects. Results support our assumption that emotion work strategies are associated with the adoption of humor in customer contact after controlling for tenure. Deep acting was positively related to positive humor use ($B = .35$, $SE = .07$, $p \le .001$; Table 3.3.2). However, as for the zero-order correlations, time pressure was not related to either positive humor (direct effect $= .09$, *ns*, 95% CI [−.059, .229]) or deep acting ($B = −.01$, $SE = .08$, *ns*). Accordingly, the indirect effect was not significant (indirect effect $= −.003$, $SE = .03$, 95% CI [−.065, .056]). Thus, hypotheses 1a and 2a were not supported (see Table 3.2.2).

Table 3.3.2 Results of mediation-analysis of deep acting mediating the relationship between time pressure and adoption of positive humor (hypotheses 1a and 2a)

Predictor variable	B	SE	t	p
DV: Deep acting (mediator variable model): $R^2 = .01$, $p = .609$				
Constant	−0.00	0.08	−.01	.996
Time pressure	−0.01	0.08	−.10	.146
Tenure retail	0.08	0.08	1.00	.320
DV: Positive humor adoption: $R^2 = .05$, $p = .000$				
Constant	−0.00	0.07	−.01	.989
Deep acting	0.35	0.07	4.85	.000
Time pressure	0.09	0.07	1.17	.245
Direct effect of time pressure on positive humor adoption	0.09	0.07	1.17	.245
Indirect effect of time pressure on positive humor adoption	Unstandardized Boot indirect effects	Boot SE	Boot LLCI	Boot ULCI
Index of mediation (by deep acting)	−0.003	.030	−.065	.056

Note: Listwise $N = 169$. All variables are z-standardized. DV = dependent variable. LL = lower limit. CI = confidence interval. UP = upper limit. Bootstrap sample size = 1,000. CI = 95%.

Table 3.3.3 Results of mediation-analysis of surface acting mediating the relationship between time pressure and adoption of negative humor (hypotheses 1b and 2b)

Predictor variable	B	SE	t	p
DV: Surface acting (mediator variable model): $R^2 = .05$, $p = .010$				
Constant	0.00	0.08	.00	1.00
Time pressure	0.15	0.08	1.97	.051
Tenure retail	−0.18	0.08	−2.47	.015
DV: Negative humor adoption: $R^2 = .09$, $p = .000$				
Constant	0.00	0.07	.00	1.00
Surface acting	0.20	0.07	2.65	.009
Time pressure	0.21	0.07	2.81	.006
Direct effect of time pressure on negative humor adoption	0.21	0.07	2.81	.006
Indirect effect of time pressure on negative humor adoption	Unstandardized Boot indirect effects	Boot SE	Boot LLCI	Boot ULCI
Index of mediation (by surface acting)	0.029	.018	.003	.073

Note: Listwise $N = 170$. All variables are z-standardized. DV = dependent variable. LL = lower limit. CI = confidence interval. UP = upper limit. Bootstrap sample size = 1,000. CI = 95%.

Time pressure was directly related to negative humor use (direct effect = .20, $p \le .01$, 95% CI [.062, .356]), and this association was partially mediated by surface acting (Table 3.3.3). Time pressure was significantly positively related to surface acting ($B = .15$, $SE = .08$, $p = .051$), and surface acting was positively associated with negative humor use ($B = .20$, $SE = .07$, $p \le .01$). The indirect effect was significant (indirect effect = .03, $SE = .02$, 95% CI [.003, .073]) and accounted for 13.8% of the direct effect of time pressure on negative humor use in customer contact. Thus, hypotheses 1b and 2b were supported by the results (see Table 3.3.3).

Discussion

In our study we investigated the relationship between time pressure, emotion work strategies and the use of positive and negative humor in customer contact on a cross-sectional retail sample. The results are summarized in Figure 3.3.2.

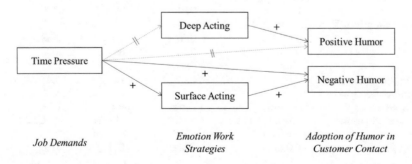

Figure 3.3.2 Summary of results

First of all, we assumed that the strategies of surface and deep acting influence the kind of humor adopted during customer contact, which was supported by the results of the survey. Deep acting seems to foster pleasant customer relations through affiliative and enhancing humor use while surface acting seems to challenge positive customer interactions through deprecating and aggressive humor use. Therefore, our findings correspond well to the theoretical assumptions and well-established empirical findings on the effects of emotion work strategies on employees' emotional experience, performance and customer satisfaction[30] and add further support for the beneficial effects of deep acting and the undesirable effects of surface acting on interpersonal performance in customer service.

Furthermore, our results support our assumption that time pressure increases the likelihood that employees will engage in surface acting which in turn is associated with a higher tendency to adopt negative humor in customer contact. These findings are in line with Ego Depletion Theory[31] which predicts that time pressure disrupts employees' capability to purposefully adopt humor in customer contact due to an increased need for and consumption of self-regulatory resources accompanied by impairments of subjective well-being and higher levels of affective irritation. However, we found no negative effects of time pressure on either deep acting or on the adoption of positive humor in customer contact. Thus, time pressure seems to increase the likelihood of dysfunctional strategies of emotional regulation, while leaving the tendency of deep acting rather unaffected. These differential effects of time pressure on deep and surface acting may be attributed to different levels of conscious control required by the emotion work strategies. While surface acting always involves deliberate monitoring of one's own emotional experience and purposeful regulations of emotional expression in order to fit situational demands, deep acting may develop into an automatic reaction to emotional conflict through processes of instrumental learning, also referred to as passive deep acting.[32] This may explain why there was no relationship between time pressure and deep acting in our sample, and could also indicate that in contrast to surface acting deep acting may be largely unaffected by stressful work demands in general.

Conclusions and managerial implications

Based on the beneficial effects of deep acting on the adoption of positive humor, we suggest that service providers should support their employees to develop and apply deep acting behaviors (e.g., through supervisor's feedback and behavior modeling, trainings and coaching). Such interventions may increase the likelihood of deep acting even in stressful work situations since deep acting was unrelated to time pressure in our sample. Deep acting may be even more effective than surface acting when employees' resources are stressed by high work demands as some authors have suggested that deep acting may require less regulatory resources.[33] Since surface acting keeps the original emotional experience intact, it constantly consumes regulatory resources in order to disconnect the emotional expression from the inner feelings. In contrast, deep acting is proposed to require less regulatory resources, because once the emotional experience is aligned to the situational demands, there is no further need to purposefully influence the emotional display. Thus, applying the emotion work strategy of deep acting may restrict employees' resources for shorter terms and to a lesser degree than surface acting, enabling them to quickly refocus their attention and efforts to the creation of pleasant customer interactions.

Nevertheless, time pressure appears to impair the quality of customer contact through an increased likelihood of surface acting and negative humor use. Thus, employees should not only be qualified in deep acting but should also be encouraged to prefer deep acting strategies over surface acting when situational demands may provoke the adoption of the latter. Over and above the effects on the adoption of humor, deep acting may be more effective in provoking desired effects on customers than surface acting. Organizational rules for emotional display are often based on the assumption that certain emotional expressions will result in desired customer reactions (e.g., higher sales by friendly shop assistants, less cancellations and complaints about sympathetic insurance salesmen). However, research shows that positive emotional expressions only evoke positive reactions to the extent that they are perceived as authentic.[34] Since surface acting results in inauthentic emotional displays, organizational interventions should aim at promoting the adoption of deep acting which involves authentic expressions of emotions and supports positive interactions between employees and customers.

Limitations and recommendations for future research

Our results are based on a cross-sectional sample from a German retail company. Thus, they do not allow for causal interpretations and generalizability is restricted. Future studies should test our theoretical model in longitudinal designs, such as diary studies, and larger as well as more diverse samples. Including nearly three quarters of the entire staff of four retail stores, our sample is likely to reliably represent a major industrial sector of service work. However, there are other fields of work requiring employees to deliberately regulate their emotions in different ways, which may also include the suppression of affiliative emotional expressions (e.g., security agents required to appear repellent rather than kind, debt collectors who have to control their sympathy and compassion for debtors, judges who are expected to remain unaffected by emotions of defendants and witnesses). It is reasonable to assume that these diverging demands will affect the adoption and effects of emotion work strategies and humor in service interactions. Replication studies should also introduce and evaluate more reliable scales for measuring the adoption of humor in customer contact. We assessed time pressure and emotion work strategies through well-established scales that also proved to be sufficiently reliable in our sample. Since there was no evaluated scale in the literature we tried to capture humor adoption through self-constructed items that showed an acceptable reliability for positive humor and a positive correlation between the items capturing the adoption of negative humor. We therefore assume that our items can be interpreted as a general indicator of humor use. Further investigations of the adoption of humor in customer contact and the integration of results will nevertheless benefit from more elaborated models and empirical measures that could for instance apply models of individual humor styles[35] to customer interaction. For instance, sense of humor as well as the self-enhancing humor style are associated with amusement by the incongruences of life (including adversities), i.e., these kinds of humor help people to distance themselves from problems in stressful situations. Thus, self-enhancing humor could be an effective coping strategy for employees during stressful periods of (emotion) work. Also important for future research is the inclusion of customer ratings or mystery shopping results in order to test whether customers actually perceive a similar type of humor as rated by the employee, and whether specific kinds of humor are actually related to (un)favorable customer reactions.

Replications and extensions of our findings would allow for causal interpretations and generalization of effects and would therefore offer a solid framework for the design and implementation of effective intervention strategies to foster positive customer relations through the purposeful use of humor.

References

1 Romero, E. J., & Cruthirds, K. W. (2006), The use of humor in the workplace. *The Academy of Management Perspectives*, *20*(2), 58–69.
2 Martin, R. A., Puhlik-Doris, P., Larsen, G., Gray, J., & Weir, K. (2003), Individual differences in uses of humor and their relation to psychological well-being: Development of the Humor Styles Questionnaire. *Journal of Research in Personality*, *37*(1), 48–75.
3 Fisher, M. L., Krishnan, J., & Netessine, S. (2006), *Retail Store Execution: An Empirical Study*. Philadelphia, PA: The Wharton School. http://knowledge.wharton.upenn.edu/wp-content/uploads/2013/09/13361.pdf [Accessed October 26, 2016].
4 PwC (2016), *They say they want a revolution. Total Retail 2016*. http://pwc.com/totalretail [Accessed October 26, 2016].
5 MacKenzie, I., Meyer, C., & Noble, S. (2013), How retailers can keep up with consumers. *McKinsey Quarterly*. http://www.mckinsey.com/industries/retail/our-insights/how-retailers-can-keep-up-with-consumers [Accessed October 26, 2016].
6 Romero, E. J., & Cruthirds, K. W. (2006), The use of humor in the workplace. *The Academy of Management Perspectives*, *20*(2), 58–69; p. 59.
7 Martin, R. A., Puhlik-Doris, P., Larsen, G., Gray, J., & Weir, K. (2003), Individual differences in uses of humor and their relation to psychological well-being: Development of the Humor Styles Questionnaire. *Journal of Research in Personality*, *37*(1), 48–75.
8 Martineau, W. H. (1972), A model of the social functions of humor. In J. Goldstein, & P. McGhee (Eds.), *The Psychology of Humor* (pp. 101–125). New York: Academic Press.
9 Baumeister, R. F., Bratslavsky, E., Muraven, M., & Tice, D. M. (1998), Ego-depletion: Is the active self a limited resource? *Journal of Personality and Social Psychology*, *74*, 1252–1265; Muraven, M., & Baumeister, R. F. (2000), Self-regulation and depletion of limited resources: Does self-control resemble a muscle? *Psychological Bulletin*, *126*(2), 247–259.
10 Kleiner, S. (2014), Subjective time pressure: General or domain specific? *Social Science Research*, *47*, 108–120; p. 108.
11 De Jonge, J., & Dormann, C. (2006), Stressors, resources and strains at work: A longitudinal test of the Triple Match Principle. *Journal of Applied Psychology*, *91*(6), 1359–1374.
12 Zapf, D., Vogt, C., Seifert, C., Mertini, H., & Isic, A. (1999), Emotion work as a source of stress: The concept and development of an instrument. *European Journal of Work and Organizational Psychology*, *8*, 371–400; p. 371.
13 Zapf et al., op. cit.
14 Grandey, A. A. (2000), Emotion regulation in the work place: A new way to conceptualize emotional labor. *Journal of Occupational Health Psychology*, *5*(1), 95–110.
15 Gross, J. J. (1998), The emerging field of emotion regulation: An integrative review. *Review of General Psychology*, *2*, 271–299.
16 Gross, op. cit.
17 Grandey, op. cit.
18 Gross, J. J., & John, O. P. (2003), Individual differences in two emotion regulation processes: Implications for affect, relationships, and well-being. *Journal of Personality and Social Psychology*, *85*, 348–362.
19 Gross & John, op. cit.
20 Huelsheger, U. R., & Schewe, A. F. (2011), On the costs and benefits of emotional labor: A meta-analysis of three decades of research. *Journal of Occupational Health Psychology*, *16*(3), 361–389.
21 Gross & John, op. cit.; p. 361.
22 Grandey, op. cit.

23 Gross & John, op. cit.

24 Huelsheger & Schewe, op. cit.

25 See also Scheel, T., Putz, D., & Kurzawa, C. (2017), Give me a break: Laughing with colleagues guards against ego depletion. *European Journal of Humour Research*, 5(1), 36–51.

26 Semmer, N. K., Zapf, D., & Dunckel, H. (1999), Instrument zur Stressbezogenen Tätigkeitsanalyse (ISTA) [Instrument for stress-related job analysis (ISTA)]. In H. Dunckel (Ed.), *Handbuch psychologischer Arbeitsanalyseverfahren* (pp. 179–204). Zürich: vdf Hochschulverlag.

27 Brotheridge, C. M., & Grandey, A. A. (2002), Emotional labor and burnout: Comparing two perspectives of "people work." *Journal of Vocational Behavior*, 60, 17–39.

28 Hayes, A. F. (2015), The PROCESS macro for SPSS and SAS. Retrieved on January 26, 2015, from http://www.processmacro.org/download.html.

29 Model 4 of Hayes PROCESS macro, op. cit.

30 Huelsheger & Schewe, op. cit.; Grandey, op. cit.

31 Muraven & Baumeister, op. cit.

32 Zapf, D. (2002), Emotion work and psychological wellbeing: A review of the literature and some conceptual considerations. *Human Resource Management Review*, 12, 237–268.

33 Totterdell, P., & Holman, D. (2003), Emotion regulation in customer service roles: Testing a model of emotional labor. *Journal of Occupational Health Psychology*, 8, 55–73.

34 Grandey, A. A., Fisk, G. M., Mattila, A. S., Jansen, K. J., & Sideman, L. A. (2005a), Is "service with a smile" enough? Authenticity of positive displays during service encounters. *Organizational Behavior and Human Decision Processes*, 96, 38–55.

35 Martin et al., op. cit.

3.4 Did you get it?

Newsjacking: what it is and how to do it well

Robert J. Angell, Matthew Gorton, Juliet Memery, and John White

Introduction

In early 2009, around the same time that 44th President of the United States of America, Barack Obama, took his seat in the Oval Office for the first time, women's cosmetic brand, Veet, ran an advertising campaign with the tagline "Goodbye Bush." When the Duchess of Cambridge gave birth to Prince George in 2013, Johnson & Johnson posted a picture of a baby in the bath with hair washed into the shape of a crown. Likewise, confectionary brand, Oreo, ran a promotion with the tagline: "long live the crème."

All of these examples have a common thread—a similar DNA: (i) they are all household brands; (ii) they all have a high level of consumer awareness; and (iii) they are all leveraging current affairs and topical news stories to promote a message. Whilst the first two attributes are evident in most advertising appearing on our televisions, computers and in our newspapers, the latter is a recent and growing phenomenon. This third element is known as newsjacking—the referencing of news stories in paid-for communication.

Why is it appropriate for newsjacking to appear in a book focusing on better understanding the topic of *humor*? As we will demonstrate, *newsjacking* certainly does not, by definition, need to contain any semblance of humor—but the most successful exemplars from market practice are quick-witted and amusing. In this chapter we will introduce several of the key tenets of 'good' newsjacking practice. Then we turn our attention to the issue of humor, and the challenge of 'being funny.' Finally, we investigate whether newsjacking is only as beneficial as the number of people that understand its underlying reference to a news story. To address this question we present the results of an empirical study undertaken using stimuli from a real-life newsjacking advertisement for BMW Mini.

Attributes of "good" newsjacking

To begin, it is useful to provide another (successful) example of newsjacking advertising. In 2014 during the FIFA World Cup, soccer superstar Luis Suarez from Uruguay bit into the skin of an opposing team's player (Italian defender Georgio Chiellini). Bud Light ran an advertisement with a picture of a man (who looked uncannily like Luis Suarez) attempting to open a beer bottle with his teeth, with the tagline: "Relax, they're twist off." The ad quickly went viral with thousands of shares and retweets.

But why? The first reason is that the advertisement involved *news*. Consumer psychologist, Jonah Berger, explained in his 2013 book *Contagious*[1] that people like to read and share information that is current, up-to-date, and innovative. It explains why people who have no formal (higher) qualifications in science or medicine, share with others in their network via social media, news of groundbreaking discoveries in either field.

Relatedly, evidence suggests that we cognitively process novel messages in a slightly different way to less novel information. Imagine you are walking into work and see a monkey swinging in the trees of a nearby garden. Would this have your attention? Would you be intrigued? Would you stop walking? Would you begin to ask yourself questions like: "How did that monkey get there?" and "Is that a wild monkey, or a pet monkey?" Now ask yourself when was the last time you saw a bird in a neighbor's garden? The majority of people will not remember, but it is quite likely to have been very recently. However, seeing a bird for most of us is such a commonplace occurrence, we do not choose to deeply process this event.[2] In their theory known as the Elaboration Likelihood Model (ELM), psychologists Richard E. Petty and John T. Cacioppo[3] suggested that humans process information via two routes—a central processing route, which provides a deeper, more involved, assessment of information, and the peripheral route which is shallower, and less long-lasting in a working memory sense. Whilst there are many antecedents for either route, information that is novel and personally relevant is more likely to be centrally processed—and this leads to higher working memory *and* affective evaluations. We can apply this logic to the Bud Light advertisement. You are likely to have seen dozens of beer commercials, many of which will involve 20–30 second acted scenes using phrases like "refreshing," "crisp," "cool." But how many of these can you remember? Moreover, how many of these ads did you really like? Would you be likely to forget, or dislike, the Luis Suarez ad though? Our guess would be "no."

The second component of successful newsjacking is *timing*. The Bud Light ad was circulated within less than two hours of the biting incident. Would it have received so much attention and interest if it were released after two weeks, or a month? PR gurus often argue that bad news will end up being tomorrow's chip wrapping.[4] David Meerman-Scott—an expert in newsjacking—suggests that an ideal window of time exists for a newsjacking ad to be successful. Generally speaking this is midway between the story breaking, and the point that journalists realize the story will be a big one and scramble to get copy together. Of course, this requires some skill in itself. The company needs to be firmly on the pulse when it comes to current affairs, but also be just as good at deciding whether a story (in journalistic terms) will "blow up." Too early, no one will understand the reference (the risks of which we empirically demonstrate later in the chapter). Too late, people might not remember, or again "realize" what the reference pertains to.

It could be argued that some newsjacking adverts have a greater longevity than others. Some news is not here today and gone tomorrow—contrary to the PR adage. Take for instance the recent US Presidential election, or Brexit. The latter has, at the time of writing, been a constant fixture in the news for over a year. World events like war and economic recessions similarly occupy far more copy space than a single day of news. So is there always a need to be swift? Although it has not been explicitly researched in a newsjacking context, *exclusivity* might be a reason why the answer to this question is 'yes.' It is possible that multiple brands piggybacking on the same news story works to reduce the novelty of the message and undermines the ability of the ad to 'cut-through' the cluttered media environment.[5] Take for instance the world of celebrity endorsement, where research has shown that the higher the number of concurrent sponsorships a brand engages in, the more negative become consumer evaluations for each of its released ads.[6, 7] Of course, the latter are governed (most of the time) by legal contracts, which is not possible in a newsjacking context. Being agile and first to the market may carry its own advantages (i.e. a first mover advantage) but this has not, to date, been researched or verified.

Congruence or *fit* has been studied in a wide variety of advertising, media and sponsorship contexts.[8] Advertising that is perceived as congruent with the product and/or brand's image is usually met with less skepticism and requires less effortful cognitive processing to understand (which is normally a good thing!). We tend to be more comfortable with partnerships—people and objects—when we consider them to be a more obvious fit. The same logic is critical for newsjacking advertising. Tenuous connections between the news story and the brand may appear as crass and opportunistic. For instance, DiGormo Pizza attempted to 'newsjack' the 'why I stayed' hashtag (referencing the plight of women affected by domestic violence), to promote its pizzas. *Fit* can be manipulated but requires a skillful marketer. Consider that Budweiser has little organic fit to Luis Suarez, but still managed to manipulate the story, actor and product to have a logical connection to its product and brand, through just a single tagline.

Does newsjacking work better when humor is used?

Until now we have not looked at the role humor plays in successful newsjacking. For every 'great' piece of newsjacking advertising that we see or hear about, a much larger number disappear into the ether. Of the countless 'how to do' newsjacking articles, blogs, and websites available to marketers online, the most cited examples tend to have employed, to some extent, humor. Indeed, you will have noticed that all of the illustrations provided at the beginning of the chapter contained an amusing tagline. That is not to say that humor *has* to be used. For example, the Golf Channel tweeted "Tweet your golf dream" on the 50th anniversary of Dr. King's famous speech, which was well responded to by the golf community. However, a large number of research studies have shown that humor successfully captures people's attention[9] and aids the comprehension of more difficult to process messages.[10] Humor may also be a *double-edged sword*. If an attempt at humor is inappropriate for the audience and context, the result can cause offense and stimulate negative behaviors such as complaints and boycotting.[11] This is very pertinent for newsjacking, with a large number of attempts ending in complaints by recipients (especially via Twitter and other social media platforms). For example, when Hurricane Sandy hit the East Coast of the US, Urban Outfitters tweeted "This storm blows (but free shipping doesn't)!" with the hashtag #allsoggy. In a world where media can be shared instantly, a single newsjacking mistake can be extremely damaging for the unprepared brand. Twitter users responded by berating the brand for its insensitivity to those affected.

Ability to decode news stories

A critical component of newsjacking is the recipient's ability to decode and recognize the underlying message. Indeed, if you had not known about the Luis Suarez incident, would you (or anyone) have found the Bud Light ad amusing and engaging? As other chapters in this book discuss, a good joke tends to be one in which the receiver has to perform some mental activity to decode its underlying message. Theory suggests that solving a puzzle—be it a cryptic message or a joke—provides the recipient with gratification. In contrast, a lack of ability to process new information tends to result in shallow (peripheral) processing and suppressed affective evaluations.[12] We posit that a fundamental component of newsjacking requires the recipient to be able to recognize the news story from which the ad arose, but this notion has never been formally tested. In other words, newsjacking is expected to only work well as long as the audience can decode the underlying news story—in the same way as using humor in advertising requires the audience to 'get' the joke. To test this assertion we undertook a study using real-life stimuli.

The study

We recruited 126 people from a city center location in the North of England using a quota sampling procedure with an even split of men and women. Most people (86.1%) claimed to engage with the news on a daily basis. Data was collected via a face-to-face survey.

We chose to use the newsjacking advertisement by BMW Mini to promote its Mini John Cooper Works Roadster in 2013—a high-performance version of the Mini. The ad had the tagline "Beef: with a lot of horses hidden in it," referencing the Meat Adulteration Scandal which broke in January 2013 after the Food Safety Authority of Ireland reported detecting horse DNA in 37% of the beef burger products it tested. The story ran for several weeks in the UK and other affected countries. To the best of our knowledge, no other brand used the story for the purpose of newsjacking. When we collected the data, the story was established but still regularly discussed in the media.

Before being shown the ad, respondents were asked to complete scales pertaining to: (i) their involvement with the news, and (ii) product involvement with automobiles. Both were anchored on five-point Likert scales and adapted from an original brand involvement scale.[13] Next, respondents were shown the BMW newsjacking ad, and asked to complete three separate scales pertaining to their: (i) attitude towards the ad (Aad),[14] (ii) brand attitude (Ba)[15] and (iii) intentions towards purchasing the car (PI).[16] Each was measured on seven-point semantic differential scales (−3 to +3). Finally, and most critically, at the end of the questionnaire, respondents were asked to state whether or not they 'recognized' the news story referenced in the ad, and then to describe it to the interviewer. In total, 61 people were 'able' to do so accurately, with 61 'unable.' It is worth noting that six of the latter had previously believed they had decoded the reference but were unable to explain why.

See the image of the advertisement here: http://www.newsworks.org.uk/Opinion/mini-capitalises-on-horsemeat-scandal/44279.

Since we were interested in whether *ability* to decode the news story led to differing affective evaluations of the ad, we used a multiple-group confirmatory factor analysis (MGCFA). This allowed us to compare the relative mean scores for both 'able' and 'unable' groups outlined before, across each of the five scales, but with the added benefit of accounting for measurement error in each of the measures.[17] We performed all of the necessary preliminary tests for this type of analysis—including tests of validity and reliability,[18] but also the necessary assessment of measurement invariance (i.e. scalar invariance). Scalar invariance means that factor loadings and intercepts are equivalent in the groups specified,[19] which allows latent mean scores to be compared.

In MGCFA one of the (in our case, two) groups is used as a reference category, meaning that mean scores for constructs in other groups are presented relative to the reference group (or category). In this case we specified the 'unable' group to be the reference category and then investigated whether any of the variables in the 'able' group were significantly different in their mean score. We found that people in the two groups did not differ in their rated *product involvement* (with automobile cars) (i.e. $\Delta \bar{x} = .29$, $p > .10$).[20] This served as a strong test of face validity, since there should be no rationale why one group would be more (or less) interested in cars. Next we looked at whether *news involvement* differed. Unsurprisingly, those in the 'able' group were significantly higher in their interest/involvement with current affairs ($\Delta \bar{x} = 1.13$, $p < .01$). Again, this served as a useful test of face validity since it would be expected that those able to recognize the news story in a newsjacking message should be higher in news involvement than those who could not.

Most importantly we investigated whether Aad, BA, and PI differed between the groups. We found significant differences with those respondents who correctly identified (able) the story having higher levels of *attitude towards the advertisement* ($\Delta \bar{x} = 1.32$, $p < .01$), *brand attitude* ($\Delta \bar{x} = 0.57$, $p < .01$), and *purchase intention* ($\Delta \bar{x} = 0.52$, $p < .01$) than 'unable' respondents. Overall, the data indicates that an ability to decode a newsjacking message is therefore an important antecedent for higher affective evaluations; essentially, the results provide evidence that recipients *do* need to 'get it' for newsjacking advertising to work effectively.

Conclusions

In this chapter, we introduced *newsjacking*, a practically important, but under-researched, advertising methodology. In the last five years it has been used increasingly—with differing degrees of success. Of course, for a method that, to some extent, relies on consumer sharing and pass-on, the vast majority of newsjacking attempts never arrive in our consciousness. In fact, consumers tend to be most exposed to the best and worst examples. It is not our intention to debate whether the worst examples still have their place. We do argue, however, that 'good' newsjacking is an effective and efficient method for building brand affect, and that the willing marketer can follow the attributes presented here, to steer their efforts in the right direction of success—although we acknowledge that far more research is required in this area.

We conclude by drawing similarities between the properties of a successful newsjacking advertisement and a very good joke. Both should involve content (i.e. news) that interests people, delivered at the optimal time, which makes sense (i.e. is a good fit) for the deliverer to tell, the receiver to hear, and requires the latter to possess the ability to understand and decode its underlying message. It also helps if it is funny!

References

1 Berger, J. (2013), *Contagious: How to build word of mouth in the digital age*, London: Simon & Schuster.
2 In some countries, seeing a monkey in a garden is the equivalent of seeing a bird or squirrel in terms of novelty.
3 Petty, R.E., & Cacioppo, J.T. (1986), The elaboration likelihood model of persuasion, *Advances in Experimental Social Psychology*, 19(C), 123–205.
4 Fish and chips were traditionally wrapped in newspaper. Albeit far from hygienic, the phrase is still widely used.
5 Scott, D.M. (2011), *Newsjacking: How to inject your ideas into a breaking news story and generate tons of media coverage*, Chichester, UK: Wiley.
6 Choi, S.M., Lee, W.-N., & Kim, H.-J. (2005), Lessons from the rich and famous: A cross-cultural comparison of celebrity endorsement in advertising, *Journal of Advertising*, 34(2), 85–98.
7 Tripp, C., Jensen, T.D., & Carlson, L. (1994), The effects of multiple product endorsements by celebrities on consumers' attitudes and intentions, *Journal of Consumer Research*, 20(4), 535–547.

8 Olson, E.L., & Thjømøe, H.M. (2011), Explaining and articulating the fit construct in sponsorship, *Journal of Advertising*, 40(1), 57–70.

9 Madden, T.J., & Weinberger, M.G. (1984), Humor in advertising: A practitioner view, *Journal of Advertising Research*, 24(4), 23–29.

10 Stewart, D.W., & Furse, D.H. (1985), The effects of television advertising execution on recall, comprehension, and persuasion, *Psychology and Marketing*, 2(3), 135–160.

11 Weinberger, M.G., & Gulas, C.S. (1992), The impact of humor in advertising: A review, *Journal of Advertising*, 21(4), 35–59.

12 McQuarrie, E.F., & Mick, D.G. (1999), Visual rhetoric in advertising: Text-interpretive, experimental, and reader-response analyses, *Journal of Consumer Research*, 26(1), 37–54.

13 O'Cass, A., & Choy, A. (2008), Studying Chinese generation Y consumers' involvement in fashion clothing and perceived brand status, *Journal of Product & Brand Management*, 17(5), 341–352.

14 Holbrook, M.B., & Batra, R. (1987), Assessing the role of emotions as mediators of consumer responses to advertising, *Journal of Consumer Research*, 14(3), 404–420.

15 Leclerc, F., Schmitt, B.H., & Dubé, L. (1994), Foreign branding and its effects on product perceptions and attitudes, *Journal of Marketing Research*, 31(2), 263–270.

16 Bruner, G.C., Hensel, P.J., & James, K.E. (2009), *Marketing scales handbook*, Chicago, IL: American Marketing Association. Scale number 483.

17 Hair, J.F., Black, W.C., Babin, B.J., Anderson, R.E., & Tatham, R.L. (2010). *Multivariate data analysis* (7th Edition). Upper Saddle River, NJ: Prentice Hall.

18 Hair et al., op. cit.

19 Williams, L.J., Vandenberg, R.J., & Edwards, J.R. (2009), Structural equation modeling in management research: A guide for improved analysis, *The Academy of Management Annals*, 3(1), 543–604.

20 The mean score difference suggests that respondents in the 'able' group were .29-points on the five-point Likert scale higher than the 'unable' group, for product involvement.

3.5 Promoting, informing, and identifying

The case of Foody, the humorous mascot of Expo Milan 2015

Carla Canestrari and Valerio Cori

Expo Milan 2015: between communication and business

Since the early editions of the Great Exhibition of Industries of All Nations, such as the famous one held in London in 1851, the main goal of every Expo has been to give nations, politics, the business world, and society a shared space in which to discuss and cooperate in a crucial area of interest common to all the participating parties.[1] Topical themes and subjects are discussed during each edition of Expo. For example, in the earlier editions, the main subjects were related to technology, as the industrial revolution and colonialism were the topical subjects of that period. Later on, even after World War II, human progress and international dialogue have taken centre stage at every Expo, in addition to technology.[2]

With the beginning of the new millennium, a number of important issues have raised common awareness about the importance of finding strategies to make progress and human development more sustainable.[3] In particular, in this day and age, malnutrition is still a serious problem for a large number of people (estimated at 805 million). Nevertheless, the increasing world population and the relative growing demand for food raise many questions about resource management.[4] The theme chosen for Expo Milan 2015 was therefore "Feeding the Planet, Energy for Life" and the event was devised to give nations, the business world, politics, and society in general an opportunity to discuss and share potential solutions for answering important questions in this field, such as:

- Is it possible to ensure access to sufficient, good, healthy, sustainable food for everyone?
- How can we ensure that everyone has access to healthy food?
- How can we use resources in a sustainable way?
- How can we reduce waste?
- How must our need for wholesome, healthy food influence our choices in energy production and the use of natural resources?[5]

The last edition of Expo was a "mega-project" as its theme touched many sectors and the event was designed to have a heavy impact on economics and society.[6] Since Expo Milan 2015 was such a huge event, it offered a platform and a shared space in which nations from all over the world could address the above-mentioned questions.

Expos are part of the business tourism sector[7] and they are an "important element of industry marketing communications".[8] The impact of these mega-events is a very complex matter.[9] Nonetheless, the popularity of these special events is increasing and their organisers are challenged to refine the communicative strategies used[10] in order to engage attendees emotionally, affectively, and cognitively.[11] Therefore, communicating effectively and strategically is clearly of key importance.[12]

To get an idea of the communicative impact of the last edition of Expo, it is sufficient to consider that the event witnessed 150 participants organising approximately 5,000 events for more than 20 million visitors, in 184 days of exposition.[13] The communication strategies for the event targeted both the visitors attending it and those who participated in it, arriving from all over the world. Due to its nature, the exposition was an opportunity for nutrition experts and researchers to meet, and it also had a strong educational slant. In fact, its visitor categories ranged from business people and experts to families and schools. Therefore, it seems reasonable to wonder how Expo reached these many different kinds of people. How did it succeed in communicating its themes, values, and knowledge? There are many answers to these questions, one of which is the use of a brand mascot, named "Foody".

Why Foody and his friends?

Foody is a colourful smiling face inspired by the work of Italian painter Giuseppe Arcimboldo (1526–1593), famous for his grotesque portraits created by wittily assembling realistic elements such as objects, vegetables, fruits, or flowers, as shown in Figure 3.5.1, right. Foody is composed of 11 anthropomorphised fruits and vegetables (i.e. his friends) and metaphorically represents the synergy of a community composed of the 140 countries from all over the world that participated in Expo Milan 2015.[14] The fact that they are fruits and vegetables immediately recalls the subject of the exhibition, namely healthy nutrition. Foody is not only a static mascot: he and the various characters composing him also come to life as lively dynamic creatures thanks to the animation project created by "Disney Italia".[15] Each fruit or vegetable that composes Foody's face is introduced in an animated cartoon, defining the character and conveying some of the topics on which Expo Milan 2015 focuses ("Feeding the Planet, Energy for Life"). The humorous communication performed by Foody's friends in the animated cartoons is the focus of our analysis.

Figure 3.5.1 Foody's face (left)[16] and the famous painting "Vertumno" by Giuseppe Arcimboldo (1591) (right)[17]

Being a mascot, Foody and his friends convey several communicative functions, such as: entertaining,[18] eliciting positive responses,[19] obtaining easy acceptability, prolonging association and recall with the brand they represent,[20] grabbing attention, connecting with a type of personality in order to reach a certain audience,[21] and making "the ideas promoted by the mascot [. . .] less alien".[22] In fact, brand mascots are acknowledged as having the potential to ensure that the values and characteristics of a corporation immediately spring into the minds of their perceivers (consumers and stakeholders). This has been shown to be particularly true in the case of anthropomorphised mascots, which are perceived by consumers as having specific personalities and ethical values.[23] At the same time, they are perceived by the organisation members as "organizational totems",[24] and the consolidators of an identity practice.[25] Using a mascot is a type of communicative strategy that is increasing with the rise of social media.[26] There are many reasons for choosing a brand character in order to communicate. Particularly, this is the case for companies trying to establish a lasting connection with the audience based on loyalty and brand advocacy,[27] as consumers are able to identify with the values and personality embodied by the brand character.[28] Brand mascots can be useful within organisations too: they have rallying power, they help to define and differentiate the organisations they represent from others and they can also have a role in orienting strategies.[29]

The Arcimboldesque figure of Foody makes the anthropomorphic nature of this brand mascot quite clear. Since anthropomorphism can be considered as a "pervasive, perhaps universal, way of thinking",[30] it can be a powerful tool for communication due to its "attention-grabbing power and its inferential potential".[31] Anthropomorphism is also one of the key components of a brand's active role in building a relationship with the customer.[32] Moreover, consumers' responses can be affected by this "process of assigning real or imagined human characteristics, intentions, motivations or emotions to non-human objects".[33] The effectiveness of anthropomorphism can be enhanced by proto-typicality and schema congruency, as in the case where the mascot is an animal that shares some features with humans (e.g. bipedalism).[34] As far as Foody is concerned, there are a number of fruits and vegetables that share some features with humans and this makes Foody an anthropomorphic mascot.

Based on the facts stated above in relation to the communicative impact of mascots in general, and in particular anthropomorphic mascots, it is important to focus on the communicative aspects of Foody. Specifically, at first glance, the elements that characterise the mascot are humour and fun, distinguishing him from previous Expo mascots. For example, the only humorous aspect of Haibo, the mascot of Expo 2010, held in Shanghai (China), was that he personified the Chinese ideogram "Ren", which means "people".[35]

The same is true for Kiccoro and Morizo, two anthropomorphic creatures of the forest, who were adopted as the official mascots of Expo 2005, held in Aichi (Japan).[36] They have a grandfather–grandson relationship and this contributes to their anthropomorphisation.

Foody shares the characteristics of personification and anthropomorphisation with his precursors, but due to his Arcimboldesque inspiration, he is markedly funny, both when we consider him as a whole and when we consider him "piece by piece". The first funny thing that pops up is that each singular element is a complete structured form in itself (i.e. a Gestalt) and at the same time it plays a specific role in Foody's face (e.g. a bulb of garlic is his nose, a banana his smiling lips, and so on). Foody's face is made of the following 11 sub-characters, also referred to as "Foody's friends": an orange (Arabella), a pear (Piera), a pomegranate (Chicca), a banana (Josephine), a corn cob (Max Mais), a watermelon (Gury), a bulb of garlic (Guaglià), a fig (Rodolfo), a mango (Manghy), and an apple (Pomina). The names of the various components of Foody's face were assigned by a group of Italian students who participated in a public competition designed to raise the awareness of young students (from kindergarten to high school) about the themes of Expo. One of the activities involved inviting the students to invent names for Foody's friends. The best names suggested were then chosen and used.[37]

Each friend comes to life in 11 short cartoons made by Disney Italia.[38] The main characteristic of these cartoons is that Foody's friends behave as if they were humans and not fruits or vegetables. In this way, the anthropomorphic figures look much more human and realistic as they are set in a dynamic background that asserts their identity.[39]

It is acknowledged that there are several reasons for favouring the decision to use humorous communication. Humour can be used for the purposes of persuasion, particularly in mass communication,[40] to build group identity and strengthen group cohesion,[41] to tease,[42] and to amuse.[43] As humour and fun are the salient features of Foody, our goal is to identify the types of messages and functions conveyed humorously in the 11 short cartoons starring Foody's friends.

Humorous communication: a qualitative analysis

Aims

The general aim of the paper is to show how humour can be used in association with a mascot and to discover the purpose for which it can be used. This goal can be achieved by analysing the humorous strategies associated with Foody and his friends and their communicative functions. In particular, our qualitative analysis aimed to pinpoint the humorous occurrences in the 11 cartoons, analysing the thematic issues on which these focus, and inferring what the authors of the cartoons hoped to gain by using humorous communication.

Method

The 11 short cartoons (described in the following section) were downloaded and the instances of humour contained therein were located by searching for humorous incongruities. Incongruity is acknowledged as being the key element of humour and it has been defined and approached in several ways within the literature.[44] Generally speaking, the key element of humour is the presence of an incongruity: humour occurs when "something unexpected, out of context, inappropriate, unreasonable, illogical, exaggerated, and so forth"[45] happens and "when the arrangement of the constituent elements of an event is incompatible with the normal or expected pattern".[46] The general framework of humour as a concept derived from incongruity, when developed from the cognitive-linguistics[47] and cognitive-perceptual perspectives,[48] provides us with useful tools for identifying humorous occurrences in the corpus.

According to the cognitive-perceptual perspective, humorous experiences are based on the perception of an incongruity and its cognitive elaboration. For example, the "weight judging paradigm"[49] demonstrates experimentally how the perception of pure incongruity can be the basis for amusing experiences: participants were asked to lift a series of weights, unaware that only the last weight was much heavier (or much lighter) than the previous ones, and so laughed when they lifted the last weight. This humorous response is due to the fact that the participants perceived a considerable incongruity between their cognitive expectations (built on the basis of the previously perceived weights) and the facts. According to the cognitive-perceptual perspective, the perception of an incongruity can also be elicited by jokes and texts playing on sensorial (i.e. perceivable) aspects.[50] In these cases, it has been demonstrated that the perception of a humorous incongruity is facilitated when it lies between elements that are clearly contrary to one another (global contrariety), rather than when they either differ too much (additive contrariety) or too little (intermediate contrariety), as in the following joke:

> Yesterday at school we celebrated my classmate Marcellina's birthday so I gave her a cherry and she kissed me to say thank you. Today I gave her a watermelon . . . . But she didn't get it![51]

Global contrariety is embodied by two elements that are invariant in many respects and opposites with reference to a key dimension. In the above joke, a cherry, and a watermelon are globally contrary to one another in terms of size yet at the same time they both share many other invariant properties (they are both fruits, round, juicy, and so on). In this case, the relationship of contrariety between the two elements is evident. Replacing the watermelon with an apple, or a big polystyrene box elicited lower levels of amusement.[52]

The cognitive-perceptual perspective was selected as the tool used to identify perception-based humorous occurrences in our corpus, based both on the perceptual aspects of the same, given that the corpus is characterised by the presence of objects (i.e. fruits and vegetables) with strong sensorial elements (olfactory, tactile, visual, and relative to taste), and on it largely being based in a visual dimension (as it is a series of animated cartoons).

We also used tools based on the cognitive linguistic perspective in a bid to find other types of humorous incongruities. According to the cognitive linguistic approach to humour, which is particularly suitable for humorous texts based on linguistic ambiguity and double meaning, the incongruity derives from the contrast between the explicit and hidden interpretations of the text. For example, the punchline of the above-mentioned joke forces the reader to switch from a childish situation (i.e. explicit meaning of the text) to a sexual innuendo (i.e. hidden interpretation of the text). In this case, the text contains a "covert incongruity" and the reader/listener is forced to backtrack through the whole text to decipher the humorous logic (i.e. resolution) that leads to the hidden interpretation of the text. The incongruity is not sudden and lies in the *comparison*[53] of the two sets of meanings unveiled by means of the punchline. In this sense, the incongruity refers to the incompatibility of two *frames of reference*,[54] or to the *script opposition* as conceptualised by Attardo from a cognitive linguistic perspective.[55] The replacement of the initial frame of reference, usually more commonplace (i.e. familiar/*salient*) with a second one (i.e. one that is less familiar/*salient*), resolves the incongruity and produces the humorous effect.[56]

As exemplified by the short analysis of the above-mentioned joke, the two frameworks used to identify humorous incongruities, namely cognitive-perceptual and cognitive linguistic perspectives, are not mutually exclusive. As a result, a humorous occurrence can be detected according to both of them, when it is based on both perceptual and covert incongruities.

Once the humorous occurrences were pinpointed according to the theoretical tools mentioned above, the messages (i.e. the issues on which the humorous communication revolves around) and the communicative functions (i.e. the communicative acts) associated with them were analysed. To serve this purpose, we applied multimodal discourse analysis[57] for the following reasons, dictated both by our corpus and our aims.

Communication through technology is a relevant domain for multimodal discourse analysis[58] and our corpus fits into this domain. Moreover, multimodal discourse analysis is particularly apt when it comes to capturing the communicative acts (i.e. functions) in texts made using different modes of communication (e.g. verbal and non-verbal texts), such as in our corpus.[59] For example, a multimodal analysis, carried out on a number of visual commercials, which are composed of visual and non-visual modes, revealed that "boundary marking, attributing qualities to entities, calling to attention" are some of the communicative functions fulfilled via multimodality.[60] Finally, this framework approaches discourse as a global communicative event.[61] In other words, a discourse is considered as a Gestalt and this is in line with our intent to focus not only on the potential humorous events occurring second by second, but also on humorous aspects emerging from a global analysis of each cartoon.

Corpus

The analysis focuses on the 11 short cartoons about Foody's 11 friends. Each cartoon revolves around one or more of the problematic issues chosen to characterise the last edition of Expo (e.g. unhealthy nutrition, food and energy waste) and suggests possible solutions (e.g. eating and drinking healthily, frugality, recycling). This common structure makes the 11 cartoons an appropriate corpus which can be analysed to discover how the thematic issues of Expo Milan 2015 are approached via humour.

Each cartoon lasts approximately 2'.30". The 11 cartoons run for a total of 27'.06" and they have been viewed 389,558 times to date (although other viewings could follow, since the cartoons are still available on YouTube).[62]

The 11 cartoons share the same setting and structure. They begin and end with the same leitmotif, lasting approximately 20 seconds. What happens in the middle can be divided into three phases. In the first one, a talent show setting appears, with a stage and a screen behind it. On that screen, Foody's face appears and quickly disappears when the main character takes to the stage. In this phase, Foody introduces the character and his voice is provided by Claudio Bisio, a famous Italian presenter of comedy shows. The character appears on the stage, does not speak but moves his body. After approximately 1 minute, a brief report on the character's biography is shown on the screen behind the stage, and this is the second phase. After approximately 50 seconds, the third phase begins: the focus is on the stage, where the character performs a skill test, a common occurrence in talent shows.

Findings

The tools of analysis described in the method section were applied by the first author of the paper to the dataset and the identified humorous occurrences were verified by the second author. In this paper, we report on the findings pertaining to the humorous occurrences upon which both analysers agreed. As pointed out in the previous sections, the aim of the paper is to focus on the possible humorous strategies that can be associated to a mascot like Foody and his friends and their communicative functions. Therefore the results of a qualitative analysis of the humorous occurrences, and not their frequencies, are provided.

Globally, the 11 cartoons share the pervasive use of humorous communication, embodied in several strategies. These include the personification of Foody and his friends, a key feature in each second of the 11 cartoons. In addition, the following humorous strategies can be found spread throughout the cartoons: incongruity-resolution forms of humour and pure humorous incongruities. In the first category, there are double meanings, allusions, verbal irony, puns, wordplay, and global contrariety-based incongruities. In the second one, there are examples of nonsense and global contrariety-based incongruity with no resolution.

For the sake of clarity, the results of the analysis conducted are reported following the three phases that structure each cartoon, as described in the previous section. In the first phase, a character, moving silently onto the stage, is introduced by Foody's voice over. As a consequence, Foody performs verbal humour and the character performs non-verbal humour. In this phase, we found occurrences of humorous incongruities based on sensorial or non-sensorial aspects, followed only in some cases by a resolution. The humorous messages mostly convey information about the vegetable/fruit in question, and sometimes aspects related to the character. In the first case, the main function associated with the humorous mode of communication is informing the audience about specific qualities of healthy food (i.e. fruits and vegetables), in the second case the main function is amusing the audience and promoting a funny image of the character.

For example, when Guagliò (the bulb of garlic) sprays perfume around his face he is playing on the sensorial contrast between a good and bad smell and humorously alluding to a salient feature of garlic (see Figure 3.5.2). In this case, non-verbal humour playing on the perception of contrasting sensorial aspects is used, with the aim of drawing the attention to a specific quality of a type of healthy food. A similar aim is achieved via verbal humour in the following example. When Foody introduces the pop musician Max Mais (a corn cob), he says: "he is the king of Pop . . . corn". Getting this joke means comparing the commonplace meaning of "pop" as the abbreviation of "popular music", with the intended meaning "burst", perfectly coherent with a corn cob. The function associated with this humorous occurrence is promoting a quality (specifically, a culinary one) of the vegetable in question. Another function of the humorous occurrences in the first phase of the cartoons is amusing the perceiver for the sake of amusement. This function is usually associated with the introduction of qualities related to the character, more than qualities related to the vegetable/fruit on stage. For example, Foody says: "Rodolfo the fig is so cool" (*"Che fico, Rodolfo fico"*). This humorous occurrence plays on the Italian homonymy between *"fico"* as "fig" and *"fico"* for the slang meaning of "cool". The incongruity between the two frames of reference conveys a humorous message aimed at introducing a quality of the character (Rodolfo) rather than one pertaining to the fruit (the fig). In this case, the elicitation of amusement and humour is not supposed to inform the audience about the sensorial, historical, geographical, or culinary qualities of figs but to elicit humour and amusement *per sé*.

Similarly to the first phase, in the second phase we found verbal and non-verbal occurrences of humorous incongruities based on sensorial or non-sensorial aspects, followed only in some cases by a resolution. In addition to messages conveying information related to the fruit/vegetable or the character on stage, we also found a new type of message delivered via humour, namely messages linked strictly to the thematic issues of Expo Milan 2015. This category characterises this phase and we report on the analysis of a couple of examples that also show different modes of communication and humorous strategies. The first case we would like to examine comes from the cartoon featuring Arabella (an orange), who undergoes several beauty treatments, while neither changing her diet nor playing sports. Foody comments on Arabella's behaviour negatively, using a

Figure 3.5.2 Humorous incongruity playing on olfactory perception[63]

simile: beauty treatments on their own are as useful as soup forks. This verbal humorous case plays on sensorial properties eliciting the perception of a global contrariety: solid and liquid are the two extreme properties of the same dimension (i.e. consistency) epitomised respectively by forks (used for solid food) and broth (that requires spoons to be eaten). At the same time, forks and spoons share several features: they are both small, they are pieces of cutlery, made of the same material, lightweight, and so on and so forth. The same can be said for solid food and broth: they are opposite in terms of consistency and they share invariant properties (in that they are both types of food). The coexistence of opposite and invariant properties makes this case an example of humour that plays on global contrariety. From the communicative and functional points of view, the message promoted by the simile presented by Foody is strictly linked to healthy nutrition. The amusement associated with this humorous case is designed to make people think about bad habits and good dietary practices. Another set of humorous examples focusing on one of the thematic issues of Expo Milan 2015 and promoting good practices is in Max Mais' cartoon. The character performs exaggerated activities that are humorous in that they are the opposite of the expected or normal behaviour. For example, when he leads a non-sustainable lifestyle, he uses a high fashion car that burns too much petrol simply when moving from one room to another in his house (Figure 3.5.3, top). After his conversion to recycling, he uses a broken shoe as a plant vase, a cathode-ray tube TV as an aquarium, an old suitcase as a bathtub (Figure 3.5.3, bottom). These humorous exaggerations convey the message that recycling is a better practice than wasting and the function associated with it makes people think about environmental problems – derived from malpractices – and possible solutions.

Finally, the cartoons end in the third phase. The consistent humorous strategy of the third phase, which is also a new one in comparison to the previous phases, is the clown-like performances of the characters in each cartoon. For example, Pomina, the apple, casts spells and ends up in four slices after having inserted a sword in her mouth (see Figure 3.5.4). Max Mais, the corn cob, makes a big soap bubble that swallows him up and makes him float in the air, until he damages the chandelier and the resulting sparks transform him into popcorn. The recursive humorous pattern in this last phase of each

Figure 3.5.3 Two extreme examples of opposite behavioural patterns in the cartoon with
        Max Mais[64]

cartoon is always linked to the character and aims to show his or her clumsiness. Eliciting
humour and amusement *per sé* is the main function of this kind of humorous mode. In
this phase of the cartoon, there are few occurrences of verbal humour, mainly based on
the incongruity-resolution paradigm, always performed by Foody. Also in these cases, the
humorous messages are designed to promote a clumsy and funny picture of the characters,
for the sake of amusement.

Figure 3.5.4 Clownish performance by Pomina[65]

To sum up, the main results of the descriptive analysis are as follows: (1) the humorous strategies vary from verbal to visual and sensorial-based humour, and from pure incongruity to incongruity-resolution-based humour; (2) the issues on which the humorous occurrences play range from the thematic issues of Expo Milan 2015 (e.g. health, nutrition, recycling, eco-sustainability) to the sensorial, historical, geographical, or culinary qualities of the specific fruits and vegetables and also to the anthropomorphic qualities of the characters; (3) depending on the issues on which the humorous occurrences focus, different functions emerge, such as promoting good practices, informing the audience about the benefits of healthy food, building characters' identities, or simply amusing the audience for the sake of entertaining.

Conclusions and discussion

In order to create deep, meaningful, and long-term relationships with customers, companies refine their communication strategies.[66] One of the most topical strategies is the use of brand mascots, which can serve as tools to capture the target audience's attention, obtain good acceptability of the products, advocate a prolonged association with the brand, or recall it.[67] The use of Foody to promote Expo Milan 2015 is perfectly in line with these purposes. The point of the analysis we have carried out on the corpus was to describe some of the communicative aspects it contains. In particular, we have striven to identify the messages and values conveyed by the humorous strategies and define their communicative functions.

Starting from the general framework of incongruity theories of humour, approached from the cognitive linguistic and cognitive-perceptual points of view, we identified humorous incongruities and analysed whether these were followed by a resolution or were based on sensorial aspects. The resulting patterns are epitomised in different humour strategies and modes, such as jokes, wordplay, exaggerations, non-verbal behaviours, and so on. We have shown that in some cases, these humorous occurrences have an informative value. Specifically, they communicate certain properties of the fruits and vegetables involved in the cartoon. They served to draw the attention to healthy nutrition and the values related to it. This result is consistent with Meyer's approach to the functions of humour: incongruity-based humour can be used to *clarify* an issue and, at the same time, differentiate the points of view involved in it.[68] Humour, even a humorous line, can be used to clarify a point of view in a creative and memorable manner, since the message is presented in an unexpected and incongruous way. Moreover, humour can serve to reinforce social norms and emphasise an expected behaviour, rather than focusing on the seriousness of the violation.[69] In the case of Foody, we showed some humorous occurrences that have the function of clarifying, introducing, or reinforcing a number of good habits related to nutrition. In a sense, some of the humorous occurrences were also construed specifically to *differentiate* between two behavioural patterns (e.g. unhealthy vs healthy nutrition habits, dis-respectful vs respectful attitude towards the environment) yet in a mild way (i.e. without resorting to aggressive forms). For example, some of Foody's humorous lines were designed to differentiate healthy from unhealthy food, in a communicative form that was not aggressive at all. Furthermore, humour, by means of differentiation, can serve to objectify an inadequate aspect and manage it.[70] It seems realistic that the creators of Foody wanted to make people recognise their own bad nutrition habits and render these laughable in order to promote change.

We also found some cases where humorous occurrences had a more playful value. This type of occurrence was useful for telling amusing stories related to Foody's friends and describing their personalities in order to make them look more human and realistic. As we noticed in the theoretical section, anthropomorphism is a feature that accompanies Foody's humour and amusement in order to make a stronger connection with the audience. Brands are seen more favourably when an anthropomorphic advertising campaign is used, as shown by Patterson et al.[71] Therefore, we can conclude that humour functions to enrich anthropomorphism in Foody. In fact, showing Foody as having a sense of humour, which is considered as a desirable characteristic in interpersonal relationships,[72] surely contributes to making this mascot more human. Telling funny anecdotes about Foody's friends helps to create their stories and build their identities. As a result, the referent anthropomorphic figure appears more realistic to consumers.[73]

In addition, it is worth remembering that humour can also be a good tool for advertising communication: advertisements based on a humorous communication are easily recalled[74] and can be perceived as more appealing.[75] We can suppose that the decision to make Foody incorporate humorous elements was taken with a view to making the whole Expo communication campaign more attractive. It could be interesting to test this kind of hypothesis with a survey or with an experimental design capable of capturing how a particular sample of the audience can recall the campaign or find it appealing.

The data under consideration in this study are examples of mass media communication; therefore, the cartoons were obviously created with the intention of generating a number of effects on the audience. However, the focus of the analysis was on the cartoons and not on the audience. In other words, by applying the qualitative tools provided by multimodal discourse analysis, we could depict a reliable picture of the communicative functions conveyed by the cartoons, and not their actual effects on the audience. Therefore, a further phase of this research might verify the efficiency of the campaign for the last edition of Expo, with particular reference to Foody and his friends. This could be done by surveying people who have viewed the cartoons after having set up various different conditions in order to test the effects of the humorous communication conveyed by Foody and his friends with an appropriate experimental design. Moreover, it can be considered that this campaign has a very wide target audience, so it would be interesting to analyse its communicative effects on different samples from different populations (in statistical terms), dividing groups according to their ages or cultural backgrounds. Even though our analysis does not represent an attempt to evaluate the efficacy of the Expo advertising campaign, as a first step we aimed to analyse the role of humour in enriching this particular anthropomorphic mascot and to highlight the main functions that humorous communication can have in a context such as this.

References

1 BIE Paris. (2015a), *A short history of expos*. Available from BIE Paris: http://www.bie-paris.org/site/en/expos/past-expos/past-expos-a-short-history-of-expos [Accessed 14 January 2016].
2 Ibid.
3 Ibid.
4 Expo Milano 2015. (2015a), *The theme*. Available from Expo Milano 2015: http://www.expo2015.org/archive/en/learn-more/the-theme.html [Accessed 17 January 2016].
5 BIE Paris. (2015b), *Feeding the planet, energy for life*. Available from BIE Paris: http://www.bie-paris.org/site/en/expos/past-expos/expo-milano-2015/theme-feeding-the-planet-energy-for-life [Accessed 14 January 2016].

6 Locatelli, G., & Mancini, M. (2010), Risk management in a mega-project: the Universal EXPO 2015 case, *International Journal of Project Organisation and Management*, 2(3), 236–253.

7 George, R. (2008), *Marketing tourism in South Africa* (3rd ed.), Cape Town; New York: Oxford University Press Southern Africa.

8 Gregry, J. J., & Swart, M. P. (2013), *The moderating effect of biographic variables in the relationship between expo product and expo promotion – HuntEx 2012*, Presented at the XXX Pan Pacific Conference, Johannesburg, South Africa, 3–6 June 2013.

9 Hiller, H. H. (1998), Assessing the impact of mega-events: a linkage model, *Current Issues in Tourism*, 1(1), 47–57.

10 Hede, A. M., & Kellett, P. (2011), Marketing communications for special events: analysing managerial practice, consumer perceptions and preferences, *European Journal of Marketing*, 45(6), 987–1004.

11 Close, A. G., Finney, R. Z., Lacey, R. Z., & Sneath, J. Z. (2006), Engaging the consumer through event marketing: linking attendees with the sponsor, community, and brand, *Journal of Advertising Research*, 46(4), 420–433.

12 Bhattacharya, C. B., & Sen, S. (2003), Consumer–company identification: a framework for understanding consumers' relationships with companies, *Journal of Marketing*, 67(2), 76–88; Delre, S. A., Jager, W., Bijmolt, T. H. A., & Janssen, M. A. (2007), Targeting and timing promotional activities: an agent-based model for the takeoff of new products, *Journal of Business Research*, 60(8), 826–835; Holm, O. (2006), Integrated marketing communication: from tactics to strategy, *Corporate Communications: An International Journal*, 11(1), 23–33; Pitta, D. A., Weisgal, M., & Lynagh, P. (2006), Integrating exhibit marketing into integrated marketing communications, *Journal of Consumer Marketing*, 23(3), 156–166; Rotfeld, H. J. (2006), Understanding advertising clutter and the real solution to declining audience attention to mass media commercial messages, *Journal of Consumer Marketing*, 23(4), 180–181; Sneath, J. Z., Finney, R. Z., & Close, A. G. (2006), An IMC approach to event marketing: the effects of sponsorship and experience on customer attitudes, *Journal of Advertising Research*, 45(4), 373–397.

13 Expo Milano 2015. (2015b), *Rivivi Expo Milano 2015*. Available from Expo Milano 2015: http://www.expo2015.org/rivivi-expo/ [Accessed 4 February 2016].

14 Expo Milano 2015. (2015c), *Ti presento Foody, Progetto Scuola*. Available from Expo Milano 2015: http://www.progettoscuola.expo2015.org/mascotte/ti-presento-foody [Accessed 27 July 2016].

15 Expo Milano 2015. (2015d), *The mascot*. Available from Expo Milano 2015: http://www.expo2015.org/archive/en/learn-more/the-theme/the-mascot.html [Accessed 17 January 2016].

16 Expo Milano 2015 World's Fair. (2015a), *With Guaglià the Garlic, there's always something new cooking* [screenshot]. Available from YouTube: https://www.youtube.com/watch?v=nmJUzubq4IA [Accessed 21 March 2016]. Kindly licensed by Expo 2015 S.p.a. and The Walt Disney Company Italia S.r.l.

17 Wikimedia Commons. (2007), *Rudolf II as Vertumnus*. Available from Wikimedia Commons: https://commons.wikimedia.org/wiki/File:Arcimboldovertemnus.jpeg [Accessed 21 March 2016].

18 Patterson, A., Khogeer, Y., & Hodgson, J. (2013), How to create an influential anthropomorphic mascot: literary musings on marketing, make-believe, and meerkats, *Journal of Marketing Management*, 29(1–2), 69–85.

19 Connell, P. M. (2013), The role of baseline physical similarity to humans in consumer responses to anthropomorphic animal images, *Psychology & Marketing*, 30(6), 461–469.

20 Malik, G., & Guptha, A. (2014), Impact of celebrity endorsements and brand mascots on consumer buying behavior, *Journal of Global Marketing*, 27(2), 128–143.

21 Stone, S. M. (2014), The psychology of using animals in advertising, in *Hawaii University International Conferences Arts, Humanities & Social Sciences*, Honolulu, 3–6 January 2004.

22 Hayden, D., & Dills, B. (2015), Smokey the Bear should come to the beach: using mascot to promote marine conservation, *Social Marketing Quarterly*, 21(1), 3–13.

23 Aaker, D. A. (1991), *Managing brand equity: capitalizing on the value of a brand name*, New York: Free Press; Aggarwal, P., & McGill, A. L. (2007), Is that car smiling at me? Schema congruity as a basis for evaluating anthropomorphized products, *Journal of Consumer Research*, *34*(4), 468–479; Delbaere, M., McQuarrie, E. F., & Phillips, B. (2011), Personification in advertising, *Journal of Advertising*, *40*(1), 121–130; Fournier, S. (1998), Consumers and their brands: developing relationship theory in consumer research, *Journal of Consumer Research*, *24*, 343–373.

24 Cayla, J. (2013), Brand mascots as organisational totems, *Journal of Marketing Management*, *29*(1–2), 86–104.

25 Harquail, C. V. (2008), Practice and identity: using a brand symbol to construct organizational identity, in Lerpold, L., Ravasi, D., von Rekom, J., & Soenen, G. (Eds.), *Organizational identity in practice*, 135–150. London: Routledge.

26 Schultz, E. J. (2012), Mascots are brands' best social-media accessories, *Advertising Age*, *83*(13), 2–25.

27 Bhattacharya & Sen, op. cit.

28 Aaker, D. A. (2009), *Managing brand equity, US*, New York: Simon & Schuster; Delbaere et al., op. cit.

29 Cayla, op. cit.

30 Mithen, S., & Boyer, P. (1996), Anthropomorphism and the evolution of cognition, *The Journal of the Royal Anthropological Institute*, *2*(4), 717–721.

31 Boyer, P. (1996), What makes anthropomorphism natural: intuitive ontology and cultural representations, *The Journal of the Royal Anthropological Institute*, *2*(1), 83–97.

32 Fournier, op. cit.

33 Connell, op. cit.

34 Ibid.

35 Shanghai China. (2010), *Shio*. Available from Information Office of Shanghai Municipality: http://en.shio.gov.cn/expo.html [Accessed 17 January 2016].

36 Expo Aichi 2005. (2005), *Official mascots / Official music*. Available from Expo 2005 Aichi, Japan: http://www.expo2005.or.jp/en/whatexpo/mascot.html [Accessed 17 January 2016].

37 Expo Milano 2015. (2015e), *Foody and friends, Progetto Scuola*. Available from Expo Milano 2015: http://www.progettoscuola.expo2015.org/docenti/video-gallery/foody-friends [Accessed 17 January 2016].

38 Expo Milano 2015, op. cit.

39 Patterson, Khogeer, & Hodgson, op. cit.

40 Weinberger, M. G., & Gulas, C. S. (1992), The impact of humor in advertising: a review, *Journal of Advertising*, *21*(4), 35–59.

41 Terrion, J. L., & Ashforth, B. E. (2002), From "I" to "we": the role of putdown humor and identity in the development of a temporary group, *Human Relations*, *55*(1), 55–88.

42 Drew, P. (1987), Po-faced receipts of teases, *Linguistics*, *25*(1), 219–253; Shapiro, J. P., Baumeister, R. F., & Kessler, J. W. (1991), A three-component model of children's teasing: aggression, humor, and ambiguity, *Journal of Social and Clinical Psychology*, *10*(4), 459–472.

43 Apter, M. J. (1982), *The experience of motivation: the theory of psychological reversals, UK*, London: Academic Press.

44 Dynel, M. (2009), *Humorous garden paths*, Newcastle upon Tyne: Cambridge Scholars Publishing; Martin, R. A. (2007), *The psychology of humor: an integrative approach*, Burlington, MA: Elsevier; Ritchie, G. (2004), *The linguistic analysis of jokes*, London: Routledge; Canestrari, C., & Bianchi, I. (2013), From perception of contrarieties to humorous incongruities, in Dynel, M. (Ed.), *Developments in linguistic humour theory*, Amsterdam: John Benjamins Publishing Company, 3–24; Canestrari, C., Dionigi, A., & Zuczkowski, A. (2014), Humor understanding and knowledge, *Language & Dialogue*, *4*(2), 261–283; Forabosco, G. (1992), Cognitive aspects of the humor process: the concept of incongruity, *Humor. International Journal of Humor Research*, *5*(1/2), 45–68.

45 McGhee, P. E. (1979), *Humor: its origin and development*, San Francisco, CA: Freeman.

46 Ibid.

130 *Carla Canestrari and Valerio Cori*

47 Attardo, S., & Raskin, V. (1991), Script theory revis(it)ed: joke similarity and joke representation model, *Humor. International Journal of Humor Research*, 4(3/4), 293–347; Giora, R. (2003), *On our mind: salience, context, and figurative language*, New York: Oxford University Press; Brône, G., Feyaerts, K., & Veale, T. (2006), Introduction: cognitive linguistic approaches to humor, *Humor. International Journal of Humor Research*, 19(3), 203–228.

48 Maier, N. R. F. (1932), A Gestalt theory of humour, *British Journal of Psychology*, 23, 69–74; Canestrari, C., & Bianchi, I. (2012), Perception of contrariety in jokes, *Discourse Processes*, 49(7), 539–564.

49 Deckers, L. (1993), On the validity of weight-judging paradigm for the study of humor, *Humor. International Journal of Humor Research*, 6(1), 43–56; Nerhardt, G. (1970), Humor and inclination to laugh: emotional reactions to stimuli of different divergence from a range of expectancy, *Scandinavian Journal of Psychology*, 11, 185–195; Nerhardt, G. (1976), Incongruity and funniness: towards a new descriptive model, in Chapman, A. J., & Foot, H. C. (Eds.), *Humour and laughter: theory, research and applications*, London: Wiley, 55–62.

50 Canestrari & Bianchi, op. cit.

51 Ibid.

52 Ibid.

53 Ritchie, G. (1999), Developing incongruity-resolution theory, in *Proceedings of the AISB 99 Symposium on Creative Language* in Edinburgh, Scotland, 6–9 April 1999, 78–85.

54 Koestler, A. (1964), *The act of creation*, London: Hutchinson.

55 Attardo, S. (1997), The semantic foundations of cognitive theories of humor, *Humor. International Journal of Humor Research*, 10(4), 395–420.

56 Giora, R. (1991), On the cognitive aspects of the joke, *Journal of Pragmatics*, 16, 465–485.

57 LeVine, P., & Scollon, R. (2004), *Discourse and technology: multimodal discourse analysis*, Washington DC: Georgetown University Press; O'Halloran, K. (2004), *Multimodal discourse analysis: systemic functional perspectives*, London: Continuum; Kress, G., & van Leeuwen, T. (2001), *Multimodal discourse: the modes and media of contemporary communication*, Oxford, UK: Oxford, University Press.

58 Davis, B., & Mason, P. (2004), Trying on voices: using questions to establish authority, identity, and recipient design in electronic discourse, in LeVine, P., & Scollon, R. (Eds.), *Discourse and technology: multimodal discourse analysis*, Washington DC: Georgetown University Press, 47–58; Jewitt, C. (2004), Multimodality and new communication technologies, in LeVine, P., & Scollon, R. (Eds.), *Discourse and technology: multimodal discourse analysis*, Washington DC: Georgetown University Press, 184–195; Jones, R. H. (2004), The problem of context in computer-mediated communication, in LeVine, P., & Scollon, R. (Eds.), *Discourse and technology: multimodal discourse analysis*, Washington DC: Georgetown University Press, 20–33.

59 Erickson, F. (2004), Origins: a brief and intellectual technological history of the emergence of multimodal discourse analysis, in LeVine, P., & Scollon, R. (Eds.), *Discourse and technology: multimodal discourse analysis*, Washington DC: Georgetown University Press, 196–207.

60 Van Leeuwen, T. (2012), The reasons why linguists should pay attention to visual communication, in LeVine, P., & Scollon, R. (Eds.), *Discourse and technology: multimodal discourse analysis*, Washington DC: Georgetown University Press, 7–19.

61 Erickson, op. cit.

62 Expo Milano 2015 World's Fair. (2015b), *Arabella, la dolce acidella*. Available from YouTube: https://www.youtube.com/watch?v=Z2OkxiF986Y [Accessed 5 March 2016]; Expo Milano 2015 World's Fair. (2015c), *Chicca, la super melagrana*. Available from YouTube: https://www.youtube.com/watch?v=kVjB04PGX2s [Accessed 7 October 2016]; Expo Milano 2015 World's Fair. (2015d), *Con Guagliò non è la solita minestra*. Available from YouTube: https://www.youtube.com/watch?v=sxOY0vMAflQ [Accessed 7 October 2016]; Expo Milano 2015 World's Fair. (2015e), *Gury, un talento natural*. Available from YouTube: https://www.youtube.com/watch?v=4LEvE_Q679Y [Accessed 7 October 2016]; Expo Milano 2015 World's Fair. (2015f), *Josephine, la banana matura*. Available from YouTube: https://www.youtube.com/watch?v=owGSrH96hH0 [Accessed 7 October 2016]; Expo Milano 2015 World's Fair. (2015g), *Manghy, il bello di Bollywood*. Available from YouTube: https://www.youtube.com/watch?v=vdSheRMbUu4 [Accessed 7 October 2016]; Expo Milano 2015 World's Fair. (2015h), *Max Mais, il musicista pop-corn*.

Available from YouTube: https://www.youtube.com/watch?v=TBl5Y1w-T2E [Accessed 7 October 2016]; Expo Milano 2015 World's Fair. (2015i), *Piera, fiera del fisico a pera*. Available from YouTube: https://www.youtube.com/watch?v=ohvVdhNSMro [Accessed 7 October 2016]; Expo Milano 2015 World's Fair. (2015j), *Pomina, l'attrice acerba*. Available from YouTube: https://www.youtube.com/watch?v=UrjLeFPlGVI [Accessed 7 October 2016]; Expo Milano 2015 World's Fair. (2015k), *Rap Brothers, fratelli & rapanelli*. Available from YouTube: https://www.youtube.com/watch?v=6uHiaN-t1UE [Accessed 7 October 2016]; Expo Milano 2015 World's Fair. (2015l), *Rodolfo, il vero fico*. Available from YouTube: https://www.youtube.com/watch?v=HEBFkb2miYQ [Accessed 7 October 2016].

63 Expo Milano 2015 World's Fair, op.cit. Kindly licensed by Expo 2015 S.p.a. and The Walt Disney Company Italia S.r.l.

64 Ibid.

65 Ibid.

66 Bhattacharya & Sen, op. cit.

67 Malik, G., & Guptha, A. (2014), Impact of celebrity endorsements and brand mascots on consumer buying behavior, *Journal of Global Marketing*, 27(2), 128–143.

68 Meyer, J. C. (2000), Humor as a double-edged sword: four functions of humor in communication, *Communication Theory*, 10(3), 310–331.

69 Ibid.

70 Goldstein, J. H. (1976), Theoretical notes on humor, *Journal of Communication*, 26(3), 104–112.

71 Goldstein, op. cit.; Patterson et al., op. cit.

72 Martin, R. (2003), Sense of humor, in Lopez, S. J., & Snyder, C. R. (Eds.), *Positive psychological assessment: a handbook of models and measures*, Washington DC: American Psychological Association; Sprecher, S., & Regan, P. C. (2002), Liking some things (in some people) more than others: partner preferences in romantic relationships and friendships, *Journal of Social and Personal Relationships*, 19(4), 463–481.

73 Patterson et al., op. cit.

74 Kellaris, J. J., & Cline, T. W. (2008), Humor and ad memorability: on the contributions of humor expectancy, relevancy, and need for humor, *Psychology & Marketing*, 24, 497–509.

75 Narwal, P., & Kumar, A. (2011), A study on challenges and impact of advertisement for impulse goods, *Research Journal of Social Science & Management*, 6, 25–40.

3.6 Controversial humor in advertising

Social and cultural implications

Margherita Dore

Introduction

As Nash observes, "[v]irtually any well known forms of words—from the language of politics, of advertising, or journalism, of law and social administration—will serve the requirements of wit"[1] (my emphasis). As a matter of fact, witticisms, puns, jokes, satire, parody, etc. are examples of the different forms and guises in which humor can come. Be it scripted (e.g., jokes) or naturally occurring, humor can be used to enhance or challenge interpersonal and social relations.[2] It is therefore not surprising that it has been often used in advertising to seek the involvement of the audience while promoting products, services and, consequently, the brand or corporate company that provides them. As Berger explains, humor can create what he calls the "halo effect," meaning "a feeling of well-being that becomes attached to the products being advertised."[3] Nonetheless, humor in advertisement has often been considered risky, especially due to its potential offensiveness, which can be inadvertent or intentional.[4] Moreover, the (non) appreciation of a humorous advert may very well depend on various factors (e.g., personal situation, beliefs, etc.) that often escape the marketers' control. It is therefore interesting to explore the possible reasons that can lead to a negative response by the receivers of controversial adverts that consciously or unconsciously entail humor. In particular, this paper concentrates on adverts that have been considered offensive by their receivers at the local, national or global level, on the basis of their themes, language and culture-specific references. Considering that such adverts or campaigns set out to address and/or seek the involvement of their target clientele in today's hyper-politically correct world, the latter's (unexpected) reaction is worth exploring, as it can be of great interest to advertising companies and marketers alike. Before proceeding with an in-depth analysis of the issue at hand, I will offer a brief overview of humor and how it can be defined for the purposes of this paper.

Humor theories

Humor is a pervasive feature of human life. As Raskin explains, "the ability to appreciate and enjoy humor is universal and shared by all people, even if the kinds of humor they favor differ widely."[5] Humor can indeed be seen as a universal phenomenon, which varies, however, according to different cultures and historical periods. It comes as no surprise, therefore, that scholars in various fields of research have struggled to provide a unified definition.[6] Moreover, individual reactions to a potentially humorous stimulus may differ greatly and depend on factors such as personal beliefs and specific situations, as well as an individual's cultural background. In general, the most obvious and predictable response to humor is laughter. However, Raskin cautiously suggests that laughter is one of the factors that best characterize this aspect of human emotion. Chiaro and Nash maintain that humor and laughter have an implicit relationship,[7] while Palmer and Morreall are more inclined to see laughter as an integral part of humor.[8] By contrast, Oring talks about laughter and humor as separate phenomena,[9] while Attardo points out that, more often than not, humor is incorrectly assimilated to laughter, as the latter may depend on factors such as the use of hallucinogens; it may even serve other purposes (e.g., express embarrassment).[10] The different ways humor is perceived deserve a thorough analysis that, however, falls beyond the scope of this chapter. It may suffice to note that these observations confirm the difficulties involved in defining humor and its perception (and/or appreciation). For the purposes of this study, I shall accept Attardo's broad definition of humor as "whatever a social group defines as such,"[11] as it offers sufficiently solid grounds for its analysis. Moreover, I consider laughter as one of the ways human beings may consciously or unconsciously respond to humor.

From a functional point of view, some scholars have attempted to detect the mechanisms underlying humor and its effect(s) on society by means of different approaches drawn from fields such as anthropology, psychology, philosophy and linguistics.[12] Space limitations rule out an extensive review of the substantial body of literature on humor produced to date. It will suffice to mention the most recent approaches developed in the field. Raskin's analysis of a series of jokes has led him to put forward the Semantic Script Theory of Humor (SSTH) which postulates that to be humorous, a text has to partially or fully oppose and overlap two different scripts, where a script is defined as "a large chunk of semantic information surrounding the word or evoked by it."[13] To this, Attardo adds: "It [a script] is a cognitive structure internalized by the speaker which provides the speaker with information on how things are done, organized, etc."[14] The linguistic ambiguity of a text is due to the fact that the scripts are in opposition and such oppositions are virtually infinite. Attardo sees the SSTH as unable to distinguish between *verbal humor* (based on language) and *referential humor* (based on content), which can, however, be subsumed under the umbrella term of Verbally Expressed Humor.[15] Moreover, he considers the incongruity-resolution model developed in psychology to be better suited to explaining the interpretative process of a humorous text. According to this model, the interpretation of a joke involves two steps. At first, the receiver interprets the text according to the linguistic cues and the script they activate. Subsequently, the punchline forces the receiver to detect the incongruity and then reinterpret the linguistic cues in the text according to another script, which is in opposition to the one activated previously. This step is called the "resolution" phase.[16]

Hence, although retaining the SSTH's main tenets, Attardo (together with Raskin) has developed the General Theory of Verbal Humor (GTVH) to detect the humorous instances in texts longer than self-contained jokes. The GTVH entails six Knowledge Resources (KRs), including the already established features of script opposition. These six KRs are conceived according to a hierarchical structure, at the top of which the script opposition (SO) is found. The KR that follows is called the logical mechanism (LM); it is the parameter that explains how the two scripts are brought together (i.e., by juxtaposition, ground reversal, etc.). As per the incongruity-resolution model mentioned above, the SO is the parameter that reveals the incongruity, while the LM is the parameter that resolves it. The situation (SI) describes the context (e.g., objects, participants, activities, etc.) while the target (TA) defines the "butt" of the joke. The narrative strategy (NS) is responsible for the organization of the text (e.g., a dialog, narrative, figure of speech, etc.).

At the bottom, we find the KR called language (LA), which contains the information regarding the verbalization of the text.[17] As Tsakona observes, in the case of matching verbal and non-verbal text, the Language KR should be revised to account for both.[18]

Since it first appeared, the GTVH has been extensively applied to, and revised to account for, texts longer than jokes, as well as instances of humor in texts other than verbal. For example, drawing on Attardo's notion of *hyperdetermination* (i.e., the simultaneous presence of more than one source of humor at the same time[19]), Tsakona analyzes a series of newspaper cartoons to demonstrate how *hyperdetermined* humor is the result of the interaction of the language and/or the image. Consequently, cartoons become multilayered compositions made up of one or more script oppositions that are retrieved from our encyclopedic or world knowledge. Since several script oppositions and *hyperdetermination* can be detected in the same text, this may also explain why people react differently to the same cartoon.[20] For her part, Gérin uses the GTVH in conjunction with iconography theories to detect the humor in visual art. In particular, she proposes to redefine the Target KR so that it can distinguish between the butt of the joke that is visually represented and the targeted public or ideal viewer of the image.[21] This distinction is crucial for the analysis of adverts that, like visual art, make ample use of visuals, music and sound, alongside spoken and written text.[22] Moreover, in the specific case of controversial ads, it stands to reason that in some cases the ideal receiver does not coincide with the real one, which results in mismatching communication between advertisers and consumers. Hence, all these findings and caveats can also be taken into account when applying the GTVH to the analysis of controversial humorous adverts, as well as to the task of understanding the reasons why some people find such ads amusing while others consider them distasteful or even appalling.

Humor in advertising

From a general point of view, an advertisement can be described as a message conceived by an advertiser (or advertising company) that is sent to its target receivers. Adverts are conceived by marketers in order to reach a prospective pool of local, national and/or international customers. Simpson and Mayer summarize the categorizations thus far produced for the different types of ads (cf. Table 3.6.1).[23]

As may appear evident, such a categorization is not clear-cut, and some advertisers may use soft-sell strategies in space- and time-base ads. Others may attempt to persuade target customers of the exceptional quality of their product by using long-copy text (e.g., iPhone campaigns). Moreover, ads are categorized according to their inherent features: (1) the headline, with a catchy line that may or may not interact with the visual image; (2) the body copy, which is a longer stretch of text explaining, for instance, the main features of the product; (3) the signature, which is a small picture reporting the trade name of the product (e.g., Unilever); (4) the slogan, which is a memorable phrase accompanying a signature (e.g., I'm lovin' it, McDonald's); and (5) the testimonial, normally a famous celebrity endorsing a product (e.g., George Clooney for Nespresso). Interestingly, MacInnis *et al.* explain how all these ad types have been designed to enhance consumers' motivation, opportunity and ability (MOA) to process brand information in an advertisement. These variables are respectively described as the desire to process information in adverts, the time devoted to them and the consumers' skill or proficiency in understanding ads. Humor seems particularly effective in increasing the processing of brand information; yet research has not been able to confirm whether or not its positive effect is due to the surprise value

Table 3.6.1 Summary of advertisement types

Ad Type	Explanation	Examples
Product vs. non-product	The attention drawn to the product	Coca-cola, Mercedes cars, H&M, etc.
	The attention drawn to the activities or proposals by political parties or organizations	"CHANGE. We can believe in" (Barak Obama's 2008 presidential campaign)
Hard sell vs. soft sell	Overt, explicit advertising of the product's merits	5.0 megapixel camera, 50 horsepower engine
	Covert advertising, aiming more to amuse	Wordplay, music and pictures (Fresh Up with Seven up)
Reason vs. tickle	Supporting reasons to purchase	"Because you're worth it"
	Appeal to humor, emotions and mood	Think Fast (BMW car)
Slow drip vs. sudden burst	Launched on several media and in installments	Telecommunication company advertising campaigns
	Sudden appearance of the ad on the media	An ad for a new movie in cinemas; a sales campaign
Short copy vs. long copy	Displaying low textual matter embedded in a big visual context	"Have a break. Have a Kit Kat"
	Displaying a large amount of text	Advertorials (advertisements in the form of an editorial)
Space-based vs. time-based	Appears in print media	Newspaper ads
	Appears on television or in cinemas	Multimedia ads

of the brand information in the ad.[24] In other words, the humor in an ad may be effective for the online processing of an advert, but it may not result in a tradeoff effect for the brand itself. This point is particularly relevant to the analysis of the examples at hand. Indeed, it could be argued that although controversial humor involves a great deal of surprise, it may not imply a positive customers' response regarding the product and the brand itself, especially if the humor in the ad is not relevant to the message conveyed.[25] In addition, use of humor may produce the so-called "vampire effect," sucking attention away from the product or message that is advertised.[26]

The present study will be looking at tickle adverts in particular. As mentioned earlier, such ads, which aim to elicit people's curiosity and participation,[27] are likely to comprise verbal and non-verbal text (i.e., even a written ad on a plain white newspaper page still involves using both verbal and non-verbal elements). In order to provide a systematic analysis of the data under scrutiny, I will refer to Speck's categorizations of five humorous advert types.[28] Speck suggests that four out of five humor types are based on the incongruity-resolution mechanism, which can also be used in conjunction with the arousal–safety mechanism (related to relief and release theories, which see laughing at others as a form of releasing pleasure[29]), and/or humor disparagement (related to hostility theories, which suggest that humor is created by the speaker's aggressive attitude towards the object of her/his humorous utterance[30]). As Speck further explains, *comic wit* in humorous adverts involves incongruity-resolution alone, whereas *satire* is based on a combination of incongruity-resolution and disparagement; *sentimental comedy* involves both arousal–safety and incongruity-resolution, while *full comedy* involves all three processes. Conversely, the fifth humor type, sentimental humor, entails the arousal–safety process only.[31]

As Gérin points out, the incongruity-resolution approach mainly focuses on its cognitive mechanism, whereas considering hostility and release theories can shed light on the function of humor.[32] Indeed, drawing on Speck, Beard renames sentimental humor as *resonant humor* and explains that it implies a sort of mild social aggression (e.g., using taboo themes and/or words) that aim to surprise receivers and attract their attention. He also renames sentimental comedy (which produces pleasure when the incongruity is resolved) as *resonant wit* and points out that, unlike resonant humor, it does not involve offense. Interestingly, Beard has analyzed a series of complaints put forward by New Zealanders against what they deemed to be offensive adverts. The data examined has shown that humor is not the cause of the offense *per se*; rather it is the theme used in adverts that is potentially offensive, regardless of its humorous or non-humorous content.[33] For instance, a humorous advert may be based on the "sex–no-sex" concrete script opposition[34] but may not be intentionally offensive; however, if the main theme is "oral sex," a series of further associations and script oppositions may arise. Thus, one part of the target audience may find it offensive (i.e., some men and women) while others may find it amusing (i.e., other men and women) (cf. the Burger King example below).

As a matter of fact, humor appreciation may depend on one's personal disposition and/or contingent factors (cf. for instance, Hatzithomas *et al.*'s study on the influence of economic conditions on the appreciation of humor in advertising[35]). Besides, what may determine the (in)appropriateness of humor in general (and in an advert, in this case) is often due to the norms established in a given socio-cultural setting.[36] Therefore, the issue of appropriateness becomes paramount when investigating the social and cultural implications that humor in advertising may have. For instance, one famous and much debated example is the 2008 Absolut Vodka advert, which showed a 19th-century map of Mexico with its borders extending further north to include part of the US territory. Despite being aimed at the Mexican public, the ad was picked up by the US media, which roundly criticized this campaign and encouraged US citizens to boycott Absolut Vodka and its products. Eventually, the company was forced to withdraw the ad and publicly apologize.[37] Such a drastic action was a clear attempt to ward off business losses in a market that is likely to ensure high returns to Pernod Ricard, the French group that owns the brand.

In the following sections, therefore, the focus will not only be on *overtly* intentionally offensive humorous adverts, but also on some instances of advertising that were accidentally offensive (or supposedly so), hence failing to obtain a positive response. Be that as it may, it is interesting to notice how the resulting negative emotions and feedback have also led to the receivers getting actively involved, taking action against some of these ads and forcing them to be withdrawn or modified. In other cases, the corporation also issued official apologies, as we shall see below.

Controversial humor in the local and global market

Global corporations' advertising campaigns are often motivated by two needs: to cut advertising costs and to build a unified image of the brand. Yet cultural barriers can often make such an approach impracticable, and opting for an unlocalized campaign may be detrimental to the message in the ad and the brand itself.[38] Nonetheless, even localized campaigns are no guarantee of success, especially if they are based on sensitive or taboo topics. Moreover, the concept of localization in today's globalized world needs to be challenged, since any advert designed for a given target culture can easily be viewed, shared and commented on over the Internet. In the following subsections, I discuss a series of ads that show how national and multinational corporations or organizations try to exploit humor to generate product appreciation among their prospective buyers. However, other ads will demonstrate how adverts can become inadvertently humorous, thus confirming that the perception and appreciation of such ads are relative concepts. For the sake of clarity, the sections below are divided according to the different types of humor employed. Firstly, I shall discuss some instances of adverts based on verbal humor, in which the image is only used in the background to support the verbal text. I shall then move on to examine instances based on referential humor that are supported by the visual component. This will include adverts based respectively on stereotyped and culture-specific humor. All the examples discussed below are considered to be controversial, given that they have encountered the opposition of their potential receivers.

Verbal humor

From a purely linguistic point of view, adverts manipulate language and violate the language code in the attempt to extract more meaning, as poetry does. In the case of verbally humorous ads, the different levels of manipulation include spelling and phonology (e.g., "nite" rather than "night," "donut" instead of "doughnut"), vocabulary (neologisms such as "innervigoration": in+nerve+vigor+tion), the use of collocations and clichés as well as the exploitation of morphology and syntax (e.g., proliferation of compound nouns and modifiers as in "record-breaking machine"). Along with the playful manipulation of language structures that violate syntax, morphology, etc., advertisers may insert puns and wordplay in headlines, body copy and slogans to promote products and win customers.

Soft and tickle ads rely heavily on such exploitation because they resort to linguistic witticism and can therefore be considered as instances of sentimental comedy/resonant wit, according to Speck's and Beard's categorizations discussed above. For instance, the body copy in the Sharp advert "From **Sharp** minds come **Sharp** products" is based on words having the same sound, spelling and meaning (i.e. synonymy). The receiver's pleasure derives from detecting the incongruity-resolution mechanism in the text, which uses the same linguistic item (i.e. sharp) to trigger two different scripts ("intelligent minds" and "IT products"). Conversely, the "Every**wear**—Burton Menswear" advert is based on homophony (i.e. words having the same sound but different spelling); in this case, the incongruity-resolution mechanisms is based on the activation of the script opposition between "where" and "wear," and the pleasure stems from the detection of such opposition. Last but not least, London Transport's advert "Less **bread**. No **jam**" deserves mention, as it exploits the spelling similarity of some words with different meanings (i.e. homography). In this case, the "money/no-money" concrete script opposition[39] is triggered by the word "bread," which in this context is slang for "money." Similarly, the word "jam" activates both the literal and referential meaning of "traffic jam" and the "actual/non-actual" abstract script opposition.[40]

As I have suggested earlier, some companies and advertising agencies may choose a more sensationalist or provocative approach, which may provoke opposing reactions among the target receivers. From a language-specific standpoint, the 2003 Ryanair (a well-known low-cost airline based in Ireland) "FawKing great offers" advert is a case in point. The campaign was launched a few days before Bonfire Night and advertised flights to the UK in *The Daily Telegraph*. It played on the homophony between the "F***" word and Guy Fawkes's name. The latter had famously tried and failed to blow up the House of Parliament in London in 1605, and each year on November 5 people in the UK celebrate the foiling of the Gunpowder Plot with fireworks.[41] The potential humor stems exclusively from the verbal text, while the people depicted in the advert merely play a supporting role.[42] Clearly, the humor is conveyed when the receiver is able to resolve the incongruity of the first interpretation (the F*** word) with the most relevant and amusing reference to Guy Fawkes's name.

From a GTVH standpoint, the SO is "obscene/non-obscene," while the LM is also "referential ambiguity,"[43] the SI is "discount flights offer" and the TA is "Guy Fawkes." In the data discussed here, the NS is always "advertising"; LA is verbal text only, as the image plays no role in humor production here. Interestingly, the (British) Advertising Standards Authority criticized the advert after receiving complaints from the public who deemed it offensive. Ryanair commented that the ad was "intended to be humorous."[44] As we can see, in this case the proponent of the advert and the receivers disagree on what is offensive or humorous. One possible explanation could be that the customers felt they were the target of the implied reference to the swearword, whereas Ryanair intended Guy Fawkes to be the butt of the joke. Moreover, it could be argued that instead of enjoying the pleasure of resolving the incongruity, these members of the public were disturbed by it. The consumers' protest also led the ASA to order Ryanair not to run similar campaigns in future.[45]

The last example I would like to discuss in this section is an instance of a controversial ad that plays on the taboo topic of defecation. The campaign launched in 2011 to promote Sheet Energy Strips, edible strips containing vitamins and nutrients. The billboards offer a clear demonstration of the humor in the three body copies and how the images serve as backdrop to the entailed *incongruity*.

See the images of the campaign here: http://www.adweek.com/creativity/worst-ad-campaign-year-sheets-energy-strips-134913/ [accessed 05/09/2017].

These billboard adverts are based on the humorous homophonic wordplay between "take a sheet" and "take a shit," thus implying defecation and all the composing elements of this script. They display three examples of similar body copy (respectively "I take a sheet in the pool," "I've taken a sheet in the library" and "I take a sheet right on the stage") that should suggest that using these energy strips can help consumers to perform better in different contexts: during physical exercise (swimming), intellectual work (at the library) or a musical performance (at a concert). Interestingly, the "right on the stage" example features Pitbull, an internationally acclaimed rapper who endorsed the campaign. Another endorsement is provided by the famous basketball player LeBron James, who also happens to be a co-founder of the company that produces the energy strips. Unlike the Ryanair example above, the marketers of this ad blatantly confirmed their intention to shock the receivers of the ad so as to make it more memorable. These energy strip producers also claimed they obtained substantial returns on the investment.[46] Nonetheless, the adverts were the targets of much humor and negative comments over the Internet. Also, this series of adverts may have proved detrimental to both celebrities' images.[47]

According to the GTVH, the SO is "obscene/non-obscene" while the LM is again "referential ambiguity"; the SI is respectively "physical exercise," "intellectual activity" and "live performance." The TAs of this campaign are probably "the product," "the brand" and "the testimonials" themselves. This example shows how punning and the creative manipulation of language can also boomerang. On the one hand, it can be argued that the potential offensiveness of the ad has served the goal of the ad's becoming a trend topic on the Internet. Yet part of this success resulted in the receivers ridiculing the brand and its products.

All in all, it can be claimed that advertisement campaigns based on punning are a risky business because they can often backfire. In the Ryanair ads, the company was forced to pay a fine and apologize publicly. In the Sheet Energy Strips campaign, formal apologies were not needed, yet the ads were deemed distasteful, with consequent detrimental effects on the company itself.

Verbal and visual humor

As mentioned earlier, advertisers can also exploit both the verbal and the referential content (i.e. meaning) that language ambiguity brings about. However, as Forceville suggests, adverts can make use of multimodal metaphors. Their target domain, which may be presented in the verbal or visual text (or a combination of the two), is placed where we would normally find something else, thus giving rise to a whole set of conceptualizations based on our background knowledge.[48] Therefore, this composition produces an opposition between what is expected and what is actually presented in the advert. Bearing this in mind, I will examine a series of billboard and TV adverts that have made use of such creative devices in the attempt to be amusing and appealing, yet received the opposite response due to their controversial themes.

In 2006, the multinational corporation Sony published a billboard ad to launch its full white PlayStation Portable (PSP). In the attempt to cunningly show the battle between the previous all-black PSP and the brand-new white version, they created an advert featuring a stern white woman clutching a black woman by the chin with the accompanying copy "PlayStation Portable. White is coming." The possibility of choosing between a white and black PSP visually punned with the color of the two models' skin. However, the personified representations (a multimodal metaphor, as suggested above) of the two consoles are particularly interesting, as the white model appears to be in a dominant position. Interestingly, this campaign was launched in the Netherlands and was not intended to appear in the American market, or at least this is what the company maintained.[49] Yet, as reported by *The Guardian*, Sony entrusted the campaign to TBWA, a notoriously provocative agency that tends to challenge conventions.[50] Such an ad would be unthinkable in America, and it could be argued that Sony was very well aware of this. It stands to reason to suggest that, since ten years ago "viral videos" on YouTube and other platforms were in their infancy, they thought the ad could go unnoticed. Nonetheless, this image-based ad soon reached the USA and provoked opposing reactions. Some people suggested it had racist connotations, while others claimed it simply flagged the difference in color of the two products and was therefore harmless. Hence, the issue of intentionality here cannot be discounted altogether. Be that as it may, the audience's negative reaction eventually led the company to withdraw the advert.

From a GTVH standpoint, the SO is "black/white"; yet I would argue that, as Tsakona suggested, this ad seems to elicit a multiple set of other SOs (e.g., "appropriate–inappropriate," "black/white race," "good–bad") depending on the audience's individual sensitivity to the underlying "black/white" opposition and the controversial theme of racialization it (inadvertently?) evokes. The LM in this case is "analogy" as it is based on a "multimodal metaphor" that maps the features of the two consoles onto the two models; the SI is "a battle." In general terms, the TA can be said to be the black console that is being challenged by the white one. If we consider Sony's claim, their prospective audience was the Dutch market, where they probably thought the "black/white" joke would not be taboo. Conversely, the American audience perceived it in more offensive terms as it flies in the face of the political correctness movement. Clearly, the line between what is considered humorously acceptable is extremely blurred here and it may depend on several factors, including the cultural and historical background.

Research in marketing has demonstrated that appealing to intrinsically hedonic needs, such as sexual instincts and appetites, is likely to enhance consumers' motivation, opportunities and ability to process brand information in an advertisement.[51] Yet, like humor, sex is culture-bound. As Biswas *et al.*'s analysis of humor and sex appeal in advertising has demonstrated, the French and Americans do make different uses of these phenomena. However, these scholars have looked at these variables separately. By contrast, the ad shown at the webpage link below is an interesting example that combines humor and sex via its verbal text and image. It was launched in 2009 in Singapore by Burger King (a.k.a. BK), a global chain of fast-food hamburger restaurants founded in 1954 in Miami, Florida.

See the image of the advertisement here: http://www.telegraph.co.uk/women/womens-life/11018413/Burger-King-raped-my-face-claims-model-on-angry-YouTube-video.html.

As can be seen, the billboard shows a girl facing a large seven-inch hamburger. The image referentially plays with the idea of oral sex since the sandwich roll is metaphorically associated with a penis that is placed just in front of a wide-eyed girl with an open red-lipsticked mouth. The incongruity breaks the frame of expectations[52] (regarding food) that is recast on the sex domain, thus resulting in a humorous effect. Moreover, the copy of the advert "It'll blow your mind" is a homonymic reference to the slang expression for fellatio (i.e. "give someone a blow job"). From the GTVH point of view, the SO is "sex/no-sex" or "obscene/non-obscene," while the LM is again "analogy" and "multimodal metaphor"; the SI is fast-food eating and sexual intercourse while the TA (strictly speaking) is the girl in the picture.

The sexual innuendo in this sudden burst advert was immediately criticized as distasteful and repulsive. It is likely that the audience also transferred the disparaging humor targeting the girl in the picture to women at large, since the ad also seems to give rise to further opposition such as "men's domination versus women's oppression," etc. Once again, the corporation's spokesperson tried to respond to the customers' ire by saying:

> [t]his print ad is running to support a limited time promotion in the Singapore market and is not running in the U.S. or any other markets. The campaign is supported by the franchisee in Singapore and has generated positive consumer sales around this limited time product offer in that market.[53]

Interestingly, this campaign also stirred even more controversy a few years later, when the model seen in the billboard claimed the picture was taken without her knowledge or consent. As reported in *The Telegraph* by Radhika Sanghani, the woman posted a video on YouTube stating "Burger King raped my face" and encouraged people to boycott the fast-food chain.[54] Although the video is no longer available and the model's boycotting campaign was probably unsuccessful, reactions and debate revolving around the controversy this advert unleashed can still be found on YouTube, along with several related comments.[55]

The likelihood of carrying out successful boycotting campaigns is further demonstrated by the next two examples. Unlike space-based (i.e. print) adverts, these are instances of time-based (i.e. TV) ads, which stirred up a great deal of controversy from the social point of view and forced the company proposing the ads to withdraw them. Both adverts under scrutiny here were created to advertise Huggies diapers by Kimberly-Clark, an American multinational corporation that produces mostly paper-based products. Interestingly, each advert was conceived to target respectively the US and the Italian market by playing with stereotyped and biased ideas. In the case of the American advert launched in 2012, the ad playfully joked about the fact that fathers are not used to changing diapers or helping their wives/partners with babies in general. The video advert shows a group of fathers left alone in a house for five days with their children while the mothers enjoy some time to themselves. A peppy, fast-paced soundtrack accompanies the images while a voiceover message is broadcast. The fathers are shown struggling to change their babies' diapers because they were more interested in watching sport events on the television, etc.:

> To prove Huggies diapers and wipes can handle anything, we put them to the toughest test imaginable: dads! Alone with their babies in one house for five days . . . While we gave moms well deserved time off. How did Huggies products hold up to daddyhood? The world is about to find out.

The final headline read: "Huggies Dad Test. Coming Soon."

From a GTVH point of view, the humor appears to stem from the "normal–abnormal" SO, which produces an *incongruity* between the script of normal parental duties and related expectations (e.g., efficient care of their offspring) and fathers' (expected) ineptitude. The LM here is "exaggeration" and "role exchanges"; the SI is "father attending to toddlers and children" while the NS is "TV advertisement" and the TA is "the fathers on the ad" and "fathers in general." The generalization and stereotyped ideas the advert reflects resulted in a heated debate among those fathers who probably felt they were the butt of the joke, rather than fathers in general. On Facebook, they gave vent to their disappointment at being pictured as utterly helpless.[56] Chris Routhly launched the "We're Dads, Huggies. Not Dummies" petition, which received more than 1,000 signatures in less than a week. This led Kimberly-Clark to withdraw the offending advert and publish the following statement: "We have heard the feedback from dads (. . .) We recognize our intended message did not come through and that we need to do a better job communicating the campaign's overall message (. . .)." Interestingly, the video can still be found on YouTube and thus far it has been watched 7,094 times with the following feedback: 12 dislikes and only 2 likes. One of the comments found below is:

> It is so utterly wrong to continually depict husbands and fathers as infantile buffoons, unable to grasp simple concepts or make decisions. How many ads have we seen where the kids and wife roll their eyes, as "stupid Dad" has no clue what he's doing? As others have said, reverse the gender and see how funny it is.[57]

In 2015, Kimberly-Clark launched an advertising campaign for Huggies in Italy. This time the supposed overall message of the advert was to encourage parents to buy diapers specifically made for baby girls or baby boys on the basis of the physical differences. However, in order to underline these physical differences, the advertiser exploited stereotyped images regarding gender roles. In the TV advert a mother is shown playing with two toddlers (a girl and a boy) while the voiceover message reported in Table 3.6.2 is heard (an English translation is provided in the right-hand column).

Each of the statements that fosters a polarized gender difference is matched with images that contribute to create visual metaphors in different parts of the whole text. For instance, the baby girl on screen looks more feminine and caring while playing with dolls; the boy plays with a ball and later runs to hug his mother. They can therefore be seen as

Table 3.6.2 Italian "Baby boy and baby girl Huggies" advert

Italian	Gloss
Lei penserà a farsi bella, lui a fare goal. Lei cercherà tenerezza, lui avventure. Lei si farà correre dietro, lui invece ti cercherà. Così piccoli e già così diversi. Allora perché usare gli stessi pannolini? La rivoluzione Huggies: bimbo e bimba. L'unico pannolino progettato sulle loro differenze per catturare la pipì proprio lì dove la fanno. Per un asciutto su misura: Huggies bimba e Huggies bimbo	She will think about making herself beautiful; he will think about scoring a goal. She will look for tenderness; he will look for adventures. She will let the guys chase her; he will look for you [his mother]. So young and already so different. So why are they using the same diapers? The Huggies revolution: baby boy and baby girl. The only diaper designed for their differences, which can capture pee exactly where they do it. For a tailor-made stay-dry feeling: Huggies for baby girls and baby boys

instances of *punctual hyperdetermination*.[58] Hence, according to the underlying message of this advert, boys are likely to grow up to become footballers (and womanizers) while girls will mainly concentrate on being beautiful and getting chased by men. In addition, girls are pictured as constantly searching for love and affection and boys as mother-dependent. In GTVH, the advert can be explained as SO "normal–abnormal," as not all baby girls will want to become loving Barbie-like women and not all baby boys will want to be mother-dependent footballers. The LM is again "exaggeration" and the TA are "babies that will be adults." It stands to reason that this attempt to humorously play on gender-based stereotypes has given rise to a series of script oppositions ("sex/no-sex," "men are womanizers/women are stupid, etc.) that were obviously unintended or unforeseen by the marketers. The problem here lies in the fact that the target audience, mostly comprising mothers, felt particularly offended by the advert as they probably perceived their own children and themselves to be the butt of the joke. Therefore, they generated petitions to remove the advert and boycott Huggies in the stores. Eventually the ad was modified to avoid such references.[59] Clearly, the topic itself here is not taboo, but its inherent sexism was perceived as more disturbing than its potential humor.

These examples show the extent to which the world has changed in the last couple of decades. Waller's 1999 study found that, out of all issues, women were most offended by sexist behavior.[60] Conversely, the Huggies ads targeted men from a sexist point of view, which was demonstrated to be equally disturbing for men. It is also worth noting that in the past, such ads might have done limited damage, but today's interconnected world allows for fast and easy access to news by virtually everyone. The line between businesses influencing the public and vice versa is undoubtedly becoming blurred. More than ever, companies are not willing to risk losing their positive image and potential returns over unhappy customers. Hence, they quickly react to their feedback.

Concluding remarks

The examples presented in this study have attempted to offer both a local and global view of the function(s) of humor in advertising, be it inadvertent or intentional. Some examples have shown how advertisers creatively manipulate language. The adverts by Sharp etc. demonstrate their ability to play with language and involve the target buyers so as to promote a positive image and enhance sales. Nevertheless, some adverts have proved to be unsuccessful (if not total failures) due to the customers' negative reactions and/or the community's active participation in the debate the ads sparked. The Sony PSP and BK campaigns have shown how the exploitation of the verbal and visual texts can evoke a series of script oppositions at different levels within the same pool of target buyers. Adverts based on sensitive topics such as race and gender may involve metaphoric representations that can boomerang (e.g., by stirring up the customer's discontent and fomenting boycotting campaigns) and have social and economic implications for the brands. The present analysis has benefited from the application of the GTVH, which has been able to show how several billboard and TV adverts can exploit the verbal text, or the verbal text in combination with the non-verbal text, to evoke a set of multilayered script oppositions and incongruities. In the case of potentially humorous adverts based on controversial themes, the oppositions and incongruities also seem to result in different targets of disparagement. This is proved by the audience's different reactions to the adverts.

The analysis could certainly be expanded to include other local contexts and sectors, which may contribute to a better understanding of the social and cultural implications of the phenomenon of humor in ads. For example, further research could concentrate on the cross-cultural use and appreciation of humor by looking at instances of translated adverts. Due to space limitations, this issue could not be addressed here, but many examples of (un)intended humorous adverts can be found online and in literature.[61] In addition, the linguistic and cultural reasons for the failure of cross-cultural communication via advertising certainly deserve further investigation. Unfortunately, statistical data regarding returns from challenging or controversial adverts are probably extremely difficult to retrieve, and it is unlikely that companies will provide them. Nonetheless, it would be of enormous interest to verify the empirical effectiveness, or lack thereof, of such selling strategies.

In any case, this chapter has hopefully contributed to shedding some light on the importance that various forms of humor have in advertising. Most importantly, it has offered a wealth of examples showing how humor is a delicate issue that needs to be handled carefully, especially in today's hyper-politically correct world, in which seeking social involvement via advertising may backfire, resulting in the potential buyers' turning against the company or brand itself.

References

1 Nash, W. (1985), *The Language of Humour: Style and Technique in Comic Discourse*, London and New York, Longman.
2 Norrick, N. R. (1993), *Conversational Joking: Humor in Everyday Talk*, Bloomington, Indiana University Press.
3 Berger, A. A. (2015), *Ads, Fads, and Consumer Culture: Advertising's Impact on American Character and Society*, Fifth Edition, Lanham, Rowman & Littlefield Publishers.
4 Beard, F. K. (2008), Advertising and audience offense: The role of intentional humor, *Journal of Marketing Communications* 14 (1): 1–17.
5 Raskin, V. (1985), *Semantic Mechanisms of Humour*, Dordrecht, D. Reidel.
6 Attardo, S. (1994), *Linguistic Theories of Humour*, Berlin, Mouton de Gruyter; Attardo, S. (2001), *Humorous Texts: A Semantic and Pragmatic Analysis*, Berlin and New York, Mouton de Gruyter; Oring, E. (2003), *Engaging Humour*, Urbana and Chicago, University of Illinois Press.
7 Chiaro, D. (1992), *The Language of Jokes. Analysing Verbal Play*, London and New York, Routledge; Nash, W. (1985), *The Language of Humour: Style and Technique in Comic Discourse*, London and New York, Longman.
8 Palmer, J. (1994), *Taking Humour Seriously*, London and New York, Routledge; Morreall, J. (1983), *Taking Laughter Seriously*, Albany, State University of New York.

 9 Oring, op. cit.
10 Attardo (1994), op. cit.
11 Attardo (1994), op. cit.
12 Norrick, op cit., Palmer, op. cit.; Critchley, S. (2002), *On Humour*, London, Routledge; Billig, M. (2005), *Laughter and Ridicule: Towards a Social Critique of Humour*, London, Sage.
13 Raskin, op. cit.
14 Attardo (1994), op. cit.
15 Ritchie, G. (2000), Describing verbally expressed humour, in *Proceedings of AISB Symposium on Creative and Cultural Aspects and Applications of AI and Cognitive Science*, April 2000, Birmingham: 71–78, Chiaro, D. (2005), Foreword: Verbally expressed humour and translation: An overview of a neglected field, *Humor: International Journal of Humor Research* 18 (2): 135–145.
16 Attardo (1994), op. cit.
17 Attardo (1994), op. cit.
18 Tsakona, V. (2009), Language and image interaction in cartoons: Towards a multimodal theory of humor, *Journal of Pragmatics* 41: 1171–1188.
19 Attardo (2001), op. cit.
20 Tsakona, op. cit.
21 Gérin, A. (2013), A second look at laughter: Humor in visual arts, *Humor: International Journal of Humor Research* 26 (1): 155–176.
22 Forceville, C. (2007), Multimodal metaphor in ten Dutch TV commercials, *The Public Journal of Semiotics* 1 (1): 15–34.
23 Simpson and Mayr, op. cit.
24 MacInnis, D. J., Moorman, C., and Jaworski, B. J. (1991), Enhancing and measuring consumers' motivation, opportunity, and ability to process brand information from ads, *Journal of Marketing* 55 (4): 32–53.
25 MacInnis, Moorman, and Jaworski, op. cit.
26 Catanescu, C. and Tom, G. (2001), Types of humor in television and magazine advertising, *Review of Business* 22 (1): 92–96.
27 Bernstein, D. (1974), *Creative Advertising*, London, Longman.
28 Speck, P. S. (1991), The humorous message taxonomy: A framework for the study of humorous ads, *Current Issues & Research in Advertising* 13 (1): 1–44.
29 Morreall, J. (1983), *Taking Laughter Seriously*, Albany, State University of New York Press.
30 Raskin, op. cit.
31 Speck, op. cit.
32 Gérin, op. cit.
33 Beard, op. cit.
34 Raskin, op. cit.
35 Hatzithomas, L., Boutsouki, C., and Zotos, Y. (2016), The role of economic conditions on humor generation and attitude towards humorous TV commercials, *Humor: International Journal of Humor Research* 29 (4): 483–505.
36 Attardo (1994), op. cit.
37 Reuters (08/04/2008), http://www.reuters.com/article/us-mexico-absolut-idUSN0729018920 080409 [Accessed March 24, 2016].
38 Biswas, A., Olsen, J. E., and Carlet, V. (1992), A comparison of print advertisements from the United States and France, *Journal of Advertising* 21 (4): 73–81.
39 Raskin, op. cit.
40 Raskin, op. cit.
41 Durant and Lambrou, op. cit.
42 Tsakona, op. cit.
43 Attardo (2001), op. cit.
44 BBC (04/02/2004), Ryanair advert dubbed "offensive," http://news.bbc.co.uk/2/hi/business/3456423.stm [Accessed March 24, 2016].
45 BBC, op. cit.

46 Del Rey, J. (31/10/2011), How LeBron and an unusual adman linked up to launch for Sheets Energy Strips, http://adage.com/article/news/lebron-unusual-adman-linked-sheets-energy-strips/230723/ [Accessed November 24, 2016].

47 Nudd, T. (16/09/2011), *Worst Ad Campaign of the Year? Sheet Energy Strips*, http://www.adweek.com/adfreak/worst-ad-campaign-year-sheets-energy-strips-134913 [Accessed November 24, 2016].

48 Forceville, op. cit.

49 Tolilo, Stephen (12/07/2006), Sony pulls Dutch PSP ad deemed racist by American critics, http://www.mtv.com/news/1536222/sony-pulls-dutch-psp-ad-deemed-racist-by-american-critics/ [Accessed November 24, 2016].

50 *Guardian* (05/07/2006), Sony ad provokes race accusations, http://www.theguardian.com/technology/gamesblog/2006/jul/05/sonyadcasues [Accessed March 24, 2016].

51 MacInnis, Moorman, and Jaworski, op. cit., 35.

52 Tsakona, op. cit.

53 Miller, R. J. (2009), Critics cringe at ad for Burger King's latest sandwich, *FoxNews*, June 30, http://www.foxnews.com/story/2009/06/30/critics-cringe-at-ad-for-burger-king-latest-sandwich.html [Accessed November 24, 2016].

54 Sanghani, R. (2014), "Burger King raped my face", claims model on angry YouTube video, *The Telegraph*, August 7, http://www.telegraph.co.uk/women/womens-life/11018413/Burger-King-raped-my-face-claims-model-on-angry-YouTube-video.html [Accessed March 24, 2016].

55 Cf. "Model Says She Was 'Face Raped' by Burger King's 'Seven Incher' Blowjob Ad," and related comments, https://www.youtube.com/watch?v=B2ePS90LZvE [Accessed November 30, 2016].

56 Harrison, J. (2012), Huggies pulls ads after dads insulted, *ABC Network*, March 14, http://abcnews.go.com/blogs/lifestyle/2012/03/huggies-pulls-ads-after-dads-insulted/ [Accessed March 24, 2016].

57 *Huggies Dad Test*, https://www.youtube.com/watch?v=j7kX8ZKylD4 [Accessed March 24, 2016].

58 Attardo (1994), op. cit.; Tsakona, op. cit.

59 *Successful petition to remove the Huggies advert in Italy*, https://www.change.org/p/huggies-rimozione-campagna-pubblicitaria-huggies-bimbo-bimba [Accessed March 24, 2016].

60 Waller, D. S. (1999), Attitudes toward offensive advertising: An Australian study, *The Journal of Consumer Marketing* 16 (3): 288–294.

61 Durant and Lambrou, op. cit.; Simpson and Mayr, op. cit.

Part 4

Society within business

Humor's use and roles in the workplace and in organizations

4.1 Humor styles in the workplace

Nicholas A. Kuiper and Nadia B. Maiolino

Humor styles in the workplace

Over the past decade there has been an increasing recognition that humor can play an important role in many different facets of business. Some of the positive benefits of workplace humor include greater team unification, enhanced idea generation, and frustration relief.[1] It has also been proposed that humor can be used as a multifunctional management tool to help achieve a number of positive organizational objectives, including reductions in employee stress, improvements in communication, fostering creativity, and the enhancement of both leadership and group cohesiveness.[2] This deliberate use of humor by supervisors to help generate greater problem solving and creativity in employees of an organization is also a prominent aspect of a model of management humor.[3]

It has been further suggested that humor use can be beneficial in terms of increasing organizational commitment, making negotiations more effective, raising employee satisfaction, increasing productivity, and reducing both absenteeism and turnover. Indeed, a recent meta-analysis found a number of positive benefits that were significantly associated with increased humor use.[4] For employees that used benign humor in the workplace, these benefits included not only a greater ability to cope with workplace stress, enhanced work satisfaction, and increased performance, but also decreases in stress, burnout and work withdrawal. Supervisors that used more humor were also rated more positively by their subordinates, and these subordinates displayed greater workgroup cohesion and better performance, along with reduced absenteeism.

Despite these advances, several investigators have suggested that the investigation of humor in the workplace still remains limited.[3, 4, 5, 6] One major concern relates to the limited research on the detrimental negative effects of humor in the workplace.[4] This is not to say that researchers have been unaware of possible negative effects. It has been long recognized that the use of certain styles of humor, such as aggressive humor, can have a strong negative interpersonal impact that may lead to quite detrimental repercussions in the workplace.[2] The notion of a hostile work environment resulting from the use of negative humor has also resulted in the notion that humor in a business context can be a "double-edged sword." In particular, humor can be positive by facilitating intercultural business meetings, or negative when it leads to undue collusion and exclusion.[7] The downside of negative humor in the workplace is that it may not only be distracting, but may also hurt an employees' credibility or even cause serious offense in a diverse workplace.[1] This negative humor, which is often intended to belittle or intimidate, can thus contribute to an increasingly hostile work environment.

Taken together, these comments suggest that it is important for humor-related research in workplace settings to move towards models of humor that have a multidimensional perspective that considers both positive and negative forms of humor. Accordingly, one goal of the present chapter is to describe and then build upon one contemporary model that clearly asserts that different humor styles can have either positive or negative intrapersonal or interpersonal effects. As described below, this humor styles model was developed by Rod Martin and colleagues to examine four distinct humor styles that individuals may vary on, namely, self-enhancing, affiliative, self-defeating, and aggressive humor.[6, 8]

The present chapter focuses on this humor styles model, as it offers several advantages.[6, 9, 10] First, it is a relatively comprehensive multidimensional model of individual differences in sense of humor that covers both the positive and negative aspects of humor for either self (intrapersonal) or others (interpersonal). To elaborate, self-enhancing humor is an adaptive style that uses positive self-focused humor as an effective coping technique for dealing with stressful life events and experiences. This humor style, which is non-detrimental to others, involves the ability to generate a humorous perspective on life in order to reduce negative emotional and cognitive responses to upsetting events and circumstances. Affiliative humor is also an adaptive humor style, but here the focus is on using benign positive humor to enhance and facilitate social relationships and interactions with others, often leading to enhanced group morale and relationships, and reduced conflict. In contrast to these two adaptive styles, both self-defeating and aggressive humor are considered maladaptive. Self-defeating humor consists of the use of self-focused negative humor that is extremely disparaging and puts oneself down. This excessively critical humorous ridiculing of the self is used in a misguided attempt to ingratiate oneself with others, and seek their acceptance and approval. Aggressive humor is also a maladaptive humor style that involves ridicule, sarcasm, teasing, and disparagement. However, the focus here is outward, with the deliberate aim of insulting and hurting others in a demeaning and derogatory manner. At a more general level, the advantage of using this 2×2 theoretical framework (adaptive/maladaptive humor style by self/other focus) is that it ensures that a very broad range of positive or negative effects of both positive and negative humor use can be captured in any setting of interest, including the workplace.

A second reason for focusing on the humor styles model as our primary theoretical framework for guiding humor-based research in the business environment is that this model has received a large amount of empirical support over the past decade or so.[6, 10, 11] In a recent interview, Rod Martin indicated that, by now, a large number of empirical studies have examined various facets of his humor styles model, and more continue to appear.[10] These humor studies typically employ the Humor Styles Questionnaire (HSQ), which is a 32-item, self-report measure assessing an individual's level on each of the four humor styles. Sample items from each HSQ subscale are as follows:

- Self-enhancing: *"Even when I am by myself, I am often amused by the absurdities of life."*
- Affiliative: *"I laugh and joke a lot with my close friends."*
- Self-defeating: *"I will often get carried away in putting myself down if it makes my family or friends laugh."*
- Aggressive: *"If someone makes a mistake, I will often tease them about it."*

The associated body of research literature, which includes cross-cultural studies on humor, has offered considerable empirical support for the theoretically expected four-factor structure of the HSQ, corresponding to the four humor styles.[9, 10, 11]

A large number of studies in the humor styles literature also provide evidence of good reliability, validity, and predictive utility for the HSQ and its underlying 2×2 theoretical model.[6, 10, 12] These studies have found that each of the four humor styles are related to various indices of psychological well-being in the expected manner.[9, 10, 12, 13, 14] At the intrapersonal level, for example, those high on self-defeating humor typically show greater levels of depression and anxiety, reduced self-esteem, and a much less positive life orientation; whereas those high on self-enhancing humor show the opposite pattern. Furthermore, higher levels of self-enhancing humor and affiliative humor are also associated with increased levels on other positive psychological indices, such as happiness, gratitude and savoring; whereas higher levels of aggressive and self-defeating humor are linked to significantly lower levels of happiness and gratitude.[13] Interpersonally, a number of studies have also confirmed the theoretically expected relationships between the various humor styles and relevant psychosocial constructs. For example, higher levels of both affiliative and self-enhancing humor were associated with increased empathic concern for others, and significantly greater perspective-taking empathy.[15, 16] In contrast, those high on aggressive humor showed significantly lower levels of empathy for others.

Our final reason for focusing on the humor styles model is that this theoretical platform has already received some initial consideration by investigators interested in examining humor in the workplace. As described below, the work conducted thus far appears to be promising in terms of supporting the utility of using this model to provide a comprehensive examination of sense of humor issues in a business environment.

Current workplace research using the humor styles model

Considerable research has now firmly established that the four humor styles are differentially associated with positive and negative psychological well-being. Both self-enhancing and affiliative humor are often linked to higher levels of well-being (e.g., greater happiness and higher self-esteem); whereas self-defeating humor is linked to a much more negative pattern of well-being (e.g., greater depression and anxiety). These types of relationships have also been examined in the workplace, but with a special emphasis on psychological well-being indices that are of particular relevance to the workplace. As one example, a two-week-long daily diary study in the Dutch automotive sector found that on the days that employees expressed more adaptive humor (affiliative), they were much more engaged in their work; and that on days when they expressed more maladaptive humor (self-defeating), they appeared more emotionally exhausted.[17] This pattern indicates how differential relationships between the humor styles and well-being can also impact directly on performance in the workplace.

Further research has examined the impact of individual humor styles on broader organizational outcomes, such as organizational commitment and satisfaction with co-workers.[18] This survey of over 300 workers in a number of large and small organizations found that both adaptive humor styles (affiliative and self-enhancing) were related to higher organizational commitment, whereas higher levels of aggressive humor showed the opposite relationship. Furthermore, higher levels of affiliative humor, and lower levels of aggressive humor were both associated with greater satisfaction with co-workers.

The effects of supervisor humor styles on employee job-related well-being has also been examined in several studies. As one example, it has been found that when leaders used more self-enhancing humor, their subordinates displayed more job-related positive affect, which could then be associated with greater job satisfaction and other positive job attitudes, such as higher job commitment.[19] However, when leaders displayed more aggressive humor, this had a mild negative impact on the job-related affect displayed by their subordinates. This pattern suggests that self-enhancing humor may play a key role in supervisory–subordinate relationships and well-being.

A similar pattern was also evident in a survey of over 300 supervisor–subordinate dyads in several South Korean organizations.[20] This study also found that greater self-enhancing humor use by a supervisor was positively associated with better job performance and psychological well-being in subordinates. In addition, they also found that greater supervisor affiliative humor was associated with more positive employee psychological well-being, whereas greater supervisor aggressive humor showed the opposite relationship.

A different aspect of the humor styles relationship between supervisors and subordinates was examined in a study determining whether or not the quality of the working relationship between supervisors and subordinates was related to humor styles. Findings indicated that subordinates with higher levels of adaptive humor (self-enhancing and affiliative) liked their supervisors more, showed greater support and loyalty, and also displayed a greater willingness to contribute positively to organizational goals.[21] The pattern was opposite, however, for employees that displayed higher levels of aggressive humor, as they showed much less respect for their supervisors. Interestingly, the humor styles of the supervisor had little impact on the subordinate's perceptions of the quality of their relationship with their supervisors.

Other business-related research has found that an individual's humor styles may also play a role in task persistence. Here, it was found that the amount of time and effort a person spends on a task was the greatest when that individual was high on self-enhancing humor.[22] This persistence to achieve goals is an important element of success in a variety of different business settings (e.g., in pursuing sales, in establishing and building up a business), and it is proposed that the use of self-enhancing humor helps an individual restore and revitalize self-regulatory resources that contribute to enhanced persistence, including resiliency.[9]

Research in the workplace domain has also examined cross-cultural distinctions in the patterns of humor styles displayed by individuals. One study reported that American business managers working in the Middle East were significantly higher on both self-enhancing and self-defeating humor than their Egyptian and Lebanese employees.[23] Based on this pattern, it was suggested that American managers should be careful in using either of these two self-focused humor styles when attempting to make themselves more approachable to their employees. In particular, it was suggested that Arab employees might misinterpret the use of self-defeating humor, and consider it to be indicative of a less capable manager. In turn, this negative impression could then have a detrimental impact on manager–employee relationships, contributing to more difficulties in the workplace.

More generally, our brief overview suggests that the continuing use of the humor styles model to guide further research in the business domain is a promising and worthwhile endeavor. By highlighting the fundamental multidimensional nature of sense of humor, this model can help expand and clarify our knowledge regarding the beneficial workplace effects of using adaptive humor styles, such as affiliative or self-enhancing humor. Equally important, however, the use of this model can help to focus our attention on the need to greatly increase our understanding of the possible detrimental impact of the maladaptive humor styles, such as aggressive or self-defeating humor. While workplace investigators have long acknowledged the possibility of detrimental effects of humor use in business settings,[2] the actual amount of research on negative aspects of humor in these settings has been relatively circumscribed.[4] As such, the remainder of this chapter suggests some directions that this research might take.

Extensions of the humor styles model in a business context

The first extension we consider builds upon a recent humor climate approach that has stressed the importance of much more broadly considering the positive or negative nature of the humor typically evident in the workplace, including humor in groups of employees.[5] As highlighted below, this more extensive humor climate may then have pervasive positive or negative effects on other individuals and groups, both within and outside of the organization.

Humor climate approach

Most of the humor styles research to date has considered the primary unit of analysis to be the individual. In other words, this research has typically focused on measuring the humor styles displayed by a given individual (e.g., a supervisor), and then determining how this person's humor styles may have a systematic impact on the workplace construct being investigated (e.g., job satisfaction of employees). Although this focus on individual differences in humor styles has revealed interesting findings, it does not really capture the broader presence and tone (positive or negative) of the typical humor displayed by an entire group of employees. In other words, we still know very little about the more general humor environment the entire group works in; and how this humor climate may then impact on various work-related constructs of interest, such as job commitment, satisfaction, or productivity.

The humor climate model directly addresses this limitation by assessing the predominant positive or negative forms of humor experienced by employees, as an integral component of their workgroup setting.[24] Interestingly, some of these broader humor forms, which include affiliative and aggressive humor, derive, in part, from the original humor styles approach.[8] The resulting model then offers a means of studying these positive and negative humor forms, and their associated effects, at a broad group level, rather than an individual level of analysis.

To illustrate for positive humor use, each member of a workplace group can be asked to complete a Humor Climate Questionnaire (HCQ),[24] which captures overall positive affiliative humor evident in that group (e.g., "*Humor is often used to encourage or support coworkers*"). This positive humor climate within a group provides a non-confrontational technique for workers in that group to interpret work-related events in a humorous and benign manner that can diffuse tension. Ultimately, this can serve to improve both intra-group and other organizational relationships, be they for an individual or an entire group.[5]

The HCQ also assesses two forms of aggressive humor.[24] The first of these, which is labeled negative humor, is directed at another member of the same group of employees (e.g., "*If someone makes a mistake, they often will be ridiculed by others in the group*"). This aggressive in-group humor involves demeaning and berating group members (e.g., "*My coworkers sometimes use humor to belittle each other*"). Disparaging treatment of a group member may initially foster greater conformity, but often comes at a high cost. In particular, a negative humor climate leads to the erosion of trust and respect within the group, breaking down group solidarity and isolating group members from one another and the organization. Ultimately this can lead to a serious deterioration in work performance that severely undermines group effectiveness in meeting organizational commitments and expectations.[5]

The second form of aggressive humor captured by the Humor Climate Questionnaire is labeled "out-group humor."[24] Group members can use this form of negative humor to derogate and denigrate those outside of their specific group of co-workers. This can include both immediate and upper managers (e.g., "*My coworkers often make jokes about management*"), as well as more general put-downs of the entire organization and its policies (e.g., "*Management policies are often a target for jokes or ridicule among my coworkers*"). This out-group directed humor can have some positive functions by fostering greater group cohesiveness. Again, however, this can come at considerable cost, as the excessive use of out-group aggressive humor can lead to social and professional isolation of the group from the rest of the organization, and its goals and aspirations.

Although the humor climate model is a very recent addition to the psychological literature on humor in the workplace, it has already generated some promising initial empirical support. To begin, it has been demonstrated that the self-report measure central to this model, namely, the Humor Climate Questionnaire (HCQ), has very good psychometric properties pertaining to reliability and validity.[24] Even more importantly, however, this broad humor climate measure can predict additional levels of job commitment and satisfaction, above and beyond what can be accounted for by individual differences in humor styles. In other words, these researchers found that a more positive workgroup humor climate, as assessed via the HCQ, predicted significantly more job satisfaction and commitment than could be attributed to any of the individual humor styles displayed by workgroup participants in a group. Similarly, a higher level of negative humor climate for a given workplace group predicted significantly lower levels of job commitment and satisfaction than would be expected from a consideration of individual humor styles alone. As such, these findings clearly support the importance and increased utility of considering group-related humor climate in the workplace, in addition to a focus on individual differences in humor styles.

More generally, these findings argue for the further development of an integrative theoretical model of humor styles in the workplace that factors in considerations of group-level humor, as well as individual differences in sense of humor. In refining and testing this model it would be quite beneficial for further research in this domain to explore not only how these group versus individual difference aspects of humor in the workplace may relate to a much wider set of workplace relevant constructs, but also how these two different aspects of humor use in the workplace may interact with one another. To date, very little is known about humor use in the workplace beyond the individual level, and the integration of a group-level perspective with an individual differences approach would result in a more comprehensive theoretical model for guiding further research.

In the remainder of this chapter we suggest that such a model could be used to help explore the possible role of humor with respect to several important societal concerns that are also highly relevant to the workplace, such as sexism, racism, prejudice, and discrimination. We further suggest that the development of this integrated model could be informed by drawing from recent work that focuses specifically on aggressive humor styles that are derogatory in nature.[25, 26] This work offers a number of insights at both the individual and group level, in terms of furthering our understanding of both the positive and negative effects of using aggressive humor styles that are derogatory.

Derogatory aggressive humor in a business environment

Derogatory humor (also referred to as disparagement humor) has been defined as "a humorous communication that is intended to elicit amusement through the denigration, derogation or belittlement of a given target" (p. 163).[25] Although still relatively limited in scope, most of the contemporary humor theory and research investigating the social impact of this aggressive humor style can trace its origins back to Martineau's seminal work on disparagement humor.[27] Martineau's theory is briefly highlighted below, followed by an application to the workplace context.

Martineau's theoretical perspective

Fundamental to Martineau's theory is the concept of in-group versus out-group. As one example, an in-group might consist of a small tightly-knit group of male employees that work closely together in the same department. For this particular in-group, an example out-group might be upper level managers, or female employees that work together in another department of this same company. Building on these group distinctions, the positive or negative social consequence of derogatory humor then depends upon two additional factors. The first is whether the derogatory humor is directed at either an in-group (intragroup) or an out-group (intergroup). The second is whether the person using this derogatory humor is a member of the in-group or the out-group. Using these concepts, it has been proposed that derogatory humor delivered by an out-group member may lead to members of the recipient in-group showing greater group cohesion and solidarity, as they bond together and rally against these highly abrasive comments. As such, this derogatory humor style can have a positive in-group effect by serving as a social lubricant and enhancing relationships among members of the in-group. At the same time, however, these denigrating humorous comments can also lead to negative intergroup effects by fostering a collective hostile attitude that may contribute toward further intergroup conflict. In addition, depending on the in-group's ability to deal with such abrasive humorous comments over a substantial period of time, there may also be negative effects that emerge, such as severe demoralization and disintegration of the in-group.[25]

According to Martineau's theory, other combinations are also possible.[27] For example, the use of derogatory humor by one member of a group that is directed towards another member of that same group may have some positive effects by encouraging group members to conform to prevailing group norms. In fact, this pattern was found in a recent study that demonstrated that participants who observed the aggressive humorous ridicule of others actually inhibited their own behaviors to conform more to group values and opinions, thus avoiding "jeer pressure."[28]

Further illustrations are provided in a recent review which concludes that derogatory humor can help shape social relationships and result in social consequences that range from positive to negative, depending on the specific group context and factors described above.[25] This conclusion has been reinforced in a recent theoretical review on the use of derogatory humor as a delegitimization strategy, to both devalue and dehumanize members of an out-group.[29] This theory points out that humor is a fundamental aspect of social life, and that the use of negative aggressive humor styles, such as derogatory humor, can have very serious negative intergroup consequences, including heightened discrimination, prejudice, sexism, and racism. As such, this review concludes that derogatory humor can play a key role in devaluing out-group members, with this type of aggressive humor style evident in much of everyday life, including the workplace.

Derogatory humor and the humor styles model in the workplace

From the preceding theoretical overview, it is clear that derogatory aggressive humor can have important ramifications in the work setting. As such we propose that a humor styles model that is applied to the workplace should expand to include a more detailed focus on derogatory humor and its consequences. This aggressive humor style has direct application to the business and society interface, as the use of a derogatory humor style can serve to develop and maintain a negative organizational environment. In turn this toxic climate can help foster serious detrimental effects in the workplace that are associated with both sexist and racist prejudice and discrimination. From a business and society perspective, these detrimental effects may span a number of issues, including reduced leadership effectiveness, reduced employee well-being, a poor organizational climate, less group cohesiveness, and reduced productivity.[30]

Empirical work has demonstrated some of the damaging effects of derogatory humor in the workplace. In this research, both male and female participants were first exposed to either a non-sexist or sexist joke.[31] Following this, participants then evaluated a work scenario in which a female employee was being patronized by her male boss. Consistent with the position that societal sexism is also quite evident in a business environment, it was found that those participants exposed to a sexist joke subsequently showed more tolerance of this discriminatory behavior by the male boss towards the female employee. This increased tolerance was then attributed to a prejudice releasing function for sexist humor. In other words, the use of sexist humor served to make it more socially acceptable to engage in subsequent discriminatory behaviors that can then demean and diminish others in this workplace.

Measuring derogatory humor in workplace settings

Findings such as those described above indicate that it would be very worthwhile to continue with additional research on the detrimental impact of derogatory humor in a business environment. In pursuing this work, we would encourage the use of a variety of recent measures of derogatory humor. One candidate, for example, is to use the Humor Climate Questionnaire (HCQ).[24] As described previously, this measure assesses both negative humor within an in-group, as well as negative humor that is out-group focused. This fundamental group distinction maps directly onto Martineau's original formulations regarding derogatory humor,[27] as well as subsequent theoretical extensions by other researchers.[25, 26] Accordingly, using the HCQ in further research in this domain is certainly warranted, from both a theoretical and empirical perspective.

We would also encourage the use of other measures of derogatory humor, such as the Negative Humor Questionnaire.[30] Much like the HCA, this brief 13–item scale was also developed specifically for use in organizational settings, but captures two slightly different dimensions of negative humor. The first is 'domination' ("*Telling a put-down joke about someone to their face could help me gain an advantage over them*"); whereas the second is 'denigration' ("*It is not OK for my good friend who is from another ethnic group to tell jokes about my ethnic group*").

The NHQ provides an assessment of a person's tendency to use these two negative dimensions of humor to enhance their own power and privilege in an organization.[30] This individual power focus is distinct from the organizational humor climate focus of the HCQ, suggesting these two scales could be used to examine different research issues pertaining to derogatory humor use in the workplace. For example, it has been suggested the NHQ might be used as an employee screening tool, with careful thought being given to the appropriateness of hiring those that obtain high derogatory humor scores on this measure.[30] In addition, it has also been proposed that those scoring low on the Negative Humor Questionnaire might be those too easily offended by more harmless humor in the workplace.[30] Both of these suggestions could be empirically evaluated in further research on derogatory humor use in the workplace. Such research, with its focus on the effects of an individual's level of derogatory humor (as assessed by the NHQ), could also include a broader organizational focus on in-group versus out-group humor climates (as assessed by the HCQ). Furthermore, if these assessments also included the original four humor styles (as assessed by the HSQ), then future work employing this combination of humor measures could yield a much more comprehensive theoretical–empirical picture of humor use, and its effects, in the workplace.

Refining derogatory humor theory

Over the years, Martineau's theory has provided a useful conceptual framework for examining various societal effects of disparaging humor. Further research has spurred the development of additional explanatory constructs involving the use and effects of derogatory humor. These additional constructs can then enhance our understanding of the various factors that may be relevant to the use of derogatory humor in the workplace. One example of such a construct is perceived norm theory.[32] This concept derives from reviews of the literature on disparagement humor, which have revealed that not all of the hypotheses advanced by Martineau in his original theory have been supported by subsequent research. In particular, some research shows that being exposed to derogatory humor does not necessarily instigate a more negative view of the targeted group. Instead, this derogatory humor functions as a release mechanism for prejudices that already exist in some members of the group, but are not typically revealed as outward behavioral expressions of disparagement or discrimination. In other words, for group members that already have sexist attitudes, the telling of a demeaning sexist joke or humorous sexist comment is perceived by these individuals as evidence of the existence of work-setting norms that are highly tolerant of discrimination against women. In turn, this perception of increased tolerance or acceptance serves to release their own prejudices in this setting, which are then expressed in the form of additional demeaning and discriminatory behaviors towards women. Several examples of research studies showing this perceived norm effect in a business context are described in a recent review.[25]

Effects of individual differences on derogatory humor

In addition to providing support for perceived norm theory, contemporary research highlights the importance of individual differences between group members that can either limit or enhance the negative effects of derogatory humor in a business setting. As one example, in the study described previously, it was also found that the effects of sexist humor on the degree of tolerance for the male boss's patronizing behaviors towards his female employee were most evident for participants that scored high on an individual difference construct of hostile sexism.[25]

Further research studies have examined the effects of social power and disparagement humor on the evaluations of subordinates. Of particular relevance in the present context is that the demeaning effects of derogatory humor regarding subordinate employees was most pronounced when this humor was directed at individuals in leadership positions of power.[33] In contrast, this same derogatory humor, when directed towards those in low power positions, showed virtually no evidence for subsequent discrimination and devaluation of the employees.

Taken together, these studies suggest that it is important for any future research examining the effects of derogatory humor in a business context to also consider the potentially important role of individual difference factors. These individual differences could then be incorporated into an extended humor styles model that could provide a more complete theoretical framework for guiding future research. To illustrate further, building on prior work,[26] one aspect of this research approach might further explore the relationships between the humor styles and other well-established individual difference predictors of prejudice-related behaviors. In this study, it was reported that those scoring higher on individual difference predictors of intergroup prejudice, including modern racism and social dominance orientation, also endorsed much higher levels of aggressive humor use.[26] Accordingly, further research in a business context might determine how the specific dimensions of denigrating and dominating humor identified previously, may also relate to these racist attitudes and social dominance views. This identification of prejudice-prone individuals would then help determine more precisely the most important individual difference characteristics that can serve to enhance the negative sexist or racist effects of derogatory humor use in a business setting.

A theoretical–empirical elaboration of the humor styles model might also determine if "cavalier humor beliefs" should be incorporated as an important individual difference construct that is related to the expression of sexist or racist behaviors in the workplace. Individuals endorsing cavalier humor beliefs have the uncritical view that "a joke is just a joke."[34] In other words, these individuals adopt a nonchalant and lighthearted approach to all forms of humor, including derogatory humor that can be quite harmful or detrimental to others. By dismissing the possibility of any harm coming to the groups or individuals that are being made fun of, these cavalier humor beliefs provide a psychologically benign cover of acceptance and legitimacy for further devaluations of out-groups that are not liked. Future work in a business setting might thus establish if those with heightened cavalier humor beliefs also show greater acceptance of the prejudicial attitudes and views that underlie much of derogatory humor.[34] If this is the case, then this work might also consider means of challenging these beliefs and replacing them with more grounded perceptions of the true negative impact of derogatory humor, be it in the workplace or elsewhere.

Concluding comments

Research to date has clearly shown the importance of humor in the workplace. This research is also beginning to reveal the complex relationships that exist between humor, different aspects of the workplace, and their interaction with broader societal issues such as sexism, discrimination, and prejudice. In the past, considerable emphasis has been placed on the notion that humor is positive, and can thus only serve to provide many benefits to business and society. This traditional view, however, has been challenged by current theory and research that provides increasing evidence that not all humor is good. In fact, this work has described several very detrimental aspects of humor that can have a profound negative impact on the workplace and society

It is against this theoretical–empirical backdrop that we have proposed the humor styles model as a particularly useful theoretical tool to explore humor-related issues in the business environment, and how these issues may then intersect with broader societal concerns. A fundamental tenet of this model is the consideration of the effects of both positive and negative humor in the workplace. This makes the humor styles model an ideal vehicle for redressing the imbalance towards positive humor that is often seen in the workplace research domain. Moving towards a more balanced theoretical–empirical framework provides the opportunity to more fully consider the pros and cons of such business-related issues as attempting to teach humor skills or styles in the workplace, or examining how group-level constructs of humor, such as humor climate, may interact with individual differences in humor styles. Using this integrative model also allows us to draw from the associated domains of social psychology and personality research to investigate the potential positive and negative effects of using derogatory aggressive humor in workplace settings. By proposing a theoretical orientation that combines several different levels of analyses, including group effects of humor as well as individual difference factors, our proposed extensions of the humor styles model may thus help us understand more clearly major societal issues that impinge heavily on the workplace, including sexism, racism, prejudice, and discrimination.

References

1 Lyttle, J. (2007). The judicious use and management of humor in the workplace. *Business Horizons, 50*, 239–245.
2 Romero, E. J., & Cruthirds, K. W. (2006). The use of humor in the workplace. *Academy of Management Perspectives, 20*(2), 58–69.
3 Wood, R. E., Beckman, N., & Rossiter, J. R. (2011). Management humor: An asset or liability? *Organizational Psychology Review, 1*(4), 316–318.
4 Mesmer-Magnus, J., Glew, D. J., & Viswesvaran, C. (2012). A meta-analysis of positive humor in the workplace. *Journal of Managerial Psychology, 27*(2), 155–190.
5 Blanchard, A. L., Stewart, O. J., & Cann, A. (2014). Making sense of humor at work. *The Psychologist-Manager Journal, 17*(1), 49–70.
6 Martin, R. (2007). *The psychology of humor: An integrative approach.* New York: Academic Press.
7 Rogerson-Revell, P. (2007). Humor in business: A double-edged sword—A study of humor and style shifting in intercultural business meetings. *Journal of Pragmatics, 39*, 4–28.
8 Martin, R. A., Puhlik-Doris, P., Larsen, G., Gray, J., & Weir, K. (2003). Individual differences in the uses of humor and their relation to psychological well-being: Development of the Humor Styles Questionnaire. *Journal of Research in Personality, 37*, 48–75.
9 Kuiper, N. A. (2012). Humor and resiliency: Towards a process model of coping and growth. *Europe's Journal of Psychology, 8*(3), 475–491.
10 Martin. R. A., & Kuiper, N. A. (2016). Three decades investigating humor and laughter: An interview with Professor Rod Martin. *Europe's Journal of Psychology: Special Issue on Psychological Investigations of Humor and Laughter, 12*(3), 498–512.
11 Kuiper, N. A. (2016). Psychological investigations of humor and laughter: Honoring the research contributions of Professor Rod Martin. *Europe's Journal of Psychology: Special Issue on Psychological Investigations of Humor and Laughter, 12*(3), 312–319.
12 Kuiper, N. A., Grimshaw, M., Leite, C., & Kirsh, G. (2004). Humor is not always the best medicine: Specific components of sense of humor and psychological well-being. *Humor: International Journal of Humor Research, 17*, 135–168.
13 Maiolino, N. B., & Kuiper, N. A. (2014). Integrating humor and positive psychology approaches to psychological well-being. *Europe's Journal of Psychology: Special Issue on Humor, Well-being and Health, 10*(3), 557–570.
14 Maiolino, N., & Kuiper, N. A. (2016). Examining the impact of a brief humor exercise on psychological well-being. *Translational Issues in Psychological Science: Special Issue on Humor, 2*(1), 4–13.
15 Ford, T. E., McCreight, K. A., & Richardson, K. (2014). Affective style, humor styles and happiness. *Europe's Journal of Psychology: Special Issue on Humor, Well-being and Health, 10*(3), 451–463.
16 Guenter, H., Schreurs, B., Van Emmerik, H., Gijsbers, W., & Van Iterson, A. (2013). How adaptive and maladaptive humor influences well-being at work: A diary study. *Humor: International Journal of Humor Research, 26*(4), 573–594.
17 Hampes, W. (2014). The relation between humor styles and empathy. *Europe's Journal of Psychology: Special Issue on Humor, Well-being and Health, 10*(3), 34–45.
18 Romero, E. J., & Arendt, L. A. (2011). Variable impacts of humor styles on organizational outcomes. *Psychological Reports, 108*(2), 649–659.

19 Unal, Z. M. (2014). Influence of leader's humor styles on the employee's job-related affective well-being. *International Journal of Academic Research in Accounting, Finance, and Management Sciences, 4*(3), 201–211.

20 Kim, T. Y., Lee, D. R., & Wong, N. Y. S. (2015). Supervisor humor and employee outcomes: The role of social distance and affective trust in supervisor. *Journal of Business Psychology*, online version April 22, 2015.

21 Wisse, B., & Rietzschel, E. (2014). Humor in leader-follower relationships: Humor styles, similarity and relationship quality. *Humor: International Journal of Humor Research, 27*(2), 249–269.

22 Cheng, D., & Wang, L. (2014). Examining the energizing effects of humor: The influence of humor on persistence behavior. *Journal of Business Psychology*, published on-line December 27, 2014.

23 Kalliny, M., Cruthirds, K. W., & Minor, M. S. (2006). Differences between American, Egyptian and Lebanese humor styles: Implications for international management. *International Journal of Cross Cultural Management, 6*(1), 121–134.

24 Cann, A., Watson, A. J., & Bridgewater, E. A. (2014). Assessing humor at work: The humor climate questionnaire. *Humor: International Journal of Humor Research, 27*(2), 307–323.

25 Ford, T. E. (2015). The social consequences of disparagement humor: Introduction and overview. *Humor: International Journal of Humor Research, 28*(2), 163–169.

26 Hodson, G., MacInnis, C., & Rush, J. (2010). Prejudice-relevant correlates of humor temperaments and humor styles. *Personality and Individual Differences, 49*, 546–549.

27 Martineau, W. H. (1972). A model of the social functions of humor. In J. H. Goldstein & P. E. McGhee (eds.), *The psychology of humor*, 101–125, New York: Academic Press.

28 Janes, L., & Olson, J. (2015). Humor as an abrasive or a lubricant in social situations: Martineau revisited. *Humor: International Journal of Humor Research, 28*(2), 271–288.

29 Hodson, G., & MacInnis (2016). Derogating humor as a delegitimization strategy in intergroup contexts. *Translational Issues in Psychological Science, 2*(1), 63–74.

30 Cruthirds, K. W., Wang, Y. J., & Romero, E. J. (2013). Insights into negative humor in organizations: Development of the Negative Humor Questionnaire. *Journal of Business Management, 19*(3), 7–18.

31 Ford, T. E. (2000). Effects of sexist humor on tolerance of sexist events. *Personality and Social Psychology Bulletin, 26*, 1094–1107.

32 Ford, T. E., Richardson, K., & Petit, W. E. (2015). Disparagement humor and prejudice: Contemporary theory and research. *Humor: International Journal of Humor Research, 28*(2), 171–186.

33 Arguello, C., Willis, G. B., & Carretero-Dios, H. (2012). The effects of social power and disparagement humor on the evaluations of subordinates. *Revista de Psicologia Social, 27*(3), 323–336.

34 Hodson, G., Rush, J., & MacInnis, C. (2010). A joke is just a joke (Except when it isn't): Cavalier humor beliefs facilitate the expression of group dominance motives. *Journal of Personality and Social Psychology, 99*(4), 660–682.

4.2 The value of positive humor in the workplace

Enhancing work attitudes and performance

Daryl Peebles, Angela Martin, and Rob Hecker

Introduction

The purpose and value of humor as a human characteristic has been debated by philosophers for centuries. However, the use of humor in workplaces still remains a contentious issue in management theory. Some academics and philosophers praise humor and encourage its use, particularly as a coping and social cohesion mechanism; others see it as a frivolous distraction from the job at hand or as a potentially destructive form of communication.

Although the primary focus of this chapter is on the use of humor within a workplace context, the principles discussed may be applicable to many settings including families; schools (management, teaching and administrative staff and students); hospitals (medical personnel, administrative staff, patients and visitors); religious institutions; social, recreational and sports clubs; community groups, etc. Any situation in which humans congregate is a rich environment for humor use with all its potential positive benefits despite possible negative consequences.

This chapter will provide a review of the intersection between humor as a positive human attribute and its relationship to contemporary workplace management practices and outcomes. It commences with an overview of the history of humor studies and examines the potential benefits of this human attribute. It then examines the styles of humor used and discusses the appropriateness of differing humor styles within workplaces. The chapter then focuses specifically on the use of humor in workplaces, examining both the benefits and potential challenges of using humor as well as addressing in particular humor's impact on workplace stress, leadership and fun-team climates. Finally, the chapter turns to a discussion of contemporary management and the emergence of Positive Psychology. We conclude by discussing the construct of Psychological Capital (*PsyCap*), a psychological resource that enhances workplace performance, its relationship with 'positive humor,' and research opportunities associated with understanding the potential workplace benefits that may be achieved by facilitating PsyCap and positive humor development in tandem.

Humor: an overview

Humor is an inherent human trait universally existing in all cultures and throughout history, transcending language, geography and time.[1] Despite its ubiquity as a desirable human attribute, humor tended to be ignored or downplayed by organizational scientists and, until the late 1980s, comparatively little research had been done to explore humor's purpose in the overall realm of human experience.[2] Some notable exceptions to this assertion include Roy[3] who, in studying boredom among employees in organizations, became aware of rituals among small groups of workers that included joking and bantering. He concluded that worker boredom and fatigue was alleviated by this 'horseplay.'

Many theories of humor and laughter have been postulated by philosophers over the past two millennia commencing with Plato (428–348 BC) who saw humor as being one's amusement towards relatively powerless people in a malicious manner. Following Plato, philosophers including Aristotle, Cicero, Thomas Hobbes, Rene Descartes, Francis Hutcheson, David Harley, Immanuel Kant, George Santayana and Henri Bergson, as well as psychoanalyst Sigmund Freud were amongst those adding their theories to the debate.[4] Contemporary theories of humor have evolved over the past few decades.[5]

The human expression of laughter arises from a variety of situations or stimuli that have little in common, thus making the identification of an underlying principle extremely difficult if not impossible. It may be triggered by a pleasant surprise; being told an amusing story, anecdote or joke; or observing an incident or pictorial representation of something that leads to amusement. There are seven primary types of laughter: humorous, social, ignorance, anxiety, derision, apologetic and tickling.[6] Laughter may be caused by various non-humorous stimuli such as embarrassment, laughing gas (nitrous oxide), and can be triggered by other people's laughter.[7] Humor in the form of an amusing story, image or situation, as noted above, is therefore only one of the many stimuli that may lead to laughter. It is humor that remains the focus of this chapter. However, not everybody views humor in the same way. Personal taste plays a crucial part in humor appreciation, and these tastes may change over time, even within short periods of time as moods change.[8] Different responses to certain attempts at humor are also possible through misunderstandings, ambiguity, language differences or the lack of a common understanding of basic concepts on which the humor is based. Irony is particularly vulnerable to misunderstanding.[9]

Humor styles

Differing opinions around the use of humor in a business setting appear to stem from a lack of clarity around the 'style' of humor being considered in a workplace context. Research aiming to understand humor styles has considered both positive and negative forms. 'Positive humor' is the focus of this chapter and is regarded as humor that is inclusive and uplifting, and that satisfies definitions of the styles identified and labeled as 'affiliative' and 'self-enhancing.'[10] This style of humor does not target or attack others, nor does it marginalize them. It is humor that can make light of a situation or some behaviors without another person feeling compromised. This is popularly described as using humor to lift people up—not put them down.

A Humor Style Questionnaire developed by Martin et al.[11] provided a tool for researchers to differentiate the four humor style preferences being displayed in workplaces. This enabled more targeted and meaningful research to be undertaken. Researchers were now able to specifically examine the style of humor used and determine whether it is predominantly affiliative, inclusive and uplifting. This enabled organizational research regarding whether or not this positive style of humor is of value in terms of enhanced worker attitude and workplace performance leading to improvements in productivity.

The four 'styles' of humor identified are:

- affiliative humor (in which one laughs and jokes with friends and colleagues);
- aggressive humor (in which one laughs and jokes at the expense of others—usually in an attempt to belittle or demean them);

- self-enhancing humor (in which one attempts to cheer oneself with uplifting self-focused humor to help change perspective or counter stressors);
- self-defeating humor (in which one uses negative self-directed humor at one's own expense, or allows or encourages others to use negative humor toward them at their expense).

Affiliative and self-enhancing humor styles are described as being relatively healthy or adaptive, whilst aggressive and self-defeating humor styles are relatively unhealthy or maladaptive and potentially detrimental.[12] This chapter labels the two style groupings as 'positive' and 'negative' respectively, to align with the emphasis on positivity promoted through Positive Psychology which is discussed later in the chapter.

A common mistake made when trying to find universality in theories of humor and laughter is the expectation that an 'ontology of humor' exists—that is, that humor and laughter can easily cross all boundaries including cultural, generational and gender, etc.

This is clearly impractical as, for example, word-plays and puns do not translate easily across languages or jokes made within the context of cultural norms may not be understood by people with no knowledge of those cultures. However, the Humor Styles Questionnaire has been used extensively in North America, Europe and Australasia including versions being translated into other languages and successfully used within other cultures including Lebanese Armenian and Italian.[13]

Taking humor a little more seriously: a growing awareness of humor as a beneficial human attribute

Until mid-last century little research had been done in the area of workplace humor as very few organizational scientists, academics and students took the topic seriously. Despite its ubiquity as a desirable human attribute, humor tended to be ignored or downplayed as a useful organizational tool.[14] Most of the books and journal articles written about human emotion up until the 1980s tended to focus on 'negative' emotions.

Prior to studies supporting the use of humor in workplaces, the study of 'laughter' as a phenomenon may have been viewed as frivolous because laughter was not considered a serious activity. Morreall observed that 'although thousands of books and articles have appeared in our century dealing with human emotions and related phenomena, by far the greater number of these has been concerned with such things as fear and anger and anxiety.' He noted that, by comparison, little had been published about more positive phenomena such as laughter.[15]

Workplace humor usually attracted criticism as potentially being offensive, counterproductive and a waste of time. Some organizations held the view that humorous people could not be taken seriously and that if a worker was being playful he/she could not be taking the work seriously enough to actually be productive.[16] It was found that inappropriate humor, especially if used by managers, could have a detrimental effect on employee job satisfaction.[17] There were other arguments against encouraging humor in workplaces based on perceptions of reduced respect for managers;[18] the promotion of sexual harassment, especially if jokes are aimed against women;[19] and the potential for jokes to be made at the expense of any minority group.[20] Significant problems may arise should offensive humor be evident within a workplace. This is a dangerous situation for any workplace given the contemporary ramifications for employers in regard to bullying and sexual harassment.[21]

The opposing perspective suggests that humor can have a positive impact on groups of people including organizations and workplaces as long as the humor is appropriate.

The positive impacts of humor in the workplace: from anecdotal reports to scholarly evidence

In an organizational context, the value of positive humor in human resource development has begun to be recognized. Within contemporary management practices, humor and laughter, once perceived as detrimental to organizational effectiveness, are now being viewed as a potentially positive organizational attributes.[22] Humor is an effective way to promote a healthy work life and improved workplace harmony, and is an effective form of communication cutting across hierarchical boundaries by being multidirectional throughout the organization. A good indicator of an organization's culture is the shared workplace humor and joking patterns. Corporate values and assumptions may also be reflected through workplace humor enabling different insights into the nature of the organization.[23]

Popular books and magazines contain a plethora of case studies detailing the benefits of humor. Among the many case studies examining humor as an important component of organizational culture are Castelli[24] who reported on the Ben & Jerry's ice-cream franchise; Caudron[25] who examined Kodak when it held a dominant position in the photographic film sector; and Hudson[26] who explained the corporate culture of the Brady Corporation from her perspective as its CEO. Hudson reported that getting the people at Brady to loosen up and enjoy themselves fostered a company *esprit de corps* and greater team camaraderie. Humor use in the Brady Corporation started conversations that sparked innovation, helped to memorably convey corporate messages to employees, and increased productivity by reducing stress. The company doubled its sales and almost tripled its net income and market capitalization over seven years.[27] The improvements experienced by the Brady Corporation suggest that promoting fun within the workplace can not only lead to a robust corporate culture, but can also improve business performance. A similar corporate culture initiative from within Southwest Airlines helped facilitate learning, promoted increased creativity and helped employees feel less threatened by change.[28]

The work and influence of the International Society for Humor Studies has broadened the academic lenses through which humor is studied.[29] Studies on laughter and humor have moved away from philosophical and literary analysis into scientific journals where psychological, physiological, sociological and psychiatric approaches are applied to understanding humor and its impacts.[30]

Scholarly research indicates that the acceptance and use of appropriate humor within workplaces has significant benefits for both the employee and organization.[31] Increased job satisfaction and workplace involvement was reported by workers who participated in workplace humor. These workers also displayed better mental health than those who did not report enjoying humor at work. Those initiating the humor were also less likely to resign from their workplace.[32]

Many aspects of a well-functioning organization are enhanced as a result of the appropriate use of humor. Workers using such humor have a positive impact on workplace attributes and productivity indicators such as stress management, organizational commitment, teamwork and cooperation between team members.[33]

Peer-reviewed journal articles and publications reporting on specific workplace outcomes from the use of humor include:

- collaborative team and relationship building;[34]
- improved communications;[35]
- enhanced training outcomes;[36]
- greater employee motivation;[37]
- reduced work stress;[38]
- reduced staff turnover;[39]
- enhanced creativity;[40]
- improved leadership connection;[41]
- increased job satisfaction and engagement;[42]
- increased productivity;[43]
- coping with workplace boredom;[44]
- building a 'fun' organizational culture without having a detrimental effect on workplace outcomes.[45]

In addition to these specific workplace outcomes, Noon and Blyton[46] observed that joking within workplaces is important for group cohesion. They see humor as a key factor in this context as it can help suppress the potential for workplaces to alienate workers and can diminish the negative impacts of some dehumanizing aspects of work.

Humor as a potential workplace de-stressor

Humor is one way humans have historically coped with stress. It has been a useful characteristic in the evolution of the species, allowing us to cope with otherwise unbearable circumstances and enabling humans to cluster together for mutual and collective benefits.[47] From a functionalist psychological perspective, it has been suggested that there is a crucial difference between humor that is beneficial to a group and 'hostile' humor which has a predominantly splintering effect on members of a group rather than being cohesive.[48] A reduction of anxiety levels and an increase in positive moods and emotional response follows the use of humor.[49]

Assuming, as claimed, that the use of appropriate humor does play an important role in dealing with stress,[50] the question remains, how does this relationship work? Laughter may moderate the adverse effects of stress and may also increase a person's level of social support, suggesting that the social support element may be the key when it comes to fighting stress and staying happy. The role of humor in this scenario may be cyclic. A positive sense of humor appears to make a person more approachable and likable. This in turn helps them build and maintain a nurturing social network, resulting in increased social interaction that helps generate more humor.[51]

Humor is an effective self-care option. Tensions can be reduced through recognizing the humor in a situation and having an ability to find something delightful in a current circumstance. To experience joy and laughter, especially if it is with others, will reduce tensions and can be a significant antidote to stress.[52] A sense of humor may moderate stress. An individual taking a humorous perspective on an otherwise stressful situation may be able to make a positive reappraisal of the circumstance and use this as a coping strategy.[53]

Workplaces can be stressful, and strategies for coping with stress and antidotes to stress are needed. Short-term, quick-fix solutions for stress management are inadequate. Longer-term strategies are needed involving preventative stress management and workplace culture changes.[54] In addition, where stressors are inevitable, it would be helpful for organizations to encourage their employees to develop the skills necessary to cope with those stressors.[55]

Killian reported lower levels of burnout in stressful occupations where humor use was prevalent,[56] and Fry reported higher levels of humor-inspired psychological well-being.[57] For example, the use of humor by British sex workers and descriptions of the way humor contributes to the range of defense mechanisms that prostitutes use to cope with their 'extreme' profession have been reported.[58] Humor used by emergency workers within the Queensland State Emergency Service, primarily as a mechanism for coping with the daily stresses of their work, has also been reported.[59]

Humor and leadership

The growing significance of humor as a legitimate addition to a manager's skill-set is evident from colleges and universities responding to a demand from the business sector that humor be included in leadership and management studies. For example, the Singapore Government's Public-Sector Leadership and Management program conducted by the Civil Service College includes a course entitled, 'How Leaders and Managers Can Engage Staff through Humor.' The course synopsis suggests that 'humor provides an important key to creating a more open and responsive workplace.' The synopsis details the potential benefits of humor including less 'burnout,' improved communication, enhanced problem-solving skills and better employee relations. It concludes that through using humor, professionals not only become more productive on the job, but also enjoy their work more.[60]

The emotions of those in positions of power, or with a higher organizational status, have a greater influence on subordinates than the emotions of subordinates have on their superiors. How leaders control or project their emotions will either have an uplifting or a detrimental effect on their subordinates.[61] A 'sense of humor' is one of seven core skills, competencies and qualities that workers look for in their managers or leaders. The other attributes are honesty and integrity; competence and credibility; ability to motivate and inspire; good two-way communication skills; equity and fairness.[62] Earlier research suggests that managers who possess or develop a strong sense of humor make the most effective leaders;[63] will have improved management style and performance;[64] and will be better liked by their subordinates.[65]

The constructive use of humor typifies effective leadership with many incidents being reported that demonstrate a link between humor, laughter and leadership effectiveness. Using humor, even in tense situations, will send a strong positive message from the leader or manager that will 'shift the underlying emotional tone of the interaction.'[66] It was also acknowledged that certain kinds of humor were more appropriate than others.[67] There will be times when the use of humor is inappropriate and an effective leader should have the maturity and judgment to understand this. The potential for a mismatch between what a supervisor may think of as humorous and how that might be perceived by the subordinates is significant. Managerial humor may backfire by reinforcing employee cynicism.[68] Managers may use humor in ways that are offensive or oppressive, may express aggression and hostility, and may reinforce gender stereotypes. Managers who artificially incorporate joking into their control practices reduce humor to a manipulated commodity which has a number of inherent problems, including ethical issues that arise from their attempts to manipulate workplace humor.[69] These examples fall outside the parameters of 'positive humor.'

Fun teams

Workplace culture has an effect on workplace performance[70] and humor is recognized as a significant contributor to maintaining a congenial organizational climate.[71] The positive effect that a happy, 'fun' workplace may have on organizational productivity was addressed as an element of workplace culture within specific organizations.[72] A fun work environment promotes positive and happy moods within employees which may lead to increased organizational commitment and job satisfaction.[73] Providing a fun, supportive workplace may attract workers who see their work as a joy and approach tasks positively. It was proposed that such workers would provide better customer service and would have an abundance of energy and enthusiasm to focus their talents toward the organization's goals and objectives.[74]

When advertising staff vacancies, some organizations use words such as a 'fun team' or a 'fun-filled workplace' to encourage applicants. This is an indication that these businesses recognize the value of making work 'fun.' A study of 'fun workplace activities' led to the development of a framework to help create a positive work environment; aid the attraction and retention of employees and support the organization's efforts in encouraging the general well-being of employees.[75] This framework also proposes that an organization that supports a fun environment will benefit from enhanced creativity, communication, satisfaction and enthusiasm amongst its employees.

Popular management books based on practical corporate examples strongly support the view that working in a fun environment has more productive outcomes than working in a routine environment.[76] Workplace fun has a positive impact on worker attributes such as job satisfaction, morale, pride, creativity and quality,[77] counters the negative effects of stress and burnout[78] and leads to less absenteeism and staff turnover.[79] The two most important benefits of workplaces with a fun culture are increased staff commitment and the organization's attractiveness to potential employees. Increased commitment is reflected in employee attributes such as loyalty and dedication, and staff turnover.[80] The common goal implicit in all these publications is one of moving organizational culture from frustration to fun.

Critical analysis of humor in the workplace

A top-down imposition of 'fun' activities should be avoided. Observations made while witnessing employees of a company participating in games of hopscotch, frisbee throwing and kickball suggested that although there was much clapping, cheering and laughter accompanying these activities, some employees privately confessed to joining in only because they did not want to be seen as 'a bad sport or a party pooper.'[81] The inference here is that for organizational fun and humor to be productive, it should be both positive and organic; that is naturally occurring or inherent within a situation.

The role of humor in providing relief from work pressures, or as a way to counter boredom or to overcome the tedium of repetitive tasks, should not be underestimated. Nor should one ignore its satirical force, especially when directed at managerial targets.[82] Managers perceived to be applying continual pressure on workers to meet increasingly difficult targets or to achieve more productivity with fewer resources, or who are thought of as bullying or intimidating workers, will become unpopular and thus most likely become the butt of workplace jokes.

Such employee humor may include actions that are detrimental to organizations such as ridicule, resistance to instruction or, in the worst-case scenario, sabotage.[83] This is an obvious example of 'negative humor' which may be used by subordinates as a method of dealing with strict managerial control. It offers an informal mechanism through which work groups can define their own identity.[84] This is also commonly referred to as 'subversive humor.' The relationship that exists between supervisors or managers and their subordinates may determine a climate in which the humor is shared (and thus mostly affiliative) or subversive should there be a climate of antagonism between management and the workforce.

A changing work environment calls for changing management practices

Significant changes in societal and workplace values and attitudes have occurred over the past few decades. These are now being reflected in contemporary human resource management practices. Equal opportunity and pay for women, different expectations of work/life balance by younger generations entering the workforce and greater cultural diversity characterize some of these changes.[85] During this period there have been other community and societal changes that have impacted on workplaces leading to a greater focus on the 'softer' aspects of human relations. This now includes consideration being given to employee commitment as well as their capability.[86]

To meet the demands of the emerging globally competitive environment, substantial downsizing through redundancy programs has been a constant feature of many organizations in OECD countries since the 1980s.[87] The consequences for organizations undertaking redundancy programs were not always positive when assessed against organizational and social criteria.[88] Management's endeavors to rationalize staff as well as accommodating the changing workforce considerations mentioned above, have led to increased demands for greater flexibility from workers and the need for job consolidation, multi-skilling and multi-tasking from a management perspective. There has also been a shift toward organizational out-sourcing of some tasks and a greater emphasis on contract, part-time and temporary employee arrangements. These moves toward increasingly lean and efficient workplaces have resulted in employee insecurity and workplace stresses which may lead to new inefficiencies and further organizational and productivity losses.[89]

This period of increasing turbulence has resulted in constant changes within organizations and presents new challenges for their survival in the growing competitive global environment in which they now must operate. In an attempt to satisfy the two seemingly contradictory imperatives of creating lean and efficient workplaces and yet attracting and retaining the best employees available, many programs and workplace development interventions have been proposed, trialed and implemented.[90] Organizations worked on the assumption that sustained competitive advantage could be assured through maintaining a technological edge and the patent protections and government regulations on which they relied. They mostly ignored the human resource development that the changing environment was demanding.[91]

The response of workplaces to this changing environment led to new pressures on workers which necessitated a different human resource management focus to accommodate the ideology of lean production and maintaining high-performance workplace teams.[92] Initially, the organizational investment in 'human capital' had a greater emphasis on developing and maintaining the skills, knowledge and expertise of the workers. This human resource development focus has now extended beyond the job-specific activities and has embraced the broader attributes of a highly functioning worker.[93] Also, as younger people joined the workforce, the career development emphasis became one of employability rather than job security.[94] There was now an appreciation that organizations were only as good as the people within them and that if workers felt threatened, bored, undervalued or discouraged they would not be working at their optimum and therefore would not reach their full potential and value to the organization.[95]

A link between human happiness and human productivity suggests more attention needs to be given to emotional well-being as a causal force within workplaces.[96] As managers' performance impacts on organizational productivity and the economic prosperity of individual businesses, and in turn their nation-states, it is suggested that managers' jobs be changed to ensure a continuation or enhancement of 'happiness' in their work situation. Contemporary understandings about aspects of human behavior that contribute to workplace performance and productivity have been enhanced through the research concerned with the happy, productive worker hypothesis.[97]

Considerations such as worker attitudes and values, and psychological attributes are now accorded a higher prominence in developing human resources in organizations. The underlying premise of emerging Positive Psychology theories supported this approach to human resource development. Positive Psychology advocated that, by changing certain psychological attitudes and resources, a transformative effect on a person's life would follow. It suggested that a person's overall well-being relied on positive emotion together with sound relationships, a sense of accomplishment and having a meaning to one's life.[98]

Integrating Positive Psychology with the study of humor in the workplace

The number of research papers focusing on positive emotions, happiness and factors that promote positivity started to escalate in the mid-1980s.[99] Since the turn of the century, studies have emerged showing that workplaces were benefiting from the application of Positive Psychology in enhancing workplace satisfaction, motivation and productivity.[100] The need for a more positively oriented focus within social and human sciences was recognized, and since that time there has been a plethora of research studies, peer-reviewed journal articles and academic texts published.[101] This emphasis on positivity led to the establishment of a Positive Psychology movement supported by subject-specific journals and national and international conferences.

Positive Psychology has moved from within the traditional disciplinary boundaries of psychology and research has explored its applicability in a number of disciplines and professions including organizational sciences.[102] It now embraces other specific foci of research and application including virtues, excellence, thriving, flourishing, resilience and flow.[103] It has also led to other theoretical frameworks such as Positive Organizational Behavior (POB) and Positive Organizational Scholarship (POS).

Positive Organizational Behavior (POB) refers to 'the study and application of positively oriented human resource strengths and psychological capacities that can be measured, developed, and effectively managed for performance improvement in today's workplace.'[104] POB elements have been linked to higher job satisfaction, and worker happiness and commitment.[105] Additional positive employee characteristics include optimism, kindness, generosity and humor.[106] These attributes are expected to relate to higher levels of individual performance in a work environment. POS is 'concerned primarily with the study of especially positive outcomes, processes, and attributes of organizations and their members.'[107]

Psychological Capital (PsyCap)

Also emerging from the field of Positive Psychology, Luthans, Youssef and Avolio[108] developed a construct called *Psychological Capital* (or PsyCap) based on the capacities of *self-efficacy, resilience, hope* and *optimism* associated with improved employee performance. Although the above-mentioned states—*self-efficacy, resilience, hope* and *optimism*—are the original attributes included in the PsyCap model, other cognitive and affective strengths displayed by individuals were also considered. These included creativity, wisdom, well-being, flow and humor.

> We believe that today's business environment is in great need of more humor and laughter. Not only is a positive, humorous work environment likely to reduce medical and legal costs, it can also enhance teamwork, foster effective problem solving, promote wider acceptance and tolerance of one-self and others, and encourage challenge-seeking and attaining results.[109]

Humor, generally, has a positive social impact for both the deliverer and the recipient of that humor. However, there is a potential downside in which use of inappropriate humor (negative humor) may alienate others and can lead to social isolation for the deliverer and apprehension by those observing this behavior. Thus inappropriate humor may lead to reduced group cohesion.[110]

Research suggests that PsyCap has a positive correlation with performance and satisfaction, mediates between a supportive organizational climate and employee performance, and supports effective organizational change.[111] The view of organizations at the end of the twentieth century was that a competitive advantage would only be achieved if the full potential of their human resources could be realized. It was noted that the optimal use of human resources is harder to replicate by competitors than infrastructure or processes.[112] The development of PsyCap was stimulated by this observation and proposes that these states of self-efficacy, hope, optimism and resilience, in contrast to dispositional traits, can be developed within individuals and converted into commercial gain within an organization.[113]

Surprisingly little research has been done to examine the relationship between PsyCap and humor, a notable exception being Hughes[114] who examined a sense of humor and its relationship with the PsyCap construct and with each of the PsyCap capacities of self-efficacy, hope, optimism and resilience individually. The conclusion reached was that overall sense of humor and PsyCap are positively and significantly related and that there is also a positive relationship between a sense of humor and all the individual PsyCap factors with the exception of hope. Hughes also commented that there was a 'dearth of literature bridging the so-called research-practice gap' in this area.[115]

A subsequent study examined both the PsyCap scores and the use of positive humor within 50 Australian work teams and conducted a confirmatory factor analysis to determine whether or not positive humor fits empirically with the PsyCap construct.[116] Results for a model of positive humor and PsyCap achieved satisfactory fit, showing evidence of convergent validity. Linear regressions were also used to test a series of hypotheses relating to workplace attitudes and performance. Results were mixed but overall supportive of the value of using, or at least allowing, positive humor to be a part of contemporary workplace cultures.[117]

There is, however, a growing discourse as to whether other constructs such as humor should be included in the PsyCap scale.[118] Dawkins et al.[119] warn that the inclusion of additional dimensions without adequate theoretical justification may lead to conceptual confusion about the definition of the PsyCap construct.

Opportunities for future research

Despite the concerns expressed over confusing the PsyCap definition,[120] opportunities exist for further research into the relationships between positive humor, PsyCap and the potential positive effects these may have on worker attitude and performance and workplace productivity. There is also an opportunity to develop and implement specific humor interventions alongside suggested PsyCap-based interventions[121] within workplaces, and to conduct longitudinal research projects to determine the effect, it any, such interventions may have on workplace outcomes.

A fundamental challenge for future research opportunities arises from the assertion that many of the claimed benefits of positivity are yet to be demonstrated.[122] This challenge is based on the observation that only 'half the story' is being addressed by providing positive organizational scholarship tools to help individuals deal with the challenges of life and work. More research is needed within the POB paradigm to help identify and create suitable conditions within organizations to promote learning and growth. To achieve this, researchers working in this field are encouraged to shift their focus from individuals and to concentrate their efforts in determining the positive structural features that are the basis of the social systems in which people live and work.[123]

Conclusions

Combining the organizational benefits of PsyCap and the contributions that appropriate humor may make to any organization, as discussed in this chapter, suggests that workplace managers (as well as leaders of any groups) would be well served to further explore these fundamental human attributes of self-efficacy, hope, optimism, resilience and positive humor. They are all attributes that can be nurtured and developed and all have the potential to contribute to workplace harmony, efficiency and increased productivity through leadership; teamwork; workplace culture; worker health, happiness, attitudes and values; creativity and communication.

References

1 MacHovec, F. J. (2012). *Humor*. Bloomington: Authors Guild BackinPrint.com, iUniverse, Inc.
2 Brief, A. P. (1998). *Attitudes in and around organizations*. Thousand Oaks, CA: Sage, 102; Chapman, A. J. and Foot, H. C. (Eds.) (2007). *Humour and laughter: Theory, research and applications*. London: Wiley.
3 Roy, Donald F. (1959). 'Banana time': Job satisfaction and informal interaction. *Human Organization, 18*, 158–168.
4 Morreall, J. (1987). *The philosophy of laughter and humor*. New York: State University of New York Press.
5 Ziv, A. (1984). *Personality and a sense of humor*. New York: Springer; Fry, W. F. (1994). The biology of humour. *Humor, 7*(2), 111–126; Ruch, W. (1998). Sense of humour: A new look at an old concept. In W. Ruch (Ed.), *The sense of humour: Explorations of a personality characteristic* (3–14). New York: Mouton de Gruyter; Lefcourt, H. M. (2001). *Humor—The psychology of living buoyantly*. New York: Kluwer Academic / Plenum Publishers; Martin, R. A. (2007). *The psychology of humor—an integrative approach*. San Diego, CA: Elsevier Academic Press; McGhee, P. E. (2010). *Humor: The lighter path to resilience and health*. Bloomington, IN: AuthorHouse.

6 Giles, H. and Oxford, G. (1970). Towards a multidimensional theory of laughter causation and its social implications. *Bulletin of the British Psychological Society, 23*(79), 97–105.

7 Attardo, S. (2008). A primer for the linguistics of humor. *The primer of humor research.* Berlin and New York: Mouton de Gruyter, 10.

8 Ross, A. (1998). *The language of humour.* London: Routledge.

9 Ibid.

10 Martin, R. A., Puhlik-Doris, P., Larsen, G., Gray, J. and Weir, K. (2003). Individual differences in uses of humor and their relationship to psychological well-being: Development of the Humor Styles Questionnaire. *Journal of Research in Personality, 37*, 48–75.

11 Ibid.

12 Ibid.

13 Kazarian, S. S. and Martin, R. A. (2006). Humor styles, culture-related personality, well-being, and family adjustment among Armenians in Lebanon. *Humour, 19*(4), 405–423; Penzo, I., Giannetti, E., Stefanile, C. and Sirigatti, S. (2011). Stili umoristici e possibili relazioni con il benessere psicologico secondo una versione italiana dello Humor Styles Questionnaire (HSQ), in Falanga, R., De Caroli, M. E. and Sagone, E. (2014). Humor styles, self-efficacy and pro-social tendencies in middle adolescents. *Procedia—Social and Behavioral Sciences, 127*, 214–218; Falanga, R., De Caroli, M. E. and Sagone, E. (2014). Humor styles, self-efficacy and prosocial tendencies in middle adolescents. *Procedia—Social and Behavioral Sciences, 127*, 214–218.

14 Brief, op. cit.

15 Morreall, J. (1983). *Taking laughter seriously.* New York: State University of New York Press.

16 Brief, op. cit.

17 Infante, D. and Gordon, W. (1989). Argumentativeness and affirming communication style as predictiveness of satisfaction / dissatisfaction with subordinates. *Communication Quarterly, 37*, 81–90; Zillman, D. (1983). Disparagement humor. In McGhee, P. E. and Goldstein, J. H. (Eds.), *Handbook of humor research,* Vol. 1. New York: Springer-Verlag.

18 Duncan, W. J. and Feisal, P. (1989). No laughing matter: Patterns of humor in the workplace. *Organizational Dynamics, 17*, 18–30.

19 McGee, E. and Shelvin, M. (2009). Effect of humor on interpersonal attraction and mate selection. *The Journal of Psychology, 143*(1), 67–77; Hemmasi, M., Graf, L. A. and Russ, G. S. (1994). Gender related jokes in the work place: Sexual humor or sexual harassment? *Journal of Applied Social Psychology, 24*(12), 1114–1128; Smeltzer, L. R. and Leap, T. L. (1988). An analysis of individual reactions to potentially offensive jokes in work settings. *Human Relations, 41*(4), 295–304.

20 Davies, C. (2002). *The mirth of nations.* New Jersey: Transaction Publishers.

21 Quinn, B. A. (2000). The paradox of complaining: Law, humor, and harassment in the everyday work world. *Law and Society, 25*(4), 1151–1186.

22 Barsoux, J. (1996). Why organizations need humour. *European Management Journal, 14*(5), 500–508.

23 Ibid.; Robert, C. and Yan, W. (2007). The case for developing new research on humor and culture in organizations: Toward a higher grade of manure. *Research in Personnel and Human Resource Management, 26*, 205–267; Meyer, J. C. (1997). Humor in member narratives: Uniting and dividing at work. *Western Journal of Communication, 61*(2), 188–208.

24 Castelli, J. (1990). Are you weird enough? *HR Magazine, 38* (September), 1.

25 Caudron, S. (1992). Humor is healthy in the workplace. *Personnel Journal, 71*, 63–68.

26 Hudson, K. M. (2001). Transforming a conservative company—One laugh at a time. *Harvard Business Review, 07* (July/August 2001), 45–53. Retrieved from https://hbr.org/2001/07/transforming-a-conservative-company-one-laugh-at-a-time March 18, 2016.

27 Ibid.

28 Barbour, G. (1998). Want to be a successful manager? Now that's a laughing matter. *Public Management,* July 1998, 6–9.

29 McGraw, P. (2011). The importance of humor research. A serious non-serious research topic. *Psychology Today.* Retrieved from https://www.psychologytoday.com/blog/the-humor-code/201109/the-importance-humor-research.

30 Milner Davis, J. (2003). *Farce.* New Brunswick, NJ: Transaction Publishers.

31 Bass, B. M. and Avolio, B. J. (1994). *Improving organizational effectiveness through transformational leadership.* Beverly Hills, CA: Sage; Crawford, C. B. (1994). Theory and implications regarding the utilization of strategic humour by leaders. *Journal of Leadership Studies, 1*(4), 53–67; Rizzo, B. J., Wanzer, M. B. and Booth-Butterfield, M. (1999). Individual differences in managers' use of humour: Subordinate perceptions of managers' humour. *Communication Research Reports, 16,* 360–369; Mesmer-Magnus, J., Glew, D. and Viswesvaran, C. (2012). A meta-analysis of positive humour in the workplace. *Journal of Managerial Psychology, 27*(2), 115–190.

32 Abramis, D. J. (1992). Humor in healthy organizations. *HR Magazine, 37*(8), 72–75.

33 Romero, E. and Arendt, L. (2011). Variable effects of humor styles on organizational outcomes. *Psychological Reports, 108,* 649–659.

34 Bennis, W. (1997). *Organizing genius: The secrets of creative collaboration.* Reading, MA: Addison-Wesley; Hudson, op. cit.; Dziegielewski, S. F., Jacinto, G. A., Laudadio, A. and Legg-Rodriguez, L. (2003). Humor: An essential communication tool in therapy. *International Journal of Mental Health, 32*(3), 74–90; Chapman and Foot, op. cit.; Romero, E. and Pescosolido, A. (2008). Humor and group effectiveness. *Human Relations, 61,* 395–415.

35 Dziegielewski et al., op. cit.; Zinker, J. C. (2003). Beauty and creativity in human relationships. In Lobb, M. and Amendt-Lyon, N. (Eds.), *Creative license: the art of gestalt therapy* (142–151). New York: Springer; Romero, E. and Cruthirds, K. (2006). The use of humor in the workplace. *Academy of Management Perspectives, 20*(2), 58–69; Meyer, op. cit.; Romero and Pescosolido, op. cit.; Hill, D. (1988). *Humor in the classroom: A handbook for teachers (and other entertainers).* Springfield, IL: Charles C. Thomas.

36 Ziv, A. (1988). Teaching and learning with humor: Experiment and replication. *Journal of Experimental Education, 57,* 5–15; Abramis, D. J. (1991). There is nothing wrong with a little fun. *San Diego Union,* March 19, p. 25; Barbour, op. cit.; Dziegielewski et al., op. cit.

37 Abramis, D. J. (1989). Finding the fun at work. *Psychology Today, 23*(2), 36–38.

38 Hudson, op. cit.; Romero and Cruthirds, op. cit.; Mesmer-Magnus et al., op. cit.

39 Abramis (1992), op. cit.

40 Abramis (1991), op. cit.; Murdock, M. C. and Ganim, R. M. (1993). Creativity and humor: Integration and incongruity. *Journal of Creative Behavior, 27*(1), 57–70; Barbour, op. cit.; Hudson, op. cit.; Romero and Cruthirds, op. cit.

41 Avolio, B. J., Howell, J. M. and Sosik, J. J. (1999). A funny thing happened on the way to the bottom line: Humor as a moderator of leadership style effects. *Academy of Management Journal, 42*(2), 219–227; Romero and Cruthirds, op. cit.; Mesmer-Magnus et al., op. cit.; Priest, R. F. and Swain, J. E. (2002). Humor and its implications for leadership effectiveness. *Humor, 15*(2), 169–189.

42 Davis, A. and Kleiner, B. (1989). The value of humour in effective leadership. *Leadership and Organizational Development Journal, 10*(1), 1–3; Abramis (1989), op. cit.; Abramis (1992), op. cit.; Mesmer-Magnus et al., op. cit.

43 Avolio et al., op. cit.; Romero and Pescosolido, op. cit.

44 Collinson, D. (1988). Engineering humour: Masculinity, joking and conflict in shop floor relations. *Organization Studies, 9*(2), 181–199.

45 Romero and Cruthirds, op. cit.; Robert and Yan, op. cit.

46 Noon, M. and Blyton, P. (1997). *The realities of work.* Basingstoke, UK: Macmillan, 159–160.

47 Lefcourt, op. cit.; Kuiper, N., Martin, R. and Olinger, L. (1993). Coping humor, stress and cognitive appraisals. *Canadian Journal of Behavioral Research, 25*(1), 81–96; Abel, M. (2002). Humor, stress, and coping strategies. *Humor, 15,* 365–381.

48 Lefcourt, op. cit.

49 Abel, M. and Maxwell, D. (2002). Humor and affective consequences of a stressful task. *Journal of Social and Clinical Psychology, 21*(2), 165–190.

50 Berk, L. S., Tan, S. A., Fry, W. F., Napier, B. J., Lee, J. W., Hubbard, R. W., Lewis, J. E. and Eby, W. C. (1989). Neuroendocrine and stress hormone changes during mirthful laughter. *American Journal of Medical Science, 298*(6), 390–396; Dixon, P. (1994). *The truth about AIDS—Aids care education and training international.* Eastbourne, UK: Kingsway Publications; Gavin, J. H. and Mason, R. O. (2004). The virtuous organization: The value of happiness in the workplace. *Organizational Dynamics, 33*(4), 379–392.

51 Martin, R. A. (2004). Sense of humor and physical health: Theoretical issues, recent findings, and future directions. *Humor, 17*(1), 1–19.

52 Lefcourt, H. M. and Martin R. A. (1986). *Humor and life stress.* New York: Springer-Verlag.

53 Martin, R. A. (2001). Humour, laughter, and physical health: Methodological issues and research findings. *Psychological Bulletin, 127*(4), 504–519.

54 Matteson, M. T. and Ivancevich, J. M. (1987). *Controlling work stress.* San Francisco, CA: Jossey-Bass.

55 Jex, S. M. and Bliese, P. D. (1999). Efficacy beliefs as a moderator of the impact of work-related stressors: A multilevel study. *Journal of Applied Psychology, 84*(3), 349.

56 Killian, J. G. (2005). Career and technical education teacher burnout: Impact of humor-coping style and job-related stress. *Humanities and Social Sciences, 65*(9), 3266.

57 Fry, P. (1995). Perfectionism, humor and optimism as moderators of health outcomes and determinants of coping styles of women executives. *Genetic, Social and General Psychology Monographs, 121*(2), 211–245; Sanders, T. (2004). Controllable laughter: Managing sex work through humour. *Sociology, 38*(2), 273–291.

58 Ibid.

59 Moran, C. C. and Massam, M. (1997). An evaluation of humour in emergency work. *The Australian Journal of Disaster and Trauma Studies, 3,* 26–38.

60 Singapore Civil Service College website, https://www.cscollege.gov.sg/About%20Us/Pages/PST-Service.aspx. Accessed November 12, 2013.

61 Anderson, C., Keltner, D. and John, O. (2003). Emotional convergence between people over time. *Journal of Personality and Social Psychology, 84,* 1054–1068.

62 Foster, N. (2005). *Maximum performance: A practical guide to leading and managing people at work.* Cheltenham, UK: Edward Elgar.

63 Bass and Avolio, op. cit.; Romero and Pescosolido, op. cit.

64 Crawford, op. cit.

65 Rizzo et al., op. cit.

66 Goleman, D., Boyatzis, R. and McKee, A. (2002). *Primal leadership.* Boston, MA: Harvard Business School Press, 34–35.

67 Martin et al., op. cit.

68 Collinson, D. L. (2002). Managing humour. *Journal of Management Studies, 39*(3), 269–288.

69 Ibid.

70 Frost, P. J., Moore, L. F., Louis, M. R., Lundberg, C. C. and Martin, J. (Eds.) (1985). *Organizational culture.* Thousand Oaks, CA: Sage Publications.

71 Goleman et al., op. cit.

72 Castelli, op. cit.; Caudron, op. cit.; Hudson, op. cit.

73 Chan, S. C. H. (2010). Does workplace fun matter? Developing a useable typology of workplace fun in a qualitative study. *International Journal of Hospitality Management, 29*(4), 720–728.

74 Berg, D. (2001). The power of a playful spirit at work. *Journal for Quality and Participation, 24*(2), 57–62.

75 Chan, op. cit.

76 Von Oech, R. (1983). *A whack on the side of the head.* Menlo, CA: Creative Think; Lundin, S. C., Paul, H. and Christensen, J. (2000). *FISH!* London: Omnibus, Hodder and Stoughton; Yerkes, L. (2007). *Fun works: Creating places where people love to work.* San Francisco, CA: Berrett-Koehler Publishers.

77 Murdock and Ganim, op. cit.; Barbour, op. cit.; Deal, T. and Kennedy, A. (1999). *The new corporate cultures.* London: Perseus Books.

78 Hudson, op. cit.; Romero and Cruthirds, op. cit.

79 Abramis, op. cit.; Abner, M. (1997). Corporate America takes fun seriously. *Women in Business, 49*(5), 42.

80 Ford, R., Newstrom, J. and McLaughlin, F. (2004). Making workplace fun more functional. *Industrial and Commercial Training, 36*(3),117–120.

81 Critchley, S. (2002). *On humour.* New York: Routledge.

82 Taylor, P. and Bain, P. (2003). Subterranean worksick blues: Humour as subversion in two call centres. *Organization Studies, 24*(9), 1487–1509.

83 Linstead, S. (1985). Jokers wild: The importance of humour and the maintenance of organisational culture. *Sociological Review, 33*(4), 741–767.

84 Collinson, op. cit.

85 Nankervis, A. R., Compton, R., Baird, M. and Coffey, J. (2011). *Human resource management:
Strategy and practice* (7th ed.). South Melbourne, Victoria: Cengage Learning Australia.

86 Stone, R. (2008). *Managing human resources.* Milton, Queensland: John Wiley & Sons Australia,
Ltd, pp. 12 and 350.

87 Worrall, L., Campbell, F. and Cooper, C. (2000). Surviving redundancy: The perceptions of
UK managers. *Journal of Managerial Psychology, 15*(5), 460–476; Gandolfi, F. (2005). How do
organizations implement downsizing? An Australian and New Zealand study. *Contemporary
Management Research, 1*(1), 57–68; Zimmerer, T. W., Scarborough, N. M. and Wilson, D. (2008).
Essentials of entrepreneurship and small business management. New Jersey: Pearson Education Inc.;
Stone, op. cit.; Nankervis et al., op. cit.

88 Morris, J. R., Cascio, W. F. and Young, C. E. (1999). Downsizing after all these years: Questions
and answers about who did it, how many did it, and who benefited from it. *Organizational
Dynamics, 27*(3), 78–87.

89 Kumar, P., Murray, G. and Schetagne, S. (1999). *Workplace change in Canada: Union perceptions of impacts, responses and support systems.* Kingston, Ontario, Canada: IRC Press, Queen's
University.

90 Powell, T. C. (1995). Total quality management as competitive advantage: A review and empirical study. *Strategic Management Journal, 16*(1), 15–37.

91 Morris et al., op. cit.; Luthans, F., Luthans, K. W. and Luthans, B. C. (2004). Positive psychological
capital: Beyond human and social capitals. *Business Horizons, 41*(1), 45–50.

92 Kumar et al., op. cit.

93 Stone, op. cit.; Nankervis et al., op. cit.

94 Parker, P. and Inkson, K. (1999). New forms of career: The challenge for human resource management. *Asia Pacific HRM, 37*(3), 76–85.

95 Berg, op. cit.

96 Oswald, A. J., Proto, E. and Sgroi, D. (2014). *Happiness and productivity.* JOLE 3rd version,
retrieved from http://www2.warwick.ac.uk/fac/soc/economics/staff/eproto/workingpapers/
happinessproductivity.pdf, May 16, 2015.

97 Hosie, P. J., Sevastos, P. P. and Cooper, C. L. (2006). *Happy-performing managers—the impact of
affective wellbeing and intrinsic job satisfaction in the workplace.* Cheltenham, UK: Edward Elgar.

98 Seligman, M. E. P. and Csikszentmihalyi, M. (2000). Positive Psychology: An introduction.
American Psychologist, 55(1), 5–14.

99 Fineman, S. (2006). On being positive: Concerns and counterpoints. *Academy of Management
Review, 31*(2), 270–291.

100 Luthans, F. (2002). Positive organizational behavior: Developing and managing psychologi-
cal strengths. *Academy of Management Executive, 16*, 57–72; Csikszentmihalyi, M. (2003). *Good
business: Leadership, flow and the making of meaning.* New York: Viking; Fredrickson, B. L. (2003).
Positive emotions and upward spirals in organizations. In Cameron, K. S., Dutton, J. and Quinn,
R. (Eds.), *Positive organizational scholarship* (164–175). San Francisco, CA: Berrett-Koehle;
Peterson, C. M. and Seligman, M. E. P. (2003). Positive organizational studies: Lessons from
Positive Psychology. In Cameron, K. S., Dutton, J. E. and Quinn, R. E. (Eds.), *Positive organiza-
tional scholarship* (14–17). San Francisco, CA: Berrett-Koehler Publishers.

101 Seligman and Csikszentmihalyi, op. cit.

102 Cameron, K. S., Dutton, J. E. and Quinn, R. E. (Eds.) (2003). *Positive organizational scholarship:
Foundations of a new discipline.* San Francisco, CA: Berrett-Koehler Publishers; Luthans (2002),
op. cit.

103 Donaldson, S. I. and Ko, I. (2010). Positive organizational psychology, behavior, and scholarship:
A review of the emerging literature and evidence base. *The Journal of Positive Psychology, 5*(3),
177–191.

104 Luthans (2002), op. cit., p. 59.

105 Youssef, C. M. and Luthans, F. (2007). Positive organizational behaviour in the workplace: The
impact of hope, optimism, and resilience. *Journal of Management, 33*(5), 774–800.

106 Seligman, M. E. P. (2002). How to see the glass half full. *Newsweek*, September 16, 48; Ramlall, S. J. (2008). Enhancing employee performance through positive organizational behavior. *Journal of Applied Social Psychology*, *38*(6), 1580–1600; Luthans, F., Avolio, B. J., Avey, J. B. and Norman, S. M. (2007). Positive psychological capital: Measurement and relationship with performance and satisfaction. *Personnel Psychology*, *60*(3), 541–572.

107 Cameron et al., op. cit., p. 4.

108 Luthans, F., Youssef, C. and Avolio B. (2007). *Psychological capital—Developing the human competitive edge*. New York: Oxford University Press.

109 Ibid., p. 167.

110 Ibid.

111 Luthans, F., Avey, J. B., Avolio, B. J. and Peterson, S. J. (2010). The development and resulting performance impact of positive psychological capital. *Human Resource Development Quarterly*, *21*(1), 41–67.

112 Barney, J. (1991). Firm resources and competitive advantage. *Journal of Management*, *17*(1), 99–120; Luthans et al. (2010), op. cit.

113 Luthans et al. (2007), op. cit.

114 Hughes, L. W. (2008). A correlational study of the relationship between sense of humor and positive psychological capacities. *Economics and Business Journal: Inquiries and Perspectives*, *1*(1), 46–55.

115 Ibid.

116 Peebles, D. R. (2015). *The value of positive humour in the workplace*. Unpublished PhD dissertation, Tasmanian School of Business and Economics, University of Tasmania.

117 Ibid.

118 Newman, A., Ucbasaran, D., Zhu, F. and Hirst, G. (2014). Psychological capital: A review and synthesis. *Journal of Organizational Behavior*, *35*, 120–122.

119 Dawkins, S., Martin, A., Scott, J. and Sanderson, K. (2013). Building on the positives: A psychometric review and critical analysis of the construct of psychological capital. *Journal of Occupational and Organizational Psychology*, *86*, 348–370.

120 Ibid.

121 Luthans et al. (2007), op. cit.

122 Hackman, J. R. (2009). The perils of positivity. *Journal of Organizational Behavior*, *30*(2), 309–319.

123 Ibid.

4.3 Laughing out loud

How humor shapes innovation processes within and across organizations

Marcel Bogers, Alexander Brem, Trine Heinemann, and Elena Tavella

Introduction

Innovation processes increasingly rely on the collaboration between different stakeholders across various boundaries, including functional, hierarchical and organizational boundaries.[1] Such boundary-crossing collaborations rely on different mechanisms, activities and boundary objects. In this paper, we explore the role of one such mechanism, namely humor, which consists of a humorous stimulus and reaction,[2] in collaborative innovation processes. Humor might shape those processes as it affects the social positions of and relationships between individuals. The occurrence of humor, smiling and laughter is generally considered as having a positive influence on interactions, as it, for instance, promotes creativity, intelligence, social skills, psychological health, and conflict resolution.[3]

During the innovation process, small incremental actions are taken that cumulatively serve to shape the future of a product, process or service.[4] In this case study, we consider the role played by the individual in the micro-management of a collaborative innovation process. Specifically, we use conversation analysis to identify how proposals for future actions are designed and received in the context of an innovation workshop and what role humor plays in such proposals. By adopting a micro-level perspective on interactions and through conversation analysis, we explore how humorous expressions, smiling and laughter are employed by different participants engaged in collaborative innovation processes. Specifically, we identify how proposals for future actions are designed, received and accepted in the context of three innovation workshops and what role humor plays. Additionally, we explore which roles different workshop participants play—by employing humorous expressions, smiling and laughter—in the micro-management of the collaborative innovation process.

Our study shows how humor is employed at the micro-level of collaborative innovation processes. Based on data from workshops in which participants worked together to construct new business models for a particular company, our study reveals that humor (humorous expressions and laughter) may be an important condition for the acceptance of proposals at the interactional micro-level of innovation processes. A particular finding is that company-internal representatives' use of humor differs from company-external participants in terms of their orientation to having different rights and responsibilities in the innovation process. Moreover, we show that workshop participants orient to the shaping of proposals for future action as a joint task, rather than as something that can or should be done unilaterally by one participant. Thus, though proposals for future action can in principle be formulated and designed in a variety of ways, participants largely rely on a very specific pattern of proposing and accepting future actions, a pattern in which humorous expressions and laughter play a significant role. However, slight variations in terms of which participant makes a proposal, who produces humorous expressions, and who smiles and laughs reveal that different participants embrace different social positions during the workshops. Those positions vary depending on who has equal, primary and secondary rights to shape the innovation process.

Background

Corporate innovation management and its related processes can be seen as a main trigger for successful innovation activities for which management scholars propose a set of tools that often relate to the efficiency of these activities.[5] However, innovation must also be seen as a social and communicative process that requires the participation and collaboration of interdisciplinary teams to achieve success.[6] It is only through diversity among team members that participants can "overcome possible blind spots"[7] and create more and different insights,[8] allowing for a more comprehensive analysis of the problem at hand.[9] In this view, innovation becomes a social construction, shaped and negotiated through an "evolving pattern of interaction between people that emerges in the local interaction of those people with its fundamental aspects of communication, power, and ideology and evaluative choices."[10] Individual social positions held by participants and the normative expectations associated with those positions[11] can influence the overall organization of the innovation process, as well as the potential outcome.

Scholars interested in exploring the micro-interactions occurring during social and communicative processes have increasingly paid attention to the emergence and effects of emotions. Strategy scholars, for instance, have recently investigated the emotional dynamics emerging during strategic conversations. Liu and Maitlis[12] have analyzed how members of top management teams display emotions, as well as the relationship between the emotional display and the way they propose, discuss, and evaluate strategic issues, and make or postpone related decisions. Cornelissen et al.[13] explored how commitment to sense-making frames emerges and escalates under pressure during communication, emotional turmoil, and use of materials. Håkonsson et al.[14] examine how past performance and emotions dynamically influence and are influenced by group decisions to adopt and implement new routines, as well as the effect of performance and emotions on group decisions.

Similarly, and more specifically, research on humor, smiling, and laughter has gained presence in the literature with studies covering a wide range of disciplines. Scholars have, for instance, identified that humor can be used to creatively build, nurture, and contest workplace relationships, as well as enhance collaborative creative thinking and behaviors at work.[15] Maemura and Horita[16] investigated the role of humor in conflict resolution through negotiations, in particular, whether humor and laughter affect the structure, content, and process of negotiations. This study has shown that the occurrence of humor can enhance cohesion, cooperation, and the ability to tackle difficult situations, as well as reduce tensions. Besides, humor and laughter help structure the exchanged arguments, as well as pose new arguments and break out of deadlocks, thereby altering the content and process of negotiations. Humorous expressions and laughter have also been found to enhance negotiation processes and the achievement of goals, as well as to strengthen interpersonal relationships.[17]

Employing humor and proposing future actions constitute two interactional activities that each in different ways encompass the social positions held by individuals, as well as the relationship between them. Hatch[18] argues that cultural and emotional contexts of contradictions, namely, the complexity of "open social construction processes," are constructed through humorous discourse. Moreover, even though laughing together may be a way to reduce power distance, asymmetrical use of humor in organizations reveals the local constraints and obligations of individuals,[19] where hierarchical and organizational positions and relevancies can be "laughed into being."[20]

These same relevancies can play a role when participants propose future actions in the context of organizations. Asmuss and Oshima[21] thus demonstrate how institutionally defined positions such as being the CEO or the HR manager are made relevant through the way in which the participants negotiate proposal sequences, so that "institutional roles are local achievements and are subject to continuous renegotiation throughout interaction" (p. 83). Similarly, Stevanovic and Peräkylä[22] argue that authority, that is, "the exercise of power that the subject of authority understands as legitimate" (p. 297), is exercised and recognized through interaction. Landgrebe and Heinemann[23] illustrate that knowledge and authority are intertwined, so that participants "in the know" have the authority to determine future joint actions.

Method and data

In this case study, we consider how the individual's social position and the normative expectations associated with this position emerge through the local interaction of participants within an innovation process, specifically by investigating humor and its relation to the proposal for future action. For this purpose, we use conversation analysis, an ethnomethodological approach that focuses on how members interpret each other's actions and display that interpretation moment by moment.[24]

Our analysis draws on video-recordings of three workshops carried out by a research center in collaboration with a national industry network for middle- and top-managers from various companies in Denmark. The workshops aimed at helping one of the involved companies, here referred to as Lightoman, create a tangible business model[25] for new markets. The workshop participants—three representatives of Lightoman and several network members from other companies—were tasked with collaboratively developing proposals for future business models. Due to the innovative, future-oriented and collaborative nature of the workshops they can be viewed as processes of innovation.

Following the principal method of "unmotivated looking"[26] which is usually employed in conversation analysis, a first analysis of the video-records identified a noticeable pattern: humorous expressions, smiling and laughter were almost exclusively employed within one particular type of workshop activity, namely, when a participant was making what we here term a "proposal for future action." Those proposals typically followed a particular sequenced pattern of interaction: (i) a participant identifies an object for representing a particular stakeholder in the value network being constructed, and (ii) other participants either accept or reject this proposal. This pattern is illustrated with a representative excerpt from the data in the next section (Table 4.3.1).

Findings

The pattern of proposals for future action

In the case of Lightoman, the pattern of making proposals for future action emerged through the following steps:

1   A stakeholder is identified and named as relevant for the value network.
2   An object is selected and proposed to represent that stakeholder.
3   Participants orient to the proposal as humorous by giving the object a label in the form of a pun-like expression, and/or by smiling and laughing.
4   The object is placed on the table as part of the value network.
5   Participants move on to identifying the next relevant stakeholder.

As an illustration of this process, the excerpt below in Table 4.3.1 provides a transcript of an actual proposal sequence that follows the pattern described above. It starts by participants B and C (lines 01–04) identifying the need for a particular stakeholder, in this case a bank, to be included in the value network. Next, one of the participants finds and grabs an object, sometimes verbally proposing to use that object for the

Table 4.3.1 Transcript of proposal sequence

(1) Tangible business 1: Bank

01 B:	*hvordan ser en bank ud*
	what does a bank look like
02	(2.9)
03 C:	*Ja, den ska vi li' ha (k-) positioneret*
	Yes, that we just need to position
04	*først banken*
	first, the bank
05	(0.2)
06 B:	⋆*måske*⋆
	⋆maybe⋆
07	+(2.1)
08 geB:	+picks up the ball
09 B:	Slippery.+
10 geB:	+smile
11 B:	heh [heh +heh heh +heh heh
12 A:	[ye:s +heh +huh heh heh
13 gaB:	+to C +to A
14 gaC:	+to B
15 geC:	+smile
16 C:	+hah hah hah hah [hah hah Slippery
17 B:	[.hhe hhe

representation of a stakeholder. In other instances, as illustrated in this excerpt, the participant makes the proposal non-verbally, by holding up the object for inspection by the others. In line 8, B does this with the silvery ball he has selected and picked up in line 08. B's labeling of the ball (and hence the bank) with the humorous expression "slippery" (line 09) and the other participants' reactions to this in the form of laughter, smiling, etc. (in lines 12–16) are other constitutive features of the proposals for future action as found in this excerpt.

The effect of humor on proposal design, receipt, and acceptance

Operationalizing humor as a "laughable,"[27] that is, as actions that participants themselves treat as funny through smiling, laughing or in other ways indicating the humorous nature of the proposal, our data reveals that humor is a constitutive feature of proposals for future actions in the cases we investigated. Based on these initial observations, we subsequently collected all proposal sequences in the data and coded these with respect to how the proposals were designed as humorous or not, whether they were treated by recipients as humorous or not and whether the proposals were accepted or not. A total of 38 proposals across the three workshops were found. The overall results are illustrated in Table 4.3.2.

The three main columns represent, firstly, the total number of proposals that we identified in our analysis (the above-mentioned 38), secondly the number of those proposals that we identified as being received as humorous by one or more recipients, and thirdly those (of the total 38 proposals) that were accepted by the receiver as identified through the follow-up action. The rows then indicate, for each of these categories, how many proposals were designed or intended to be humorous (with different types of indications given in parentheses), how many were transformed to be humorous by another participant, and how many proposals were not designed to be humorous.

As Table 4.3.2 illustrates, the use of humorous expressions accompanied by smiling and laughing constitute proposals for future actions in this particular context, as it is employed in 31 out of 38 proposal sequences. Our findings do not, however, suggest a direct correlation between whether a proposal is humorous or not and whether the proposal is ultimately accepted, since non-humorous proposals are at least just as likely to be accepted as their humorous equivalents. Given that humor does not appear to be a prerequisite for having a proposal accepted, what other role may it serve in proposal sequence? In order to investigate this, we looked in more detail at the way in which different participants in the workshops made use of humor in relation to the proposals. Most notably, the three representative members of Lightoman, for whom the business models were being built, behave in ways that deviate from the other participants, who were network partners from other companies. In one workshop, for instance, a Lightoman representative member refrained entirely from participating in the construction of the business models, and instead preferred to merely take notes of the other participants' contributions. The other two representative members of Lightoman, each engaging in their respective workshop group, participated more actively in the construction of the business models, making their own proposals, selecting objects for

Table 4.3.2 Proposals in relation to the use of humor

	Total number of proposals	Proposal received as humorous*	Proposal accepted*
Proposal designed to be humorous			
(Proposer smiles and produces a humorous expression)	(7)	(4)	(5)
(Proposer produces a humorous expression)	(15)	(9)	(13)
(Proposer smiles)	(2)	(0)	(1)
Total number of proposal designed to be humorous	24	13	19
Proposals transformed to be humorous by co-participant producing a humorous expression	7	4	7
Proposals designed to be non-humorous	7	3	6
Total number of proposals	38	20	32

* Note that these two categories are not mutually exclusive, that is, a proposal could be both received as humorous and accepted by the receiver. At the same time, they do not necessarily have to overlap, that is, a proposal may be accepted whether or not it is received as humorous.

representing stakeholders, producing humorous expressions and laughing. But even when engaging in the construction of the business models, Lightoman representative members and other network partners behaved differently, specifically, in terms of how they marked proposals as humorous and pushed for and joined laughter. Those behavioral differences are outlined next.

Marking a proposal as humorous

As illustrated in the excerpt above, in the case of Lightoman, proposals were treated as humorous by the participants, either through smiling and laughter, or by accompanying the proposal with a humorous expression (e.g., a bank is represented by a "slippery" ball, as in Table 4.3.1). What we here labeled as humorous expressions were typically statements of a pun-like quality, where the physical property of an object was used to ascribe a cognitive or behavioral property to the stakeholder the object was proposed to represent. Figure 4.3.1 presents a selection of these puns, taken from our data, as they were produced by the participants in the workshops.

Though such puns were regularly produced as part of the proposal sequence, we find a striking difference between participants with respect to who did or did not produce puns in response to another participant's proposal. In particular, Lightoman representatives were the only participants who would produce puns to accompany other participants' proposals, either when such a pun had not been made by the proposer, or to replace a pun produced by the proposer. At the same time, other participants only produced a pun to accompany their own proposals.

Puns and other humorous expressions that accompany proposals function as a type of account, in serving to imply and explicate why and how a particular object should

Object	Stakeholder	Pun
Petanque ball	Bank	Slippery
Petanque ball	Authorities	Having the balls to send signals
Corner bracket	A bank's technical department	Can be a bit square about what can be done/ not done
Complex bracket	Authorities	Who are a bit square and difficult to understand
Tea strainer	Buyers	Filter things, some get through, others do not
Fishing hook	Board of directors	It can be uncomfortable to sit on the board in a bank, but once there you get stuck/stay around
Ribbon	Architects	A bit decorative

(continued)

Object	Stakeholder	Pun
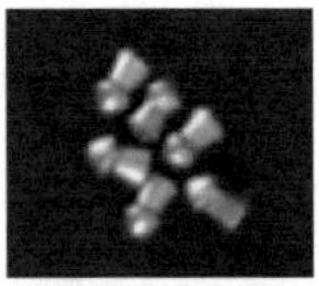 Bullets	Private customers	Are small and almost unnoticeable
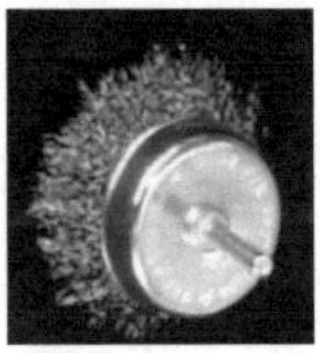 Wire brush	Architect	Longhaired (hippyish)
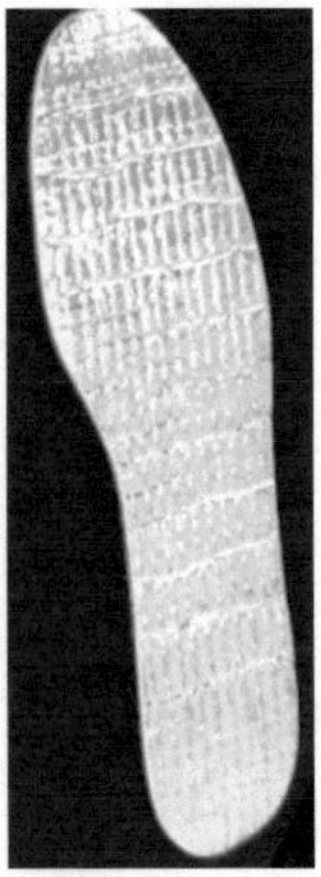 Insole	Hotel owner	Has the big foot print
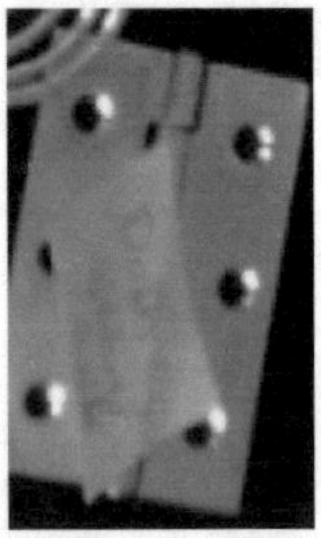 Hinge	Technical department	Connects everything
 Hooter	Customer	Complains and is never satisfied (makes a lot of noise)

Figure 4.3.1 Examples of puns used as humorous expressions

Note: Due to the translation from Danish to English, some of the humorous expressions may have been diluted.

represent a certain stakeholder. In the excerpt above (Table 4.3.1), for instance, the pun-like expression "slippery" serves to articulate why the ball is a good representation of a bank, since many might consider banks "slippery." Producing a pun is thus a way of creating meaning, by establishing a direct relationship between the selected object and the stakeholder it is proposed to represent. When producing a pun on behalf of other partici-pants' proposals, Lightoman representative members thus support the others' proposal by making sense of it.

At the same time, the production of a pun on behalf of others also constitutes a claim of independent recognition of the relationship between object and stakeholder, something which is particularly apparent when a pun is produced to replace or correct another pun already provided by the producer of the proposal. Through producing puns on behalf of other participants' proposals or replacing other participants' puns, Lightoman repre-sentative members thus seem to orient to or demonstrate their special social status as being someone who is ultimately responsible both for making sure that other participants' proposals are accepted and that they are accepted in the right way, that is, as appropriate sense-making proposals.

Pushing for laughter

As illustrated in the above description of the steps in making proposals, a requirement for a successful proposal is that others have received it with laughter. Laughter can thus be seen as the participants' orientation that the proposal sequences are generally derived through joint accomplishments. When laughter by others is not produced, most par-ticipants simply abandon their proposal, looking either for a new object or suggesting another stakeholder. The Lightoman representative members, however, did not aban-don their proposals when these were not responded to with laughter by others. Instead, they pursued laughter or other types of acceptance/evaluation of their proposal until it was finally accepted and the object could be placed on the table.

Since laughter and acceptance of the proposal are overall connected, the Lightoman representatives' pursuit of laughter and hence acceptance thus becomes a way of invoking a certain social status in which an individual has the right and authority to insist on and pursue acceptance at a point where this has otherwise not been produced.

Joining the laughter

Though Lightoman representative members clearly orient to the importance of laughter when making their own proposals or constructing puns for others' proposals (as recipi-ents), they laugh considerably less than other participants. Notably, they do not laugh even in contexts where participants make clear that their contributions are designed to receive laughter, not just in general, but specifically from a Lightoman representative.

In the case studied, laughter appears to be a constitutive feature of proposal sequences and something that is required to make the proposal come about as a joint social con-struction, rather than a unilateral decision. In not joining the general laughter and not laughing when clearly selected as the recipient of a humorous proposal, Lightoman representative members can thus be seen to exclude themselves from the more general participation framework, assigning themselves a different role than that of the other participants, that is, as someone who is not jointly responsible for establishing consensus, as the others are.

Discussion and implications

In this study, we find that proposal sequences are constituted by participants treating the proposals as humorous and joint constructions on which acceptance by other participants is contingent.[28] Though there is a constitutive pattern for these sequences, small variations in the participants' behavior reveal attributes of the kinds of roles and responsibilities they assign themselves and each other.[29] We thus conclude that humor (humorous expressions, smiling and laughter) may be an important condition for the acceptance of proposals at the interactional micro-level of innovation processes. These findings contribute to our understanding of the relationship between humor and innovation. Moreover, linking these findings to the literature aids a further elaboration of these concepts and their relation, and more generally provides a basis for discussing the implications for both research and practice.

A particular finding is that humor plays a particular role in inter-organizational relationships. Our analysis shows that internal representatives from Lightoman behave differently from other participants, who are external contributors, in relation to the construction and use of humor in proposal sequences, and the acceptance of proposals. In doing so, the fact of a contributor being an internal versus external stakeholder effectively acts as a moderating variable that affects the relationship between humor and the acceptance of proposals, as illustrated in Figure 4.3.2. In particular, internal contributors assign themselves particular roles within the workshop more generally and within the decision-making sequences (proposing future actions) more specifically. As such, they act as someone who is not responsible for making the future actions a joint action, as the others are, but rather as someone who is ultimately responsible for (and able to determine whether) the proposal is "just right."

While humor appears to play an important role in the cross-fertilization of knowledge across organizational boundaries, it would be useful for future research to explore whether and how the type of boundary matters, and what the impact would be on different types of performance.[30] In particular, it would be useful to investigate how humor affects the obtaining and integration of external knowledge[31] and also how such an effect may differ for various stakeholders in the value network,[32] especially considering the role internal versus external stakeholders adopt in the generation and use of humor. Our findings could then also contribute to the emerging interest in individual-level attributes, such as behavior and cognition in the literature on open innovation, which has been conceptualized

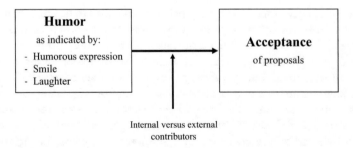

Figure 4.3.2 Relationship between humor and acceptance of proposals

as knowledge flows across organizational boundaries.[33] On this basis, we would propose a contingency view of such openness and the use of humor, although our results would initially support the assumption that the occurrence of humor is generally considered as having a positive influence on interactions.[34]

Considering the contribution of this chapter, our findings highlight some conditions that are important when "managing" humor. Previous research in the area of management and organization has identified humor as a managerial tool, with both positive and negative elements.[35] Humor has, for instance, been found to support people in unpacking the nature and substance of paradoxical conflicts they might face in carrying out particular organizational tasks, thereby helping them to respond to those conflicts. Interactional micro-practices that involve humorous expressions thus potentially influence how actors perform tasks as they have implications for their actions and how paradoxical conflicts are addressed at different organizational levels.[36] Our study then illustrates how humor may be used as a managerial tool for the micro-management of interactional processes between individuals. Moreover, given that suppression and manufacturing of humor are two overlapping managerial control strategies, in which humor can be linked to "power relations and management control through joking relations,"[37] further exploration is required to identify how such strategies relate to individual social positions and rights of the interacting participants.[38] Other perspectives, such as psychology, may also add to a more complete understanding of the attributes and types of humor.[39] Researchers who are active in this domain may build on our initial findings and further develop the specific framework and propositions that are implied in these findings. For example, our study links to various related concepts and theoretical perspectives that call for a more integrative perspective on managing humor. More generally, we hope that the findings offer a basis for a better understanding and further investigation of the enabling and/or constraining role of humor in collaborative innovation processes.

Our results also have some important implications for managers. Based on our results, we found two types of behaviors that influence the perception of innovation in companies. The first one is the use of laughter as acceptance. Supporting a positive sentence about a new product or service, accompanied with laughter, creates a positive response. This is perceived as support for the idea, and also for the person who elaborates on it. The second type is the one which is less obvious. Through a deliberate denial of laughter, the introduced idea might lack the needed support to proceed within the innovation process. A common way to express such a positive or negative attitude is the use of a pun. Such a pun can create meaning as well as independent relationships between the involved objects and stakeholders. Apparently, this is highly dependent on the innovation culture in the company on the one hand, and also on the overall cultural background of the company's employees on the other hand. Indeed, earlier studies show distinctive differences of innovation behavior in Europe and countries such as India or China.[40] Hence, these factors have to be considered in applying humor in corporate contexts. Otherwise, activities and their implications might have a different effect from the one that was intended. Finally, it is worthwhile mentioning that humor in general has a positive effect on innovation in companies. Company leaders should consider allowing and fostering humor in their organizations, even though the industry norm would indicate that this is not serious enough.

References

1 Bogers, M., and Horst, W. (2014), Collaborative prototyping: Cross-fertilization of knowledge in prototype-driven problem solving. *Journal of Product Innovation Management*, 31(4): 744–764; Bogers, M., and Lhuillery, S. (2011), A functional perspective on learning and innovation: Investigating the organization of absorptive capacity. *Industry and Innovation*, 18(6): 581–610; Dahlander, L., and Gann, D. M. (2010), How open is innovation? *Research Policy*, 39(6): 699–709.

2 Malone, P. B., III. (1980), Humor: A double-edged tool for today's managers? *Academy of Management Review*, 5(3): 357–360.

3 Hauck, W. E., and Thomas, J. W. (1972), The relationship of humor to intelligence, creativity, and intentional and incidental learning. *Journal of Experimental Education*, 40(4): 52–55; Martin, R. A., Puhlik-Doris, P., Larsen, G., Gray, J., and Weir, K. (2003), Individual differences in uses of humor and their relation to psychological well-being: Development of the Humor Styles Questionnaire. *Journal of Research in Personality*, 37(1): 48–75; Yip, J. A., and Martin, R. A. (2006), Sense of humor, emotional intelligence, and social competence. *Journal of Research in Personality*, 40(6): 1202–1208; Maemura, Y., and Horita, M. (2012), Humor in negotiations: A pragmatic analysis of humor in simulated negotiations. *Group Decision and Negotiation*, 21(6): 821–838.

4 Bogers, M. (2016), Innovating by doing: Promoting on-the-job experimentation through a climate for innovation. *International Journal of Entrepreneurial Venturing*, forthcoming; de Brentani, U. (2001), Innovative versus incremental new business services: Different keys for achieving success. *Journal of Product Innovation Management*, 18(3): 169–187; Larsen, H., and Bogers, M. (2014), Innovation as improvisation "in the shadow." *Creativity and Innovation Management*, 23(4): 386–399; Murray, F., and O'Mahony, S. (2007), Exploring the foundations of cumulative innovation: Implications for organization science. *Organization Science*, 18(6): 1006–1021.

5 Brem, A., and Voigt, K. I. (2009), Integration of market pull and technology push in the corporate front end and innovation management: Insights from the German software industry. *Technovation*, 29(5): 351–367; Cooper, R. G. (2014), What's next? After Stage-Gate. *Research-Technology Management*, 57(1): 20–31.

6 Leonard, D. A., and Sensiper, S. (1998), The role of tacit knowledge in group innovation. *California Management Review*, 40(3): 112–132; Doughtery, D. (1992), Interpretative barriers to successful product innovation on large firms. *Organization Science*, 3(2): 179–202.

7 Holzer, J. (2012), Construction of meaning in socio-technical networks: Artefacts as mediators between routine and crisis conditions. *Creativity and Innovation Management*, 21(1): 49–60, at page 50.

8 Jehn, K. A., Nortcraft, G. B., and Neale, M. A. (1999), Why differences make a difference: A field study of diversity, conflict and performance in workgroups. *Administrative Science Quarterly*, 44(4): 741–763.

9 Akrich, M., Callon, M., and Latour, B. (2002), The key to success in innovation, Part II: the art of choosing good spokespersons. *International Journal of Innovation Management*, 6(2): 207–225.

10 Stacey, R., and Griffin, D. (2005), *A Complexity Perspective on Researching Organizations*. Routledge: London, p. 19.

11 Tsoukas, H. (1996), The firm as a distributed knowledge system: A constructionist approach. *Strategic Management Journal*, 17 (Winter Special Issue): 11–25.

12 Liu, F., and Maitlis, S. (2014), Emotional dynamics and strategizing processes: A study of strategic conversations in top team meetings. *Journal of Management Studies*, 51(2): 202–234.

13 Cornelissen, J. P., Mantere, S., and Vaara, E. (2014), The contraction of meaning: The combined effect of communication, emotions, and materiality on sensemaking in the Stockwell Shooting. *Journal of Management Science*, 51(5): 699–736.

14 Håkonsson, D. D., Eskildsen, J. K., Argote, L., Mønster, D., Burton, R. M., and Obel, B. (2015), Exploration versus exploitation: Emotions and performance as antecedents and consequences of team decisions. *Strategic Management Journal*, 37(6): 985–1001.

15 Holmes, J. (2007), Making humor work: Creativity on the job. *Applied Linguistics*, 28(4): 518–537.

16 Maemura, and Horita, op. cit.

17 Vuorela, T. (2005), Laughing matters: A case study of humor in multicultural business negotiations. *Negotiation Journal*, 21(1): 105–130.

18 Hatch, M. J. (1997), Irony and the social construction of contradiction in the humor of a management team. *Organization Science*, 8(3): 275–288, p. 277.

19 Glenn, P. (2010), Interviewer laughs: Shared laughter and asymmetries in employment inter-
    views. *Journal of Pragmatics*, 42(6): 1485–1498.

20 Vöge, M. (2010), Local identity processes in business meetings displayed through laughter in
    complaint sequences. *Journal of Pragmatics*, 42(6): 1556–1576, p. 1556.

21 Asmuss, B., and Oshima, S. (2012), Negotiation of entitlement in proposal sequences. *Discourse
    Studies*, 14(1): 67–86.

22 Stevanovic, M., and Peräkylä, A. (2013), Deontic authority in interaction: The right to announce,
    propose, and decide. *Research on Language and Social Interaction*, 45(3): 297–321.

23 Landgrebe, J., and Heinemann, T. (2014), Mapping the epistemic landscape in innovation work-
    shops. *Pragmatics and Society*, 5(2): 191–220.

24 Heritage, J. (2010), Conversation analysis: Practices and methods, in D. Silverman (Ed.), *Qualitative
    Sociology* (3rd edition). London: Sage, 208–230.

25 Buur, J., Ankenbrand, B., and Mitchell, R. (2013), Participatory business modelling. *CoDesign*,
    9(1): 55–71.

26 Psathas, G. (1995), *Conversation Analysis: The Study of Talk in Interaction*. Thousand Oaks, CA:
    Sage Publications.

27 Jefferson, G. (1979), A technique for inviting laughter and its subsequent acceptance declina-
    tion, in G. Psathas (Ed.), *Everyday Language: Studies in Ethnomethodology*. New York: Irvington
    Publishers, 79–95.

28 Hatch, op. cit.; Stacey, and Griffin, op. cit.

29 Asmuss, and Oshima, op. cit.; Stevanovic, and Peräkyllä, op. cit.; Landgrebe, and Heinemann, op. cit.

30 Asmuss, and Oshima, op. cit.; Bogers, and Horst, op. cit.; Eftekhari, N., and Bogers, M. (2015),
    Open for entrepreneurship: How open innovation can foster new venture creation. *Creativity
    and Innovation Management*, 24(4): 574–584; Faems, D., de Visser, M., Andries, P., and van Looy,
    B. (2010), Technology alliance portfolios and financial performance: Value-enhancing and cost-
    increasing effects of open innovation. *Journal of Product Innovation Management*, 27(6): 785–796;
    Laursen, K., and Salter, A. (2006), Open for innovation: The role of openness in explaining
    innovation performance among U.K. manufacturing firms. *Strategic Management Journal*, 27(2):
    131–150.

31 West, J., and Bogers, M. (2014), Leveraging external sources of innovation: A review of research
    on open innovation. *Journal of Product Innovation Management*, 31(4): 814–831.

32 Bogers, M., and West, J. (2012), Managing distributed innovation: Strategic utilization of open
    and user innovation. *Creativity and Innovation Management*, 21(1): 61–75; Chesbrough, H.,
    and Bogers, M. (2014), Explicating open innovation: Clarifying an emerging paradigm for
    understanding innovation, in H. Chesbrough, W. Vanhaverbeke, and J. West (Eds.), *New
    Frontiers in Open Innovation*. Oxford: Oxford University Press, 3–28.

33 Bogers, M., Zobel, A.-K., Afuah, A., Almirall, E., Brunswicker, S., Dahlander, L., Frederiksen, L.,
    Gawer, A., Gruber, M., Haefliger, S., Hagedoorn, J., Hilgers, D., Laursen, K., Magnusson, M. G.,
    Majchrzak, A., McCarthy, I. P., Moeslein, K. M., Nambisan, S., Piller, F. T., Radziwon, A., Rossi-
    Lamastra, C., Sims, J., and ter Wal, A. L. J. (2016), The open innovation research landscape: Established
    perspectives and emerging themes across different levels of analysis. *Industry and Innovation*, 24(1):
    8–40.

34 Hauck, op. cit.; Martin, op. cit.; Yip, op. cit.; Maemura, op. cit.

35 Malone, op. cit.

36 Lynch, O. (2010), Cooking with humor: In-group humor as social organization. *Humor*, 23(29):
    127–159; Jarzabkowski, P., and Lê, J. K. (2016), We have to do this *and* that? You must be joking:
    Constructing and responding to paradox through humor. *Organization Studies*, published online
    ahead of print, DOI: 10.1177/0170840616640846.

37 Collinson, D. L. (2002), Managing humour. *Journal of Management Studies*, 39(3): 269–288, p. 269.

38 Asmuss, and Oshima, op. cit.; Stevanovic, and Peräkyllä, op. cit.; Landgrebe, and Heinemann, op. cit.

39 Martin, R. A. (2007), *The Psychology of Humor: An Integrative Approach*. Burlington, MA: Elsevier.

40 Brem, A., and Wolfram, P. (2017), Organisation of new product development in Asia and Europe:
    Results from Western multinationals [sic] R&D sites in Germany, India, and China. *Review of
    Managerial Science*, 11(1): 159–190.

4.4 Laughing apart

Humor and the reproduction of exclusionary workplace cultures

Danielle J. Deveau and Rebecca Scott Yoshizawa

Introduction

Humor has great potential as an untapped business resource; however, we are here concerned with the ways in which enthusiasm about the value of humor in social relations may mask the extent to which jokes, pranks, gags, and laughs can also instantiate negative effects in the social relationships that constitute the work environment. As scholars Penelope Brunner and Melinda Costello argue in relation to women in leadership positions, "sexual humor may be used, consciously or unconsciously, to undermine control."[1] They find that in these instances sexual humor is used not only to undermine female authority in the workplace, but also to preserve problematic organizational structures that are implicitly hostile to women's participation in certain industry sectors. While there are many ways that humor can serve a positive organizational role, it must also be acknowledged that social inequalities and prejudices which feed discriminatory practices can be reinforced by humorous exchange. Positive appraisals of the social role of humor too often overlook some of the negative consequences of joking. Not all humor is in good fun. When used against outsiders or minority groups in the workplace, it can result in discomfort, unwelcoming work environments, social exclusion, the exclusion of newcomers, and the reinforcement of inequalities within organizations.

It remains, however, that regulating such humor poses a challenge. Why is this the case? According to humor scholar Michael Billig, there is a persistent emphasis on the positive social effects of humor, rooted in an ideological aversion to negativity. He writes that a

> pattern of accentuating positives and eliminating negatives can be seen in the contemporary psychology of humour, no matter whether this is the psychology of popular writers, academics or professional psychotherapists. The negatives of ridicule, sarcasm and mockery seem to be eliminated in a view that positively praises the warm-heartedness of humor.[2]

This persistent emphasis on the positive effects of humor, such as enhancing social bonds, can be explained by the nature of humor itself. Sharing a sense of humor is incredibly important for thick social relations: for instance, we know that a shared sense of humor ranks highly in spousal selection.[3] What we find funny is particularly enduring. Humor is also remarkably culturally specific, and one of the most difficult things to understand or translate inter-culturally.[4] Our social networks therefore tend to reinforce our own sense of humor rather than refine it. As such, our experiences of humor can be very affirming for our identity and sense of belonging.

Yet is laughter always positive? Surely not when you are the butt of a cruel joke. Does humor always bring people together? Not if you are on the outside looking in. We all remember times when our attempts at humor went wrong or when we were hurt by the jokes of another. While sharing a sense of humor with a hiring committee or supervisor can open up career doors and strengthen professional networks, making the wrong joke at the wrong time can result in social ostracization. In other words, humor not only reinforces social bonds between 'in-groups,' but it also reinforces the social exclusion of 'out-groups.'

With this insight in mind and in the scope of this textbook's consideration of humor in business and society relationships, this chapter steps outside of the context of humor as a positive social force or as a tool for business management. Positive functions of humor are important to understand, but so too are the negative aspects of workplace humor that we address here. We argue that positive aspects of humor cannot be considered in isolation; the problematic social functions of humor and laughter such as exclusion, ridicule, and harassment must also be addressed. Such uses of humor can of course be seen in a range of other types of harassment, including bullying, and discrimination based upon race, class, ability, and sexual orientation. While in this chapter we focus on sexual harassment, many of the issues that we raise are relevant to any number of other forms of harassment and discrimination in the workplace. These issues offer important clues as to the persistence of systemic inequalities in the workplace: as Brunner and Costello argue, "while societal norms and discrimination laws target the obvious discrimination practices in organizations, subtle methods of prejudice, such as sexual humor, retain and support an organization's historical structure and are often overlooked."[5]

To illustrate this issue, we consider three case studies drawn from Canadian media and public discussions about workplace humor and harassment in 2016. The first is a video that was circulated at Simon Fraser University to promote "Sweater Day," an initiative whereby students and faculty are encouraged to don sweaters and lower their thermostats as a gesture towards environmental consciousness. In the video, a female faculty member is complimented on her physical appearance by a male undergraduate student and responds with girlish giggles. The video received significant backlash and resulted in backpedaling and a formal apology from the administration. The second case study considers the media and public response to a female firefighter's complaints about a pornographic video played during a training course as a 'joke.' The third case study is a discussion of the fallout from the *External Review into Sexual Misconduct and Sexual Harassment in the Canadian Armed Forces*, released in 2015, which found that humor was used to reinforce a problematic sexualized work environment, enabling other forms of more significant harassment.

Combined, these examples serve to reinforce our argument that workplace humor can produce a toxic workplace culture. Specifically, in this chapter, we argue three points: (1) humor reinforces social hierarchies; (2) humor is intimately related to gender harassment in the workplace; and (3) humor can contribute to a hostile environment within workplace culture. The theoretical underpinnings of this chapter are grounded in the perspective that the use of humor in the workplace both constructs social bonds and enacts power. We draw upon sociological discussions of humor, as well as organizational communication and discourse analyses of humor in the workplace. We suggest that business managers and leaders who are attempting to promote jovial workplaces must also equally focus on promoting social inclusion through other means, and remain cognizant of the ways in which joking can serve to reinforce problematic and exclusionary structures of power in the workplace.

Humor as an ambivalent social gesture

Although humor is a distinctly shared and social experience, it is the 'subjective' aspect of a 'sense of humor' that tends to be emphasized in critical discussions and cautionary tales of humor in the workplace. The reality is that not all people share the same sense of humor, and what is considered funny to one person, might be considered not funny— or worse, offensive—to another. Some analyses overemphasize the extent to which the offensiveness of humor is merely subjective; indeed, studies have shown, for example, that men and women are equally adept at perceiving sexist jokes as offensive, and do not differ as much in interpretation as often thought.[6] However, it is true that humor, like all discourses, is open to interpretation. Likewise, its interpretation cannot always be predicted. This renders humor an ambivalent social gesture.

Indeed, even the scholarship of humor cannot necessarily produce consistent readings of humorous texts. For example, in an introductory excerpt from his essay "Performing Media: Toward an Ethnography of Intertextuality," Mark Allen Peterson offers an anecdote to illustrate his observation that humorous references to mass culture provide vital means of producing social bonds. Peterson provides an analysis of a humorous exchange that differs significantly from our own interpretation of the scenario. In the anecdote, a group of male spectators (Peterson among them) are watching their daughters' softball practice:

> The scene is a baseball field in Midwestern Pennsylvania. The first practice for the Teal Tigers Girls' Softball Team has just ended. The coach is playing a game with the girls to test their knowledge of baseball rules, asking them questions and tossing them candies when they answer correctly. The parents, mostly fathers, stand awkwardly in a circle watching. We are waiting to collect our daughters and take them home. We do not know one another yet.
>
> The coach runs out of questions. She still has two girls who have not earned a candy and she does not want them to go home empty handed. She looks up at the parents, hopefully. "Can anybody think of another question?"
>
> "Who's on first?" says one of the fathers. Several of us grin.
>
> "What's on second?" asks another.
>
> "I don't know," says the first man.
>
> "Third base!" I offer. Two other men say it simultaneously with me. We are all grinning at each other now. The ice has been broken. We still do not know one another, yet some kind of connection has been made. The coach rolls her eyes. Our children gaze at us in perplexity.[7]

With this anecdote, Peterson intended merely to illustrate the way in which reference humor is used to form social bonds. In this case, the reference is to a Vaudeville routine, popularized by Abbott and Costello in the 1930s, in which Costello attempts to learn the names of the basemen, only to be frustrated by the exchange as each of the players has an unusual name which produces confusion (the players are named 'Who,' 'What' and 'I don't know'). However, this excerpt does much more than illustrate the use of humor to create social bonds in everyday life. Reading a little deeper into the description, it is evident that Peterson's anecdote is heavily gendered. The male spectators enjoy a joke, while the female coach responds humorlessly, perhaps even with passive annoyance. In fairness to Peterson, it is entirely coincidental that the coach happened to be a woman, and that a majority of parents present at that particular practice happened to be men. However, Peterson is very careful in his description of the scenario, noting that it is a *girls'* softball team, that the coach is in fact *female*, and that the majority of parent spectators are *male*; such specificity would suggest that gender must have something to do with it. Furthermore, as Karim H. Karim has argued, "humor is an essential part of social bonding, and those who are left out of the circle of laughter also find themselves excluded from the vital occasions for societal participation."[8]

The softball dads did not simply use humor to produce a social bond. They used humor to produce a social bond by creating an in-group who participated in the joke, and two distinct out-groups who did not. Their group was constituted as much by exclusion as it was by inclusion. The separation between the coach and the fathers is made more notable because she had asked them for help. She attempted to construct a different group, one in which the fathers participated in the coaching of the team by coming up with other questions for their daughters. If mere cultural knowledge were the main factor in forming a social bond, the fathers could have exchanged their softball knowledge including regulations, statistics, and beer-league triumphs. Instead, the fathers rejected the coach's group invitation, using humor to enter into an alternative group formation. The daughters are also excluded, being too young to understand the joke. While the coach may well have understood the reference, in the given context she does not choose to participate in the shared performance of referential humor. Indeed, it is unlikely that she was an intended participant to begin with.

However, even as it creates exclusion, humor has a knack for extending beyond its intended context. In this instance, the joke (and its retelling) includes a social meaning through the production of a relationship between the fathers, a cultural meaning through the use of shared references and signifiers, and a political meaning through the (in this case, gendered) production of an exclusionary group. Peterson did not offer his anecdote as a critical discourse on the exclusionary consequences of joking, and yet from our perspective this is precisely what this anecdote has done. Humor does not only produce social groups, but it produces groups with specific common interests. In the case of the softball dads, this commonality was based in gender, age, and a collective boredom with softball spectatorship. In all likelihood the participants did not *intend* to use humor in an exclusionary manner, nor did they intend to constitute such a relatively homogenous group. It simply occurred, seemingly on its own, seemingly *naturally*, as if it were an inevitable social progression.

Indeed, the supposed 'naturalness' of humor is a key element of its efficacy. What is funny must be obvious to the insiders, and cannot easily be explained to those who don't get the joke. As Simon Critchley notes, "a theory of humour is not humorous. A joke explained is a joke misunderstood."[9] This renders critical analyses of humor suspect. To engage with a debate about the merits of a humorous utterance can mark you as humorless. Getting the joke means getting it intrinsically. The ability to disguise itself as 'natural' is one of humor's greatest subversive powers. This is also how it can work as a tool of oppression or discrimination. The rhetorical power of humor is in its ability to disguise its socio-cultural origins. The humor of the joke teller is disguised as natural; this is an exercise of power, as the joke teller always has recourse to the claim that they were *only joking*. This is why we cannot rely on the 'intention' of the joker when deciding whether to absolve them of any offense they may cause. The more forceful accusation, *you don't have a sense of humor*, when the joke fails or causes offense is also particularly effective because we live in a society that values humor. A sense of humor is a vital human quality, and not having one is an undesirable personality trait.[10] Indeed, it is this privileged position of humor that gives it much of its rhetorical sway. As Michael Mulkay has suggested, the serious mode and the humorous mode are two distinct forms of discourse which operate according to different discursive rules.[11] However, humor can be used to great effect to put forward serious messages, disguised behind the non-serious language of joking. The claim that one was *only joking* in the context of a workplace environment where harassment has been perceived must be considered in relation to what the serious interpretation of, for example, a sexist joke might be. As Brunner and Costello argue, humor and similar utterances are "subtle methods of prejudice" which "retain and support an organization's historical structure."[12]

In the workplace, humor can play a significant role in the maintenance of social hierarchies. For example, in an ethnography of workplace communication conducted at a hospital in the late 1950s, Rose Laub Coser found that the use of humor, or witticisms, in formal staff meetings correlated strongly with relative status. That is, those in positions of authority (senior staff members) were more likely to make jokes than those who occupied lower positions (such as junior staff members and paramedical staff such as social workers). Notably, in observations made outside of the context of the formal meeting, junior staff and paramedical workers proved to be adept joke tellers, but within the context of formal meetings humor use was always hierarchically distributed. This distinction also fell along gender lines, with female participants seldom making jokes during meetings; these individuals instead expressed a sense of humor by laughing heartily at the witticisms of their senior male colleagues. When junior staff members did make jokes, they were never at the expense of senior staff present, whereas the senior staff regularly made jokes at the expense of the junior staff members. Coser found very clearly, then, that "in a hierarchical social structure [tensions] seem to be released downward" and that this process reinforces the existing status structure.[13]

This reinforcement of status is a characteristic of social joking. As Coser notes,

> humor and wit always contain some aggression, whether or not it is directed against a manifest target. The mere fact of taking the initiative to invite the group to withdraw their focal attention from the topic under discussion constitutes a daring act.[14]

This is a characteristic of humor even when it is not offensive or harassing. The act of exercising power as the joke teller engages with, and is rooted in, existing power dynamics. Joking is never neutral. As Hemmasi, Graf and Russ find in their analysis of gender-related workplace humor,

> It is expected that subordinates and newcomers to an organization are more likely to refrain from joke telling, and when they do engage in such activities tend to mitigate the threatening nature of their act by making the content of the joke non-threatening (e.g., making themselves the object of a deprecating joke).[15]

Notably, the authors did not find significant differences between men and women in terms of their tolerance for sexual jokes. However, it is worth pointing out that humor in the workplace infrequently takes the form of formal joke telling. More subtle uses of humor, such as more direct teasing that could be construed as in good fun (or a normal part of workplace culture) or as bullying and harassment (or an aspect of producing a hostile work environment), are more likely to be experienced by workers regularly, and have a greater likelihood to be potentially problematic depending upon the social context in which the humor takes place. In this sense, the use of humor in the workplace correlates with Edgar Schein's theory of "group evolution" in organizations, where workers navigate positions of authority and subordination, gradually building group conformity through increased cohesion and emotional commitment to the preservation of harmony within the group overall.[16] In this process, outsiders who hope to gain access to the group may need to strategically (though often unconsciously) minimize their difference. In our examples of sexual humor and harassment, this would entail women having to 'choose' to find the harassing humor funny, rather than offensive.

The challenge with policing humor in the workplace is that it serves many diverse and important social functions. As Holmes and Stubbe find in their analysis of workplace communication, humor creates solidarity and reinforces a sense of belonging within groups; it also maintains and constructs power relationships; and it can be used as a hedging device to soften directives as well as a means of enacting politeness or "doing collegiality."[17] As Holmes and Stubbe suggest about understanding power negotiations in speech acts more generally,

> Relative power needs to be assessed not only in the particular social context in which an interaction takes places, but more particularly in the specific discourse context of any contribution. [. . .] [T]he particular topic of discussion may be relevant in identifying where power or authority lies in a particular section of talk, as well as how it is enacted.[18]

This presents something of a challenge to any workplace with an interest in regulating speech acts. In the highly regimented workplaces that we consider in two of our case studies, a fire department and the military, power is enacted in very explicit ways, and individuals are socialized to accept and in turn enact power (and behavioral norms) down the chain of command. This serves to define (and regulate) appropriate and inappropriate discursive power plays in complex ways, with humor offering a sometimes ambiguous means of enforcing hierarchy (through for example, teasing) and group cohesion (through a shared sense of humor). It can also be used subversively amongst in-groups to deflect frustrations amongst the rank and file, or regulate participation and behavior. These uses of humorous speech acts are neither fundamentally positive nor negative; their relative power is context specific.

The power dynamics inherent in humor make its use within the work environment potentially fraught. In practical terms, the reinforcement of hierarchy through humor entails subordinates feeling obligated to find their supervisors' jokes funny, or laughing at humor that might be experienced as harassment. When fitting into workplace culture involves sharing a sense of humor, those in subordinate positions are at a disadvantage as they have a disproportionate obligation to be receptive to the humor of others, while having limited space to define the terms of humorous discourse through their own joking. When joking is experienced as harassment, these power dynamics are further exacerbated.

Case study one: Sweater Day at Simon Fraser University

Simon Fraser University in Burnaby, Canada, was recently the locus of a significant controversy over a video posted to its Facilities Management social media accounts that, by all appearances, was meant to promote SFU "Sweater Day." This event encourages students, faculty, and staff to wear a sweater so that building temperatures may be turned down in an effort to promote energy saving on campus. The video features Mrs. (not Dr.) Pinkham, donning a pink sweater and playing solitaire on her computer just as a young male student walks by. His sexually suggestive compliments are received with flattery by Mrs. Pinkham. Fairly quickly after the video was posted, there was significant backlash from students, staff, faculty and the public, promptly followed by institutional backpedaling and an apology.

Elise Chenier, professor at the university, wrote a blog post detailing her concerns about the video and what it signifies about institutional culture:

> When the very place you work promotes the kind of sexism that your intellectual work seeks to contest and ultimately, destroy, you feel like you are being eaten from the inside out. There was once a time when I would have seen the video as simply outdated, idiotic, and yes, offensive, but now I see it much differently. Now I feel the harm it does.[19]

In manifestations of institutional sexism (or racism, ableism, etc.), the intent behind an utterance or gesture doesn't matter so much as entrenched policies or practices that result in injury or exclusion of certain groups. Individual senses of humor, laughing, offense, or non-offense do not reflect on the extent to which something is, in fact, sexist. It is obvious that the video was a gaffe and huge mistake, so its semiotics need not be discussed here—even as comments such as the following appear on articles related to the gaffe, which shows the degree to which sexism masked with humor is an ongoing problem:

> Raise your hand if you have a sense of humor. If you like compliments. If you think people who overreact to silly videos have nothing better to do in their lives. My hand is in the air.[20]

Notwithstanding the major problematic of this view, what is more relevant to consider here is the chain of command that contracted the video, and the chain of approval that enabled it to be posted on official university social media accounts. Clearly, numerous people had to have been involved in the production and dissemination. This video and its sharing by university personnel is not merely an example of 'getting it wrong' in 'good fun' with regards to what people find funny. Rather, it reflects a systemic issue with the use of humor in the workplace to promote what, indeed, is something positive. That positivity is at the expense of women. We need to look more closely at the ways in which such lines of joking are reflected in common workplace disparities. For example, we know that female professors are consistently ranked below male counterparts in student and peer evaluations, which are often very gendered, including comments on appearance and physical attractiveness. The authors of this chapter have both received such comments in student evaluations of our teaching. Likewise, women are consistently paid less, are not seen in representative numbers in administration or dean positions, are promoted more slowly, and so on.

The kind of cheeky humor that the SFU video intended to emulate is widespread in popular culture. Indeed, as Beth Montemurro has found, sexual harassment is regularly used as comic fodder in popular television comedies. In an analysis of five workplace-based situation comedies, Montemurro found that, "although sexual harassment is rarely discussed in situation comedies, gender harassment is frequently used as 'material,' which leads to further trivialization of a serious problem."[21] The use of gender harassment as friendly banter in situation comedies further clouds general understandings of what 'counts' as harassment, and normalizes sexual humor in the workplace. A current example of this kind of banter can be seen in the popular program *Brooklyn 99* (Dan Goor and Michael Schur, 2014–). A recurring gag in the series involves fictional New York detective Jake Peralta (Andy Samberg) lampooning fellow detective Amy Santiago (Melissa Fumero); whenever Santiago says something banal and self-critical such as "I'm sorry about tonight," Peralta follows up with a line such as, "'I'm sorry about tonight' is the name of your sex tape." This 'sex-tape' gag is part of a flirtatious repartee between the two characters that eventually evolves into an on-screen relationship.

It is notable that this kind of low-level sexualized joking is normalized, especially as the program is a police sitcom—and policing is precisely the kind of male-dominated workplace where this kind of harassment is likely to reinforce a hostile work environment. No doubt viewers are not intended to interpret the sexual banter as harassment. Indeed, the *Brooklyn 99* work environment is ethnically diverse and includes strong female leads. The precinct police captain is African-American and gay, and there is no indication that any of the characters are overtly discriminated against. The only detectives who are regularly portrayed as incompetent are a couple of middle-aged white male detectives who are meant to represent the 'old guard' whose time has passed. All this is to say that within the scope of the program, the female detective who is the butt of sexual humor is portrayed as competent and respected by her peers. The harassment is intended to be interpreted as *just a joke*, and she does not appear to *take it personally*. It is precisely this sort of popular portrayal of sexual humor in the workplace that contributes to the normalization of this kind of banter. In everyday culture, we receive mixed signals about what constitutes appropriate workplace joking; at the same time that workplaces seek to avoid sexual harassment controversies which might result in public backlash and costly litigation, our popular culture presents representations of workplace relationships that are "rife with sexual innuendo and power trips."[22]

As we can see from the SFU Sweater Day example, this normalization can have very problematic consequences when this kind of humor is taken up in real workplaces. This is especially evident when sexualization of the work environment crosses the line into intimidation, bullying and harassment, as is the issue in the next case study that we consider.

Case study two: pornography in the firefighter classroom

In January of 2016, firefighting instructor Jeremy Hall of Newfoundland's Bay de Grave regional fire department came under media scrutiny for revelations that he had shown a pornographic video during a two-day vehicle-extrication training course in April 2014. The video in question involves a woman masturbating in a kitchen. Brenda Seymour, a Spaniard's Bay City councilor and volunteer firefighter, brought forward allegations of sexual harassment, citing the use of pornography in the course as a manifestation of a general culture of harassment that she has endured as the only female in the brigade.

When asked about his use of the video, Hall admitted that he has used it a number of times, but downplayed its significance, claiming that the video was only played as a joke, that no harassment was intended, and that his practices of warning participants about the X-rated nature of the video and offering the option of leaving the room were sufficient to mitigate any feelings of discomfort.[23]

In the aftermath, the Spaniard's Bay City council considered the removal of then-Fire Chief Victor Hiscock for his perceived failure of leadership stemming from ongoing accusations of rampant sexual harassment within the department. Although the motion for his dismissal was narrowly defeated, Hiscock resigned anyway along with 19 other firefighters who quit in a show of solidarity. The mayor, Tony Menchion, claimed that the incident was in no way a "gender issue," and an article published in *Vice Magazine* found that women in Spaniard's Bay were particularly publicly critical of Seymour for bringing forward her complaints, with one resident suggesting, "if [Seymour]'s going to be in a room of men, she has to be able to take the heat and take a joke."[24] In media discussions, public supporters of the Fire Department and its male volunteers were critical of Seymour, suggesting that her own interpersonal challenges and difficult relationship with the fire chief were the real reason for her complaints, and that the "gender issue" was simply a scapegoat.[25]

What is important to note here is that the issue of whether Seymour is a good colleague and the debate around what behaviors do and do not cross the line are moot. The use of pornographic material in a workplace or training environment results in the sexualization of the workplace. This inappropriate action is rendered even more problematic when the workplace in question has such a disproportionately low number of women; that is to say, the workplace is already structurally gendered, and the pornographic video intensifies and reinforces this. To hide behind the argument that the video, and other potentially harassing behaviors, were only intended as 'jokes' is a clear manifestation of the problematic role that humor can play in reinforcing exclusionary workplace cultures.

In cases such as this one, it is apparent that the exclusion, ridicule, and harassment functions of humor must be addressed in ways that do not reinforce the assumption that when joking is poorly received, blame can be deflected onto the individual who does not find the joke funny. This occurs in workplace disagreements over whether a particular line of joking constitutes sexual or gender harassment, or whether it is simply good-natured fun.[26] In the case of the Spaniard's Bay Fire Department, the deflection of Seymour's complaints about workplace humor through an indictment of her supposed lack of a sense of humor operates to cover up deeper systemic issues present in the work environment. The point is not simply that individuals might perceive humor differently, but rather that humor is regularly invoked in workplaces to reinforce problematic (or hostile) workplace cultures which in turn reinforce traditional exclusions. The humor in a workplace can therefore act as an index of other systemic issues, such as sexism. This can play out not only in whether or not one finds a joke offensive, but also in who is given space to tell jokes and who is expected to laugh at them. In this case, we need to consider the extent to which joking is part of a hierarchical system in which not all parties can expect to participate equally. While the context of a fire department in a relatively small community might be taken as an isolated incident, rather than a systemic issue that can characterize an entire industry, it is made clear in our final case study that problematic and harassing humor cultures do exist on a much more widespread scale in other male-dominated workplaces such as policing and the military.

Case study three: the sexualized environment of the Canadian Armed Forces

Sexual harassment in hierarchical, predominantly male organizations such as fire departments, police forces, and the military is increasingly an object of scrutiny in Canada. In the fire department example considered above, it is notable that internal resistance remains a barrier to effecting cultural change. Not all organizations remain so entrenched in their opposition to considering the "gender issue," however. In October of 2016, the RCMP commissioner offered a public apology to female members of the force who had experienced systemic gender harassment; the apology coincided with the settlement of two proposed class-action lawsuits and an announcement that new strategies would be put in place to alter the force's problematic workplace culture.[27]

In an even more significant public admission of wrongdoing, the Canadian Armed Forces recently publicly acknowledged that they have been inadequate in addressing significant and widespread sexual harassment within their ranks. This admission was precipitated by the release of retired justice of the Supreme Court of Canada Marie Deschamps' report, *External Review into Sexual Misconduct and Sexual Harassment in the Canadian Armed Forces*. Commissioned by the Canadian Armed Forces as an independent review of its policies, procedures, and programs related to sexual harassment, the report found that the problem was not simply that quid-pro-quo sexual harassment and sexual assault were found to be occupational hazards for women and LGBTQ members of the Canadian Armed Forces, but more significantly, that the entire system reinforced a "sexualized environment [. . .] characterized by the frequent use of swear words and highly degrading expressions that reference women's bodies, sexual jokes, innuendos, [and] discriminatory comments."[28]

In an analysis of discrimination in the military, Elizabeth Kier argues that the need for a strong, unified organizational culture is particularly significant due to its reliance on commitment, obedience, discipline, and group cohesion. In practice, humor can be used to reinforce such a culture by establishing camaraderie and reinforcing group norms. However, it is also evident that such organizational culture can play a role in reinforcing problematic and discriminatory practices. As Deschamps has found, some of this camaraderie includes engaging in joking that creates a sexualized work environment. According to Kier, the positive identification that comes with a strong regimental culture and collective identity has a negative counterpart:

> military cultures help create commitment but they also define and sharpen boundaries. Members of a group identify *with* as well as *against* others. Comparison and opposition are always present; there can be no in-group without an out-group, no "we" without a "they."[29]

In their discussion of workplace humor, Holmes and Stubbe find that "jocular abuse" or joking insults are often expressions of solidarity. As such, women in male-dominated workplaces experience a "double-edged sword" with regards to "boys club" sexualized joking. If they are spared this joking because it only occurs when they are absent, they are not fully part of the in-group and as such are excluded from some spaces of social bonding. If, however, they want access to this level of camaraderie, they must accept and perhaps even participate in this joking, even if it is disproportionately offensive to women. In terms of organizational culture, this acceptance is required for women to reach what Edgar Schein describes as "group maturity," which is characterized by an "emotional focus on preserving the group and its culture" and where "member differences are seen as a threat."[30] In the case of the pornographic video clip offered as a 'joke' in the previous case study, it was expected that the lone female participant in the course would simply be *cool*, and accept this sexualized joking as part of belonging to the club.

In the case of the Canadian Armed Forces, Deschamps argues that cultural change within the organization, at all levels of the chain of command, is essential to altering this hostile environment. It is not enough to clamp down on instances of harassment and assault; rather there needs to be a more general alteration to the culture of jokes, innuendos, and comments that contribute to the reproduction of this hostile environment. In a study of a non-military workplace, Beth Quinn finds that resistance tactics exist within the work environment, which enable sexual harassment to be interpreted as mere joking. In particular, Quinn finds that women who experience harassment are reluctant to identify it as such, preferring instead to interpret sexual joking as common "chain yanking" and to "not take it personally."[31] For this reason, very few instances of harassment are legally defined as such, and many employees who experience harassment do not report it. What is clear from both the Deschamps report and the Quinn study is that, in workplaces where harassment is systemic, significant changes to workplace culture are required, and existing processes for the reporting of harassment are inadequate.

Conclusions

Studies evaluating the receptivity of men and women to sexist and sexual jokes in the workplace have found that, in general, the majority of managers and employees perceive sexist joking as inappropriate.[32] Despite this general agreement, 40% of survey respondents also indicated that they regularly encounter sexist and sexual jokes in their own workplaces.[33] Humor in the workplace, therefore, continues to be a challenging issue, especially with regards to harassment.

Scholarly considerations of workplace humor tend to focus on its relationship to sexual and gender harassment. In their study of gender-related jokes in the workplace, Hemmasi, Graf and Russ grounded their discussion of offensive humor in the issue of subjectivity in humor perception, noting that what is "'just good fun' for one person could be 'sexual harassment' for another."[34] This perspective is prevalent in discussions of workplace harassment, where humor is simply 'misinterpreted' as sexual harassment.

How the issue of harassment is taken up can vary greatly, and not all those concerned about the issue of harassment are primarily focused on the needs of the potential victims of this joking. Instances of the trope of blaming the offended party, rather than the offending one, are widespread. For example, Howard Scott, a consultant writing for a dry-cleaning trade publication, characterizes the issue of workplace humor as being a dangerous terrain in which "You never know what will be considered 'humor' by one person and 'offensive smut' by another. [. . .] Moreover, when an individual sees the possibility of financial gain you don't know how far the truth will be stretched."[35] In this instance, the real concern for employers is the potential for lawsuits fought on the grounds that workplace humor might constitute harassment. This perspective takes up the 'employee making trouble' perspective, in which good-natured workplace humor is just misinterpreted and misconstrued by a sensitive or conniving member. Fitting in to this workplace culture can require the acceptance of inappropriate uses of humor, absolving the utterer of wrongdoing by accepting that they were ostensibly 'only joking.' Claiming humorous intent therefore reinforces systemic exclusions, operates as a means of social intimidation, and can be used to deflect accusations of sexual harassment.

Along similar lines, journalist Cathy Young noted in 2003,

> Women's claims of "hostile environment" harassment are often based on a bawdy workplace atmosphere which seems to affect men and women alike, and to which other women may contribute. [. . .] [W]hat seems to be nearly extinct is any appreciation of diverse cultural norms in the workplace—of the fact that some work

environments may be relatively straitlaced while others may be raunchy and free-wheeling, and that people unhappy with the culture of their current job might simply seek other employment.[36]

Young's perspective here is that the kind of humor that might be misinterpreted as contributing to a "hostile environment" in the workplace might have more to do with workplace culture. This is precisely what public criticisms of firefighter Brenda Seymour alluded to: that her complaints about harassment were invalid given the expectation that she ought to be more amenable to the raunchy workplace culture of the firehall. What these arguments overlook, is that this is indeed the problem. Humor is the shortest and surest path to the reproduction of problematic and exclusionary workplace cultures. While systems are often in place to deal with quid-pro-quo sexual harassment, or explicit verbal and physical expressions of sexual interest, it is much more difficult to address the subtle ways in which the underlying cultures of workplaces enable the exclusion of certain types of participants, especially, though not exclusively, through humor. It is important to note that humor is problematic in the workplace not only when it is harassment. The performance of the right kind of a 'sense of humor,' or the affective labor of laughing at the boss's jokes, can also be part of defining 'fit' with workplace culture. As Karim H. Karim has argued, being able to engage in certain types of discussions of popular culture become "the entry point into casual conversations [. . .] or 'water cooler talk.'"[37] In this sense, humor can act as a more subtle, everyday aggression of gendered exclusion.

Changing these problematic cultures is not easy. Indeed, in the case of the Canadian military, it is clear that all levels of command are implicated in the reproduction of a sexualized work environment, and that changing this culture must come through the chain of command. In instances such as the Spaniard's Bay Fire Department example, we see a clear reluctance on the part of high-ranking officials (the fire chief, the mayor) to admit that a problematic culture exists. In this case, pressure for change likely needs to come from an authoritative external source (for example, a labor association or other government body). While evaluating and altering organizational culture is possible (and indeed necessary to ensure the long-term health of the organization and its workforce), this change is only possible with buy-in from organizational influencers, and in some instances may be very difficult to achieve in the short-term.[38]

With the case studies that we have addressed above, we consider the ways in which the presumption of the inherent positivity of humor is particularly problematic for the reproduction of certain aspects of workplace culture. When emphasizing the positive role that humor plays in workplace cultures, there is a risk of reinforcing barriers to participation which are themselves often produced and reproduced through unwritten social codes. In other words, while speaking optimistically about the value of humor in daily life, we must also consider carefully the role of humor in relations and negotiations of power. While sexual harassment is perhaps the most obvious place to perceive the ways that humor can reproduce problematic power dynamics, it is important to emphasize that even non-sexualized humor can operate in this way. Indeed, when scholars and critics of humor emphasize the problem of joke perception (that is, the subjectivity of finding something funny or not), they overlook the role that humor plays in contexts of inequality, of producing in-groups and out-groups, and of reinforcing traditional biases and exclusions within workplace cultures. Humor in this sense acts as an index of other systemic issues within organizations. Furthermore, humor plays a gatekeeping function whereby workplace cultures are reinforced, and those who hope to succeed within that culture must assimilate to dominant humor expectations, or face potential alienation. Therefore, the problem is not whether individuals *get the joke* or can endure a little so-called *chain yanking* and *not take it personally*, but rather to what extent individuals are able to accept these aspects of workplace power dynamics as part of their daily working conditions.

References

1 Brunner, P. W., and Costello, M. L. (Spring 2002), Where's the joke? The meaning behind sexual humor, *Advancing Women in Leadership*, retrieved from http://www.advancingwomen.com/awl/spring2002/BRUNN~37.HTM [Accessed March 30, 2017].

2 Billig, M. (2005), *Laughter and Ridicule: Towards a Social Critique of Humour*, London: Sage, 11.

3 Bressler, E., Martin, R., and Balshine, S. (2006), Production and appreciation of humor as sexually selected traits, *Evolution and Human Behavior*, 27, 121–130.

4 Karim, K. H. (2005), The elusiveness of full citizenship: Accounting for cultural capital, cultural competencies, and cultural pluralism, in Andrew, C., Gattinger, M., Jeannotte, M. S., and Straw, W. (Eds.), *Accounting for Culture: Thinking through Cultural Citizenship*, Ottawa: University of Ottawa Press, 146–158.

5 Brunner, P. W., and Costello, M. L., op. cit.

6 Hemmasi, M., Graf, L., and Russ, G. (1994), Gender-related jokes in the workplace: Sexual humor or sexual harassment? *Journal of Applied Social Psychology*, 24(12), 1114–1128.

7 Peterson, M. A. (2005), Toward an ethnography of intertextuality, in Rothenbuhler, E. and Coman, M. (Eds.), *Media Anthropology*, London: Sage, 129.

8 Karim, op. cit., 151.

9 Critchley, S. (2002), *On Humour*, London: Routledge, 2.

10 Billig, op. cit., 13.

11 Mulkay, M. (1988), *On Humor: Its Nature and Its Place in Modern Society*, Boston, MA: Blackwell.

12 Brunner, P. W., and Costello, M. L., op. cit.

13 Coser, R. L. (1960), Laughter among colleagues: A study of the social functions of humor among the staff of a mental hospital, *Psychiatry*, 23, 86.

14 Coser, op. cit., 83.

15 Hemmasi, Graf, and Russ, op. cit., 1117.

16 Schein, E. H. (2010), *Organizational Culture and Leadership*, San Francisco, CA: Jossey-Bass.

17 Holmes, J., and Stubbe, M. (2015), *Power and Politeness in the Workplace: A Sociolinguistics Analysis of Talk at Work*, London: Routledge, 3; see also Coser, op. cit.; Morreall, J. (1991), Humor and work, *Humor*, 4(4), 359–373.

18 Holmes, and Stubbe, op. cit., 4–5.

19 Chenier, E. (2016), When your institution treats you like a sex object, retrieved from http://elisechenier.com/2016/02/03/when-your-institution-treats-you-like-a-sex-object/?platform=hootsuite [Accessed April 4, 2016].

20 Daro, I. N. (2016), A Canadian university made this blatantly sexist video objectifying female professors, *BuzzFeed News*, retrieved from http://www.buzzfeed.com/ishmaeldaro/sfu-sweater-day-video#.bfBRvNEoN [Accessed April 4, 2016].

21 Montemurro, B. (2003), Not a laughing matter: Sexual harassment as 'material' on workplace-based situation comedies, *Sex Roles*, 48(9–10), 433.

22 Brunner, and Costello, op. cit.

23 Roberts, T. (2016, January 21), Porn in the classroom 'just for a laugh,' firefighting instructor says, *CBC News*, retrieved from http://www.cbc.ca/news/canada/newfoundland-labrador/porn-classroom-jeremy-hall-1.3413176 [Accessed October 31, 2016].

24 Brown, D. (2016, January 22), 20 male firefighters quit after only female colleague complains of harassment in Newfoundland town, *Vice*, retrieved from http://www.vice.com/en_ca/read/20-male-firefighters-quit-after-only-female-colleague-complains-of-harassment-in-newfoundland-town [Accessed October 31, 2016].

25 Hopper, T. (2016, January 21), Crashed trucks, dead mice and porn, *National Post*, retrieved from http://news.nationalpost.com/news/canada/crashed-trucks-dead-mice-and-porn-inside-the-firefighting-scandal-tearing-apart-a-newfoundland-town [Accessed October 31, 2016].

26 Hemmasi, Graf, and Russ, op. cit.

27 Quan, D. (2016, October 5), RCMP to settle in workplace harassment class-action cases, apologize to victims, *National Post*, retrieved from http://news.nationalpost.com/news/canada/canadian-politics/rcmp-to-settle-in-workplace-harassment-class-action-cases-apologize-to-victims-sources [Accessed October 31, 2016].

28 Deschamps, M. (2015), *External review into sexual misconduct and sexual harassment in the Canadian Armed Forces*, External Review Authority, ii.

29 Keir, E. (1999), Discrimination and military cohesion: An organizational perspective, in Katzenstein, M. F. and Reppy, J. (Eds.), *Beyond Zero Tolerance: Discrimination in Military Culture*, Oxford: Rowman & Littlefield, 27.

30 Schein, op. cit., 205.

31 Quinn, B. A. (2000), The paradox of complaining: Law, humor, and harassment in the everyday work world, *Law and Social Inquiry*, 25(4), 1151–1185.

32 Hemmasi, Graf, and Russ, op. cit.; Graf, L., and Hemmasi, M. (1995, November), Risque humor, *HR Magazine*, 40(11).

33 Graf, and Hemmasi, op. cit.

34 Hemmasi, Graf, and Russ, op. cit., 1126.

35 Scott, H. (2002, December), Is it humor; or harassment? *American Drycleaner*, 69(9).

36 Young, C. (2003, January), Man trouble, *Reason*, 34(8), 19.

37 Karim, op. cit., 150.

38 Schein, E. H., and Bennis, W. G. (1965), *Personal and Organizational Change through Group Methods: The Laboratory Approach*, New York: Wiley.

4.5 Does verbal irony have a place in the workplace?

Roger J. Kreuz

Introduction

After one's family, the workplace stands at the center of most adults' lives. We spend half our waking hours each day in the presence of others with whom we share a tangle of social relationships. Just as one cannot choose one's family, most of us have no control over who our supervisors or our coworkers are. Nonetheless, we are expected to maintain harmonious relationships with others, even with those who may be competitors for advancement or resources. In other cases, we attempt to foster closer relationships with coworkers we happen to like. It is also the case that relationships between employees can change as their institutional roles change. The workplace, therefore, can be characterized as a complex social milieu in which actors pursue a multitude of diverse agendas, and even innocent or well-meaning statements may be scrutinized by their recipients for subtext or multiple messages. These issues are exacerbated in computer-mediated communication (e.g., e-mail and social media), which typically lacks the contextual cues of face-to-face interaction. Given all of this, it is easy to see how workplace communication can lead to miscommunication.

Problems in communication often revolve around the expression of emotion. The expression of strong emotion via language is problematic in many cultures, and the direct expression of negative emotions is often taboo. As a result, hostility or anger may be expressed indirectly, but this indirectness also creates ambiguity about a message's intent. Different recipients may perceive the same message as humorous or as threatening, depending on their relationship with the speaker or author, and the context in which the message is delivered and received.

The importance of emotions and emotional expression in the workplace were relatively neglected topics of research until the mid-1990s.[1] Since that time, however, researchers have begun to explore the communication of emotion via language in a variety of contexts, including in the workplace.

Some terminology

Information about emotional states is often conveyed indirectly, by using so-called non-literal language. If we were to imagine a very angry coworker, we could use a variety of such forms to describe her, her thoughts, and her behaviors. This could include the use of idioms ("she flipped her lid"), metaphors ("she was a volcano"), similes ("her anger was like a tsunami"), exaggeration ("she wanted to kill someone"), as well as exaggeration's polar opposite, understatement ("she was slightly vexed").

The communication of negative emotion is also frequently accomplished through the use of verbal irony, in which a speaker says the opposite of what she means. An example would be a coworker remarking "Gee, what lovely weather we're having!" during a heavy downpour. Most theorists characterize verbal irony as conceptually distinct from other phenomena also referred to as irony. Examples include dramatic irony, in which an audience is aware of something that an actor is ignorant of,[2] and situational irony, which is the juxtaposition of two incongruous things (e.g., the fire station that catches fire).[3]

Verbal irony's close cousin is sarcasm, and the dividing line between these two forms is not entirely unclear. Different researchers define and use the two terms differently, and they are frequently conflated in nonacademic usage, particularly in the United States.[4] To muddy the waters further, some have argued that sarcasm does not necessarily entail irony; from this perspective, sarcasm is synonymous with any disparaging remark that involves some element of humor.[5] When a distinction is made, however, sarcasm is typically viewed as a subtype of verbal irony, and as a form of language that has a clear victim or target (as in "The boss has made another brilliant business decision!" when he has not).[6]

It should therefore come as no surprise to learn that the relations between the terms "humor," "irony," and "sarcasm" are also ill-defined. Many conventional ironic statements (such as muttering "Oh, that's just great!" when dropping one's car keys into a puddle) aren't humorous at all.[7] A barbed sarcastic remark is not very funny either—if you happen to be on the receiving end of such a statement. However, many ironic and sarcastic utterances are perceived as clever or witty, and this may be a principal reason for why this form of language is used so frequently.[8]

For the purposes of this chapter, I will generally employ the terms "verbal irony" or "irony," since they are the broadest and most inclusive. However, I will use "sarcasm" if that was the term employed by the original theorists and researchers whose work is under discussion.

Varieties of verbal irony

Verbal irony is often employed to highlight the difference between one's expectations and a particular outcome. For example, we hope that people will be helpful, that our enterprises will meet with success, and that the weather will be pleasant. This bias toward the positive, dubbed the "Pollyanna principle,"[9] can be thought of as reflecting implicit cultural norms. When reality doesn't align with our hopes, we can ironically *echo* these cultural expectations. If a coworker agrees to assist you with something and then fails to appear at the appointed time, you might greet him with "Gee, thanks for all help!" at your next meeting. (Since your coworker is the clear target of the remark, this would be an example of sarcasm.)

The idea of an implicit or explicit echo has been an important component of many theories of verbal irony. In echoic mention theory,[10] for example, the echo is of a thought, attitude, or cultural norm that is attributed to a person or to a group. In echoic reminder theory,[11] the ironic utterance reminds the addressee of the thought, attitude, or norm being echoed. In both cases, the critical idea is that the addressee is forced to consider the gap that exists between what was said and the current state of affairs, which should allow her to arrive at the speaker's intended meaning. In a later refinement of this approach, referred to as Allusional Pretense Theory,[12] it was proposed that pragmatic insincerity is also a key feature of ironic language. That is, it must be clear to the addressee that the speaker has violated a pragmatic norm of literal language use (such as the expectation that people say things which are true). However, the necessity of pragmatic insincerity has also been called into question in later research.[13]

If verbal irony is characterized by a mismatch between expectations and outcome, then a negative evaluation of a positive outcome should, in theory, work just as well. In practice, however, this isn't the case. A remark about "lovely weather" during a heavy downpour (a positive evaluation of a negative outcome) is an example of what has been labeled *canonical* irony, and such statements are quickly and reliably interpreted as non-literal.[14] Non-canonical ironic statements, by contrast, are *negative* evaluations of *positive* outcomes. Since there is, once again, a mismatch between a remark and reality, it might be expected that such statements would also be interpreted unambiguously.

Interestingly, however, this isn't what happens. Imagine that one's boss says "Gee, what terrible weather we're having!" on a pleasant, sunny day. This would seem odd, at least in part because it is a violation of the Pollyanna principle described above. Participants in comprehension experiments take longer to read such statements, and aren't as certain that such remarks are intended to be ironic.[15] In fact, when asked why a person might say such a thing, research participants offer up a host of potential reasons: maybe the speaker is in a bad mood, or perhaps they're mocking some earlier, incorrect prediction about stormy weather.[16] What they are less likely to do is to interpret the statement as implying its opposite, and to understand it as an ironic acknowledgment of a pleasant day.

As we know all too well, ironic statements can and do go awry. To be understood as intended, they require knowledge of one's conversational partner, as well as the correct interpretation of linguistic and paralinguistic cues, such as the use of exaggeration and a certain tone of voice.[17] However, some of the problematic issues in the use of verbal irony may have as much to do with the acceptance of the ironist's attitude as with the propositions themselves.[18] In addition, there may also be differing pragmatic standards with regard to the use of verbal irony, even within the same culture. It has been demonstrated, for example, that college students in a northern US sample perceived sarcasm as more humorous than critical, but this was not the case for participants attending a university in the southern US. Perhaps as a consequence, the southern participants spontaneously employed sarcasm to a lesser degree in a free response task designed to elicit such language.[19]

In trying to make sense of the multitude of theoretical perspectives that have been advanced, some researchers have highlighted criticism as an essential component of ironic language.[20] A crucial issue, however, may be whom this criticism is directed towards—the hearer or some other party. Other theorists have attempted to bring verbal irony under the umbrella of Politeness Theory.[21] In this theoretical approach, it is proposed that individuals minimize the impact of face-threatening acts (like making requests of others) by going "off record." That is, instead of directly asking for something, which might be perceived as face threatening, the requester can instead make a related statement, and leave it to the listener to infer the speaker's intent, as in, "Say, do you happen to have any change?" in place of directly asking to borrow some money. Several studies have shown that people automatically interpret such statements according to their off-record intent, and not as literal questions about knowledge or ability.[22]

One issue with Politeness Theory, however, is that a clean division between on- and off-record strategies is problematic: some statements seem to contain a mixture of both.[23] This can occur, for example, when someone makes a prediction that is proven incorrect. Imagine a nervous employee who predicts to a friend that his presentation will not be well received. If, in fact, the presentation goes well, his friend could mockingly echo the prediction, which would be a combination of praise (you did well) and criticism (you worry too much). The on-record compliment is tempered by the off-record critique, and such ironic compliments are perceived as more muted than literal compliments.[24]

Later research, however, has called this muting function into question. Far from diluting condemnation, ironic criticism can actually enhance its critical impact, at least in some circumstances.[25] However, this negativity depends very much on one's perspective. It has also been reported that participants who take the point of view of an aggressor find sarcastic comments to be less aggressive, and more humorous, than when they are assigned the point of view of the being the target of such statements. As the authors of the study conclude, the effects of sarcasm are truly in the eye of the beholder, and that "the same comments are understood quite differently when one utters a barb than when one is stung by it" (p. 232).[26] Finally, more recent work suggests that ironic criticism can be simultaneously more mocking and more polite.[27] Clearly, the pragmatic functions of ironic criticism are complex and deserving of additional study.

Verbal irony in close relationships

Many of the negative concepts we associate with verbal irony and sarcasm, such as hostility and belittlement, do not seem to apply when such language is used by friends and intimate partners. In an analysis of conversations between college students and their friends, it was found that ironic statements occurred frequently, at a rate of about one in twelve conversational turns,[28] which is comparable to an estimate made by another researcher in a different discourse context.[29] In addition, a positive correlation has been found between the likelihood that two people will use sarcasm and the perceived closeness of their relationship.[30] Clearly, ironic remarks made by friends are fulfilling very different discourse goals than those made by adversaries.

To speak nonliterally is to run the risk of being misunderstood. But that risk will be minimized if the speaker and hearer share sufficient common ground. In such a case, the hearer will be able to see through the apparent ruse, and interpret the remark as meaning something different from what was literally said. Common ground has been defined as including factors like shared community membership (be it a family, team, profession, religion, or culture), or the same physical environment.[31] A shared environment explains why a remark about gorgeous weather on a rainy day will be interpreted as ironic, since both parties are experiencing the same foul weather, and the mismatch between statement and reality is obvious.

But what if shared community membership is unknown, or if the speaker wants to refer to something that is not physically present? In such cases, people might employ a heuristic of inferability: a rough calculation of whether a hearer is likely to interpret a nonliteral remark correctly.[32] If inferability is high, as it would be among intimates, then would-be ironists should feel free to make completely outrageous statements, secure in the knowledge they will not be interpreted literally. And in such cases, the need to use facial, gestural, or intonation cues to signal ironic intent drops away as well. Among intimates, in fact, it is not unusual for ironic statements to be made in a totally deadpan way.[33]

However, when conversing with a stranger, the would-be ironist might decide to play it safe, and to speak in a very literal way. Like all rules of thumb, however, this heuristic is not infallible, and a given speaker may over- or underestimate the common ground that she shares with her addressee. This is likely to occur in environments like the workplace, in which employees share the common ground provided by their occupations, but possibly little else. Many workplaces are quite diverse, and similar beliefs and attitudes concerning politics, sexuality, or religion, to name just a few, are unlikely to be shared by all.

In fact, the use of verbal irony or sarcasm can function as a signal of allegiance or even as a marker of intimacy. In this way, such statements become a signifier that the addressee is part of an in-group. This idea forms the basis of Pretense Theory.[34] According to this formulation, the ironic speaker is pretending to be an ignorant and injudicious person, speaking to a credulous audience. The addressee, however, is able to see through this ruse, and understands the real meaning of the speaker. Viewed in this way, the speaker invites the addressee to become a member of an exclusive club: one of the few who possess the requisite knowledge to understand the remark as intended.

This idea of exclusivity has found some empirical support.[35] A study was designed to test the idea that such language may promote and be emblematic of solidary relationships (those in which the participants have a shared past, a collective identity, and interact as equals[36]). The researchers found, for example, that ironic statements made to solidary recipients were perceived as more humorous and playful than those made to nonsolidary addressees.

The flip side of intimacy, of course, is exclusion. So while verbal irony may foster intimacy between the speaker and addressee, by definition there will be others (e.g., side participants, bystanders, and overhearers) for whom such remarks will function in an exclusionary way. In addition to creating and promoting an in-group, the ironist, intentionally or not, also creates an out-group: those who fail to understand the remark due to a lack of context or familiarity with the speaker. And if someone isn't in on a joke, they may start to worry that they are the unwitting target of such remarks.

To take things a step further, we can consider cases in which verbal irony is used to express hostility, albeit indirectly. This type of sarcastic speech is characteristic of passive-aggressive behavior,[37] since it allows the ironist to protest that he or she was "only teasing" or "just kidding." In this way, the wielder of such statements can turn the tables and ask why the addressee can't take a joke. Unfortunately, the line that separates good-natured teasing from subtle forms of hostility is highly variable and subjective, especially in the workplace,[38] and the lack of clarity about an ironist's true motivation can make it very difficult to determine his intent. To complicate matters further, some have argued that men and women use language in very different ways,[39] so ironic banter directed at a female employee by a male may be perceived as threatening, and possibly even as harassment. In 2011, a supervisor in Queensland had her employment terminated when she was accused of bullying and harassing another employee over a two-year period. As an example of hostile behavior, it was reported that the supervisor told the worker that she "deserved the employee-of-the-year award" while using a sarcastic tone of voice. In this case, however, the supervisor appealed the decision, and Fair Work Australia ruled in her favor, noting that the supervisor's "unprofessional and inappropriate" behavior did not rise to the level of harassment.[40] Would the outcome have been different if the supervisor of the female employee had been a man instead?

Verbal irony has traditionally been studied in the laboratory in the speech of dyads or small groups.[41] Undoubtedly, however, this form of language serves important communicative functions in larger groups as well,[42] and it is reasonable to assume that similar factors affect verbal irony use within larger social contexts, such as within a business or corporation.

Verbal irony in the workplace

The general orientation of the workplace literature has been to view verbal irony, and sarcasm in particular, in a relatively negative light. Some have characterized it almost exclusively as a way of expressing hostility.[43] Furthermore, many online sources that purport to dispense business advice are full of warnings about this form of language. One such webpage begins with the following: "Sarcasm is used far too often by people . . . it weakens teamwork and reduces morale."[44] Another equates the use of sarcasm with being a "smart mouth person," the type responsible for the undermining of others and the lowering of productivity. The author goes on to discuss the pros and cons of confronting or ignoring such disruptive individuals.[45] A third online source recommends taking a strong stand against workplace sarcasm, characterizing it as "humor at its worst."[46]

As we have seen, this one-dimensional view of verbal irony is problematic at best. Just as a screwdriver can be used as a tool or as a weapon, verbal irony can be employed to fulfill a variety of discourse goals, including the positive goals of expressing humor[47] and showing solidarity with one's conversational partner.[48] Verbal irony, therefore, should not be conceptualized in positive or negative terms, but rather as a means of achieving multiple communicative ends.[49] Some of these communicative ends, such as expressing frustration in a socially acceptable way, would be difficult, if not impossible, to convey via literal language.[50]

Some researchers have argued that previous theoretical accounts of verbal irony fail to take into account the more confrontational aspects of such language.[51] And it is in environments like the workplace that humor and irony can take on more of a hard edge. Why might this be? One major difference is that, in comparison to relations with friends and intimates, the workplace involves a hierarchy. In fact, most workplaces are largely defined by the existence of asymmetrical power relationships. Subordinates can find it difficult to directly contradict or to criticize their superiors, and the use of humor and irony provide a more socially acceptable way to carry out such face-threatening acts. Importantly, however, the reverse is also true: superiors have to cajole and occasionally reprimand their subordinates, and they need to do so in ways that won't create conflict, or injure a worker's pride or morale.

One study of ironic humor in the workplace, specifically involving the statements of senior managers during staff meetings, revealed that such utterances were employed to discuss serious issues in a less threatening and more playful way. For example, after a series of discouraging reports about attempts to reduce inventory, the general manager of the firm commented, "Right, other than that, everything went great!" (p. 280).[52] This remark led to an outburst of laughter from the other managers. The statement was interpreted as an attempt to neutralize the negative emotional response of the team to some unwelcome news. The use of contradiction to create humor reveals yet another way that such statements allow their speakers to satisfy multiple discourse goals. A literal acknowledgment of the inventory reduction problems would have been damaging to the morale of the management team. By responding ironically, the general manager acknowledged the seriousness of the issue, but also signaled confidence that the problems could be overcome.

A recent and intriguing report found that the use of sarcasm can lead to higher perceptions of conflict, but also to greater levels of creativity.[53] In one experiment, online subjects participated in a simulated conversation task, and were exposed to either sarcastic or sincere statements that had been generated earlier by a different set of participants.

Next, creativity was assessed by having the subjects complete a widely used measure of creativity, the Remote Association Task (RAT; e.g., thinking of the word "pool" as the common element linking "hall," "car," and "swimming"). Afterwards, the participants completed scales that assessed their perception of conflict. Not surprisingly, the subjects who had been repeatedly exposed to sarcasm reported higher perceived conflict than those in the sincere condition, but they also solved significantly more RAT items than participants in the sincere condition, or in a control condition.

A second study used a different sarcasm induction technique: participants were asked to recall a personally relevant experience of sarcasm, or their last conversation with someone who asked them for directions (a control condition). The measure of creativity was also different: subjects attempted to solve the Duncker Candle Problem (participants are asked to attach a candle to a wall, which requires overcoming functional fixedness about using a tack box as a candle stand). Once again, the subjects who had thought about sarcasm reported experiencing more conflict, but they were also more likely to solve the Candle Problem than the control participants.

In a final experiment, participants were asked to imagine that the same sarcastic statements used in an earlier study were being spoken by someone they greatly trusted, or by someone they distrusted. Participants in the distrust condition reported greater perceived conflict, but those in the trust condition did not. Significantly, however, both groups performed better on yet another measure of creativity than control participants who imagined non-sarcastic conversations. (In this case, the participants were asked to solve the Olive in a Glass problem, which involves overcoming assumptions about the position or orientation of a glass in order to move an olive.)

Taken as a whole, the authors interpret their results as suggesting that sarcasm may be a catalyst for abstract thinking, and that such thinking is an important antecedent of creative behavior. To quote the authors, sarcasm "helps people think creatively even as they seethe in conflict."[54] However, their results also suggest that the beneficial effects of sarcasm may only accrue to members of a team who trust each other. The finding that sarcasm can boost creativity without increasing conflict has obvious implications for the workplace.

Verbal irony online

Finally, some of the issues raised earlier become even more problematic when we consider computer-mediated communication, such as via e-mail, text messaging, tweets, and Facebook postings. These impoverished communication channels lack the paralinguistic cues, such as intonation and gesture, that normally aid in the detection of nonliteral intent in face-to-face communication. The example of a boss making a brilliant business decision mentioned earlier takes on a clear nonliteral meaning if the speaker accompanies her statement with heavy stress and a slow speaking rate, or by rolling her eyes. Not surprisingly, therefore, recognizing humor and irony in social media has been described as especially problematic.[55]

Although most of us believe that our e-mails and status updates are clear enough, we have all been on the receiving end of online messages in which the actual intent of the sender was far from transparent. A series of experiments has demonstrated that a pervasive egocentric bias exists with regard to detecting sarcasm in e-mail messages.[56] It appears that people are largely unable to imagine that their own messages, in which the humorous or sarcastic intent seems clear enough, might be ambiguous to someone else. In fact, one study found that participants were *more* likely to use irony in computer-mediated communication than they were conversing face to face.[57]

In an attempt to cope with the challenges of online communication, language users have created new conventions, such as emoticons and emoji. Although they can serve a variety of purposes, emoticons are commonly used to mark nonliteral intent.[58] An early study of how these typographic conventions are employed in e-mail found that the "wink" emoticon ; -) was most strongly associated with sarcasm.[59] However, these researchers also reported that a wink plus a positive verbal message was not perceived as more sarcastic than the same message accompanied by a smile : -) , a frown : - (, or when paired with no emoticon at all. The study found that emoticons had a relatively small effect on the communication of emotion in general, and sarcasm in particular. It is worth noting, however, that a later experiment, in which secondary school students were the participants, found that emoticons did strengthen the intensity of a message.[60] This suggests that the use of, and pragmatic agreement about, such conventions may have increased over time.

Researchers have also explored whether nonliteral language is stereotypic enough to be identified through the use of specific features. It has been suggested, for example, that ironic language might be identified by the use of extreme exaggeration, such as via collocations of adverbs and extreme positive adjectives (e.g., "just delightful" or "absolutely incredible").[61] These researchers demonstrated that participants perceived nonliteral statements that contained clear exaggeration to be more ironic than similar statements that were not as extreme (e.g., "I'll never be able to repay you for your help!" versus "Thanks for helping me out").

One issue in analyzing the nonliteral language that appears in texts is the difficulty of determining whether a given statement was originally intended as ironic or sarcastic. Fortunately, the hash tags used in social media, such as "#sarcasm," allow researchers to unambiguously determine the intentions of the author. One team of researchers studied sarcastic posts to Twitter, and found that a variety of factors distinguished them from tweets expressing positive or negative sentiment. Specifically, they found that textual factors (like the use of punctuation) and pragmatic dimensions (such as whether the tweet was directed at another person) allowed their machine classifier to perform about as well as human raters.[62]

A different group of researchers focused on the use of word-level cues in sarcasm, such as interjections (such as "gee," "gosh," or "well") and positive affect terms (which would be indicative of canonical irony). Once again, the model performed almost as well as human classifiers.[63] It should be noted, however, that even humans, when asked whether a tweet expressed or did not express sarcasm, were correct only about 70% of the time. Although such performance is better than chance, it does suggest that misinterpretations are fairly common. The impoverished context, imposed by the 140-character limit of this micro-blogging service, makes it challenging to determine sarcastic intent—for humans and machines alike.

Unfortunately, online communication has also created the potential for cyberbullying in the workplace. However, a survey administered to workers in Australia suggests that it may not be as prevalent as cyberbullying among other groups, such as children, 24% of whom report having been cyberbullied at some point.[64] Thirty-four percent of the adult survey respondents reported having been bullied face to face in the workplace, while only

11% reported having been cyberbullied. Specifically, just 3% of those bullied face to face reported experiencing "excessive teasing and sarcasm." And none of those who reported being cyberbullied cited this particular behavior.[65]

Conclusions

Clearly, the workplace is an environment in which verbal irony can function as a double-edged sword, cutting more than one way.[66] On the one hand, the use of such language can make people feel excluded or less valued. It can distance speakers from their addressees.[67] Irony and sarcasm can also be misinterpreted, particularly in online communication. And like any other form of language, it can be used for ill and not just for good.

However, it is also true that verbal irony can be used to foster and maintain intimacy. It can promote solidarity and a sense of teamwork. It can allow people to express negative emotions in a socially acceptable way, which is particularly helpful when a differential power relationship exists. Ironic statements are also associated with humor, and with being perceived as witty or clever.[68] When used in unexpected ways, as in advertising, it can promote interest and attention.[69] It can be employed after the fact to allow people to dissociate themselves from previous problematic statements. And, as we have seen, such language can even foster creativity without creating conflict.[70] The review of the literature presented here makes clear that verbal irony does have a place in the workplace after all. Far from being seen only as a conduit for hostility and aggression, under the right circumstances it can be employed in a number of positive ways, as summarized in Table 4.5.1.

Clearly, a great deal has been learned about this complex linguistic form. It would be extremely premature, however, to conclude that all relevant issues have been fully explored and explained. As we have seen, even basic definitional issues concerning use of the terms "irony" and "sarcasm" have not been fully answered. And the generalizability of results from studies of college students (and more recently, online participants) to adults in the workplace is an open question. It is increasingly clear that the use of verbal irony is enmeshed in a host of cognitive, social, and cultural factors, and untangling this complex skein will require patience and ingenuity. Nonetheless, considerable progress has been made, and the increasing amount of research devoted to this intriguing form of language creates some basis for optimism.

Table 4.5.1 The benefits and drawbacks to using verbal irony

	Benefits	*Drawbacks*
Intimate settings	• Humor • Fosters and maintains intimacy	
Workplace settings	• Humor	• Differing standards for humor
	• Signifies in-group membership • Express negative emotion in socially acceptable ways • Makes serious issues less threatening	• Creates out-groups
	• Promotes solidarity and teamwork • Promotes creativity	• May promote conflict
Online communication	• Humor	• Ambiguity (egocentric bias)

References

1 Ashforth, B. E., & Humphrey, R. H. (1995). Emotion in the workplace: A reappraisal. *Human Relations*, *48*, 97–125.

2 Beckson, K., & Ganz, A. (1989). *Literary Terms: A Dictionary* (3rd edition). New York: Noonday.

3 Lucariello, J. (1994). Situational irony: A concept of events gone awry. *Journal of Experimental Psychology: General*, *123*, 129–145.

4 Dynel, M. (2010). Friend or foe? Chandler's humour from the metarecipient's perspective, in I. Witczak-Plisiecka (ed.), *Pragmatic Perspectives on Language and Linguistics Volume II: Pragmatics of Semantically-restricted Domains*. Cambridge: Cambridge University Press, 175–205; Giora, R., & Attardo, S. (2014). Irony, in S. Attardo (ed.), *Encyclopedia of Humor Studies, Volume One*. Thousand Oaks, CA: Sage Publications, 397–402; Nunberg, G. (2001). *The Way We Talk Now: Commentaries on Language and Culture*. Boston, MA: Houghton Mifflin; Wasserman, P. G., & Schober, M. F. (2006). Variability in judgments of spoken irony. *Abstracts of the Psychonomic Society*, *11*, 43.

5 Fowler, H. W. (1965). *A Dictionary of Modern English Usage* (2nd edition). Oxford: Oxford University Press.

6 Attardo, S. (2000). Irony as relevant inappropriateness. *Journal of Pragmatics*, *32*, 793–826; Kreuz, R. J., & Glucksberg, S. (1989). How to be sarcastic: The echoic reminder theory of verbal irony. *Journal of Experimental Psychology: General*, *118*, 374–386.

7 Norrick, N. R. (2002). Issues in conversational joking. *Journal of Pragmatics*, *35*, 1333–1359.

8 Roberts, R. M., & Kreuz, R. J. (1994). Why do people use figurative language? *Psychological Science*, *5*, 159–163.

9 Matlin, M. W., & Stang, D. J. (1978). *The Pollyanna Principle: Selectivity in Language, Memory, and Thought*. Cambridge, MA: Schenkman Publishing Co.

10 Wilson, D., & Sperber, D. (2012). Explaining irony, in D. Wilson & D. Sperber (eds.), *Meaning and Relevance*. Cambridge: Cambridge University Press, 123–145.

11 Kreuz & Glucksberg, op. cit.

12 Kumon-Nakamura, S., Glucksberg, S., & Brown, M. (1995). How about another piece of pie: The allusional pretense theory of discourse irony. *Journal of Experimental Psychology: General*, *124*, 3–21.

13 Colston, H. L. (2001). On necessary conditions for verbal irony comprehension. *Pragmatics & Cognition*, *8*, 277–324.

14 Kreuz, R. J., & Link, K. E. (2002). Asymmetries in the perception of verbal irony. *Journal of Language and Social Psychology*, *21*, 127–143.

15 Kreuz & Link, op. cit.

16 Kreuz & Glucksberg, op. cit.

17 Caucci, G. M., & Kreuz, R. J. (2012). Social and paralinguistic cues to sarcasm. *Humor: International Journal of Humor Research*, *25*, 1–22; Kreuz, R. J. (1996). The use of verbal irony: Cues and constraints, in J. S. Mio & A. N. Katz (eds.), *Metaphor: Implications and Applications*. Mahwah, NJ: Lawrence Erlbaum Associates, 23–38; Kreuz, R. J., & Caucci, G. M. (2009). Social aspects of verbal irony use, in H. Pishwa (ed.), *Language and Social Cognition: Expression of the Social Mind*. Berlin: Mouton de Gruyter, 325–345.

18 Piskorska, A. (2014). A relevance-theoretic perspective on humorous irony and its failure. *Humor*, *27*, 661–685.

19 Dress, M. L., Kreuz, R. J., Link, K. E., & Caucci, G. M. (2008). Regional variation in the use of sarcasm. *Journal of Language and Social Psychology*, *27*, 71–85.

20 Garmendia, J. (2014). The clash: Humor and critical attitude in verbal irony. *Humor*, *27*, 641–659.

21 Brown, P., & Levinson, S. C. (1978/1987). *Politeness: Some Universals in Language Usage*. Cambridge: Cambridge University Press.

22 Gibbs, R. W. Jr. (1983). Do people always process the literal meanings of indirect requests? *Journal of Experimental Psychology: Learning, Memory, and Cognition*, *93*, 524–533.

23 Alba Juez, L. (1995). Irony and politeness. *Revista Española de Lingüística Aplicada*, *10*, 9–16.

24 Dews, S., & Winner, E. (1995). Muting the meaning: A social function of irony. *Metaphor and Symbolic Activity*, *10*, 3–19.

25 Colston, H. L. (1997). Salting a wound or sugaring a pill: The pragmatic functions of ironic criticism. *Discourse Processes, 23*, 25–45.

26 Bowes, A., & Katz, A. (2011). When sarcasm stings. *Discourse Processes, 48*, 215–236.

27 Boylan, J., & Katz, A. N. (2013). Ironic expression can simultaneously enhance and dilute perception of criticism. *Discourse Processes, 50*, 187–209.

28 Gibbs, R. W. Jr. (2000). Irony in talk among friends. *Metaphor and Symbol, 15*, 5–27.

29 Tannen, D. (1984). *Conversational Style*. Hillsdale, NJ: Lawrence Erlbaum Associates.

30 Kreuz, op. cit.

31 Clark, H. H., & Marshall, C. R. (1981). Definite reference and mutual knowledge, in A. K. Joshi, B. Webber, & I. Sag (eds.), *Elements of Discourse Understanding*. Cambridge: Cambridge University Press, 10–63.

32 Kreuz, op. cit.; Kreuz, R. J. (2000). The production and processing of verbal irony. *Metaphor and Symbol, 15*, 99–107.

33 Kreuz, R. J., & Roberts, R. M. (1995). Two cues for verbal irony: Hyperbole and the ironic tone of voice. *Metaphor and Symbolic Activity, 10*, 21–31.

34 Clark, H. H., & Gerrig, R. J. (1984). On the pretense theory of irony. *Journal of Experimental Psychology: General, 113*, 121–126.

35 Pexman, P. M., & Zvaigzne, M. T. (2004). Does irony go better with friends? *Metaphor and Symbol, 19*, 143–163.

36 Seckman, M., & Couch, C. (1989). Jocularity, sarcasm, and relationships. *Journal of Contemporary Ethnography, 18*, 327–344.

37 Vensel, S. R. (2015). Passive-aggressive personality disorder, in L. Sperry (ed.), *Mental Health and Mental Disorders: An Encyclopedia of Conditions, Treatments, and Well-being*. Santa Barbara, CA: ABC-CLIO/Greenwood Press, 813–816.

38 Norrick, N., & Chiaro, D. (2009). *Humor in Interaction*. Amsterdam: John Benjamins.

39 Tannen, D. (1990). *You Just Don't Understand: Women and Men in Conversation*. New York: Ballantine Books.

40 Sarcasm is the lowest form of wit . . . but is it bullying? http://www.ihraustralia.com.au/news-and-opinion/sarcasm-is-the-lowest-form-of-wit-but-is-it-bullying (retrieved March 30, 2016).

41 Gibbs, op. cit.

42 Hatch, M. J. (1997). Irony and the social construction of contradiction in the humor of a management team. *Organization Science, 8*, 275–288.

43 Calabrese, K. R. (2000). Interpersonal conflict and sarcasm in the workplace. *Genetic, Social, and General Psychology Monographs, 126*, 459–494; Neuman, J. H., & Baron, R. A. (1998). Workplace violence and workplace aggression: Evidence concerning specific forms, potential causes, and preferred targets. *Journal of Management, 24*, 391–419.

44 Clay, C. (n.d.). Workplace communication: What about sarcasm? http://www.deskdemon.com/pages/uk/career/workplacesarcasm?cl=wn-sep-sarcasm (retrieved March 30, 2016).

45 Maleta, Z. (2016). How to deal with a smart mouth person in the workplace. http://work.chron.com/deal-smart-mouth-person-workplace-19093.html (retrieved March 30, 2016).

46 Patterson, K. (2011, March). Confronting workplace sarcasm. http://www.crucialskills.com/2011/03/confronting-workplace-sarcasm/ (retrieved March 30, 2016).

47 Roberts & Kreuz, op. cit.

48 Seckman & Couch, op. cit.

49 Gibbs, R. W. Jr., & Colston, H. L. (2001). The risks and rewards of ironic communication, in G. Anolli, R. Ciceri, & G. Riva (eds.), *Say Not to Say: New Perspectives on Miscommunication*. Amsterdam: IOS Press, 181–194.

50 Kreuz (2000), op. cit.

51 Holmes, J. K. (2000). Politeness, power and provocation: How humour functions in the workplace. *Discourse Studies, 2*, 159–185.

52 Hatch, op. cit.

53 Huang, L., Gino, F., & Galinsky, A. D. (2015). The highest form of intelligence: Sarcasm increases creativity for both expressers and recipients. *Organizational Behavior and Human Decision Processes, 131*, 162–177.

54 Huang, op cit., p. 14.

55 Reyes, A., Rosso, P., & Buscaldi, D. (2012). From humor recognition to irony detection: The figurative language of social media. *Data & Knowledge Engineering, 74*, 1–12.

56 Kruger, J., Eply, N., Parker, J., & Ng, Z. (2005). Egocentrism over e-mail: Can we communicate as well as we think? *Journal of Personality and Social Psychology, 89*, 925–936.

57 Hancock, J. T. (2004). Verbal irony use in face-to-face and computer-mediated conversations. *Journal of Language and Social Psychology, 23*, 447–463.

58 Kreuz (1996), op. cit.; Lebduska, L. (2014). Emoji, emoji, what for art thou? *Harlot, 12*, http://harlotofthearts.org/index.php/harlot/article/view/186/157 (retrieved March 30, 2016).

59 Walther, J. B., & D'Addario, K. D. (2001). The impacts of emoticons on message interpretation in computer-mediated communication. *Social Science Computer Review, 19*, 324–347.

60 Derks, D., Bos, A. E. R., & von Grumbkow, J. (2008). Emoticons and online message interpretation. *Social Science Computer Review, 26*, 379–388.

61 Kreuz & Roberts, op. cit.

62 González-Ibáñez, R., Muresan, S., & Wacholder, N. (2011). Identifying sarcasm in Twitter: A closer look, in *Proceedings of the 49th Annual Meeting of the Association for Computational Linguistics: Human Language Technologies*. Portland, OR: Association for Computational Linguistics, 581–586.

63 Kovaz, D., Kreuz, R. J., & Riordan, M. A. (2013). Distinguishing sarcasm from literal language: Evidence from books and blogging. *Discourse Processes, 50*, 598–615.

64 Cyberbullying Research Center. (2013). Cyberbullying research: 2013 update. http://cyberbullying.org/cyberbullying-research-2013-update (retrieved March 30, 2016).

65 Privitera, C., & Campbell, M. A. (2009). Cyberbullying: The new face of workplace bullying. *CyberPsychology and Behavior, 12*, 395–400.

66 Huang et al., op. cit.

67 Gibbs & Colston, op. cit.

68 Kreuz, R. J., Long, D. L., & Church, M. B. (1991). On being ironic: Pragmatic and mnemonic implications. *Metaphor and Symbolic Activity, 6*, 149–162.

69 Gibbs & Colston, op. cit.

70 Huang et al., op. cit.

4.6 Just kidding

When workplace humor is toxic

Linda Weiser Friedman and Hershey H. Friedman

Introduction

Over the past several decades, humor has evolved into nothing less than a platform for human communication. Wit is the hallmark of intelligent beings. While humor has been part of the essence of being human since ancient times (Friedman & Friedman 2014), the infiltration of modern computer technology into all human endeavors has brought with it a sort of playfulness (Friedman & Friedman 2003), including the proliferation of irony on the Internet, and even the (non-ironic) reference to ours as the post-ironic age.

Humor has been shown to be useful and effective in many different areas of human endeavor, including medicine, counseling, advertising, education and, of course, communication (see, e.g., Weinberger & Gulas 1992; Holden 1993; Honeycutt & Brown 1998; Goldin & Bordan 1999; Witkin 1999; Friedman et al. 2002). In the study of leadership, recent scholarship emphasizes skills of employees over degrees, in particular the so-called "soft" skills that contribute to an individual's ability to work smoothly with others (Fischer & Friedman 2015). A survey of 225 employers conducted by Millenial Branding and Experience, Inc. (2012) found that the five major skills/traits employers seek are communication skills (98%), having a positive attitude (97%), being adaptable to change (92%), having teamwork skills (92%), and being goal oriented (88%). A paper from the National Bureau of Economic Research (NBER) suggests that social adeptness—the ability to work with others—will become even more important in the future. Although quantitative/computer skills are essential, they must be combined with social skills (Torres 2015).

In the knowledge economy, the ability to be a productive member of a team has become crucial in almost every occupation. This is the reason that the soft skills involving social adeptness are indispensable. Today, an employee must have the ability to work with people from all over the world. A sexist or bigoted individual can only cause problems for most firms. What qualities make a group more effective than the sum of its constituents? Research indicates that it is the social sensitivity of group members—the ability to correctly perceive, interpret, and respect the feelings, viewpoint, and opinions of others in the group—rather than their intelligence that matters. Interestingly, women are better than men when it comes to social sensitivity, which is a kind of empathy. According to Thompson (2015):

> A general collective intelligence factor explains a group's performance on a wide variety of tasks. This "c factor" is not strongly correlated with the average or maximum individual intelligence of group members but is correlated with the average social sensitivity of group members, the equality in distribution of conversational turn-taking, and the proportion of females in the group.
>
> (Thompson 2015: para. 4)

While there is no doubt that humor is a powerful tool, it is not necessarily benign. In fact, it can cause serious problems within an organization and even across society. It certainly can affect the c factor of a team which requires mutual respect. As we shall see, the right kind of humor can probably help the c factor by getting people to bond (Plester & Sayers 2007).

Recently, several notable tempests have arisen in online social media, each in reaction to statements that were supposed to be funny; indeed, some were part of the routines of professional comedians such as Louis CK and Trevor Noah (Dickson 2015). In April 2016, New York City Mayor Bill de Blasio had to apologize for a racial joke—a reference to "colored people's time"—that was not intended to mock anyone but himself, as he is perpetually late (Howard 2016; Wofford 2016). In June 2015, Madrid city councilman Guillermo Zapata felt compelled to apologize for a Holocaust-themed joke he had tweeted back in 2011 (Minder 2015). Hillary Clinton used the gender card in the election campaign: "She jokingly tells audiences that after more than 200 years and 44 male presidents, 'It's time.' She also gushes about being a grandmother and jokes about coloring her hair" (DelReal & Gearan 2016). Bob Sutton, Chairman of the Broward County GOP Executive Committee in Florida, made a particularly insensitive remark to indicate how easy it would be for Donald Trump to defeat Hillary Clinton in the presidential race: "I think when Donald Trump debates Hillary Clinton she's going to go down like Monica Lewinsky" (Gearan & Zezima 2016).

In addition to those who may lose the love of long-time fans, this sort of negative humor is sometimes responsible for loss of employment, for example, Tex Antoine (Tex Antoine 2016), Don Imus (Guttenberg 2009), and Adria Richards (Smith 2013b); loss of sponsorships, for example, Gilbert Gottfried (Quinn 2011); and, of course, the creation and support of a toxic work environment.

When humor is mocking, disparaging of groups or individuals, it can indeed be toxic. Where is the line separating "dark" humor from the truly toxic, and how is it that so many professional humorists stumble when they cross it? Does context matter? Have we become too sensitive? According to Scott (2015), "the world is full of jokes and also of people who can't take them" (AR1).

Humor can be beneficial in the workplace (Romero & Cruthirds 2006)—for example, humor by the leader can improve performance of the group—but it can also contribute to a toxic work environment. At the same time, the targets of disparaging humor in the workplace make do by using humor themselves in order to cope.

Surprisingly, the published research in the area of workplace humor, while on the rise, is still fairly small. We can expect this to change over the next decade or two as this is a very fertile field for scholarly research, of interest to scholars across a wide variety of academic and scientific disciplines. These include psychology, sociology, humor studies, diversity studies, management, and business, among others.

This paper will examine the many effects of humor and demonstrate how it can be used as a powerful tool to build workplace cohesiveness and result in more productivity. It will also show that workplace humor can be used as a tool to exclude certain groups (e.g., women, minorities, foreigners, etc.) and thus hurt group cohesion. Moreover, it is one of the tools that workplace bullies employ to abuse, harass, and intimidate coworkers.

Humor in the workplace

Skalski et al. (2012) discuss four theories of humor: superiority/disparagement, incongruity, arousal/dark humor, and social currency. They note that as far back as Aristotle it was known that humor may be used to make one group feel superior by mocking another group. Freud made a distinction between tendentious humor, which has a purpose, and non-tendentious jokes which are innocent, such as wordplay (Freud 1960: 90–91). Three major types of tendentious jokes he describes are "exposing or obscene jokes, aggressive (hostile) jokes, and cynical (critical, blasphemous) jokes." He also briefly describes a fourth type, skeptical jokes (Freud 1960: 115). There are no victims in "Knock-knock" or "Why did the chicken cross the road?" jokes, so they are non-tendentious (Sayre & King 2010: 88). Freud (1960: 103) made the following observation regarding tendentious jokes with a hostile, aggressive purpose: "By making our enemy small, inferior, despicable or comic, we achieve in a roundabout way the enjoyment of overcoming him." Freud avers that "[s]mut [dirty jokes] is like an exposure of the sexually different person to whom it is directed . . . It cannot be doubted that the desire to see what is sexual exposed is the original motive of smut" (Freud 1960: 98). Thus, obscene jokes, according to Freud, also are aggressive and have a victim.

Skalski et al. (2012) assert that humor can be used as a social interaction tool for "the establishment of a sense of group belonging or understanding" and "a means of building and maintaining relationships." This is why humor is quite important, even essential, in the workplace. It helps create a sense of belonging and contributes to group solidarity. All humor is to some extent cultural and, perhaps to that same extent, humor serves to define, explain and enhance our understanding of a particular culture. Much like the parable of the blind men and the elephant, humor is one of the ways with which we can grasp a level of understanding of a highly complex cultural environment.

According to McGhee (2013: 1999), humor is a useful tool in the workplace, specifically for team building, where it can result in: removal of barriers that separate management from other employees; emotional bonding; open communication; enhancement of trust; improved morale; reduced job stress; and increased creativity. Duncan and Feisal (1989) note that a self-deprecating joke may be a signal to employees that the manager is actually a real person. They also feel that joking improves the cohesiveness of the group, which then has a positive effect on group performance. Other studies have found a connection between the use of humor by a leader and the performance of followers (Vecchio, Justin & Pearce 2009). Sanders (2004) found that workplace humor was an important coping strategy for women working in the sex industry. The prostitutes working in this industry often deride clients behind their backs and might ridicule the way they look or how they perform. Sanders (2004: 287) feels that "joking relations are important in extreme professions that require intense physical and emotional labor that potentially threatens personal well-being." If humor helps prostitutes cope, it certainly can help workers in all kinds of stressful professions.

Shellenbarger (2013) observes that employers prefer hiring people with a good sense of humor. One survey of 737 CEOs found that 98% preferred hiring someone with a sense of humor over one without (Bannister 2006). A smart boss uses humor to create a friendly workplace. One executive asserts: "humor breaks down silos and flattens the organization, fostering employee loyalty and productivity" (Shellenbarger 2013). Smith (2013a) quotes a researcher who states:

> At an organizational level, some organizations are tapping into what I'd call "the humor advantage." Companies such as Zappos and Southwest Airlines have used humor and a positive fun culture to help brand their business, attract and retain employees and to attract customers.

Romero and Cruthirds (2006) demonstrate how humor is relevant to the discipline of management by influencing several factors including: group cohesiveness, communication (humor can be used to enhance the ability of audiences to comprehend, appreciate, and accept messages), stress reduction, creative thinking, communication of the organizational culture (e.g., that the workplace is a happy, fun place), and leadership.

Teasing banter in the workplace, while facilitating cohesiveness (Vinton 1989), may have implications regarding the in-group positioning of an employee. Plester and Sayers (2007) demonstrate how people working at three different IT companies use humorous "banter" to strengthen workplace relationships. The term "banter" (they also referred to it as "taking the piss") is a kind of playful teasing whose purpose is to deflate another person's ego. It is part of what employees see as a "fun" organizational culture. They also note that it strengthens the cohesion of the in-group, but also has the ability to be exclusionary to outsiders:

> Observing exchanges of banter defined 'in' and 'out' groups within these organizations. Banter created group bonds and was used to exclude some individuals from the group. Groups developed 'in-jokes' only understood by members and these types of jokes highlighted the group's identity. Banter highlighted many demographic differences such as ethnicity, gender or age diversity inside work groups. Rather than denigrating the differences the jocular insults used in the banter appeared to emphasize and perhaps even celebrate diverse individual characteristics of coworkers. Demographic differences such as ethnicity and gender had effects on the types of banter shared.
>
> (Plester & Sayers 2007: 183)

In-group humor can be used to help new recruits or trainees develop a feeling of belonging. In general, this type of humor tends to bond together members of the profession. This type of bonding humor helps people find common ground (Holden 1993: 67).

In exploring computer-oriented humor (Friedman & Friedman 2002, 2003), the authors noted that much of this type of humor has a social purpose. It serves as a bonding device. Indeed, there are several kinds of humor whose primary function appears to be the creation of a feeling of belongingness and togetherness. Some of this humor is almost generic, in that the same joke works well for one subgroup and then can be reworked and recycled to be just as funny to another group of people.

This category of humor covers a wide variety of comic endeavors, including the humor of various ethnic groups, racial groups, religions, professions, scientific disciplines— indeed, any group of individuals who share a body of knowledge, rituals, experience, lore, and, of course, a sense of humor.

This type of humor is found in many professions. WorkJoke (2017) is an example of a popular web site containing a wide variety of professions and their humor, ranging from accountant to zookeeper. Sometimes humor of this type seems to operate under the theory of superiority, as when another (outsider) group is the object of the joke. The definitive computer-oriented joke in this category may be the anecdote, told as if it had really happened, about the technical support specialist who fields a call from a user about a defective cup holder at the front of the computer: it was the CD-ROM drive. At other times, there is no superiority; the humor may be of the self-deprecating type. For example,

A doctor, a civil engineer, and a computer scientist got to discussing which was the oldest profession. The doctor pointed out that according to Biblical tradition, God created Eve from Adam's rib. This obviously required complicated surgery, so therefore medicine was surely the oldest profession in the world. The engineer countered with an earlier passage in the Bible stating that God created order from chaos, and since this was most certainly the biggest example of civil engineering, it proved that his profession was the oldest profession. Smiling, the computer scientist responded: "Who do you think created chaos?"

In fact, this joke is frequently recycled and appears among the humor of several different professions (for example, lawyers).

Negative humor and its repercussions

Over on the dark side, negative humor can indeed be toxic and can have severe consequences. The Nazis, for an extreme example, were not exactly tolerant of wit at their own expense. Surprisingly, even under the vicious Nazis, who apparently did not have a sense of humor (unless it was directed against their victims), some Germans secretly told anti-Nazi jokes (Herzog 2011: 167). This is the joke that got a woman executed by the guillotine.

Hitler and Göring were standing on top of the Berlin radio tower. Hitler says he wants to do something to put a smile on the Berliners' faces. Göring says, "Why don't you jump?"

Execution for a jokester may seem a little extreme to us but, still, are we too sensitive regarding offensive humor? In a recent example of jokes gone wrong, Trevor Noah, who replaced Jon Stewart as host of *The Daily Show*, was accused of insensitivity to women, obese people, and Jews for these tweets (Dickson 2015).

"Oh yeah the weekend. People are gonna get drunk & think that I'm sexy!"—fat chicks everywhere.
    Almost bumped a Jewish kid crossing the road. He didn't look b4 crossing but I still would hav felt so bad in my german car!
    Behind every successful Rap Billionaire is a double as rich Jewish man.
    Messi gets the ball and the real players try foul him, but Messi doesn't go down easy, just like jewish chicks.

(Dickson 2015)

Dickson (2015) had the following to say about these tweets:

There is a sharp distinction between a subversive joke, and something that's merely offensive, existing purely for the sake of hurting people's feelings. In truth, Noah's tweets about billionaire Jews and JAPs who don't like to go down were neither; they were just stupid. But that doesn't mean that there aren't folks out there who agree with the underlying sentiments.

In scholarly and popular literature (Anderson 2015; Quinn 2015), a number of individuals are trying to characterize ethnic, racial, often bigoted humor in terms of its intentions and effects. Not necessarily merely positive or negative, such humor may be considered subversive, insensitive, a device that allows us "to say those things that cannot be normally expressed" (Aufrecht 2001: 11), or "raising issues about the racial divide" (Obeidallah 2015: 8). While Bergmann's (1986: 74) view—that "sexist humor presupposes sexist beliefs on the part of the audience"—fairly insists that bigoted jokes are always bigoted, this view may be too simplistic and one-dimensional. Anderson (2015) argues for a wider spectrum in characterizing offensive humor.

Moss (2012) describes how a supposedly harmless joke can create a hostile workplace environment. She was working at an Italian restaurant and the boss was lecturing employees on the correct way of cleaning mini-fridges under the counter. This involved kneeling in order to get at the difficult-to-reach back corners. The boss then pointed to one of the waitresses and said: "Come on, Kari, you know what it's like to spend plenty of time on your knees . . . And then while the entire staff looked on, he made the classic tongue-in-cheek gesture."

Moss (2012) also describes a meeting many years later at a work event with several male coworkers, where she was the only female. One of the men used the expression "sucking dick" as a seemingly innocuous phrase since it was not used in a sexual manner. Apparently, he realized that it might be offensive and turned to her and asked: "Oh man . . . I'm uh, really sorry . . . Was that offensive? Did that bother you? I didn't mean to . . . Well, I hope you weren't . . . Yeah . . . Sorry." When she assured him his language did not bother her, he tried to make things better by asking her if she was a lesbian. Moss concludes:

> For many professional women, depending on their industry, the feeling of exclusion is much more subtle and potentially damaging than outright sexism. Had this guy made a sexist comment at me, I know my rights and my options for defending them. This guy, however, was singling me out for specific comment because of my gender. It's equivalent to a teacher calling on a black student to ask how he feels about reparation politics. From the moment he asked me, and only me, my feelings on his word choice, it was obvious that I was somehow a different type of colleague than the rest of the table. It was as if, since I didn't have a penis, I was an obstacle to the flow of conversation, instead of a contributor to it.
>
> (Moss 2012: para. 8)

One of the underpinnings of humor and humor research is that all humor will not necessarily be funny to all people. Schutz (1995) feels that ethnic humor plays an important social function by helping in-groups bond and reinforce their values. Humor can be used to deride others (e.g., racist jokes, lawyer jokes) but it can also be used to enhance the image of a group. Of course, one joke can sometimes do both jobs at the same time: mock one group while at the same time making another group appear smarter than everyone else. The jokes of victims and oppressed groups very often have this dual purpose. Lowe (1986) makes this observation about certain kinds of ethnic humor: "it produces simultaneously a strong fellow-feeling among participants and joint aggressiveness against outsiders" (448).

Perhaps, certain jokes are only appropriate if you belong to a particular group. Outsiders have to be careful because the same joke may make them appear to be bigots. The following joke has been used as such an example in research by Gruner (2000: 101).

Two Jews are about to face a Russian firing squad. The two condemned men are offered blindfolds. One of them accepts it, but the other does not, defiantly saying: "I don't want your blindfold." His friend urges: "Shh, Izzy, don't make trouble."

When this joke is told by one Jew to another, it is a gentle acknowledgment of the tendency of Jews in the Diaspora to keep quiet at all costs, rather than attract unwanted attention. On the other hand, when this joke is told by one non-Jew to another, especially with humorous Jewish-sounding names and dialect as in Gruner (2000: 101), it definitely comes across as disparaging to Jews.

When a joke is told to exclude, to mock those who are the targets of the joke, there is definitely something offensive about it. When this sort of negative humor appears in the workplace, even in a teasing manner, it can hurt the teller, the listener, the target and, of course, the organization.

Toxic workplace humor

Humor can be very beneficial in the workplace but it has to be used carefully. Humor is a powerful tool and can be used for positive and negative purposes. Humor can be inclusive and serve to break down barriers and bring people together, but it can also be divisive and quite harmful. In the workplace, it is especially important for humor to be used in a constructive manner.

Workplace humor should be used to bring people together, not to tear them apart. Romero and Cruthirds (2006) make the point that humor is a double-edged sword. Used improperly it can cause serious problems in organizations. This is especially true of humor that is perceived as racist, sexist, or humiliating. Aggressive, nasty humor of this sort can result in lawsuits and cause conflict in an organization. The wrong kind of humor can result in huge problems including the loss of employment. Unsuitable humor can result in legal problems since it can be seen as workplace harassment which creates a "hostile work environment" (Volokh 1997). In fact, blonde jokes or any kind of sexual humor can be seen as contributing to a hostile work environment (Volokh 1997). Wolfe (2013: para. 7) provides the following guidelines:

> Humor should be inclusive to be well-received. But sexist, racist, ageist jokes, and crude remarks label certain individuals, or groups of people, as inferior in some way and create exclusions. Not only is this inappropriate, but offensive displays of humor, even when not directed at a specific person, can lead to sanctions, terminations, and lawsuits.

Racist and sexist humor is often used for the purpose of perpetuating stereotypes about women and minorities and thus to keep them "in their place." Boxer and Ford (2010) see sexist humor as an example of insidious workplace misbehaviors that have a hidden agenda—to spread dishonest stereotypes about women and thus hurt their status in the organization. The same can be said about most kinds of aggressive jokes directed at vulnerable populations including short people, obese people, unattractive people, or those from another culture, ethnic group, nationality, or religion.

As Quinn (2000: 1180) points out, "When the content of humor is sexist or sexually demeaning and the context is a workplace, the possibility of defining it as hostile work environment sexual harassment exists." Quinn's research found that negative humor targeting women boosts male group solidarity and women's disempowerment. In addition, the survival strategy of not taking it "personal," a common response in the workplace and elsewhere, may be unwitting collaboration.

In the workplace, bullies often use humor to belittle others. In fact, sarcastic, belittling humor is a tool used by workplace bullies to make victims uncomfortable (Conley 2013). Humor can also be used as a weapon to end bullying. Hayden (2013: para. 1) states: "When used correctly and at the right time humor will confuse bullies and stop them in their tracks, because it's the last thing they expect to hear." In a classic episode of *Seinfeld* called "The Comeback" (Trainor 1997), George Costanza tries, repeatedly and ultimately unsuccessfully, to do just that when someone makes fun of him at a business conference. The show uses humor in a clever way to illustrate how a bad joke can cause a co-worker so much aggravation.

Humor, like literature and film, often requires the listener (or audience) to suspend disbelief and exist in an alternate realm. The workplace however is very much in the real world, the one in which we actually live and work and hope to succeed. In this milieu, following an insensitive joke with "just kidding" does not negate the offense. This sort of "worlds collide" phenomenon may be why (well, one reason) the character Michael Scott in *The Office* has so much trouble with his tone-deaf attempts at humor.

Interestingly, in what may be a possible explanation, a recent large-scale study (Robert et al. 2016) found that the existing relationship between employer and subordinate was more important to job satisfaction than whether the leader's humor was positive or negative.

Real-world examples

Cited here are several examples of toxic workplace humor that boomeranged.

Tex Antoine

Tex Antoine was the meteorologist for WABC News. On November 24, 1976, his weather spot came up right after a report dealing with the violent rape of a young girl— she was five years old. Tex jokingly said: "With rape so predominant in the news lately, it is well to remember the words of Confucius: 'If rape is inevitable, lie back and enjoy it.'" He lost his job and never recovered from this gaffe (Tex Antoine 2016). Rape, especially of children, is such an ugly crime that one cannot joke about it. His so-called joke did not reduce tension but increased it. Women were quite upset about the way this remark reinforced an ugly stereotype about them. This same foolish remark torpedoed Clayton Williams's campaign for Governor of Texas against Ann Richards; he was ahead by 11 points and lost because of this. He compared the cold, foggy weather that ruined a cattle roundup at his ranch to a rape, telling people (including reporters) around a campfire, "If it's inevitable, just relax and enjoy it" (Scarce 2012).

Don Imus

Don Imus was terminated from his radio show for referring to members of the Rutgers women's basketball team as "nappy-headed hos." He was trying to be funny (Guttenberg 2009: para. 6).

Adria Richards

Adria Richards overheard two men at the PyCon technology conference in Santa Clara joking about "big dongles" in a sexual way. Dongles are devices that plug into computers. She took a picture of the two men and posted it on Twitter with the following statement: "Not cool. Jokes about forking repo's in a sexual way and 'big' dongles." When the smoke cleared, Richards, who worked for SendGrid, as well as one of the men lost their jobs (Smith 2013b).

Professor R. K. Engler

Professor Engler was terminated from Roosevelt University for telling this joke to a college class taking his course "City and Citizenship" (Ponce 2010). "A group of sociologists did a poll in Arizona about the new immigration law. Sixty percent said they were in favor, and 40 percent said, 'No habla English.'" Professor Engler is in litigation with the university. He claims that this humor was quite appropriate for the course and was being used to stimulate discussion.

Justine Sacco

Justine Sacco, a communications director at InterActive Corp., lost her job for posting the following racially-insensitive tweet after flying to South Africa: "Going to Africa. Hope I don't get AIDS. Just kidding. I'm White!" (Umansky 2014).

Fritz Darges

Fritz Darges was an army adjutant to Adolf Hitler who got himself sent to the Eastern front for telling a joke. During a 1944 strategy meeting, Hitler was bothered by a fly that kept buzzing around him and landing on a map he was studying. Hitler told Darges to kill the fly. Darges replied to Hitler that the fly was an "airborne pest" and was therefore the responsibility of the Luftwaffe (air force) adjutant, Nicolaus von Below (Hudgins 2013).

Conclusions

Aristotle said: "Pleasure in the job puts perfection in the work" (Hoppe 2017: 96). And from Winston Churchill, "Success is going from failure to failure without loss of enthusiasm" (Hoppe 2017: 68). What do we want from our employees? If we're smart, not just work. We want passion, creativity, curiosity in the world around us. We want employees who are good communicators and collaborators. Humor goes a long way towards these goals. Humor that brings people together is very different from the sort of humor that emphasizes our differences and mocks them.

Without question, humor is an extremely powerful tool: it can strengthen relationships and build rapport in the workplace. Humor can serve as a major social bond, a bond that can be used for positive or negative purposes (Friedman & Friedman 2003). Jokes, one popular type of humor, are very revealing. If you want to know whether or not someone is a bigot or sexist, listen to the jokes s/he tells. Indeed, Helmreich (2004) examines humor and anecdotes to better understand stereotypes. Telushkin (1992) feels that if you really want to understand the Jewish people, examine the humor told by both Jews and non-Jews about the Jewish people. Davies (2011) believes that jokes often tap into strongly held stereotypical beliefs: for example, politicians are seen as corrupt, Jews as money-hungry, blonde women as being stupid, psychiatrists as nutty, professors as absent-minded, lawyers as dishonest, mothers-in-law as unlikable, economists out of touch with the real world, waiters as rude, rednecks as bigoted morons, and IT experts as geeks. The following joke is a good example:

> Question: What do you call 5,000 dead lawyers at the bottom of the ocean?
>
> Answer: A good start!

This only works with lawyers and maybe a disliked religious or ethnic group. Jews or blacks would probably work at a KKK rally. Try the joke with nurses and it does not work. In fact, it would seem bizarre.

In conclusion, it is important for people to understand the many ramifications of humor and use it in the workplace in a positive manner to heal and include rather than to exclude and hurt others.

References

Anderson, L. (2015). Racist humor. *Philosophy Compass*, 10(8), 501–509.

Aufrecht, S. E. (2001). When should a manager cross the road? The appropriate use of humor in public organizations, in *Proceedings of the Critical Management Studies Conference*, July 11–13, 2001, Manchester School of Management, UMIST, England. Retrieved from http://www.mngt.waikato.ac.nz/ejrot/cmsconference/2001/Papers/Humour%20and%20Irony/Aufrecht.pdf.

Bannister, S. (2006). Making sense of humour in the workplace. *Canadaone.com*, September 30. Retrieved from http://www.canadaone.com/ezine/oct06/humour_at_work.html.

Bergmann, M. (1986). How many feminists does it take to make a joke? Sexist humor and what's wrong with it. *Hypatia*, 1(1), 63–82.

Boxer, C. F. & Ford, T. E. (2010). Sexist humor in the workplace: A case for subtle harassment, in Greenberg, J. (Ed.), *Insidious workplace behavior* (175–206), New York: Routledge.

BrainyQuote (2017). Retrieved from https://www.brainyquote.com/.

Conley, R. (2013). Six ways you're a workplace bully without even realizing it. *Leading with Trust*, April 7. Retrieved from http://leadingwithtrust.com/2013/04/07/six-ways-youre-a-workplace-bully-without-even-realizing-it/.

Davies, C. (2011). *Jokes and targets*. Bloomington, IN: Indiana University Press.

DelReal, J. A. & Gearan, A. (2016). "Trump: If Clinton 'were a man, I don't think she'd get 5 percent of the vote.'" *The Washington Post*, April 27. Available at https://www.washingtonpost.com/news/post-politics/wp/2016/04/27/trump-if-clinton-were-a-man-i-dont-think-shed-get-5-percent-of-the-vote/?utm_term=.48f3ef51e6d1.

Dickson, E. J. (2015). Trevor Noah, Lena Dunham, and the troubling persistence of anti-Semitism. *Daily Dot*, March 31. Retrieved from http://www.dailydot.com/opinion/trevor-noah-lena-dunham-anti-semitism/.

Duncan, W. J. & Feisal, J. P. (1989). No laughing matter: Patterns of humor in the workplace. *Organizational Dynamics*, 17(4), 18–39.

Fischer, D. & Friedman, H. H. (2015, August 20). Make yourself indispensable: Skills employers desperately need to succeed in the knowledge economy. Available at SSRN: http://ssrn.com/abstract=2648691 or http://dx.doi.org/10.2139/ssrn.2648691.

Freud, S. (1960). *Jokes and their relation to the unconscious* (James Strachey, translator). New York: W. W. Norton. (Original work published in 1905.)

Friedman, H. H. & Friedman, L. W. (2014). *God laughed: Sources of Jewish humor*. Piscataway, NJ: Transaction Publishers.

Friedman, H. H., Friedman, L. W., & Amoo, T. (2002). Using humor in the introductory statistics course. *Journal of Statistics Education*, 10(3), November. Retrieved from http://www.amstat.org/publications/jse/contents_2002.html.

Friedman, L. W. & Friedman, H. H. (2003, August). *A framework for the Study of Computer-Oriented Humor (Cohum)*. Available at SSRN: http://ssrn.com/abstract=907710.

Gearan, A. & Zezima, K. (2016). Trump's "woman's card" comment escalates the campaign's gender wars. *Washington Post*, April 27. Retrieved from https://www.washingtonpost.com/politics/trumps-womans-card-comment-escalates-gender-wars-of-2016-campaign/2016/04/27/fbe4c67a-0c2b-11e6-8ab8-9ad050f76d7d_story.html.

Goldin, E. & Bordan, T. (1999). The use of humor in counseling: The laughing cure. *Journal of Counseling and Development*, 77(4) (October), 405–410.

Greenberg, J. (2010). *Insidious workplace behavior*. New York: Routledge.

Gruner, C. R. (2000). *The game of humor: A comprehensive theory of why we laugh*. New Brunswick, NJ: Transaction Publishers.

Guttenberg, S. (2009, February 11). CBS fires Don Imus over racial slur. *CBS News*.

Hayden, S. (2013, March 25). *How to use humor with workplace bullies*. Retrieved from http://suite101.com/article/how-to-use-humor-with-workplace-bullies-a374488.

Helmreich, W. (2004). *The things they say behind your back: Stereotypes and the myths behind them*. Piscataway, NJ: Transaction Publishers.

Herzog, R. (2011). *Dead funny: Humor in Hitler's Germany*. Brooklyn, NY: Melville House.

Holden, R. (1993). *Laughter, the best medicine: The healing power of happiness, humour and joy!* New York: Thorsons (HarperCollins).

Honeycutt, J. M. & Brown, R. (1998). Did you hear the one about?: Typological and spousal differences in the planning of jokes and sense of humor in marriage. *Communication Quarterly*, 46(3), 342–352.

Hoppe, K. (2017). Inspirational quotations. *Bestchapterinyourlife.com*. Retrieved from http://bestchapterofyourlife.com/pdf/Motivational%20Quotes%20Volume%202.pdf.

Howard, A. (2016). Bill de Blasio's "colored people's time" joke comes at a bad time. *MSNBC.com*, April 12. Retrieved from http://www.msnbc.com/msnbc/bill-de-blasios-colored-people-time-joke-comes-bad-time.

Hudgins, A. (2013). The joke's on all of us. *New York Times*, June 8. Retrieved from http://www.nytimes.com/2013/06/09/opinion/sunday/the-jokes-on-all-of-us.html.

Lowe, J. (1986). Theories of ethnic humor: How to enter laughing. *American Quarterly*, 38(3), 439–460.

McGhee, P. E. (1999). *Health, healing, and the amuse system: Humor as survival training*. Dubuque: Kendall/Hunt.

McGhee, P. E. (2013). Team building humor strengthens a team identity or spirit. *LaughterRemedy.com*. Retrieved from http://www.laughterremedy.com/articles/team_building.html.

Millennial Branding and Experience, Inc. (2012). The student employment gap. *Millennialbranding.com*. Retrieved from http://millennialbranding.com/wpcontent/uploads/2012/05/student_employment_gap_infographic.jpg.

Minder, R. (2015). Spanish official apologizes over Twitter joke about Holocaust. *New York Times*, June 15, A6.

Moss, E. M. (2012). Sexual jokes and lewd conversations in the workplace: Where's the line? *Forbes*, April 20. Retrieved from http://www.forbes.com/sites/goodmenproject/2012/04/20/blowjob-jokes-and-exclusionary-tactics-in-the-workplace/#5f995d0059a2.

Obeidallah, D. (2015). Colin Quinn's new book: Ending racial strife one insult at a time. *Daily Beast*, June 10. Retrieved from http://www.thedailybeast.com/colin-quinns-new-book-ending-racial-strife-one-insult-at-a-time.

Plester, B. A. & Sayers, J. G. (2007). "Taking the piss": Functions of banter in the IT industry. *Humor*, 20(2), 157–187.

Ponce, A. (2010). Professor fired for immigration joke wants job back. *NBC Chicago*, October 21. Retrieved from http://www.nbcchicago.com/news/local/roosevelt-university-professor-engler-immigration-joke-105389653.html.

Quinn, B. A. (2000). The paradox of complaining: Law, humor, and harassment in the everyday work world. *Law & Social Inquiry*, 25(4) (Autumn), 1151–1185.

Quinn, C. (2015). *The coloring book: A comedian solves race relations in America*. New York: Grand Central Publishing.

Quinn, R. (2011, March 15). Gilbert Gottfried fired for tsunami jokes. *Newser.com*. Retrieved from http://www.newser.com/story/114135/gilbert-gottfried-fired-as-voice-of-aflac-duck.html.

Robert, C., Dunne, T. C., & Lum, J. (2016). The impact of leader humor on subordinate job satisfaction: The crucial role of leader-subordinate relationship quality. *Group and Organization Management*, 41(3), 375–406.

Romero, E. J. & Cruthirds, K. W. (2006). The use of humor in the workplace. *Academy of Management Perspectives*, May, 58–69.

Sanders, T. (2004). Controllable laughter: Managing sex work through humour. *Sociology*, 38(2), 273–290.

Sayre, S. & King, C. (2010). *Entertainment and society: Influences, impacts, and innovations*. New York: Routledge.

Scarce. (2012). Clayton Williams: Victims of rape should "relax and enjoy it." *Daily Kos*, August 20. Retrieved from http://www.dailykos.com/story/2012/08/20/1122097/-Clayton-Williams-Victims-of-Rape-Should-Relax-and-Enjoy-It.

Scott, A. O. (2015). A world that won't laugh with you. *The New York Times*, June 7, AR1+.

Schutz, C. (1995). The sociability of ethnic jokes. *Australian Journal of Comedy*, 1(1). Retrieved from http://www.ozcomedy.com/journal/vol1cont.html.

Shellenbarger, S. (2013). Secrets of effective office humor. *Wall Street Journal*, August 13. Retrieved from http://online.wsj.com/article/SB10001424127887324085304579008554174349982.html.

Skalski, P. D., Neuendorf, K. A., Dalisay, F., Denny, J., Campbell, R., & Egizii, M. (2012). Exploring relationships among values, political orientation, media use, and the senses and humor. *2012 Conference of the Central States Communication Association*, Cleveland, OH. Retrieved from https://www.researchgate.net/publication/278667964_Exploring_relationships_among_values_political_orientation_media_use_and_the_senses_of_humor.

Smith, J. (2013a). 10 reasons why humor is a key to success at work. *Forbes*, May 3. Retrieved from http://www.forbes.com/sites/jacquelynsmith/2013/05/03/10-reasons-why-humor-is-a-key-to-success-at-work/.

Smith, K. (2013b). A joke about dongles led to two people losing their jobs and a huge mess for the tech world. *Business Insider*, March 22. Retrieved from http://www.sfgate.com/technology/businessinsider/article/A-Joke-About-Dongles-Led-To-Two-People-Losing-4376332.php.

Telushkin, J. (1992). *Jewish humor: What the best Jewish jokes say about the Jews*. New York: William Morrow & Company.

Tex Antoine. (2016, March 2). In *Wikipedia, The Free Encyclopedia*. Retrieved from https://en.wikipedia.org/w/index.php?title=Tex_Antoine&oldid=707865522.

Thompson, D. (2015). The secret to smarter groups: It's women. *Atlantic*, January 18. Retrieved from http://www.theatlantic.com/business/archive/2015/01/the-secret-to-smart-groups-isnt-smart-people/384625/.

Torres, N. (2015). Research: Technology is only making social skills more important. *Harvard Business Review*, August 26. Retrieved from https://hbr.org/2015/08/research-technology-is-only-making-social-skills-more-important.

Trainor, D. O. (Director). Kavet, G. & Robin, A. (Writers). (1997). The Comeback [Television series episode], *Seinfeld*. Los Angeles, CA: NBC.

Umansky, N. (2014, February 21). *10 outrageous tweets that got people fired*. Retrieved from http://www.oddee.com/item_98873.aspx.

Vecchio, R. P., Justin, J. E., & Pearce, C. L. (2009). The influence of leader humor on relationships between leader behavior and follower outcomes. *Journal of Managerial Issues*, 21(2), 171–194.

Vinton, K. L. (1989). Humor in the workplace: It is more than telling jokes. *Small Group Research* 20, May 2, 151–166.

Volokh, E. (1997). What speech does "hostile work environment" harassment law restrict? *85 Georgetown Law Journal, 627*. Retrieved from http://www2.law.ucla.edu/volokh/harass/breadth.htm.

Weinberger, M. G. & Gulas, C. S. (1992). The impact of humor in advertising: A review. *Journal of Advertising*, 18(2), 39–44.

Witkin, S. L. (1999). Editorial: Taking humor seriously. *Social Work*, 44(2), March, 101–104.

Wofford, T. (2016). *Newsweek*, April 12. Retrieved from http://www.newsweek.com/de-blasio-cp-time-apology-446835.

Wolfe, L. (2013). Business laws: Humor in the workplace is restricted by law. *About.com*. Retrieved from http://womeninbusiness.about.com/od/smallbusinesslegalissues/a/legalriskshumor.htm.

WorkJoke. (2017). WorkJoke profession jokes. *Workjoke.com*. Retrieved from http://www.workjoke.com/.

4.7 Just a joke!

A critical analysis of organizational humor

Barbara Plester

Introduction

> *A bitter jest, when it comes too near the truth, leaves a sharp sting behind it.*
>
> (Tacitus, AD 117)

This chapter offers a unique critical analysis of workplace humor based on empirical research situated within a variety of different corporate organizations. The research is unique because specific analyses of humor are few and this one is based on an ethnographic approach incorporating observations, interviews, documentary data, and everyday conversations from actual workplaces. Not only are workplace analyses of humor scarce but they are mostly based on a functional interpretation of humor that assumes the uses of humor to be "self-evident"[1] and functionalist approaches are "associated with a range of presumed positive managerial and organizational outcomes."[2] Functionalist approaches do not always adequately account for the ambiguity and complexities of humor[2] and workplaces are often complex sites of history, tradition, patriarchy, power, and control. Therefore, it is important to research organizational humor in a "nuanced and radical way"[2] in order to address the complexity and depth of the concept.

Although there are many positive functions attributed to workplace humor, a critical analysis of workplace humor must consider the crucial elements of power, control, resistance, and authority. Therefore, this analysis considers the way in which humor might be co-opted by management in order to control employees' behavior, how management attempts to limit and control workplace humor, and finally it explores employees' use of humor to resist, challenge and disrupt organizational power and control. A crucial element in such an analysis is the recognition and exploration of humor with a darker agenda that may be interpreted in a more problematized manner in order to explore humor that can harm, manipulate, or disturb people at work. In other words, this chapter discusses workplace humor that shows the "dark side" of people, organizations, and work.

Humor in modern organizations is ubiquitous, complex, influential, and multifunctional.[3] In a functional sense, humor may be used to release tension,[4] reveal hidden emotions, make sense of the working environment,[5] create affiliation and harmony in groups,[6, 7] challenge powerful organizational members,[1] display cultural values and norms[8, 9, 10] and can even be used to disrupt and reframe normal everyday working processes. Although the majority of organizational humor analyses tend to emphasize the positive and potentially productive aspects of workplace humor, recent research is emerging that cautions about adopting an overwhelmingly upbeat approach and suggests instead that the dark, biting and mocking elements of humor should be recognized and considered.[11, 12, 13, 14] It is therefore important to understand humor in a comprehensive way that encompasses both the happy, optimistic and upbeat aspects alongside the contentious, problematic dark humor that may create disruption and dissonance in modern organizations.

The bodily expression of laughter offers verbal and visual clues that people find something humorous.[13] Simon Critchley[15] cites Descartes among others and defines laughter as an "*explosion* expressed with the body." There are physical, philosophical, psychological components to laughter and it may occur when people cerebrally perceive a stimulus to be amusing which may engender the response of laughter. Conversely, when a person experiences a supposedly humorous incident as *not* amusing they may indicate displeasure or disapproval, through withholding laughter—a phenomenon known as "*unlaughter.*"[11, 13] Laughter then has twin aspects that combine physical, embodied components with a metaphysical or intellectual element.[13] Laughter can be a paradoxical occurrence[11] because it involves "those who laugh as well as those who are laughed at."[13]

Of course laughter does not always denote amusement and can be a polite social response, an expression of embarrassment or it may even be "pathological" and an involuntary disorder.[16] Moreover laughter may be caused by tickling, which is a completely different response from laughter caused by mirth.[16] In theorizing laughter in modern workplace contexts, Butler[13] highlights the social significance of laughter in workplaces and suggests that it has two key functions that are either "collective" or "corrective." The collective aspect creates collegiality, goodwill, and enjoyment but laughter may also be used to *correct* behavior. People do not like being laughed *at* and thus the threat of laughter may ensure behavioral conformity in work groups. This type of laughter may ensue from mocking and derisory teasing, sometimes called jocular abuse,[17] and although it is still humor, it is barbed, biting, and aimed humor that may have the specific purpose of changing behavior or inhibiting specific activities. Although mocking humor is still functional and may have a specific purpose, it is also associated with elements of organizational power and control, and the quick-witted workplace joker can wield fierce social power and influence through jests, barbs, and witticisms—all delivered as jokes.[18]

In order to explore and understand the concept of organizational humor from a critical perspective, a rich understanding of the organizational contextual factors such as norms, activities, assumptions, and power restructures is highly important and relevant. Therefore, the methodological approach adopted in this research is an ethnographic one, whereby I entered, affiliated and socialized (full-time) into several different organizational contexts in order to interpret the prevailing social cultural conditions that influence everyday humor events and enactments. Correspondingly, the humor displays offer a reflection of organizational norms and values assumed by power holders, workers, and the organization itself.

Methodology and data

My empirical workplace humor research, conducted over the last 12 years, adopts an ethnographic approach which is based on observing and participating in humor first-hand as it occurs in its natural setting and context. The philosopher Bergson[19] in his famous essay *Le Rire* asserts:

> To understand laughter we must put it back in its "natural environment."

Contemporary humor scholars also contend that context is an extremely important element when examining organizational humor.[20] Therefore empirical research needs to account for the rich contextual elements important to the experience of humor, which leads to a deeper, more nuanced understanding of workplace humor and its associated implications. Thus, my empirical examples include detailed situational descriptions of humor events, the organizational actors participating, the preceding and contributing factors and wherever possible the outcomes, reaction, and consequences of workplace humor. These examples are gathered from a variety of different organizations, including a prestigious law firm; a large financial institution; an energy provider; and four different information technology (IT) companies. These organizations range in size from one small owner-operated company of only 25 employees, to some larger institutions with global operations and comprising upwards of 900 staff. The data has been collected using (1) participant observation; (2) formal semi-structured interviews with staff from all hierarchical levels (90+); (3) document collection; and (4) ad hoc discussions with organizational members. This has resulted in a wide range of empirical material comprising verbatim examples of everyday banter, canned jokes, practical jokes and horseplay, email jokes, visual jokes, cartoons and a myriad of complex material encompassing the minutiae of daily barbs and quips, alongside complicated joke set-ups requiring coordination and planning. Only a small selection of this wide-ranging material can be used here, but data presented are representative of many similar examples collected and analyzed.

Management's imposition of humor

Although the creation and enjoyment of humor would seem to be a discretionary and voluntary behavior within an individual's suite of communication practices, my workplace research would suggest otherwise, as exemplified within several of the studied organizations. In observed humor examples and in the excerpts from interview transcripts, it seems that humor and the more common notion of fun may sometimes be imposed on workers by their managers and/or through organizational expectations. The imposition of humor may be associated with programs designed to foster and artificially create workplace fun, and for some organizations, fun and humor are endorsed as workplace objectives and/or espoused values.

Modern Western workplaces are striving hard to be considered healthy and vibrant places where people can portray themselves authentically and seemingly without restraint. There is a new imperative for work to be fun, but Fleming[21] cautions that contrary to the spirit of freedom and playfulness enthusiastically espoused, only organizationally approved forms of fun are endorsed and sanctioned. According to Warren and Fineman[22] the term "managed fun" is an oxymoron and such prescribed fun is "oppressive" and silences opposing perspectives held by workers. Fleming and Sturdy[23] discuss neo-normative cultures where employees are encouraged to enjoy humor, fun, display their individuality, and even their sexuality—seemingly without restraint—as management seek to increase commitment, performance, and motivation at work.

Fleming[21] extends this argument in his book *Authenticity and the Cultural Politics of Work*, claiming that modern managerial practices embrace fun and light-hearted play and that an endorsed anti-authoritarian stance has become "chic." Such an approach seeks to stave off skepticism about corporate life in the attempt to elude workers' feelings of alienation and to encourage (apparent) authenticity in the interests of whole-person engagement in the workplace context. Yet such manufactured approaches to humor and fun, and an enthusiastic willingness by management to make work enjoyable, may have the effect of inhibiting genuine self-expressed forms of humor and fun. Genuine and spontaneous workplace humor can mock managerial actions[3] and organizational initiatives, which can be challenging to management. Thus, by appearing to embrace and create humor and/or fun, managers may try to avoid ridicule and derision from workers who may use *joke-work* to express their feelings thinking they are safe from censure and reprisals.[4] In other words, management may prefer to make the jokes before they become the target of jokes. Critical scholars highlight that management has co-opted the freedom and expressive capabilities of humor and fun in order to transform it into a tool with which to control and manipulate workers.[21, 22, 23] However, Parker[24] cautions that humor should be "central to constituting a sense of an oppositional identity at work" and when this aspect of expression is co-opted by management for organizational purposes, workers may be denied a useful form of resistance and opposition.

The next section presents examples of actual workplace humor combined with workers' reflections on humor expressions and dynamics. Obtained from a variety of the studied corporate organizations, these extracts suggest that on the surface, managerial use of humor appears to be friendly and even good-natured but it also serves to emphasize power, control, and an authoritarian perspective. Even more insidious is the sense that the concepts of humor and fun have in these instances become an organizational imperative and that subordinate workers must participate, endorse, and respond to managerial humor initiatives. Non-participation or unlaughter carries the risk of not only being considered humorless and dour, but also of disapproval and condemnation from those with organizational power. These examples suggest that humor and fun at work may (in some cases) constitute a new managerial initiative that does not promote happiness and well-being but simply represents a new form of tyranny and control which workers hesitate to condemn or resist because it is supposedly "all good fun" and "only joking."

Displaying the boss's buttocks

Ann, a woman in her fifties and the office administrator, leaves her desk unattended one Friday afternoon to go and purchase alcoholic drinks for the regular after-work "Friday drinks." During her absence, Jake (the CEO) pressgangs Adrian (a young male employee) and stepping behind a partition, Jake orders Adrian to photograph his (Jake's) naked buttocks. This is uploaded to Ann's computer screen. She returns and re-opens her computer to be greeted with the full-screen photograph of her boss's naked buttocks. She screams in shock, laughs loudly and shouts (jocular) abuse at her boss and her colleagues who have surrounded her desk. Much laughter ensues from all.[14]

The described prank was typical of the many jokes that were observed and/or physically experienced in this organization. The CEO (pseudonym *Jake*) of this small, predominantly male IT organization identified himself as a "*joker who loves humor*" and he was similarly described by all of his employees. This practical joke exhibits several significant elements relevant to a critical agenda, specifically power, dominance and a gendered aspect predicated on the ideal of hegemonic masculinity.[14] This organization was defined by an overtly masculine culture and one of the few women, Ann is subjected to a photograph of her male boss's buttocks. She is definitely shocked and screams out loud in reaction—but quickly changes her protest into laughter when she realizes it's a joke and her reaction is being observed. It is difficult to discern whether she was genuinely amused, embarrassed, or felt compelled to laugh at a prank enacted by her dominant, male boss. Adrian is also forced to comply in taking the photo, and this action could not be considered a typical or reasonable workplace task. The practical joke highlights the masculine and sexualized culture prevalent in this workplace, and the display of the boss's buttocks could be considered sexual harassment of both Ann and Adrian.[25] Elements of power and control are clearly discernible, and both employees must laugh and "take the joke" or risk being excluded from the organizational culture. The only recourse open to these employees would be to initiate legal action for sexual harassment, but as Jake is the owner and boss of the company this would be risky, time consuming, and probably fraught with stress. When questioned about his employees' reactions to the incessant and confronting humor, Jake blithely responded: "*If they don't like it they can leave!*" Laughing along is the safest and easiest option and Jake's uncompromising response suggests that employees who do not accept such humor enactments will not be welcome in the organization and their only alternative is to "leave."

One of the issues in the concept of humor is that what one person finds highly amusing and deeply funny is only mildly amusing or even offensive and outrageous to a different person or group.[3] In other words, humor is highly ambiguous. In the IT organization, Jake the CEO uses this uncertainty to enact humor that he personally finds very funny and his contentious humor reinforces his power and domination over both work activities and organizational humor and fun. Jake has crafted a notorious identity as a powerful boss and as the "*industry's biggest joker*" (participants' words). Although a prank depicting bare buttocks is considered inappropriate in most corporate (Western) organizations, Jake uses the inherent ambiguity in humor to justify his sexualized display. By claiming "*it's just a joke*" he coerces his subordinate employees to accept many similar displays. Most of the time his employees accept the "jokes" because not to do so risks termination of their employment and opposition carries the risk of further mocking and ridicule. Humor in the form of ridicule can be used to control and correct those who do not conform,[13] and to complain about a joke one risks being deemed humorless and a "spoilsport."[3] Furthermore, Freud[4] claims that sexualized humor allows a joker to "display himself" and that the "joke-work" offers safety from recriminations and condemnation.

Confidential interviews with employees of this company elicited expression of distaste at some of the humor that they felt compelled to endure. Humor was used by the powerful CEO to create a very specific and somewhat threatening organizational culture, ostensibly focused on fun and laughter—but simultaneously rife with control, aggression, sexuality, and domination. Control was achieved through the use of humor by the CEO and senior managers and employees were daily subjected to ridicule and mockery about all facets of working life. However, as a feature of this humor dynamic, workers also felt free to respond in kind and used some teasing humor back to their CEO. It was notable that the employees' jokes and pranks were much more moderate than those instigated by the CEO. In some cases when an employee instigated a prank or a teasing joke towards a co-worker, the CEO joined in enthusiastically, encouraged the interaction and even escalated it—often adding extra profanity or derisory jibes.[14] Thus, an effective way to invoke the boss's approval was to create a prank or joke, particularly when targeted at a co-worker, and specific people seemed to receive more of the teasing, particularly the younger, less-experienced workers. Senior managers mimicked the CEO's fondness for scatological and sexualized humor, and thus outrageous joking and physical jokes constantly permeated this workplace. Employees in this organization, accepted that participating in and even creating humor was a component of their job. There were rare occurrences when employees dared to complain, withhold laughter, or challenge the constant barrage of jokes, and such individuals were subsequently more ferociously mocked and derided (through "jokes" of course). During the research period two employees resigned, both stating that they could not tolerate this chaotic context any longer. The following quotes from employees reflect some of these complex dynamics:

> *It's very important that people fit in. They need to fit in because you won't be lasting very long if you didn't like humor. You need someone to enjoy the culture, the tricks, the jokes and all that. It's useless getting rid of non-fits.*
>
> (Sean, 25, Sales Consultant)

> *Someone who can't handle the culture or take the jokes is never going to really loosen up and become part of the team, and the team is a very important part of the job, being able to work with other people, etc. There are a couple of people I thought were very hard to break them in, they did eventually fit in but it took them a little while to loosen up. The culture can be a little overwhelming for new people.*
>
> (Pete, 35, Engineering Manager)

> *Someone will have to be able to take jokes. That would be quite important, if they can't then they won't enjoy it and we won't like working with them, because this is a fun kind of place.*
>
> (Adrian, 24, Engineer)

> *The humor can be a bit disturbing. A lot of the humor that I have seen is about putting someone or something down. Adrian for example, is the butt of a lot of jokes, mainly because he comes across as being really innocent and unable to stand up for himself. He gets a little upset every now and then and people pull back.*
>
> (Dylan, 34, Sales Consultant)[14]

> *The humor here is very crude, crass, rude, toilet humor. I don't know anywhere else the humor is that much in the gutter—it's better than no humor though. Whatever skeletons someone has—we will dig it all out. It's the nature of humor—the Koreans are the butt of jokes and get the piss taken out of them and ragged on—but they love it. Jake initiates it—so it's top down. Jake definitely creates the humor.*
>
> (Karen, 26, Sales Consultant)[14]

Although interpretations may be ambiguous, these quotes seem to emphasize the point that employees **must** accept the workplace jokes and "tricks" (referring to actual physical pranks, of which there were many) in order to be integrated into the workplace culture. These quotes were strongly backed up by the great number of pranks, jokes, humorous emails, and displays that were observed and experienced while researching this company. There is a sinister undertone in Dylan's quote when he talks about "*getting rid of non-fits*," suggesting that workers who are not part of the humor must be dismissed. Sean talks of "*breaking people in*," and from my participant observations I noted that this occurred through a series of practical jokes played on a newcomer whereby they were teased, tricked, and then assessed as to their reactions and ability to take the humor.

Upon observing a newcomer cope with a series of pranks involving toilet humor (fart jokes, stink bombs, and an electronic machine making simulated flatulence noises) I noticed that she very quickly developed strategies for coping with the constant jokes. Her strategies included laughing heartily at pranks whilst also retaliating with vigorous jocular abuse towards her co-workers, even when the jokes became very rude or profane. Such wholehearted embracing of the humor and fun helped her become "one of the boys" quite rapidly.[26]

Karen and Dylan (above) describe the humor as crass and disturbing and involving "*putdowns*," "*taking the piss*" and "*being ragged on*." These phrases imply that mocking, deriding, and somewhat confrontational humor is the norm in this organization. All of the IT employees identified the CEO as the instigator and main protagonist of humor and fun, and as owner/operator he was also the most powerful person in this organization. Thus, Jake seemed to enjoy total freedom to inflict any form of humor that he liked on his hapless staff. It was notable that humor in this organization was profane, highly sexual, homophobic, racist, and seemingly lacking in normal societal constraints or those limitations expected in typical corporate organizations. In Karen's words the humor is "*top down*" and therefore the elements of power and control permeate the humor and fun, and the coercive elements of "*join in . . . or leave*" are felt by all organizational members. Although earlier research suggests that workers can express dissatisfaction at managerial actions through using humor,[27] and also that satire may be used to ridicule managers or authority[28] in this IT organization, humor is used by a powerful manager to control subordinate employees and display his dominance, sexuality, and aggression.[14] The appropriation of humor makes such power less obvious because it is hidden behind the flamboyant, exuberant jokes and employees' reactions are tightly controlled because laughter is mandatory and career-enhancing.

Although humor was blatantly co-opted by management in this organization, some of these effects were also seen in less overt ways in other, larger organizations where humor was enthusiastically encouraged and fun was prescribed as an organizational value or desired attribute. The following section highlights that although fun and humor are endorsed and explicitly encouraged, they are also very much controlled by management, who take an active role in deciding what constitutes fun, humor, and good taste. Additionally, management also decide which humor and fun is deemed to have "crossed the line" and become an organizational transgression.[29]

Management controlling humor

The first tranche of interview quotes (below) all originate from a large and prestigious law firm where senior management promoted the notion that this was a *fun* company. By promoting fun at work, management sought to differentiate the company from their competitors, especially in regards to recruiting top university graduates, and thus the fun element was prominently emphasized in recruitment brochures. The following four employees discuss their reactions to being labeled a fun company:

> *I think we want to tell people that we are a fun organization but they can't use that word "fun" because that would be downright lying. We are not really a culture around fun, we don't have a value called fun but I know that HR are very aware of that. They sort of are trying to bring on people that might create that fun or introduce that fun.*

(Kim, 37, Marketing Manager)

Interestingly enough we are trying to get a bit more of our humor out there to the guys who have come on board—a lot are very straight-laced. If you have a bit of fun you will find your work a lot more enjoyable. You need a release and you've got to have a laugh . . . Join in and have fun then work is more tolerable.

(Clinton, 42, Law Partner)

Obviously there are some inappropriate things as well as appropriate things and they are restricting what comes in (via email and the internet) and there are some things that aren't appropriate that come in but then again they still let us have a little bit of fun.

(John, 26, IT Manager)

Humor is important, I seem to be the loudest—I think I am. I have only been told off once by my boss—oh no twice! I don't think there is enough humor.

(Amber, 25, Marketing Assistant)

There is palpable tension in these interview responses, and the first comment from Kim was made quite ferociously as she discussed the perceived untruth in representing the organization as a *fun* place. Later in the same interview Kim pointed out that because law firms account for their time and bill in six-minute increments, it is hard, if not impossible, to find the time to create or participate in fun activities, even though the organization aspires to be known for its fun culture. During her interview, Kim laughed ironically at management's attempt to depict this organization as a fun company. Although these law employees acknowledge that fun and humor make work more enjoyable, they indicate that there is strong managerial control around what constitutes fun and they strongly suggest that this is a matter for management (or HR) to decide and articulate. John indicates that permission for fun comes from management in his comment "*they still **let** us have a **little bit** of fun*," and Amber clearly indicates that she has been reprimanded for her humor, twice. Therefore, although this organization publicly promotes its so-called fun culture, employees perceive significant managerial control regarding when, where, and what type of activities constitute acceptable fun. Thus, the possibility of any authentic and genuine fun is minimal and the only type of fun likely to occur in this law firm is that which is managerially created and endorsed.

Similarly, the excerpts below also support the notion that management define and control fun and humor in this large financial institution. These respondents also refer to reprimands ("*smack your hand*") for perceived transgressions and they suggest that in this workplace, fun is careful, politically correct, appropriate, and dispensed by management ("*handed out*"). Fun is encouraged and ardently espoused in this organization but only if it remains within prescribed "professional" boundaries.[29] Transgressing these managerially endorsed boundaries brings about recriminations and disciplinary action.

Fun is definitely part of the culture . . . I think humor is always there in the background, because I think we do have a corporate-type company. Emails and dodgy jokes going around are frowned on if it is too politically incorrect. I think there is an unspoken understanding that people are careful with what they are sending and to whom.

(Fred, 32, Customer Services Adviser)

They'll certainly hand out the fun themselves which is kind of nice. But if you think you can do something that's inappropriate that shouldn't happen then they'll smack your hand.

(Fred, 32, Customer Services Adviser)

On the first day I came in they were all about having fun but they really do define some things such as what clothes you can wear. They do encourage the whole fun thing but there is a definite line there and as much as we do joke about it is still very professional.

(Paul, 25, Customer Service Adviser)

I think there is a line fully, and as much as it [humor] is encouraged and again just based on our team and our management. Our managers they have fun with us, it's great for the team, we all have a laugh and a joke, but I think everyone knows where the line is . . . You know where the line is with management because there is a line and you can't go over it. When you've gone beyond the line and are spoken to I think that is when you really know you've crossed the line where you shouldn't go.

(Paul, 25, Customer Service Adviser)

Thus, it seems that organizational members desire the creation and encouragement of workplace humor and fun, but at the same time management feel the need to ensure that it is firmly controlled and monitored. Obviously, management teams understand the capacity of humor and fun to create issues and disharmony and thus perceive a definite need to manage these potentially chaotic workplace dynamics. One could then question if the so-called fun activities that are organizationally manufactured are actually perceived as fun by any employees, or do such activities merely become just another imposed set of workplace demands that workers must respond to, enthusiastically endorse, and pretend to enjoy and relish? As found in the financial organization discussed above, employees can find themselves assessed on their commitment to and application of company values, and thus when fun is an espoused value, not only is work performance evaluated but also workers' fun performances and participation. Therefore it could be interpreted that for many workers, fun (and by association humor) must be embraced, endured, and outwardly enjoyed, yet it is management who decides what constitutes fun and humor. Being forced to have fun and laugh at work may be humiliating[30] and even unendurable when combined with stressful work demands and constraints, yet it is overwhelmingly assumed that having a fun culture or encouraging laughter at work is both desirable and beneficial in modern workplaces.[31, 11] Forced fun and humor then may become yet another task on the long "to do" list of harried but smiling workers. Sometimes the only way to resist such imperatives is to develop a wry or satirical sense of humor, and workers may cope with the demands of too much fun, or unfunny humor, through either non-responsiveness such as "unlaughter"[11, 13] or by using alternative humor forms to mock, challenge, or resist the managerial fun perspective and cultivate their own voice.[22, 24]

Resisting managerial directives through joking

Management cannot prescribe all behavior and expression, and one great asset of humor (and fun) is that it is freely available to all and can be used to resist managerial directives and demands. Psychological research suggests that using humor provides a safety shield whereby a person can jokingly make an aimed point that is understood, but the recipient of the jibe cannot easily react negatively to something presented in the guise of joke-work.[4] Thus humor can be dark, biting, derisory, and sometimes unkind. It can also be clever and quick-witted and make people laugh which may mitigate bad feelings towards organizational edicts or developments. Humor can allow people to save face[32] and can soften harsh criticisms, and can be effectively used by both workers and managers as a way of releasing pent up emotions caused by work events. Humor and fun activities can also go horribly wrong and cause distress, offense, and negative consequences, but if the resultant distress is not too severe jokers may be able to retract or distance themselves from adverse reactions by claiming the "only joking" defense—but this is not always successful.

People have differing communicative abilities and within all of the organizations studied, I have identified specific people who are more skilled at humor use. I call this group the *jokers*, and their organizational colleagues also easily and consistently identify these characters. Not only do the jokers use humor to insulate themselves from organizational occurrences, but they also have a tendency to create quips and jokes that make others feel better, and they provide light-hearted relief from tension and pressure.[18] The jokers play an important social role within organizations, as they use humor to soften difficult interactions, relieve tension, sometimes challenge managerial directives, and they alleviate boredom associated with dull repetitive work tasks.[33]

These final examples illustrate two different organizational jokers pushing back against managerial directives and expectations, relieving the tension for all involved.

> The sales meeting is tense and uncomfortable and sales results are not ideal, a long way beneath the forecasts. The CEO is unhappy and terse and questions each team member in turn, asking sharply what their sales figure is compared to what they had forecast for the quarter. Everyone looks tense and unhappy. Finally his gaze comes to rest on Zac, who also has poor results. Zac earnestly and seriously justifies why his sales figures are low, but with steel in his voice the CEO firmly restates Zac's forecast figure and then cites Zac's much lower actual result. With his prior justification not making any impact on the CEO's displeasure, Zac (a frequent joker) gives up trying to explain and instead quips: "*Oh well, I'm revising next week's forecast to zero sales!*"[3]

The room erupts into loud laughter at Zac's joke, which relieves the very tense atmosphere in the room. The laughter was heartier perhaps than the joke warranted, but the CEO also joins the laughter and then he changes the discussion to a new topic. Zac's well-timed quip has distracted the censorious manager from his recriminations and has obliquely challenged the CEO. Zac has jokingly suggested that the only way to escape chastisement for poor sales results is to forecast that he will make no sales, thus any sales he makes will be considered a good result. The quip protects Zac by distracting the CEO and at the same time sends the message that the workers are not enjoying this public dressing down and that they might have to take drastic steps to avoid future rebukes. The quip does not change the power dynamic or the imperative to improve sales but it does effect a change of subject, and Zac's colleagues' hearty laughter shows their support and endorsement of this mild jocular challenge to the CEO's behavior.

The example below, from one of the large IT organizations, exemplifies a similar dynamic whereby workers suggest to their manager that they will only follow his instructions if they feel like doing so. The quip suggests that these workers have an alternative choice, which is to disobey the directive. In this scenario, the manager (Colin), one of the most senior staff in the organization, quietly but firmly requests that his staff complete some specific work tasks:

> Colin: "*Can you guys please get these orders sorted out and send them off before the end of the day. Thanks, this is really important*"
>
> Mac (joker): "*we **might** do it . . . if we feel like it . . .*"[3]

Initially Colin seems quite startled by Mac's seemingly challenging response. Once he realizes that Mac is joking, Colin joins the laughter of his subordinates and a cheerful atmosphere prevails. As the group joker, Mac has indirectly challenged Colin's directive (phrased as a question but constituting a demand nonetheless). By suggesting that the subordinate workers will only complete the tasks if they *"feel like it,"* Mac has implied the possibility of free choice and worker resistance. Framing this mild challenge in a joke format creates a type of *mock* resistance because Mac and his colleagues know that they must complete these tasks as they are relevant to their continued employment. The humor comes from the incongruity created in Mac responding as if he really has a choice, making everyone laugh. No actual resistance or challenge to the manager's power is constituted in the joke, just the subtle reminder that noncompliance is an option, even if it is unlikely to occur.

These two observations exemplify effects that are consistent throughout my research. Self-nominated jokers are skilled in their humor use and through joking comments are able to respond to hierarchical power through suggesting alternative courses of action that might be considered by subordinate workers. Although the joking suggestion of a contradictory workplace response does not constitute a true challenge to authority, it does allow workers a voice and at least presents the notion that alternative actions can be contemplated. Joking also relieves tension that is created in overtly powerful scenarios (such as the censorious sales meeting). Laughter may be created from the incongruity that occurs when managerial discourse involving performance, tasks, and actions is disrupted by the cognitive mind shift required to consider alternative responses—as suggested by the quips. Jokes such as this have the additional advantage of mitigating managerial hubris by reminding managers with controlling positions that workers still retain free will and can make choices about whether or not to comply with directives. Although a challenge may be implied, the use of humor in these everyday work situations does not constitute serious defiance and therefore both managers and workers save face and may even experience shared goodwill as they join the collegial laughter.

Concluding remarks

Humor may be enjoyable and pleasurable but it can also be dark, aggressive, and disturbing. It is inadvisable to entirely attribute positively functional and optimistic attributes to workplace jokes because humor may also convey unpleasant sentiments and can contain derision and mocking. Thus it is important to understand and explore the dark elements of humor. In the workplace, dark humor may be closely associated with organizational elements of patriarchy, dominance, and power. Humor may shield authority figures as they enact hegemonic practices that oppress and subjugate subordinate workers, powerless to react in any way other than with (seemingly) supportive laughter. Therefore some humor is threatening, challenging, and dangerous and when enacted by a powerful organizational actor, this humor may be overwhelming and insurmountable for vulnerable workers.

However, workers can also use humor to jokingly defy managerial directives and actions and may lightly mock some actions and pronouncements, using the protection of a joking framework to escape disapproval. Of course, joking resistance does not actually change the organizational situation[34] but humor can at least allow workers some release of tension and frustration through having voiced their opposition, albeit in a joking manner. While humor may not alter workplace objectives and power structures it can disrupt and divert managerial discourse, and workers may experience a momentary feeling of freedom from control and domination.

Critical aspects of workplace humor are difficult to access, analyze, and interpret. There are few such organizational studies and therefore the components of power, control, dominance, and hegemony are scarce in organizational humor research. This chapter offers a distinctive critical approach to workplace humor based on unique, rich, ethnographic data, and such approaches are uncommon in the current literature. This critical analysis problematizes workplace humor and fun and thus could be considered rather dark and dour. Of course, plenty of genuine, pleasant humor and fun occurs inside organizations and this is well-documented in a wide variety of studies. The point of difference for this current chapter is to explore the less-common aspects of power, control and resistance enacted through humor and fun. Humor is sometimes used to openly display power, control, and hegemonic masculinity and such behavior may be based on the overarching (but erroneous) assumption that all humor is good humor.

References

1 Collinson, D. L. (2002). Managing humour. *Journal of Management Studies*, *39*(3), 269–289.
2 Westwood, R. & Rhodes, C. (Eds.). (2007). *Humour, work and organisation*. London: Routledge.
3 Plester, B.A. (2015a). *The complexity of workplace humour: Laughter, jokers and the dark side*. Dordrecht: Springer.
4 Freud, S. (1905). *Jokes and their relation to the unconscious* (A. Richards, Trans. 1991). London: Penguin.
5 Tracy, S. J., Myers, K. K., & Scott, W. (2006). Cracking jokes and crafting selves: Sensemaking and identity management among human service workers. *Communication Monographs*, *73*(3), 283–308.
6 Cooper, C. (2005). Just joking around? Employee humor expression as an ingratiatory behaviour. *The Academy of Management Review*, *30*(4), 765–776.
7 Cooper, C. (2008). Elucidating the bonds of workplace humor: A relational process model. *Human Relations*, *61*(8), 1087–1115.
8 Kunda, G. (1992). *Engineering culture: Control and commitment in a high-tech corporation*. Philadelphia, PA: Temple University Press.
9 Linstead, S. (1985). Jokers wild: The importance of humour in the maintenance of organisational culture. *Sociological Review*, *13*(3), 741–767.
10 Holmes, J. & Marra, M. (2002). Having a laugh at work: How humour contributes to workplace culture. *Journal of Pragmatics*, *34*(12), 1683–1710.
11 Billig, M. (2005a). *Laughter and ridicule: Towards a social critique of humour*. London: Sage.
12 Billig, M. (2005b). Violent racist jokes. In S. Lockyer & M. Pickering (Eds.), *Beyond a joke: The limits of humour*, 27–46. Hampshire: Palgrave Macmillan.
13 Butler, N. (2015). Joking aside: Theorizing laughter in organizations. *Culture and Organization*, *21*(1), 42–58.
14 Plester, B. A. (2015b). Take it like a man! Performing hegemonic masculinity through organizational humour. *ephemera*, *15*(3), 537–559.
15 Critchley, S. (2007). Humour as practically enacted theory, or, why critics should tell more jokes. In R. Westwood & C. Rhodes (Eds.), *Humour, work and organization*, 17–32. London: Routledge.
16 Martin, R. A. (2007). *The psychology of humor. An integrative approach*. Burlington, MA: Elsevier.
17 Plester, B. A. & Sayers, J. G. (2007). Taking the piss: The functions of banter in three IT companies. *Humor*, *20*(2), 157–187.
18 Plester, B. A. & Orams, M. B. (2008). Send in the clowns: The role of the joker in three New Zealand IT companies. *Humor*, *21*(3), 253–281.
19 Bergson, H. (1911). *Laughter. An essay on the meaning of the comic* (C. Brereton & F. Rothwell, Trans. 1935 ed.). London: Macmillan & Co.

20 Westwood, R. & Johnston, A. (2012). Reclaiming authentic selves: Control, resistive humour and identity work in the office. *Organization, 19*(6), 787–808.

21 Fleming, P. (2009). *Authenticity and the cultural politics of work*. Oxford: Oxford University Press.

22 Warren, S. & Fineman, S. (2007). "Don't get me wrong, it's fun here, but..." Ambivalence and paradox in a "fun" work environment. In R. Westwood & C. Rhodes (Eds.), *Humour, work and organisation*, 92–112. London: Routledge.

23 Fleming, P. & Sturdy, A. (2009). "Just be yourself!" Towards neo-normative control in organisations? *Employee Relations, 31*(6), 569–583.

24 Parker, M. (2007). The little book of management bollocks: Kitsch artefacts. In R. Westwood & C. Rhodes (Eds.), *Humour, work and organisation*, 77–91. London: Routledge.

25 Collinson, M. & Collinson, D. (1996). It's only dick: The sexual harassment of women managers in insurance sales. *Work, Employment & Society, 10*(1), 29–56.

26 Fine, G. A. & De Soucey, M. (2005). Joking cultures: Humor themes as social regulation in group life. *Humor, 18*(1), 1–22.

27 Rodrigues, S. B. & Collinson, D. L. (1995). "Having fun?" Humour as resistance in Brazil. *Organisation Studies, 16*(5), 739–768.

28 Taylor, P. & Bain, P. (2003). "Subterranean worksick blues": Humour as subversion in two call centres. *Organisation Studies, 24*(9), 1487–1509.

29 Plester, B. A. (2009). Crossing the line: Boundaries of workplace humour and fun. *Employee Relations, 31*(6), 584–599.

30 Fleming, P. (2005). Worker's playtime? Boundaries and cynicism in a "Culture of fun" program. *The Journal of Applied Behavioral Science, 41*(3), 285–303.

31 Owler, K., Morrison, R., & Plester, B. (2010). Does fun work? The complexity of promoting fun at work. *Journal of Management and Organization, 16*(3), 338–352.

32 Holmes, J. (2000). Politeness, power and provocation: How humour functions in the workplace. *Discourse Studies, 2*(2), 159–185.

33 Roy, D. (1959). "Banana time": Job satisfaction and informal interaction. *Human Organisation Studies, 18*, 158–168.

34 Westwood, R. (2004). Comic relief: Subversion and catharsis in organisational comic theatre. *Organisation Studies, 25*(5), 775–795.

Index

Taylor & Francis eBooks

Helping you to choose the right eBooks for your Library

Add Routledge titles to your library's digital collection today. Taylor and Francis ebooks contains over 50,000 titles in the Humanities, Social Sciences, Behavioural Sciences, Built Environment and Law.

Choose from a range of subject packages or create your own!

Benefits for you

» Free MARC records
» COUNTER-compliant usage statistics
» Flexible purchase and pricing options
» All titles DRM-free.

REQUEST YOUR
FREE
INSTITUTIONAL
TRIAL TODAY

Free Trials Available
We offer free trials to qualifying academic, corporate and government customers.

Benefits for your user

» Off-site, anytime access via Athens or referring URL
» Print or copy pages or chapters
» Full content search
» Bookmark, highlight and annotate text
» Access to thousands of pages of quality research at the click of a button.

eCollections – Choose from over 30 subject eCollections, including:

Archaeology	Language Learning
Architecture	Law
Asian Studies	Literature
Business & Management	Media & Communication
Classical Studies	Middle East Studies
Construction	Music
Creative & Media Arts	Philosophy
Criminology & Criminal Justice	Planning
Economics	Politics
Education	Psychology & Mental Health
Energy	Religion
Engineering	Security
English Language & Linguistics	Social Work
Environment & Sustainability	Sociology
Geography	Sport
Health Studies	Theatre & Performance
History	Tourism, Hospitality & Events

For more information, pricing enquiries or to order a free trial, please contact your local sales team:
www.tandfebooks.com/page/sales

 Routledge
Taylor & Francis Group

The home of
Routledge books

www.tandfebooks.com